Qualitative Research

Theory, Method and Practice

Second edition

edited by
David Silverman

Los Angeles | London | New Delhi
Singapore | Washington DC

Qualitative Research

In memory of Carolyn Baker and Phil Strong,
fine sociologists and good friends.

Contents

Notes on contributors

Paul Atkinson is Distinguished Research Professor in Sociology at Cardiff University. He is Associate Director of the ESRC Research Centre on Social and Economic Aspects of Genomics. His main research interests are the sociology of medical knowledge and the development of qualitative research methods. His publications include: *Ethnography: Principles in Practice* (with Martyn Hammersley) (Second Edition 1995, Routledge), *The Clinical Experience* (Second Edition 1997, Ashgate), *The Ethnographic Imagination* (1990, Routledge), *Understanding Ethnographic Texts* (1992, Sage), *Medical Talk and Medical Work* (1995, Sage), *Fighting Familiarity* (with Sara Delamont) (1995, Hampton Press), *Making Sense of Qualitative Data* (with Amanda Coffey) (1996, Sage), *Sociological Readings and Re-Readings* (1996, Ashgate) and *Interactionism* (with William Housley) (2003, Sage). Together with Sara Delamont he edits the journal *Qualitative Research*. He was co-editor of *The Handbook of Ethnography*. His ethnographic study of an international opera company is published as *Everyday Arias*.

Carolyn Baker was Associate Professor in the Graduate School of Education, the University of Queensland, Brisbane, Australia. Her interests included studies of talk and interaction in classrooms, meetings and other educational settings. In her research on literacy she applied ethnomethodology and conversation analysis to instances of 'talk around text'. An example of her distinguished research output is her paper, with Jayne Keogh, 'Accounting for achievement in parent–teacher interviews', *Human Studies*, 18 (2/3), 1995. Carolyn died in July 2003.

Isabelle Baszanger is a sociologist at the CNRS (Centre National de la Recherche Scientifique), Paris. Her main research interests are sociology of medical work, sociology of pain and of the passage from curative to palliative medicine, and interactionism. Her recent publications include *Inventing pain medicine: From the laboratory to the clinic* (1998, Rutgers University Press) and *Quelle médecine voulons-nous?* (with Martine Bungener and Anne Paillet) (2002, La Dispute).

Michael Bloor is a medical sociologist with a personal chair in the School of Social Sciences, Cardiff University. His recent publications include *The Sociology of HIV Transmission* (1995, Sage) and (with Jane Frankland, Michelle Thomas and Kate Robson) *Focus Groups in Social Research* (2001, Sage). He is currently preparing for Sage a *Dictionary of Qualitative Methods* (with Fiona Wood) and *The Sociology of Occupational Health and Safety: the case of the globalised shipping industry* (with Michelle Thomas).

Amanda Coffey is a senior lecturer in the School of Social Sciences, Cardiff University. Her research interests include education in informal settings, the role of (auto)biography in qualitative research and ethnographic representations. She is currently co-editor of *Sociological Research Online*. Her publications include *The Ethnographic Self* (1999, Sage) and *Making Sense of Qualitative Data* (with Paul Atkinson) (1996, Sage). She was one of the co-editors of *The Handbook of Ethnography*.

Robert Dingwall studied at Cambridge and Aberdeen, where he trained in medical sociology before moving on to law and society research at Oxford. Since 1990, he has been a professor at Nottingham, where he now directs an interdisciplinary institute studying developments in biology and biotechnology. He has published widely on professions, work, occupations, interaction and qualitative methods.

Nicolas Dodier is a sociologist at the INSERM (Institut National de la Santé et de la Recherche Médicale), and Professor at the Ecole des Hautes Etudes en Sciences Sociales, Paris. His research interests include sociology of technology, sociology of medicine and science, and theory of action. His recent publications include *L'expertise médicale: Essai de sociologie sur l'exercice du jugement* (1993, Métailié), *Les hommes et les machines: La conscience collective dans les sociétés technicisées* (1995, Métailié), and *Leçons politiques de l'épidémie de sida* (2003, Editions de l'Ecole des Hautes Etudes en Sciences Sociales).

Michael Emmison is Reader in Sociology in the School of Social Science at the University of Queensland, Brisbane, Australia. He works primarily in the fields of language and interaction and material culture and is currently researching the social organization of problem solving on a software helpline and the impact of technology (telephone, email and online web counselling) on troubles telling on a national children's helpline. He is the co-author (with Tony Bennett and John Frow) of *Accounting for Tastes: Australian Everyday Cultures* (1999, Cambridge University Press) and *Researching the Visual* (with Phillip Smith) (2000, Sage).

Kathryn J. Fox received her PhD in sociology from the University of California, Berkeley, USA. She is now an associate professor of sociology at the University of Vermont, USA, where she teaches courses on deviance and social control. She has completed qualitative studies of a midwestern punk scene in the 1980s, an AIDS prevention project in San Francisco and a cognitive therapy programme for violent offenders in prison. Her new research project, which is just beginning, is a study of truancy intervention and the social construction of truants.

Barry Glassner is Professor of Sociology at the University of Southern California, USA, and the author or co-author of a dozen books, including *Our Studies, Ourselves* (2003, Oxford), *The Culture of Fear* (2000, Basic) and *Career Crash* (1994, Simon & Schuster). He has published papers in *The American Sociological Review*, *Social Problems*, *American Journal of Psychiatry* and other leading journals in the social sciences.

Jaber F. Gubrium is Chair and Professor in the Department of Sociology at the University of Missouri, Columbia, USA. His research deals with the narrative organization of personal identity, family, the life course, aging and adaptations to illness. He is editor of the *Journal of Aging Studies* and author or editor of more than twenty books, including *Living and Dying at Murray Manor* (1975, St. Martin's Press), *Caretakers* (1979, Sage), *Describing Care* (1982, Oelgeschlager, Gunn and Hain), *Oldtimers and Alzheimer's* (1986, JAI Press), *Out of Control* (1992, Sage) and *Speaking of Life* (1993, Aldine de Gruyter).

Christian Heath is Professor of Work and Organisation at King's College London. With members of the Work, Interaction and Technology Research Group, he is currently undertaking studies of control centres, operating theatres, medical consultations, newsrooms and museums and galleries. His recent publications include *Technology in Action* (with Paul Luff) (2000, Cambridge University Press).

John Heritage is Professor of Sociology, at UCLA, USA. He is the author of *Garfinkel and Ethnomethodology* (1984, Polity), and *The News Interview: Journalists and Public Figures On the Air* (with Steven Clayman) (2002, Cambridge University Press) and the editor of *Structures of Social Action* (with Max Atkinson) (1984, Cambridge University Press), *Talk at Work* (with Paul Drew) (1992, Cambridge University Press), and *Practicing Medicine* (with Douglas Maynard) (2004, Cambridge University Press). He is currently working on a range of topics in doctor–patient interaction, and on presidential press conferences (with Steven Clayman).

James A. Holstein is Professor of Sociology in the Department of Social and Cultural Sciences at Marquette University, Milwaukee, USA. He is the editor of the journal *Social Problems*, and has authored or edited three-dozen books including *Court Ordered Insanity* (1993, Aldine de Gruyter), *Reconsidering Social Constructionism* (1993, Aldine de Gruyter), *Challenges and Choices* (2003, Aldine de Gruyter) and *Dispute Domains and Welfare Claims* (1996, JAI Press). In collaboration with Jay Gubrium, he has also published *What is Family?* (1990, Mayfield), *The New Language of Qualitative Method* (1997, Oxford University Press), *The Self We Live By* (2000, Oxford University Press), *Institutional Selves* (2001, Oxford University Press), *Handbook of Interview Research* (2002, Sage) and *Inner Lives and Social Worlds* (2003, Oxford University Press).

Annette Markham is an assistant professor of communication studies at the University of Illinois, Chicago, USA, where she teaches courses in communication theory, interpretive research methods, and communication technology. Her research focuses on the intersection of culture, technology and identity from an ethnographic perspective. This research is well represented in her 1998 book *Life Online: Researching Real Experience in Virtual Space* (AltaMira). Her current research explores the influence of computer-mediated communication technologies on qualitative methods.

Gale Miller is Professor of Sociology, Department of Social and Cultural Sciences, Marquette University, Milwaukee, USA. His research interests include the study of language use in organizations, the sociology of troubles, and the social construction of social problems. His interest in the paradox of control is personal as well as intellectual, having just finished a term in university administration.

Jody Miller is Associate Professor of Criminology and Criminal Justice at the University of Missouri–St Louis, USA. Her research focuses on gender, crime and victimization, particularly in the contexts of youth gangs, urban communities and the commercial sex industry. Her monograph, *One of the Guys: Girls, Gangs and Gender*, was published by Oxford University Press in 2001. She has published numerous articles and book chapters, including in *Criminology, Social Problems, Justice Quarterly, Journal of Research in Crime and Delinquency* and *Journal of Contemporary Ethnography*.

Elizabeth Murphy is Reader in Sociology at the University of Nottingham. Her interests are in the sociology of health and illness, food, gender and motherhood. She is conducting a study of the transition from child to adult services for young people with learning difficulties. She is also interested in the application of qualitative methods to policy-relevant areas. She trained at the Universities of St Andrews, Southampton and the Open University.

Anssi Peräkylä is Professor of Sociology at the University of Helsinki, Finland. He received his PhD at the University of London in 1992. His research interests include conversation analysis, medical interaction, psychotherapeutic interaction and emotional communication. His publications include *AIDS Counselling* (1995, Cambridge University Press) and numerous articles in journals such as *Sociology, Social Psychology Quarterly* and *Research on Language and Social Interaction*.

Jonathan Potter is Professor of Discourse Analysis at Loughborough University. He has studied racism, scientific argumentation and crowd disorder. He is currently working on calls to a child protection helpline. His most recent books include *Representing Reality* (1996, Sage), which attempts to provide a systematic overview, integration and critique of constructionist research in social psychology, postmodernism, rhetoric and ethnomethodology, *Talk and Cognition* (with Hedwig te Molder) (Cambridge University Press, in press), in which a range of different researchers consider the implication of studies of interaction for understanding cognition, and *Focus Group Practice* (with Claudia Puchta) (2004, Sage), which analyses interaction in market research focus groups.

Lindsay Prior is Professor of Sociology at the University of Wales, Cardiff. He is currently engaged in a number of projects that focus on lay and professional understandings of risk. These include studies of risk assessment in cancer genetics, problems of genetics and insurance, lay attitudes to vaccinations, and the use of anti-depressants in primary care. His most recent book is *Using Documents in Social Research* (2003, Sage).

David Silverman is Professor Emeritus of Sociology at Goldsmiths College, University of London. His research interests are focused on professional–client interaction, medicine and counselling, and qualitative research methods. He is author of *Doing Qualitative Research* Second Edition (2004, Sage), *Interpreting Qualitative Data: Methods for Analysing Talk, Text and Interaction* (Second Edition, 2001, Sage) and of *Discourses of Counselling: HIV Counselling as Social Interaction* (1996, Sage). He edits the Sage Series called Introducing Qualitative Methods.

Sue Wilkinson is the Ruth Wynn Woodward Endowed Professor of Women's Studies at Simon Fraser University, Vancouver, Canada. She is the founding and current editor of the international journal *Feminism & Psychology*, and author of over eighty publications in the areas of gender, sexuality and health. Her current research interests are in breast cancer and threatened feminine identities, and in conversation analytic approaches to data analysis.

Part I Introduction to the second edition

1 Introducing *Qualitative Research*

David Silverman

The first edition of this book sought to provide a guide to the latest developments in qualitative research. This second edition offers a newly updated introduction to cutting edge issues, written by leading scholars in our field. Chapters from the first edition have been revised by their distinguished authors. In addition, reflecting the changing face of qualitative research in the past decade, four entirely new and exciting chapters appear. New to this volume are chapters on visual data, focus groups, Internet data and the applicability of qualitative research to organizational behaviour. To complete these revisions, my concluding chapter on missing issues in qualitative research has been specially written for this volume. Finally, to enhance the reader-friendliness of this book, each chapter concludes with a set of annotated recommended readings.

Like the first edition, this text aims to build on the success of my *Interpreting Qualitative Data* (IQD; Silverman, 2001). Like that book, it was generated by a number of assumptions set out below:

1 The centrality of the relationship between analytic perspectives and methodological issues and the consequent requirement to go beyond a purely 'cookbook' version of research methods.
2 The need to broaden our conception of qualitative research beyond issues of subjective 'meaning' and towards issues of language, representation and social organization.
3 The desire to search for ways of building links between social science traditions rather than dwelling in 'armed camps' fighting internal battles.
4 The belief that a social *science*, which takes seriously the attempt to sort fact from fancy, remains a valid enterprise.

5 The assumption that we no longer need to regard qualitative research as provisional or never based on initial hypotheses. This is because qualitative studies have already assembled a usable, cumulative body of knowledge.
6 The commitment to a dialogue between social science and the community based on a recognition of their different starting points rather than upon a facile acceptance of topics defined by what are taken to be 'social problems'.

Each of these assumptions is, implicitly or explicitly, highly contested within contemporary qualitative research. This is largely, I believe, because such research has become a terrain on which diverse schools of social theory have fought their mock battles. Ultimately, the assumptions set out here try to move the terrain of our field towards an analysis of the everyday resources which we use in making our observations. This point, which is implicit in many of these contributions, is set out in detail in the final chapter of this book.

Of course, avoiding such battles, in the context of a commitment to a cumulative social science, is far more likely to make our trade appear relevant to the wider community. As we look outwards rather than inwards, with confidence rather than despair, the way is open for a fruitful dialogue between social scientists, organizations, professionals and community groups.

Moreover, it is worth noting that we present ourselves not only to the wider community but also to the students we teach. Both *Doing Qualitative Research* (Silverman, Second Edition 2004) and *IQD* derive from thirty years of teaching methodology courses and supervising research projects at both under-graduate and graduate levels. That experience has reinforced the wisdom of the old maxim that true learning is based upon *doing*. In practice, this means that I approach taught courses as workshops in which students are given skills to analyse data and so to learn the craft of our trade. This means that assessments of students' progress are properly done through data exercises rather than the conventional essay in which students are invited to offer wooden accounts of what other people have written.

It follows that I have little time for the conventional trajectory of the PhD in which students spend their first year 'reviewing the literature', gather data in the second year and then panic in the third year about how they can analyse their data. Instead, my students begin their data analysis in the first year – sometimes in the first week. In that way, they may well have 'cracked' the basic problem in their research in that first year and so can spend their remaining years pursuing the worthy but relatively non-problematic tasks of ploughing through their data following an already-established method.

Like *IQD*, my hope is that this book will be used by students who are not yet familiar with the approaches involved, their theoretical underpinnings and their research practice. In *IQD*, student exercises were designed to allow readers to test their understanding of each chapter. In this book, worked-through examples of research studies make the arguments much more accessible. Moreover, the chapters are not written in standard edited collection style as chapters addressed to the contributors' peers but inaccessible to a student audience. This means that the presentation is didactic but not 'cookbook' in style.

The particular contribution of this reader lies in its assembly of a very well-known international team of researchers who share my commitment to rigorous, analytically derived, but non-polarized qualitative research. Eight US researchers join eight from the UK, two from France and Australia and one from Finland and Canada. While the majority of the contributors are sociologists, the disciplines of social psychology, criminology and educational studies are also represented. In any event, I believe that all contributors have succeeded in making their presentations accessible to a multidisciplinary audience. Rather than denying their own analytic position in favour of some woolly centre ground, these authors have clearly set out the assumptions from which they proceed while remaining open to the diverse interests of their readers. Each has written a chapter which reflects on the analysis of each of the kinds of data discussed in *IQD*: observations, texts, talk, visual data and interviews. Following *IQD*, each author uses particular examples of data analysis to advance analytic arguments.

The two chapters on observational methods seek to rescue observational work from the pitfalls of mere 'description' and lazy coding and towards exciting methodological and analytic directions for observational research. In Chapter 2, Isabelle Baszanger and Nicolas Dodier begin with the need to ground research in field observations. The question they then raise is how the ethnographer actually goes about relating partial observations to broader generalizations about the 'whole'. Baszanger and Dodier show how ethnography has been dominated by traditions which seek to integrate observations either by an appeal to the concept of 'subculture' or by the understanding or writing of the individual author. Rejecting such appeals to 'culture' or 'the self', they depict a 'combinative ethnography' which seeks to generalize by applying the comparative method to groups of situations or activities collected in the ethnographic 'casebook'.

In Chapter 3, Gale Miller and Kathryn Fox show how cumulative observation can be combined with analytic vitality. In this chapter, 'Building Bridges', Miller and Fox raise the possibility of dialogue between ethnography, conversation analysis and Foucault. Beginning with the focus on naturally occurring data used by discursively oriented ethnographers, Miller and Fox point to what each of these three traditions have in common and to how they can provoke a set of fascinating research questions for the ethnographer. They then show how these questions can be addressed in the single case study as well as in comparative or longitudinal studies.

Part III on 'texts' follows Miller and Fox's call for building bridges by showing how ethnographic reading of texts can fruitfully work with a diverse set of analytic traditions. Paul Atkinson and Amanda Coffey apply theories from the literary theory of narrative and genre to the documents through which organizations represent themselves and the records and documentary data they accumulate. Taking the example of 'audit', they show how we can fruitfully analyse financial statements produced by accountants and accounts of their work by university departments. They also remind us of the 'audit trail' as documents refer to other documents. Following Atkinson and Coffey, we are given the tools to explicate systematically how texts are organized through the concepts of 'authorship', 'readership', 'intertextuality' and 'rhetoric'.

In Lindsay Prior's chapter on texts, we move from literary theory to theories of discourse. However, unlike the stultifying theoretical level of some introductions to this topic, Prior has written a delightful, accessible chapter which shows, in practice, what it is like to 'do things with documents'. Avoiding references to a knowing 'subject', Prior shows us how we can instead focus on the ways in which a text instructs us to see the world. Using examples as diverse as a statistical summary of 'causes of death' and a psychiatric interview, he reveals a thought-provoking toolbox that we can use when working with textual material.

In the twenty-first century, however, conventional documents are not the only textual material that circulate in the world. The Internet is now perhaps the prime site where words and pictures circulate. Annette Markham's new chapter develops this insight and, in so doing, offers readers an invaluable guide to interpreting such data. Markham shows the importance of distinguishing three ways in which the Internet works: as a medium of communication; as a network of computers; and as a context for social interaction. Using illuminating examples of Internet data, Markham demonstrates how researchers can use the Internet either as a means of conducting conventional interview or focus group studies (albeit with different time constraints) or as a way of studying how participants themselves constitute meaning in naturally occurring websites such as chatrooms. Following this latter option, we learn, as in the other chapters on texts, how participants actively construct meaning.

This idea of the 'active' reader is carried over into Part IV on interviews and focus groups. All four chapters in this section remind us that both respondents and social scientists actively construct meaning in each other's talk. Jody Miller and Barry Glassner address the issue of finding 'reality' in interview accounts. As I argue in *IQD*, the desire of many researchers to treat interview data as more or less straightforward 'pictures' of an external reality can fail to understand how that 'reality' is being represented in words. Miller and Glassner set out a position which seeks to move beyond this argument about the 'inside' and the 'outside' of interview accounts. Using their own research on adolescents' social worlds, they argue that interview accounts may fruitfully be treated as situated elements in social worlds, drawing upon and revising and reframing the cultural stories available in those worlds. For Miller and Glassner, the focus of interview research should be fixed upon what stories are told and how and where they are produced.

In their chapter, James Holstein and Jaber Gubrium show us how a focus on story and narrative structure demands that we recognize that both interview data and interview analysis are *active* occasions in which meanings are produced. This means that we ought to view research 'subjects' not as stable entities but as actively constructed through their answers. Indeed, in Holstein and Gubrium's telling phrase, both interviewee and interviewer are 'practitioners of everyday life'. Using examples from their research on nursing home residents and on carers of elderly family members, they invite us to locate the interpretive practices which generate the 'hows' and the 'whats' of experience as aspects of reality that are constructed in collaboration with the interviewer to produce a 'narrative drama'.

The final chapter on interview data is by Carolyn Baker. In common with Holstein and Gubrium, Baker treats interview talk as social action in which all parties draw upon their cultural knowledge in doing their accounting work. Baker's particular contribution is to show how interview data may be analysed in terms of the categories that participants use and how those categories are routinely attached to particular kinds of activity. Using this form of Sacks's 'membership categorization analysis' (see also Part IX), Baker shows how we can describe the interpretive work present in data taken from parent–teacher interviews and research interviews with teenagers and the Chair of a school welfare committee. Like the previous two chapters, Baker's appeals to the 'cultural logics' drawn upon by members in accounting for themselves and assembling a social world which is 'recognizably familiar, orderly and moral'.

Sue Wilkinson's chapter on focus groups carries forward Baker's focus on how we construct the social world with our respondents. Using illuminating extracts from her own data, Wilkinson reveals the complicated interpretive activities between members of focus groups as they try to make sense of each other (and the researcher). This close attention to the details of short data extracts is contrasted with how most focus group (and interview) research is usually conducted. Wilkinson's concern with theoretically driven, detailed data analysis stands apart from the dominant tendency to treat focus group talk as a straightforward means of accessing some independent 'reality'. Above all, Wilkinson shows us that content analysis and a concentration on the mechanics of how to run a focus group are no substitute for theoretically informed and detailed data analysis of talk-in-action. Like all the contributors to this volume, Wilkinson underlines the fact that we must never overlook the active interpretive skills of our research subjects.

Part V is concerned with audio data. Jonathan Potter discusses discourse analysis (DA) as a way of analysing naturally occurring talk. Potter shows the manner in which DA allows us to address how versions of reality are produced to seem objective and separate from the speaker. Using examples drawn from television interviews with Princess Diana and Salman Rushdie and a newspaper report of a psychiatrist's comment, he demonstrates how we can analyse the ways in which speakers disavow a 'stake' in their actions.

In its focus on how reality is locally constructed, DA shares many concerns with conversation analysis (CA). John Heritage's chapter presents an accessible introduction to how conversation analytic methods can be used in the analysis of institutional talk. After a brief review of the main features of such talk, Heritage devotes the rest of his chapter to an illuminating analysis of a short telephone conversation between a school employee and the mother of a child who may be a truant. He shows how, using CA, we can identify the overall structural organization of the phone call, its sequence organization, turn design, the lexical choices of speakers and interactional asymmetries. Finally, Heritage demonstrates how each of these elements fits inside each other – 'rather like a Russian doll', as he puts it.

The elegance of Heritage's account of institutional talk is matched by the two chapters in the next part on visual data. Like Sue Wilkinson (in her chapter on focus groups), Michael Emmison argues that visual researchers have worked with inadequate theories. For instance, most tend to identify visual data with such artefacts as photographs and, to a lesser extent, cartoons and advertisements. Although such work can be interesting, it is, in a sense, two dimensional. If we recognise that the visual is also spatial, a whole new set of three-dimensional objects emerge. By looking at how people use objects in the world around them (from streetmaps to the layout of a room), we can study the material embodiment of culture.

Christian Heath's discussion of the analysis of face-to-face interaction through video shows one way of looking at three-dimensional data in fine detail. Beginning with a clear account of CA's focus on sequential organization, Heath shows how CA can be used to study visual conduct and how the physical properties of human environments are made relevant within the course of social interaction. Like Heritage, Heath uses an extended example. In a medical consultation, a patient's movements serve to focus the doctor's attention on a particular aspect of her account of her symptoms. The example also shows that, while the visual aspect of conduct is not organized on a turn-by-turn basis, as Heath puts it: 'the sequential relations between visual and vocal actions remain a critical property of their organization'. Heath concludes by showing the relevance of these insights to studies of the workplace, including human–computer interaction.

The final four chapters of this book, by Peräkylä, Bloor, Miller, Dingwall and Murphy and myself, move on to broader themes about the credibility and wider impact of qualitative research. Anssi Peräkylä discusses how qualitative research can seek to offer reliable and valid descriptions. Following Heritage's chapter, Peräkylä illustrates his argument with CA research on institutional interaction. He shows how good transcripts of audio-recorded interactions can maintain the reliability of the data. However, Peräkylä also shows how we can accommodate the fact that tapes do not necessarily include all aspects of social interaction and addresses such 'nitty gritty' questions as the selection of what to record, the technical quality of recordings and the adequacy of transcripts. Finally, validity questions are discussed in terms of conventional 'deviant case analysis' as well as specifically CA methods, such as validation through 'next turn'. Overall, Peräkylä is right to claim that his chapter is the first systematic attempt to discuss such matters in relation to CA. At the same time, his discussion has a much broader relevance to all serious qualitative research.

Michael Bloor's chapter also deals with a topic that concerns most qualitative researchers: the ability of our research to contribute to addressing social problems. Bloor argues that our focus on everyday activities makes it particularly relevant in helping practitioners to think about their working practices. He demonstrates his argument by detailed discussions of case studies which he conducted of male prostitutes in Glasgow and of eight therapeutic communities. Both sets of studies illustrate Bloor's point about the ways in which rigorous qualitative research can have relevance for service provision, even if, at least in the UK, it is unlikely to have much impact upon policy debates at the governmental level. Finally, Bloor reviews (and rejects) the argument that social scientists should not be practitioners' helpers.

Bloor's focus on how professionals can make use of qualitative research is complemented by Miller, Dingwall and Murphy's chapter. Like Bloor, they are concerned with the wider community. However, their attention is on the variety of 'stakeholders' in the organizations that dominate our lives. Economists and management consultants hold centre stage in this arena and qualitative research receives little attention. Yet the latter's ability to reveal organizational processes suggests that we have much to offer to managers. Using illuminating examples of studies of both private corporations and public agencies, Miller, Dingwall and Murphy establish precisely what qualitative research, with its flexible research designs, can offer organizations. Organizational complexities can be recognized and, as a result, new ways of reframing organizational problems can be posited.

Not all of the contributors to this volume are in agreement about every issue. We particularly see this within Parts II and V, where contrasting views of each kind of data analysis are advanced. None the less, I believe that the contributors to this volume share enough in common to make this a coherent volume. Many of my contributors, I suspect, would agree with most of the six points at the start of this chapter. With more certainty, I would claim that we share a fairly common sense of what constitutes 'good' qualitative research. For instance, even though we come from different intellectual traditions, I would be surprised if we were to have any fundamental disagreement about, say, the assessment of an article submitted to us for refereeing.

This common sense of what we are 'looking for' derives, I believe, from an attention to the mundane properties of everyday description. Therefore, this volume concludes with a postscript, drawing upon the work of Harvey Sacks, in which I sketch out these properties and their consequences for qualitative research. I thank Geraldine Leydon, Jay Gubrium and Judith Green for their comments on an earlier draft of this chapter.

I want to conclude this introduction by mentioning an absent friend. Carolyn Baker had agreed to revise her brilliant chapter on interviews for this volume. Tragically, a serious illness prevented her fulfilling this commitment. Sadly, Carolyn died a few days before I wrote this introduction. She will be sorely missed for both her intellectual brilliance and personal qualities. In the circumstances, I have limited myself to some minimal updating of her chapter for this volume.

As always, my thanks are also due to Gilly for putting up with me and to my friends at the Nursery End for giving me summers I can look forward to.

REFERENCES

Silverman, D. (2000) *Doing Qualitative Research*. London: Sage.
Silverman, D. (2001) *Interpreting Qualitative Data: Methods for Analysing Talk, Text and Interaction*, Second Edition. London: Sage.

Part II Observation

2 Ethnography

Relating the part to the whole

Isabelle Baszanger and Nicolas Dodier

By the beginning of the twentieth century, the anthropological tradition, primarily through the influential work of Bronislaw Malinowski, Edward Evans-Pritchard and Margaret Mead, had conferred an abiding legitimacy on field observations integrated into a 'cultural whole'. The subsequent crisis in this model corresponds to two lines of questioning. First, ethno-methodological studies undermined the conventional view by revealing the interpretations and negotiations needed to decontextualize observation situations at all junctures of fieldwork. Whether that work is ethnographic or statistical, it involves invisible operations that do not generally appear in social science texts. Second, analysis of how field notes are constructed forced a revision of the traditional views of the anthropologist in the field and served as a basis for a very critical reassessment of the authority of the ethnographer.

In parallel, within the field of sociology, greater emphasis was being placed on ethnographic approaches, primarily in terms of the importance given to direct, *in situ* observation of concrete sequences of activities. This was encouraged by new developments in the theory of action including extensions of the interactionist tradition, the many studies focusing on scientific activity, and work carried out in French pragmatic sociology looking at different regimes of action.

Since that time, new conceptions of ethnography have emerged. They reassert the value of fieldwork, but focus more on demonstrating the relationship between forms of heterogeneous action rather than trying to identify a culture as a whole. This chapter will take stock of these new developments in ethnography, the underlying conception of the field and the way in which they deal with the fact of human plurality (Arendt, 1995).

We will start with the question of the totalization of ethnographic data, i.e. how to integrate the series of data collected in the field into a single whole? We suggest distinguishing between three kinds of ethnography:

1 *Integrative ethnography*: following the anthropological tradition, this constructs units of collective belonging for individuals.
2 *Narrative ethnography*: by contrast, this offers readers a first-person narrative of events for each different field.
3 *Combinative ethnography*: by working simultaneously in different fields, this brings together a casebook that can be used to identify the different forms of action in which people may engage, along with the possible combinations between them.

As the above list suggests, totalization has a methodological dimension. This involves an examination of the operations whereby a totality is built up in the course of an ethnographic study, into which each concrete item is then, finally, fitted. These operations are both external (note taking, building up a series of observations, codings, etc.) and internal (the transformation, during the work, of the researcher's own way of apprehending the world). At the same time, it is also a theoretical question, since the relationship between individual cases and a totality directly involves the status ascribed to the references to the latter (e.g. collective belonging, individual stories, forms of action) in interpreting individual behaviour or actions.

In this chapter, we show how combinative ethnography has helped find a way out of the crisis of totalization in its 'integrative' version, and also how the question of the anchoring of the wholes thus constituted is brought into new focus by initiating reflection around the mode of otherness in which persons appear in each of the three forms of ethnography listed above.

AN INITIAL CHARACTERIZATION OF ETHNOGRAPHIC RESEARCH

Ethnographic studies are carried out to satisfy three simultaneous requirements associated with the study of human activities:

1 the need for an empirical approach;
2 the need to remain open to elements that cannot be codified at the time of the study;
3 a concern for grounding the phenomena observed in the field.

Each requirement is briefly discussed below.

The need for an empirical approach

This first need is dictated by the fact that the phenomena studied cannot be deduced but require empirical observation. This is undoubtedly what Durkheim really meant by his well-known injunction to 'treat social facts as things', meaning not so much that sociology should be conducted along the same lines as the natural sciences, but as a way of distinguishing it from philosophy and the introspection that takes place upstream of an empirical approach.[1] In the current debate over the resources people mobilize to understand the world and to make reference to it, this is the major difference between the social sciences, on the one hand, and the philosophy of language, phenomenology and hermeneutics, on the other.

The need to remain open

Beyond any methodical planning of observations, the fieldworker must remain open in order to discover the elements making up the markers and the tools that people mobilize in their interactions with others and, more generally, with the world. By markers, we mean representations of the world, or normative expectations, but also the linguistic and para-linguistic resources that are displayed in contact with the environment (Bessy and Chateauraynaud, 1995; Thévenot, 1994). The objective here is to distinguish between openness to new data (*in situ studies*) and its opposite, as when individual activities are studied according to strict schedules and on the basis of previously defined items and rules (*a priori codified studies*). This second approach is intrinsically incapable of revealing the unexpected elements that come to light as a study progresses. In methodological terms, a study can be described as *in situ* if it allows each subject to behave in an endogenous manner: that is, one that is not influenced by the study arrangements.

There are many reasons for not 'aligning' the subjects of a study in compliance with the study arrangements, just as there are many theories calling for recourse to ethnographic studies: discovery of other cultures that cannot be understood in the light of pre-existing knowledge (anthropological tradition), the contingency of continually negotiated human activities (interactionist tradition) and observation of how people handle the contingencies of a given situation (ethnomethodology), and so on.

This principle of openness to what cannot *a priori* be pre-codified results in the basic tension underlying *in situ* studies. The flexibility required by this openness conflicts with the need to maintain at least a minimum of method in the conduct of the study; that is, a certain guide for the behaviour of both the fieldworker and the people observed, depending on the plan of the study. This duality is an implicit part of the general situation of the *in situ* fieldworker.

The tension is primarily epistemological. The principle of non-alignment of the people observed does not sit easily with the principle of planning that has governed the experimental sciences since the idea of scientific 'reproduction' or 'reproducibility' was elevated to the rank of a major, normative requirement of scientific research (Licoppe, 1996). Social scientists who wish, none the less, to continue openly to observe the endogenous development of human activities approach this problem in a number of different ways. Some seek to conform as closely as possible to the requirements of experimental reproducibility. Even if they allow open activity sequences to take place, they try as much as possible to standardize the time intervals of these sequences and record this activity by automatic means (tape recorder or VCR used in conversation analysis – see Parts V and VI of this volume).

Others oppose this requirement of alignment and even the whole idea of observation corresponding to the current canons of science. They insist on an approach that is opposed to any type of planning, leaving the study completely open to the uncertainties of the field. Still others recognize the need for some sort of compromise between method and openness to situations, and see ethnographic tensions as a more extreme but, ultimately, a quite banal example of the sort of negotiation that is omnipresent in science (e.g. scientists' negotiation between the need to follow standard rules, which in any case always demand local interpretations and adjustments, and the concrete course of any scientific endeavour).[2]

It is worth noting that this duality underlying the ethnographer's work also has moral implications beyond the epistemological dimension. To satisfy this principle of openness, which is deliberately taken quite far, the ethnographer must graft his/her study onto pre-existing systems of activity. As opposed to the researcher, who channels subject matter into the laboratory, the ethnographer leaves the laboratory and tries to make his/her data gathering compatible with the study population's other commitments. By definition, ethnographic study design is a hybrid approach in which the fieldworker is present in two agencies, as data gatherer and as a person involved in activities directed towards other objectives.[3]

Grounding observed phenomena in the field

A study becomes ethnographic when the fieldworker is careful to connect the facts that s/he observes with the specific features of the *backdrop* against which these facts occur, which are linked to historical and cultural contingencies. Not all *in situ* studies are field studies.

Distinctions can be made between different sorts of empirical study carried out in the social sciences. Some attempt to universalize, i.e. are formal in nature, while others, resolutely grounded in a specific context, can be considered as ethnographic – or field – studies. Formal studies dissociate collected data from any context in order to access a universal, human level from the outset. This is the approach characteristic of the philosophy of language, of Austin's pragmatics, of phenomenological analyses or ordinary language analysis based on analysis of conversations.

It is also characteristic of the 'nomothetical' approach that uses empirical observation to demonstrate consistencies between facts and to formulate general laws. Nevertheless, the ethnographic study is not only empirical or only 'open'. It is, like history, embedded in a field that is limited in time and space (Ricoeur, 1984–1988). Returning to a concept that Darbo-Peschanski (1987) applies to the studies of Herodotus, it is a 'science of the particular' and describes itself as such.

This does not exclude a second step, in which a series of ethnographic studies can serve as sources for defining universal, human phenomena, in the true sense. This is, for example, the position of Lévi-Strauss: ethnographic studies provide elements for ethnological texts that study societies one after the other. On this basis, starting from a systematic comparison between societies, anthropological work attempts to arrive at a theory of the structure of the human spirit.

In *in situ* studies, this reference to field experience nevertheless distinguishes ethnographic studies from other observation methods that are not grounded in a specific field (conversation analysis, situated cognition and ethnomethodology). This raises questions about fieldwork: what is the status of this 'specific' context in which the study takes place? How is it described? How is this framework delineated, since it is not a here-and-now situation, nor a situation in which humankind as a whole is characterized through the fundamental properties of every one of its activities?

These questions are the focal point of any analysis of the process of generalization in ethnography, particularly in terms of how a cultural whole is depicted. This is what is called here the process of 'totalization', an operation whereby the ethnographer integrates the different observation sequences into a global referential framework.

INTEGRATIVE ETHNOGRAPHY

The ethnographic tradition has long considered that it is possible to integrate sequences of ethnographic observations by relating them to a cultural whole: a global reference which encompasses these observations and within which the different data throw light on each other. This vision of an integrative ethnography has been developed in social and cultural anthropology, particularly in the study of non-Western societies, but also in similar studies carried out in Western countries. It also involves the most culturally oriented part of the interactionist tradition: that is, the study of microcultures or subcultures, and, more generally, all references in the interactionist tradition to the existence of communities of people sharing the same rules and the same understanding of the world (e.g. deviant communities).

Integrative ethnography proposes a monographic totalization that is distinct from statistical totalization or summation. In general, the latter does not meet the requirement of openness, and is therefore excluded from our classification of '*in situ*' study methods.[4]

A number of methods have been proposed to achieve this monographic totalization. First, it can result from the fieldworker's reflections, whereby s/he achieves an integrated vision of his/her subjective experience. This is the meaning behind calls for empathy with the people encountered: the fieldworker tries to immerse him/herself in the field conditions and gain access to the point of view of the others, seen as 'natives': that is, people who share a similar cultural perspective, one that differs from the perspective of the newly arrived fieldworker. As Clifford noted, a professional anthropologist is supposed successfully to 'infiltrate the expressional universe of the other' (1983: 100). By understanding the other through an empathetic relationship, the fieldworker would be able to reconstruct this other's point of view, and therefore culture (or the contents of this other's collective consciousness).

The assumption of empathy as the process through which the point of view of the other becomes transparent to the fieldworker is vulnerable to criticisms arising from hermeneutic interpretation of texts and actions (Gadamer, 1975; Ricoeur, 1991). The act of gaining access to the point of view of the other always implies an initial period of questioning, which is itself embedded in a certain tradition, that of the interpreter – s/he is always caught in the 'hermeneutic circle' of the initial questioning of the text (or action), and of its transformation, in return, as a result of this encounter.

Although certain relationships or certain moments can be better qualified as empathetic, in the sense of a type of harmony between persons, we cannot therefore conclude that the point of view of the other will be conveyed in total transparency or that it can be expressed in words. Any interpretive act is influenced, consciously or not, by the tradition to which the interpreter belongs. Lévi-Strauss (1963) proposes a variation on this process by considering the moment the experience is integrated into a whole not as a moment of access to the point of view of the other, but as a moment when the entire set of results experienced and memorized by the fieldworker crystallizes into a single, unified experience. That event takes place at the conclusion of the fieldworker's ethnographic apprenticeship in the society studied. The ethnographer's field experience 'represents a crucial moment in his/her education, prior to which he may have accumulated dissociated knowledge that might never integrate into a holistic experience; only after this moment will this knowledge "take definitive form" and suddenly acquire a meaning that it previously lacked' (Lévi-Strauss, 1963). In other words, what we are dealing with here is a genuine 'internal revolution' (Lévi-Strauss, 1963).

By treating participant observation as a method rather than 'a clinical talent' resulting from an empathetic stance,[5] a number of authors have helped to provide a new explanation for the position of the ethnographer, which becomes one of his/her own methodological tools. Just like the ethnographer in remote societies, the observer has to accept a separation from his/her familiar universe, not only in order to be physically present in the new environment, but also in order to achieve personal proximity.[6]

The observer has to enter into the group and find the right distance between him/herself and the group. There is a close relationship here between the observer's presentation of him/herself (to enter the field and throughout the study), and the place accorded to the observer by the other.

While it is paramount for a fieldworker to be attentive to the expectations and role projections of the people being observed,[7] this is less in order to achieve an empathetic attitude than because the interrelations themselves and, ultimately, the fieldworker and the work done on his/her experience are the preferential instruments of observation.

There is nothing romantic or intuitive here (Piette, 1996: 68–72). This is conscious work on the part of the observer, who has to control his/her emotional reaction to what is observed and also develop a finely tuned introspection to understand fully the process of transformation which s/he undergoes by being constantly present in the field. Hence, understanding a cultural whole is achieved through this reciprocating motion of the observer and the phenomena that s/he is observing, or, as Fox puts it, the process 'by which a participant observer gradually makes organized sense out of what he sees, hears and becomes a part of it' (1974: 230).

The observer establishes a sort of parallel between what s/he feels and what the people observed feel, or the phases they pass through. S/he uses a form of introspection to reveal how s/he develops new attitudes or borrows new roles and what that 'does for him/her'. In this way, the observer has fleeting insights into the possible functions and meanings for the people observed, which s/he then tries to verify in the field, at which point s/he either recognizes their validity or rejects them.[8]

The duration of the observation enables the fieldworker in a sense to immerse him/herself in the subject being observed, but this is closer to a process of socialization than a direct access to the point of view of the other. In order to achieve a comprehensive understanding of a group, the fieldworker has to work his/her way through the dense fabric of the culture observed, in order to arrive later at an objective understanding and, hence, a monographic totalization.[9] This brings us back to a slightly modified form of Lévi-Strauss's position.

Geertz (1973) also distances himself from the empathetic schema and reintegrates the concept of culture in a hermeneutic process: activities can be read like texts, as far as both the actors themselves and the fieldworker are concerned; the concept of 'culture' is also a tool for the actors, who use it to interpret their reciprocal behaviour. It is the discovery of the hermeneutic role of the concept of culture for all individuals in their daily relationships – based not on a representation of lived experience or on their point of view, but on a description of their oral or written production – that allows us to relate a sequence of specific scenes to a culture. In any case (empathy, the integrative experience of the ethnographer, the participant observation of the sociologist, the hermeneutic approach), access to the major features of the culture being studied, as can be seen in all ethnography manuals, implies using methods to go beyond a disparate set of ethnographic observations and discover an integrated culture which is different from other cultures.[10]

Because of its capacity to satisfy the need for concrete facts in the study and at the same time produce a discourse taking in collective wholes, this approach has for a long time exerted a great deal of fascination over the social sciences. However, it does not stand up very well to two criticisms. First, it is only valid if we are dealing with so-called 'mechanical' solidarity between individuals (Durkheim): that is, a society or group in which people are assumed to share the same elements of the collective consciousness. Difficulties arise if the coordination between human activities conforms to other types of logic. In contemporary worlds, one now has to take into account the fact that several possible references can coexist despite their contradictions, sometimes within the same person, and that they can slot into the normative guidelines for action depending on the constraints of the actual situation (Boltanski and Thévenot, 1991).

The very notion of society becomes problematical when solidarity between people is established along socio-technical networks in which individuals coordinate their activities step by step according to functional objectives and without reference to a single common framework (Dodier, 1995a). Moreover, at the methodological level, the moment at which data are integrated into a whole occurs at an unknown, almost mysterious point of the process.

Some ethnographers cultivate this sense of mystery by affirming their lack of interest in any account of methods. But others take a more ambiguous stand: monographic totalization may conceal implicit statistical totalization performed, as it were, behind the scenes. We see this particularly in the rhetoric of cultural ethnographic studies, which very easily use frequency markers when describing behaviour (often, sometimes, from time to time, always, etc.) without making more than a token attempt to justify them. These problems have been taken very seriously by some historians of ethnography and by certain ethnographers, to the point of casting doubt on the tradition of totalization presented more or less as a foregone conclusion in ethnology and field sociology.

NARRATIVE INTEGRATION

An attentive reading of ethnographers' field notes, particularly the famous example of Malinowski's notebook (1967), has led some authors to hark back to the question of the status that should be accorded to the process of monographic totalization (Marcus and Cushman, 1982). The very personal nature of the act of totalization, perceived in an almost ritual form by anthropologists, has been revealed as an experience associated with solitude.

For a long time, this experience in the field was perceived as a necessary moment of immersion in a culture for which the anthropologist could then become the legitimate representative. An analysis of field notes shows that the switch from this experience in the field to the ethnographic text is more complicated than had been thought. The role of the actual individual history of the ethnographer in his/her manner of identifying the culture became more apparent, as did the influence of the actual work of writing on the identification of cultural types, based on much vaguer and more varied encounters than might be imagined from the simple accounts given in the published texts. Once this observation was acknowledged, several channels were explored.

The first consists of claiming that the writing work itself is an essential part of ethnography. The ethnographic text is deliberately considered to be a work of fiction, stylizing people and events as a way of emphasizing their cultural traits. The ethnographer is seen as an author and due emphasis is given to the profoundly personal nature of his/her account (Clifford and Marcus, 1986).

Another channel consists of seeing the fieldwork itself not as the hidden face of ethnography, perhaps reported in a personal diary, but as the actual material of the ethnographic text. This text is no longer the 'picture' of a culture or a society revealed to the ethnographer at the end of a learning process by which, finally, s/he is able to see it as a whole, but the 'account' of events confronting the ethnographer as the enquiry progresses. The narrative is now seen as integrating these events (Ricoeur, 1991); it preserves their temporal dimension and does not banish the ethnographer from his/her text – quite the opposite, in fact.

Such narrative ethnography can take the form of an approach that we might call hyper-reflexive, more preoccupied in fact with questioning and reporting on the operations performed by the ethnographer in his/her attempt, through concepts such as 'culture' or 'society', to confer some meaning on activities, than really acknowledging the existence of the other (Moerman, 1972). The encounter between ethnologist and study population is viewed as a dialogue initiated between individuals who themselves belong to different collective wholes. The concept of 'culture' is not abandoned, but the ethnographer does not try so much to acknowledge an 'other culture' as to reveal the dialogue that is established between different cultures during the fieldwork (Dwyer, 1979).

Finally, the narrative approach in ethnography is influenced by psycho-analysis (Favret-Saada, 1980; Favret-Saada and Contreras, 1981).[11] The study is described as a process profoundly linked to the individual history of the ethnographer. The text may be a history of the events occurring in the course of the fieldwork, i.e. the field notes (Favret-Saada and Contreras, 1981).

Alternatively, in an approach that is closer to the anthropological tradition, the narrative dimensions of the ethnological study are fitted into or alternate with analyses giving a representation of the logic of the relationships (in this case, the framework surrounding enunciations about sorcery) encountered by the ethnographer (Favret-Saada, 1980). This form of narrative is interesting because it does not unfairly remove the ethnographer from his/her text, particularly if s/he is closely involved in the activities described therein. It also avoids limiting the enquiry to the trajectory of a specific person, without at least suggesting why this experience is exemplary and in what way it provides information about the type of relationship the people studied have with the world. Hence, this form of text transcends the alternative between a purely singular 'I', characteristic of narrative ethnography, and the absence of the 'I', which is typical of classic ethnography. The work of reflexivity is not limited to narratives in the first person. Through the study itself, and in a retrospective vision, the author becomes capable of describing, in the series of events which s/he is reporting, in what capacity s/he was present or what place s/he occupied in these events (and, notably, in the case of Jeanne Favret-Saada, the place of her work in the framework surrounding enunciations). Here, we are dealing, in the field of the social sciences, with texts that have the same force as 'evidence'. Often, these texts also suggest what part of this evidence is representative of a more general condition, by using all the possibilities of first-person narration and by identifying the role played by the author.[12]

THE ETHNOGRAPHIC CASEBOOK

There is another way of looking at the aggregation of specific events collected in an ethnographic study. The context of the events observed is considered neither as a 'whole' to be discovered (integrative ethnography) nor as a grounding point for an individual history (narrative ethnography), but as a disparate collection of resources between which individuals have to navigate. Unlike the cultural approach, we do not presume here that the resources mobilized by people in their behaviour can be linked up to a coherent whole. Unlike narrative ethnography, we leave behind the first-person account, the aim being to generalize from the study. This approach could be described as *combinative ethnography*. It takes several different forms in ethnographic work. In point of fact, it is present from the very beginning of the interactionist tradition.

Compared with the anthropological tradition, the originality of the early Chicago School was that it did not necessarily integrate the data collected around a collective whole in terms of a common culture, but in terms of territory, of geographic space.[13] The problem with which these sociologists were concerned was based on human ecology: the interactions of human groups with the natural environment and a given geographical milieu. Their key concept, the unit of reference, so to speak, was the biotic community, with its notion of territory.[14] The main point here was to make an inventory of a space by studying the different communities and activities of which it is composed.

This kind of ethnography sought to identify certain cases (and notably life histories) as examples of more general phenomena,[15] but with quite a high degree of freedom to move between different levels of generalization.[16] Here the ethnographer's participation in daily activities was seen as much, if not more, as a way of collecting facts as of gaining access to the meaning of situations for the subjects being studied. In this respect, we are still some distance away from the movement that was to become participant observation in the 1950s (cf. Platt, 1983) and the position of integrative ethnography.[17]

In the theory of action proposed by Glaser and Strauss (1967) as well as in its methodological implications, the method known as 'constant comparison' does not necessarily concern collective entities, but rather situations or types of activity, classified by the sociologist and studied in their relationships to each other, with a view to revealing their compatibility or the contrasts between them. Individuals can switch from one line of activity to another and the aim of the sociological study is to demonstrate the combinations – whether harmonious or conflictual – between these multiple commitments.

This methodological orientation has also emerged within the framework of new developments of the sociological theory of action. Here, in the context of 'sociological pragmatics', it is considered that individuals can be involved in different 'regimes of action', that the arrangements that provide a framework for these situations direct people towards certain forms of commitment, but that tensions or combinations can emerge between these regimes of action (Boltanski and Thévenot, 1991; Dodier, 1993, 1995a). For example, the actual work of a doctor could be studied as the articulation between different 'framings' of his/her patient (Baszanger, 1998b; Dodier, 1994; Silverman, 1987). From this viewpoint, ethnography is no longer concerned with the search for references shared by the actors, as in the integrative approach. It aims to take stock of the dynamic relationship between the real activities of individuals within the framework of complex, normative references, which are related to the situation and are not unified. Although the arrangements framing the action are assumed to have a historical origin and a particular distribution in space, they are not automatically assigned to a culture. This type of schema, which breaks with the concept of a collective consciousness shared from the outset, assumes that individuals, and their actions, are located at the intersection of a non-harmonized plurality of references, which are examined in their existential commitment.

A common characteristic of these three types of ethnographic study (the Chicago tradition, the form of interactionism inspired by Anselm Strauss, sociological pragmatics) is to *distinguish between generalization and totalization*. The study method consists of accumulating a series of individual cases and of analysing them as a combination between different logics of action that coexist not only in the field under consideration, but even within these individuals or during their encounters.

Accumulation and processing of these cases can be likened to an *ethnographic casebook*, which is gradually enriched by new examples displaying new forms of activity and patterns of articulation. The research aims at producing a combinative inventory of possible situations. The researcher has not chosen an integrated field constituting a central point from which s/he will reconstitute a collective whole. Instead, s/he circulates between several sites, depending on which dimensions appear relevant in the analysis of each case. Although the researcher sometimes seeks a field that will allow him/her to study a regime of action or a form of activity in greater depth, s/he is not surprised if this field proves to be more disparate than anticipated, a factor that forces him/her to take into consideration the way in which it is related to other forms of action. As a result, the material collected often appears as a rather vast corpus of textual data coming from very disparate sources, in terms of situations and the media used.[18]

FORMS OF TOTALIZATION AND FORMS OF OTHERNESS

In ethnography, several responses have been proposed to the question of how we aggregate our observations. Integrative ethnography suggests that it is possible, thanks to monographic totalizations, to gain access to the collective wholes that govern behaviour. Narrative ethnography has quite radically challenged any pretension to totalization on the part of the social sciences – it integrates itself in a vaster movement of critiques of totalization in the social sciences,[19] and focuses on the production of highly individualized accounts gathered in the course of the study. Finally, various ethnographic practices have sought to implement forms of generalization, which, starting from work on series of cases, aim not so much at the totalization of data as the revelation of a combinative mechanism between disparate or even contradictory forms of action within a given society.

Methodologically speaking, these last-mentioned works refer back to a non-cultural concept of the field which was already present in the Chicago tradition. However, here there is a greater concern for theoretical clarification concerning the concept of action and the methods for gathering and processing data.[20] This avoids both the mysteries of monographic totalization and the excesses of focusing on the person of the fieldworker evident in some narrative ethnographic works, or the escape back towards hyper-reflexivity.

What is the aim of each of these forms of ethnography? In this chapter, we will look at this question from the perspective of otherness: how do they represent the fact of human plurality? We suggest that these forms of ethnography propose what we might call different modes of otherness, i.e. different ways of showing the reader how the people present and acting in the texts are both similar to and different from him/her.

The relationship of individuals to the wholes or aggregates of integrative ethnography is one of belongingness. These aggregates are all tools for distinguishing among individuals between those that 'belong', so to speak, and those that do not. Hence, they are social identification markers, within the meaning given by Goffman (1961). The aggregates of classical ethnography, as noted by Piette (1996), correspond to objects supposedly 'shared' by people. These are shared only by the people presented in the ethnographic text, and not by its readers, who are, on the contrary, invited to see in ethnography faithful images of what happens 'over there', and not 'here' (Geertz, 1988). Moreover, these shared objects are only recognized as such by the ethnographer because the ethnographer him/herself does not share them.

The whole process of assembling observations, up to and including closure of the study, is based on the fact that what is shared is shared only by a circumscribed group of individuals which includes neither the ethnographer nor, in most cases, the people who read ethnography. Whether one identifies the recording of this aggregate in an integrative experience (Lévi-Strauss), in a hermeneutics of indigenous interpretations (Geertz) or in a successful socialization (Fox), the very fact that closure can be reached reflects the dual nature of this global reference. It is shared by the others, and distinct from what we ourselves are supposed to share given that we belong to other wholes. Whether or not these other wholes are explicitly mentioned in the text is unimportant – it is their implicit presence that counts. Here, we are dealing with an otherness of belonging.

Narrative ethnography is built on recording encounters between the ethnographer and the study population within an individual story, establishing a completely different relationship to the relevant whole: in this case, a biographical sequence. This sequence is built up gradually by the fieldworker, who is revealed to him/herself in the field in the narrative work of the configuration of self, according to a schema defended in a more general sense by Ricoeur (1990). The other individuals are perceived in the same way: as so many individual beings also involved in the process of the construction of self, caught up in the same tangled web of stories in the field.

Closure occurs when the ethnographer deems that s/he is capable, at a given moment, of giving his/her experience the shaping form of the narrative. Closure does not rule out further developments that might spring from later reflection by the fieldworker about him/herself, or further applications which might be directed to him/her by contacts in the field. Here the reader is faced with the otherness of the ethnographer as much as that of his/her contacts. At the centre of this otherness we find the interplay between two forms of identity proposed by Ricoeur, 'ipseity' and sameness. Ipseity comes from the Latin pronoun *ipse* and defines a form of identity referring to the singular person, which is distinct from 'sameness', a form of identity referring to categories of belongingness of the person. The interplay between these two forms of identity as a characteristic of the narrative leads, as he suggests, to the narrative identity.

Integrative ethnography proposed that the ethnographer disappear to reveal better to the reader an otherness of belonging (that of the natives). Conversely, in narrative ethnography, the presence of the ethnographer confronts the reader with a narrative otherness, grounded in the 'ipseity' of the ethnographer but none the less – thanks to the very dynamic of the narrative – offering possible avenues towards generalization beyond the individual case.

The question of belonging, which is central to integrative ethnography, and that of individual biographies, central to narrative ethnography, is replaced in combinative ethnography by the question of action. The initial point of entry into the field is generally an enquiry into a form of activity, explored in different places: disputes, judgement, scientific activity, medical activity, production, etc. In this case, the ethnographic text is very similar to a kind of inventory. It is generally presented as a list of possible operations: the resources available to people to act while taking into account situational constraints.

Nevertheless, despite the basically disparate or even conflicting nature of the forms of action envisaged, these inventories do not contradict the idea that the people involved act with reference to 'shared objects'.[21] However, these objects do not have the same status as in integrative ethnography. The resources mobilized are presented very specifically in the form of a relative availability. They are available to people because they belong to a common fund of skills, shared by all those appearing in the text.

This availability is relative since mobilization of these resources implies a cost, unless they become available owing to some unexpected opportunity or development. These resources, which are potentially available to individuals, do not, as in integrative ethnography, 'absorb' these individuals, to use the concept developed by Piette. They are too disparate or even mutually contradictory for that.

In combinative ethnography, the coherence of resources is lost, but not the existence of a shared aggregate of dispositions for understanding the world. This aggregate is presented as a common fund of possible actualizable operations. The origin and contours of this common fund vary according to the forms of activity studied and the underlying frameworks.

So we find studies referring to a common fund shared by all (or virtually all) human beings. These studies, while showing disparate forms of action, none the less relate them to a global reference as a source of shared objects. But it is a very general reference, not particularized as in the case of integrative ethnography.

Ethnomethodology refers to the skills of 'members' as shown in their mastery of natural language. Through this mastery, people are capable of demonstrating, *in situ*, the accountability of their activities. The work of Sebastian McEvoy on 'defensive invention' (1995) attributes this very general skill in handling language in a given situation to people involved in sequences of accusation and defence and in the myriad possible ramifications of the language in which disputes may be expressed. Luc Boltanski and Laurent Thévenot refer explicitly to the existence of a very general skill in people's commitment to multiple forms of action directed towards a concern with justice, renewing both for philosophy and history, the question of the genesis of these skills.

In other studies, the status of this common fund is more flexible. Erving Goffman, for instance, refers to interactional skills which are shared by all individuals in their daily lives, and skills available to people under more specific conditions. One of the attractions of his work lies in the connections he creates between very different places, even in work which, in other respects, as in *Asylums* (Goffman, 1961), presents a monographic-type unity of time and place. The contours of the common fund of resources tend to be more strictly demarcated in the interactionist tradition inherited from Anselm Strauss, notably in the sense that concepts such as 'social world' (Strauss, 1978) tend to refer to circumscribed groups of people brought together around a shared horizon of action.

Hence it is possible to build up a theory that occupies an intermediate position between combinative and integrative ethnography, oscillating between the study of a common fund of interactional skills in our societies and a demonstration of the existence of varied funds of knowledge distributed between different groups of people. Here, at the extreme, skills are so plastic that they depend completely on the eminently local context surrounding the person, social distinctions between individuals on the basis of their belong-ingness once again becoming meaningless. This is shown in the follow-up work on scientific innovation carried out by Michel Callon and Bruno Latour:[22] their narratives propose a vision of a world in which constant movement in the chain of socio-technical networks is echoed by transformation of the skills of the human beings engaged in these networks. The skills referred to are, once again, common, but in the very general sense of a capacity to maintain and keep in operation the networks of sciences and techniques.

This dual language of 'common' skills and 'possible' acts reflects the new status ascribed to closure of the ethnographic field. Here, inventories and casebooks are associated with the principle of a closure that is always envisaged as relative. In Glaser and Strauss's 'grounded theory', closure corre-sponds to a saturation of data within the framework of gradual sampling operations that take into account unexpected developments in a collection organized in different places, which are then compared with each other (Glaser and Strauss, 1967).

In the work of Boltanski and Thévenot (1991), the forms of possible actions are, to some extent, closed off by the enumeration of 'cities' to which actors are assumed to make reference when addressing the concept of justice, but the list of figures inside the model increases as observations in the field feed the 'common worlds' concretely linked to the cities. Moreover, the model does not rule out the historical emergence of new cities supplementing those that already exist, and interfering with them in unexpected combinations.[23] Francis Chateauraynaud's work on professional mistakes (1991) and, in association with Christian Bessy, on the expertise of objects (Bessy and Chateauraynaud, 1995), is characterized by an epistemology that resolutely emphasizes the endless deployment of figures that can be demonstrated from interrogation into a given form of activity, consistent with the inventions that people may propose.

The relativity of closure of an inventory of possible actions is exacerbated, in the ethnography of regimes of action, by the fact that each observed 'case' is itself considered to be open. Once we accept that each protagonist has possible resources to attempt to change the temporal outcome of the action, there is nothing (apart from the constraints specific to empirical enquiry itself) to justify closing off at any particular point following the dynamics of stories that might continue to be played out in the field and elsewhere, even in the most unexpected configurations.

Here we can see where combinative ethnography differs from the preceding forms of ethnography in terms of the mode of otherness proposed to readers. Otherness is not seen in the same way as in integrative ethnography, i.e. in terms of belongingness. No distinction is made between people as such; that is, in terms of their acquisition of dispositions differentiating them in a sufficiently stable manner inside shared, albeit circumscribed, wholes. In the case of those ethnographic works which take the most radical line, we are, as readers, authors and the people encountered in the field, assumed to share a common fund of skills, and it is this fund revealed by the analysis which is deployed along-side the other entities present in the world: artefacts, natural entities. Or, as is the case in work which allows a wider margin for distinguishing between people in terms of a flexible belongingness, the contours of common funds and their inscription within groups are not clearly specified.

This reference to a common fund of resources does not necessarily imply that we cannot differentiate between the positions taken by people, but that they are first and foremost action related. This means that they are defined by the respective positions occupied by people at the time of their encounter rather than by their belongingness to a given group or aggregate: such as victims/benefactors/spectators; care workers/patients; judges/prisoners/counsel for the defence, and so on.

Uneven distribution of skills between people is envisaged in terms of these respective positions, rather than as a function of what each party has acquired through belonging to distinct aggregates. Here, ethnography seeks to build a sociology of encounters[24] between persons occupying different action-related positions with respect to an 'anthropological' problem (i.e. linked to a general human condition). People are seen to be in possession of a fund of skills offering various possibilities of commitment in the encounter, while remaining within the constraints fixed by the arrangements created by the initial situational context.

MEASURING WHAT IS POSSIBLE

This suggests the emergence of a new mode of otherness which we might call pragmatic otherness. It proceeds from the fact that the reader is brought into contact, through the text, with individuals who share with the reader and between themselves a common fund of heterogeneous resources and who may, depending on the case, occupy varied action-related positions. From the reader's viewpoint, and despite all the myriad ethnographic details provided, the text does not present people that are 'different', either in terms of their acquired skills as in integrative ethnography, or in terms of their individual stories, as in narrative ethnography. Indeed, the criticism of 'disembodiedness' frequently levelled at the most radical texts of combi-native ethnography reflects their failure to satisfy this implicit expectation of integration of observations in persons distinguished from one another.

Whereas successful integrative ethnography offers its readers an encounter with appreciably different individuals, combinative ethnography offers an explicitation of what is in fact present in all of us, albeit not necessarily activated owing to the limited opportunities afforded us by our situated commitments. It pictures a world of common or indeed plastic capacities, with the potential for indefinite modelling in reaction to the sudden appearance of the non-human objects with which we are confronted owing to the incessant transformations of socio-technical networks.

Ultimately, combinative ethnography presents itself as a vast inventory of possibilities or potentialities regarding situated actions. Each new study observes new scenes and hence helps enlarge the spectrum of skills, arrangements and forms of action explored by earlier studies. The discourse of possibilities characteristic of these works springs from taking into account two simultaneous properties of action: individuals have to deal with situational constraints; but they always have the possibility of dealing with them by redefining the situation. However, these possibilities impose a cost for the people using them. Such costs can involve internal tensions, linked to the individual's confrontation with heterogeneous forms of activity, with the work of adjustment required to move from one form to the other, or to harmonize one with the other in the course of the action. All the cases show the efforts made by the individual to reorganize around him/herself the other people and arrangements engaged in the same situation.[25]

This brings us to the question of creating an equivalence between these costs: how do we measure possibilities and establish a comparison between them? Crucial to the different forms of combinative ethnography is the representation of fundamental possibilities or potentialities. Even if they have not hitherto been actualized, the skills referred to here are considered as being potentially in people, who draw on them primarily as a function of situational opportunities. The paramount factor in whether they deploy these potentialities is whether they have or have not yet encountered the arrangements or action-related positions allowing them to do so. The characteristics of people who have acquired distinct sets of capacities through past experience is not systematically investigated.

This does not mean that combinative ethnography is not interested in the question of acquisition of skills. Indeed, a number of researchers have reflected on the comparison between distinct processes of acquisition, linked to distinct forms of action.[26] However, in these works, differentiation between persons in terms of what they have actually mobilized is of secondary importance. This assessment of potentialities tends to compare the different situations with which a generic person might be confronted.

This manner of looking at individuals reflects a theoretical choice: the primary aim is to construct a theory of potential skills, actualized depending on the encounters of each individual with other people, with arrangements and with action-related positions, rather than a theory of differentiated acquisition of skills. However, it also highlights the limitations of combinative ethnography as a study method. Integrative ethnography proposed a simple and attractive schema, marrying close observation of behaviour with a recording of the differences between people. Measuring possible actions was comparatively clear: the society or the unit of belongingness defined for each person the range of appropriate possibilities, those of their society or group, and excluded other possibilities as so many reactions incompatible with this belongingness.

Looked at from the perspective of heterogeneous worlds, the skills acquired by people emerge less clearly. Here, we need to 'follow' individuals, and observe the very complex way in which the effects of successive commitments in composite situations are embedded in these people. There is nothing to prevent an ethnographer undertaking this follow-up of individuals and indeed this is the process found in case histories centring on a given person, whose trajectory is recounted in the light of salient moments observed by the ethnographer.[27] Nevertheless, a genuine comparative analysis of possibilities linked to the differentiated positions acquired by individuals presupposes the establishment of a common space within which the facts relating to their behaviour would be systematically recorded.

This work is not incompatible with ethnography, but it does require some additional investment at a given moment in tools capable of representing in a single item (a diagram of connections, a statistical table, etc.) the often quite large numbers of people concerned in terms of the kinds of activity that constituted the point of entry into the study. Only in this way can we hope to visualize the degree to which the positions occupied by individuals are similar or different and compare the possibilities available to individuals structured in a distinct manner within a single space of coexistence.[28]

Within such a space, individuals emerge according to a new form of otherness: the otherness of acquired skills. The reader is introduced to people who over time have acquired distinct sets of potentialities. This form of otherness provides a key for reflecting on acquired skills in heterogeneous worlds, beyond the schema of belongingness proposed, for other contexts, by integrative ethnography.

Representation of a common space of coexistence necessarily implies selecting a few fairly simple traits characteristic of the actions of the study population, given the complexity of the operations revealed by ethnography of action. The degree to which this activity is simplified depends on the resources which the fieldworker is able to invest and the limitations, at any given time, of the processing tools available to deal with complex bodies of data.[29] In addition, the different forms of commitment coincide more or less exactly with the representational arrangements required to visualize these common spaces. Certain forms of action can hardly be recorded (Dodier, 1990) and other forms can only be recorded in very specific forms of writing as Boltanski showed in his study of love as agape (1990).

Here we can measure the very reductionist effect on the pragmatic condition of individuals of ethnographic observations aimed at illustrating work which tries to represent systematically the differentiated positions acquired by individuals in a given society – notably in the sociology of Pierre Bourdieu. Indeed, in these observations, the concept of pragmatic otherness disappears, practically speaking, when all the skills of commitment in situations are related, as a matter of principle, to so-called social positions.

Ethnographic observations then exist, first and foremost, as a means of exemplifying phenomena objectified elsewhere, using other methods, mainly statistical ones. The lucidity required to unmask in each situation what is related to social positions monopolizes the interpretive effort. There is no longer any possibility to reflect on what in the relationship with the other is related to a genuine pragmatic otherness and is not simply the projection, at the moment of the encounter, of positions acquired in the specific form of the common space of coexistence that is the social space engendered by the forms of capital uncovered by Bourdieu. The question of differential assessment of possibilities for acting by virtue of acquired positions is assumed to be already resolved even before the relevant forms of action are brought to light in the study.

ETHNOGRAPHY IN THE PUBLIC SPACE OF ITS READERS

One contribution made by combinative ethnography is its capacity to explain to readers the skills for acting with which they themselves are unfamiliar as objects of reflection. Every person can see him/herself as potentially concerned both by situational constraints and by possibilities for acting. Moreover, the close observation of activities which ethnography allows here possesses a capacity to bring to light, from a critical point of view and in a public space, skills that are not acknowledged by the usual arrangements for recording activities. In particular, close observation of individual behaviour uncovers the texture of the activity by revealing the multiple operations that individuals perform in order to act in a complex universe.

Indeed, one aim of this work of combinative ethnography is to bring into the public space the elements constituting the (often hidden) pragmatic condition of individuals. This type of ethnography renders visible to an audience a whole complex web of activity which otherwise would be apparent only to those engaged in the situation, at the time and in that place, generally without leaving any durable and transportable trace of their commitment.[30]

Integrative ethnography brought into close perspective the fabric of the life of individuals belonging to other societies. Combinative ethnography shows us what we all mobilize in the course of action, or what we might be brought to mobilize if confronted with a given set of arrangements or a given action-related position. Its real aim is to bring to light what generally remains invisible in official accounts, both by revealing the work of adjustment and by acknowledging skills for acting that are typically underestimated.

The critical compass of ethnography is very sensitive, for instance, to what ethnomethodology and laboratory-based ethnographies reveal concerning the local adjustments of scientific practice which escape the remote observation formerly allotted to it by epistemology. What is true of skills is also true of the pragmatic tensions experienced by people in a heterogeneous universe. These tensions are only revealed by close observation of behaviour which force us to look beneath the smooth surface that some actors ascribe to their organizations when they undervalue, consciously or not, their costs for concrete activities.

Hence this work involves explaining concrete conditions for acting, openness to new capacities and a critique of what is ordinarily hidden in official accounts. This critique proceeds not so much by elucidating the real interests of the actors, as in much sociological work, but by revealing the adjustments that people are obliged to make, whatever their other interests, in the detailed course of their actions. Its characteristic – and also its limitation – is that it concerns itself with people who are not differentiated from each other in terms of acquired skills and of whom we can, in the last analysis, say that they are not collectively structured in terms of their differences.

This is the point at which, in an extension of research into pragmatic otherness, we might usefully undertake work concerned more with the otherness of acquired skills, which would seek to represent distinct positions in a common space of coexistence. Making reference to such a space should give readers the possibility, which combinative ethnography has temporarily neglected, of situating themselves with respect to others, as persons structured differently by time and not only as persons endowed with similar potentialities. Representing such a space also answers the concern to totalize ethnographic data in the framework of a collective entity, once the schemas of belongingness typical of integrative ethnology have been abandoned.

NOTES

1. 'To treat facts of a certain order as things is not then to place them in a certain category of reality but to assume a certain mental attitude toward them on the principle that when approaching their study we are absolutely ignorant of their nature, and that their characteristic properties, like the unknown causes on which they depend, cannot be discovered by even the most careful introspection' (Durkheim, 1982).
2. This last argument is reinforced, on the epistemological level, by the fact that the negotiated character of the design and implementation of an experiment has, in any case, generally come to light thanks to work in sociology of science. Even in the most detailed experimental plans, negotiations are often eliminated from reports, in spite of the fact that they actually exist (Collins, 1985; Knorr-Cetina, 1981; Latour and Woolgar, 1979).
3. This is why themes of duplicity, treachery and manipulation are at the heart of such narratives (Leiris, 1981). An implicit part of the ethnographer's condition is that s/he has to resolve these tensions as they appear.
4. On the opposition between monograph and statistics, see Desrosières (1998).
5. 'There is a general tendency to think of a study based on participant observation as largely the product of an esoteric, personal kind of clinical talent on the part of the fieldworker, who is considered to be endowed with qualities usually referred to as "sensitivity", "intuition" and "empathy"' (Fox, 1974: 231).
6. This separation is achieved via an initial work on oneself. 'On several afternoons and evenings at Harvard, I found myself considering a trip to Cornerville and then rationalizing my way out of it. . . . Then too, I had to admit that I felt more comfortable among these familiar surroundings than I did wandering around Cornerville and spending time with people in whose presence I felt distinctly uncomfortable at first. When I found myself rationalizing in this way, I realized that I would have to make a break. Only if I lived in Cornerville would I ever be able to understand it and be accepted by it' (Whyte, 1981: 293–4).
7. It is clearly shown in the example in the appendix of Bosk (1979).

8. The way in which Renèe Fox describes her understanding (discovery) of the meaning and function of black humour for sick people nicely illustrates this phenomenon: 'At a non-hospital gathering one evening, I *caught myself* in the act of making a macabre joke, and I can remember speculating on the source of my unlikely new talent. The next morning, as I moved to [the ward], for the first time I *noticed* how much of the ward's conversation was phrased in the language of the grim joke and how often I responded in kind. Without realizing it, I had learned to speak to the men of [the ward] in the same way that they talked to each other. Long before this insight occurred, my field notes contained many samples of ward humor. But it was only by virtue of *self-observation* that I became sufficiently *aware* of its prevalence to regard it as a phenomenon central to my study' (1974: 231; emphasis added).

9. This point appears clearly in the relationship between the initial field notes, which, in many ways, already contain 'everything', and the final analysis which came months later: 'From the very start . . . my notes contained almost all the components of the ward picture I was ultimately to assemble. However, at the time that I recorded this observation, I was not yet aware of the patterned interconnections between them. At what point did I begin to see the ward in a coherently structured way? In the sense of month and day, I cannot really answer that question. But I do know that the so-called "understanding" of [the ward] which I eventually attained was not simply the result of coming to know more about the ward in a cognitive sense. It also involved a process of attitude learning (very much akin to what social scientists mean when they refer to the process of "socialization")' (Fox, 1974: 217–18).

10. We can, for example, refer to the classical manuals of Griaule (1957), Maget (1962) or Mauss (1947).

11. See also Certeau (1987) concerning the relationship between history and narrative.

12. Evidence about working-class lifestyles are remarkable in this respect in their capacity to combine accounts of individual histories anchored in very specific contexts and preservation of a general framework of discussion (Linhart, 1978; Navel, 1945; Weil, 1951).

13. The sociological objective of this tradition was an attempt to understand the new urban space emerging as a result of industrialization and the double phenomenon of immigration that accompanied it (from the south and rural zones towards the north and the dawning metropolises, on the one hand, and from the European continent with its multiple ethnic components, on the other). Chicago, with its mosaic of ethnic groups and its different socio-ethnic neighbourhoods, was emblematic of this phenomenon. The aim was to analyse the ways in which this space in which different groups confronted each other and mixed together was structured and to study their reactions to these totally new living conditions.

14. For example, Thrasher (1927) started from the question of the geographical localization of juvenile delinquency: some sectors are more affected than others; how can this be explained?

15. The preferred approach is the study of natural history followed by a study of the community (understood here in the sense of a biotic community with its notion of territory): a town, a neighbourhood, an ethnic community located in a given geographical space (the ghettos). The central method used is the case study, which is based essentially on a life history and, to a lesser extent, on non-structured interviews using the actual words of the subject and all sorts of personal documents (personal letters, evidence collected in community notebooks, etc.).

16. The important point was to gather intensive data – for example, for *The Hobo*, Anderson (1923) collected sixty life histories, and made a preliminary study of 400 tramps, one use of which was to establish a list of the apparent physical defects of hobos and to identify both individual and more general traits. Alongside these life histories, the facts were collected via a study of administrative statistics, archives, local newspapers and the case files of social workers.

17. The fieldworker's position is different from the empathetic position of the participant–observer and is closer to that of the stranger, if we refer to Sombart and especially to Simmel. In a text written during his 1927 survey and published in 1983, Cressey shows how he attempted to build up a position as stranger in his ethnographic relationships to study the environment, the world of taxi dance halls. Referring to Sombart's analysis of 'the cultural stranger', he distinguishes between two 'stranger positions' which he used in his research. The 'sociological stranger' is a stranger with a particular status as commonly used by lawyers, doctors, social workers, public school counsellors, etc. The second, which he used much more often, is that of the 'anonymous stranger'. This is an ordinary relationship in big cities where isolated people meet up in transient relationships and with free time on their hands. For the researcher: 'it provides an opportunity for exploring aspects of human nature not ordinarily revealed' and has the effect of a 'catharsis'. This ethnographic relationship allows the fieldworker to access revelations that Cressey calls 'impersonal confessions'.

18. The work of processing these data can benefit from the development of automated techniques designed to facilitate constant two-way communication between the encoding of the material and ethnographic concentration on its special features (Chateauraynaud, 2003).

19. On the critique of statistical totalization and its limitations, see Dodier (1996).

20. See, for example, the enumerations made in Becker et al. (1961), and, in a more general sense, for the relationships between qualitative and quantitative data in theoretical elaboration, see Glaser and Strauss (1967: Chap. 8).

21. For developments on this point, and more particularly concerning interactionism and ethnomethodology, and taking a critical approach to this referring back to shared objects, see Piette (1996).

22. See for instance Callon (1998) and Latour (1987).

23. It is worth pointing out that in a recent work Boltanski and Chiapello (1999) analyse the emergence of a new city 'the city of projects' (*la Cité 'par projets'*), linked to the latest developments of capitalism.

24. The encounter is characterised by the fact that the people involved are in each other's horizon of action, whether directly or indirectly through objects of communication. At the very least, these people are in each other's horizon without this necessarily being reciprocal, as in the scene analysed by Boltanski (1999) based on an action-related schema, of the television viewer faced with the sight of another person's suffering. Encounter-driven relations can be distinguished from relations of interdependence, which includes all those situations where the action of one person has consequences for another, without one being necessarily present in the horizon of the other (see Corcuff, 1995).

25. See for instance the work of Goffman (1974) on shifts in 'framing', the analyses of Strauss et al. (1985: 151–90) on the 'work of articulation', or the revelation of the cost of moving between different 'common worlds' in Boltanski and Thévenot's model (1991).

26. We might note the observations of Thévenot (1994) on the constitution of familiarity

in the relationship to objects, and the way in which Bessy and Chateauraynaud (1995) use the concept of 'hold' to describe the embedding, in both persons and things, of moments when the body is engaged at a level that does not mobilize exercise of judgement.

27. A good example is Strauss et al.'s development (1985: 161–81) of the case of Mrs Price in the framework of an analysis of the trajectories of cumulative mess in the hospital environment.

28. This space may bring together contemporaries who live at the same point in history. It may also aim to grasp the effects of history on the internal structuring of individuals, notably to situate observations relative to the present in an historical perspective (Baszanger, 1998b; Young, 1995).

29. These limitations are fortunately tending to recede thanks to the recent development of automated techniques allowing a continuous movement back and forth between encoding of material and an ethnographic attention to its particularities (Chateauraynaud, 2003).

30. We might think here of the way in which Anselm Strauss's focus on the different dimensions of medical work and above all the difficulty of harmonizing the different lines of work allowed him to see and bring to light the work done by the patient, in all its different dimensions (Baszanger, 1998a). For an argument supporting the need for close observation in order to apprehend the intensity of the web of judgements of ability between operators responsible for ensuring the operation of technical systems, see Dodier (1995b).

Recommended reading

Adele Clarke (2004) *Grounded theory after the postmodern turn: situational maps and analyses*. London: Sage.
Clarke revisits grounded theory and offers new provocative developments, in particular ways of doing 'situational analyses'.

Paul Atkinson, Amanda Coffey, Sara Delamont, John Lofland and Lyn Lofland (eds) (2001) *Handbook of ethnography*. London: Sage.
This handbook offers a rich and stimulating vision of the range of ethnographical questions today, paralleling some of the points made in this chapter.

REFERENCES

Anderson, N. (1923) *The Hobo*. Chicago: University of Chicago Press.

Arendt, H. (1995) *Qu'est-ce que la politique?*. Paris: Seuil.

Baszanger, I. (1998a) 'The work sites of an American interactionist: Anselm Strauss, 1917–1996', *Symbolic Interaction*, 21 (4): 353–77.

Baszanger, I. (1998b) *Inventing pain medicine. From the laboratory to the clinic*. New Brunswick, NJ: Rutgers University Press.

Becker, H., Geer, B., Hughes, E. and Strauss, A. (1961) *Boys in white. Students' Culture in Medical School*. Chicago: University of Chicago Press.

Bessy, C. and Chateauraynaud, F. (1995) *Experts et faussaires. Pour une sociologie de la perception*. Paris: Métailié.

Boltanski, L. (1990) *L'Amour et la Justice comme compétences, Trois essais de sociologie de l'action*. Paris: Métailié.

Boltanski, L. (1999) *Distant suffering: morality, media, and politics*. Cambridge and New York: Cambridge University Press.

Boltanski, L. and Chiapello, E. (1999) *Le nouvel esprit du capitalisme*. Paris: Gallimard.

Boltanski, L. and Thévenot, L. (1991) *De la justification. Les économies de la grandeur*. Paris: Gallimard.

Bosk, C. (1979) *Forgive and remember. Managing medical failure*. Chicago and London: University of Chicago Press.

Callon, M. (ed.) (1998) *The laws of the markets*. Oxford and Malden, MA: Blackwell/Sociological Review.

Certeau, M. de (1987) *Histoire et psychanalyse entre science et fiction*. Paris: Gallimard. pp. 66–96.

Chateauraynaud, F. (1991) *La faute professionnelle. Une sociologie des conflits de responsabilité*. Paris: Métailié.

Chateauraynaud, F. (2003) *Prospero. Une technologie littéraire pour les sciences sociales*. Paris: Editions du CNRS.

Clifford, J. (1983) 'De l'autorité en tehnographie', *L'Ethnographie*, (2): 87–118.

Clifford, J. and Marcus, G. (1986) *Writing culture: the poetics and politics of ethnography: a School of American Research Advanced Seminar*, Berkeley, CA: University of California Press.

Collins, H. (1985) *Changing order: replication and induction in scientific practice*. London: Sage.

Corcuff, P. (1995) *Nouvelles sociologies. La réalité sociale en constructions*. Paris: Nathan.

Cressey, P. (1983) 'A comparison of the roles of the "sociological stranger" and the "anonymous stranger" in field research', *Urban Life*, 12, (1): 102–20.

Darbo-Peschanski, C. (1987) *Le discours du particulier. Essai sur l'enquête hérodotéenne*. Paris: Seuil.

Desrosières, A. (1998) *The politics of large numbers: a history of statistical reasoning*. Cambridge, MA: Harvard University Press.

Dodier, N. (1990) 'Représenter ses actions. Le cas des inspecteurs et des médecins du travail', *Raisons Pratiques*, (1), *Les formes de l'action*, 115–48.

Dodier, N. (1993) 'Acting as a combination of common worlds', *The Sociological Review*, 41 (3): 556–71.

Dodier, N. (1994) 'Dealing with complaints in expert medical decisions. A sociological analysis of judgment', *Sociology of Health and Illness*, 16 (4): 489–514.

Dodier, N. (1995a) 'The conventional foundations of action. Elements of a sociological pragmatics', *Réseaux. The French Journal of Communication*, 3 (2): 147–66.

Dodier, N. (1995b) *Les hommes et les machines. La conscience collective dans les sociétés technicisées*. Paris: Métailié.

Dodier, N. (1996) 'Les sciences sociales face à la raison statistique', *Annales. Histoire et Sciences Sociales*, (2): 409–28.

Durkheim, E. (1982) *The rules of sociological method*. New York: Free Press.

Dwyer, K. (1979) 'The dialogic of ethnography', *Dialectical anthropology*, 4 (3): 205–24.

Favret-Saada, J. (1980) *Deadly words: witchcraft in the bocage*. Cambridge and New York: Cambridge University Press.

Favret-Saada, J. and Contreras, J. (1981) *Corps pour corps, Enquête sur la sorcellerie dans le bocage.* Paris: Gallimard.

Fox, R.C. (1974) *Experiment Perilous.* Philadelphia: University of Pennsylvania Press (first published in 1959).

Gadamer, H.G. (1975) *Truth and method.* London: Sheed & Ward.

Geertz, C. (1973) *The interpretation of cultures.* New York: Basic Books.

Geertz, C. (1988) *Works and lives: the anthropologist as author.* Stanford, CA: Stanford University Press.

Glaser, B. and Strauss, A. (1967) *The discovery of grounded theory.* Chicago: Aldine.

Goffman, E. (1961) *Asylums: Essays on the situation of mental patients and other inmates.* Garden City, NY: Anchor.

Goffman, E. (1974) *Frame analysis: an essay on the organization of experience.* New York: Harper & Row.

Griaule, M. (1957) *Méthode de l'ethnographie.* Paris: PUF.

Knorr-Cetina, K. (1981) *The manufacture of knowledge.* Oxford: Pergamon.

Latour, B. (1987) *Science in action: how to follow scientists and engineers through society.* Cambridge, MA: Harvard University Press.

Latour, B. and Woolgar, S. (1979) *Laboratory Life. The production of scientific facts.* London: Sage.

Leiris, M. (1981) *L'Afrique fantôme.* Paris: Gallimard (original edition 1934).

Lévi-Strauss, C. (1963) *Structural anthropology.* New York: Basic Books.

Licoppe, C. (1996) *La formation de la pratique scientifique.* Paris: La Découverte.

Linhart, R. (1978) *L'établi.* Paris: Minuit.

McEvoy, S. (1995) *L'invention défensive.* Paris: Métailié.

Maget, M. (1962) *Guide d'étude directe des comportements culturels* (ethnographie métropolitaine). Paris: Editions du CNRS.

Malinowski, B. (1967) *A diary in the strict sense of the term.* London: Routledge & Kegan Paul.

Marcus, G. and Cushman, D. (1982) 'Ethnographies as texts', *Annual Review of Anthropology,* 11: 25–69.

Mauss, M. (1947) *Manuel d'ethnographie.* Paris: Payot.

Moerman, M. (1972) 'Analysis of Lue conversation: providing accounts, finding breaches, and taking sides', in D. Sudnow, (ed.), *Studies in social interaction.* New York: The Free Press. pp. 170–228.

Navel, G. (1945) *Travaux.* Paris: Stock (republished by Folio Gallimard).

Piette, A. (1996) *Ethnographie de l'action. L'observation des détails.* Paris: Métailié.

Platt, J. (1983) 'The development of the "participant observation" method in sociology: origin, myth and history', *Journal of the History of the Behavioral Sciences,* 19: October.

Ricoeur, P. (1984–1988) *Time and narrative.* Chicago: University of Chicago Press.

Ricoeur, P. (1990) *Soi-même comme un autre.* Paris: Seuil.

Ricoeur, P. (1991) *From text to action.* Evanston, IL: Northwestern University Press.

Silverman, D. (1987) *Communication and medical practice. Social relations in the clinic.* London: Sage.

Strauss, A. (1978) 'A social world perspective', in N.K. Denzin (ed.), *Studies in symbolic interaction.* Greenwich, CT: JAI Press. Vol. 119–28.

Strauss, A., Fagerhaugh, S., Suczeck, B. and Wiener, C. (1985) *The social organization of medical work.* Chicago: University of Chicago Press.

Thévenot, L. (1994) 'Le régime de familiarité. Des choses en personne', *Genèses,* 17: 72–101.

Thrasher, F.M. (1927) *The Gang.* Chicago: University of Chicago Press.

Weil, S. (1951) *La condition ouvrière*. Paris: Gallimard.

Whyte, W.F. (1981) *Street corner society*, Third Edition. Chicago: The University of Chicago Press.

Young, A. (1995) *The harmony of illusions. Inventing post-traumatic stress disorder*. Princeton, NJ: Princeton University Press.

3 Building bridges

The possibility of analytic dialogue between ethnography, conversation analysis and Foucault

Gale Miller and Kathryn J. Fox

This chapter extends and elaborates the analytic potential of qualitative research by considering how it may be used to construct bridges between different approaches to social life, particularly perspectives that focus on macro- and microscopic issues. The analysis deals with the ways in which the microsociological insights of ethnomethodology (Garfinkel, 1967; Heritage, 1984; Mehan and Wood, 1975; Zimmerman, 1969) and conversation analysis (Atkinson and Heritage, 1984; Boden and Zimmerman, 1991; Button and Lee, 1987; Sacks, 1992; Sacks et al., 1974) may be linked with the macro-historical emphasis of Foucauldian discourse studies (Dreyfus and Rabinow, 1982; Foucault, 1972, 1980; Lindstrom, 1990; Shumway, 1989). Our aim is to explicate the parallels between the various approaches, bringing both their differences and similarities into relief. Rather than promising an exhaustive discussion of each methodological approach, this chapter will explore particular relevant features of each approach that inform the associations we make. It is our hope to show how aspects of Foucauldian scholarship, for example, share common themes with ethnomethodology and conversation analysis.

We use the bridging metaphor self-consciously. Bridges link distinctive land formations, making it possible for people to traverse between them. While opening new opportunities for residents on each side, bridges do not blend the formations or otherwise make them indistinguishable. Where possible, bridges are also built to span the shortest distance between the land formations. The same conditions hold for this analysis. Our purpose is to show how two or more analytic formations may be linked and made mutually informative, while also respecting the distinctive contributions and integrity of each perspective. The analysis is also intended to identify the areas of greatest complementarity between these distinctive perspectives and methodological strategies.

This goal may be contrasted with triangulation, a research strategy that involves using several methods to reveal multiple aspects of a single empirical reality (Denzin, 1978). A major assumption of the triangulation strategy is that sociological research is a discovery process designed to get at an objective truth that may be systematized as a formal theory of social structure and process. Triangulation assumes that looking at an object from more than one standpoint provides researchers and theorists with more comprehensive knowledge about the object. This approach also assumes that "there is an overwhelming need for a single set of standards by which the methodological act can be evaluated" (Denzin, 1978: 339). The bridging approach discussed here differs from triangulation in its focus on using several methodological strategies to link aspects of different sociological perspectives, not to discover indisputable facts or to construct an all-encompassing theory about a single social reality.

We set the stage by demonstrating the significance of discourse in ethnographic studies, thereby uncovering the link between structural or institutional frames for interaction and the methods used to analyze the ways that discourse shapes possibilities. Next, we treat the concerns, objectives, and techniques of ethnomethodology, conversation analysis, Foucauldian discourse studies separately in order to establish correspondence between them. In addition, we will demonstrate the ways in which the questions that researchers ask and the sites they choose for study establish some parallels as well between these various methodologies. We conclude by discussing what can be gained by bridging distinct approaches.

DISCOURSE AND ETHNOGRAPHY

The significance of ethnomethodology, conversation analysis, and Foucauldian discourse studies for this chapter centers in their concerns for how language and knowledge are related and are constitutive aspects of social life. Each of these perspectives stresses how social life may be organized within multiple social realities as well as how the realities are socially constructed through our use of language, and the reflexivity of our accounts of social settings, realities, and issues. The concept of reflexivity refers to the ways in which our portrayals of social realities simultaneously describe and constitute the realities (Garfinkel, 1967). Our descriptions of social realities, then, cannot be separated from the objects, persons, or circumstances that they describe or the languages that we use to describe them.

While informed by aspects of philosophy (particularly hermeneutics and ordinary language philosophy), ethnomethodology and conversation analysis orient toward and recast classic sociological issues (Hilbert, 1992). They also emphasize how social realities are built from the "bottom up" (from ordinary interactions to general social processes). Foucauldian discourse studies, on the other hand, are part of the philosophical movement sometimes called poststructuralism (Eagleton, 1983) and other times postmodernism (Best and Kellner, 1991). This approach also treats social realities as embedded in generalized discourses which people enter into and use in conducting their everyday activities and interactions. Indeed, Foucauldian discourse studies might be characterized as moving from the "top down" (from culturally standardized discourses to the reality-constructing activities of everyday life). Schutz (1970) was concerned with a similar problem, that is, the relationship between the structural possibilities endowed by the "lifeworld" (or everyday life) and the systems of relevance which characterize social groups. In other words, meaning systems for groups may appear distinct from everyday life, yet our relevance codes emanate from practical experiences (including relationships to institutions) similar to the Foucauldian notion that discourse conditions our possible understandings.

These perspectives are also similar in their treatment of empirical research and analysis as interrelated. Ethnomethodology, conversation analysis, and Foucauldian discourse studies are not offered as integrated, all-encompassing, or grand theories of society (defined as an abstract structure or entity), but as distinctive standpoints from which concrete, empirical aspects of social life may be seen and analyzed. Their empirical focus is also reflected in the differing methodological strategies associated with each perspective. The strategies are designed to produce data that might be used to apply, extend, and elaborate on issues that are central to the perspectives. While some proponents of these perspectives and strategies describe their research as inductive (e.g., Merry, 1990) because it involves careful analysis of data, it is important to recognize that qualitative data – like other depictions of social reality – are social constructs. Thus, they are influenced by researchers' assumptions about social reality and methodological practices.

Taken together, these perspectives provide qualitative sociologists with interpretive resources for writing ethnographies of institutional discourse (Miller, 1994). These ethnographies focus on the ways in which everyday life is organized within, and through, language. They involve attending to both the discursive categories and practices associated with social settings, and how setting members use them (sometimes in distinctive ways) to achieve their practical ends. Thus, social settings might be said to "provide" their members with discursive resources and opportunities for constructing a variety of social realities. Situationally "provided" discourses shape and guide (but do not determine) what might be said in social settings (Silverman, 1987). Social realities are always locally constructed and contingent. They are "built up" through setting members' organization and use of the discursive resources and opportunities that are made available to them in concrete social settings. This analytic focus has, at least, two major implications for qualitative sociologists' orientations to their research. First, ethnographic studies of institutional discourse need to be differentiated from qualitative studies that focus on the distinctive values and perspectives of cultural and subcultural groups. These studies provide readers with "insider" knowledge about how cultural and subcultural groups orient to social reality, and explain the social significance of their distinctive practices. Schwartz and Jacobs (1979) aptly characterize this ethnographic approach as reality reconstruction, because it is concerned with accurately representing the meanings expressed by group members. The ethnography of institutional discourse, on the other hand, better fits within Schwartz and Jacobs' (1979) formal sociology category which focuses on setting members' interpretive and interactional competencies, including those that are so taken for granted that members are unlikely to mention them to one another or to qualitative researchers.

Second, ethnographies of institutional discourse extend the long-standing emphasis on observational methods in qualitative sociology. The methods include participant observation, various types of non-participant observation, and the use of less obtrusive observational techniques (such as observation from behind one-way mirrors or other "hidden" sites). Frequently (perhaps usually), qualitative researchers combine these observational strategies with other qualitative methods, such as interviews and life histories. Ethnographers of institutional discourse also rely on observational methods (usually non-participant observation) in conducting their research. But the focus of discursively oriented ethnographers' observations is different from those of other qualitative researchers.

One way of understanding this difference is by considering what it means to study social settings versus social worlds. The latter research topic assumes that everyday life is organized within relatively stable and integrated ways of life (Unruh, 1983). Qualitative researchers of social worlds use observational and related methods to identify and reconstruct the perspectives and patterns of action and interaction that organize diverse social worlds. Discursively focused research on social settings, on the other hand, emphasizes how social realities are always under construction. It considers how setting members continually assemble and use the interactional and interpretive resources "provided" by social settings to construct defend, repair, and change social realities. Hence the emphasis by discursively oriented ethnographers on observing (directly, by means of audio and video recordings, and through the careful reading of texts) the actual ways in which setting members construct social realities by making sense of practical issues.

We elaborate on these issues in the next three sections by discussing some of the major emphases of ethnomethodology, conversation analysis, and Foucauldian discourse studies. The discussion is selective, emphasizing those aspects of the perspectives that might be used to construct dialogue between them. Later, we use this discussion to identify areas of complementarity between the perspectives, and then consider how they might be bridged through comparative research.

ETHNOMETHODOLOGICAL CONCERNS AND STRATEGIES

The ethnomethodological project focuses on the common-sense methods that we use to make sense of our experiences and constitute social realities (Garfinkel, 1967). The methods of special interest to ethnomethodologists are the various interpretive procedures that we routinely use to classify aspects of our experience and to establish connections between them. Smith (1978), for example, takes an ethnomethodological stance in analyzing how persons are assigned to mental illness categories by way of contrast structures. Contrast structures are oppositional distinctions that cast some circumstances, behaviors, or persons as normal, natural, or preferred and cast others as abnormal, unnatural, or undesired. An example is the following statement made by Angela about K.

(i)   We would go to the beach or pool on a hot day,
(ii) I would sort of dip in and just lie in the sun
(iii) while K insisted that she had to swim 30 laps. (Smith, 1978: 43)

Angela's claims are expressed as straightforward, declarative statements that might be treated as descriptive of her own and K's behavior. For ethnomethodologists, however, such descriptive practices are reality-creating activities through which behaviors, circumstances, and persons are cast as instances of cultural categories and may be assigned moral and political significance. Also, two of the several assumptions about mental illness underlying Angela's description are that mental illness is a departure from what might be called a normal state of mind, and that signs of mental health and illness may be discerned from persons' behavior.

Foucault (1975) shares an analogous fascination with such categorization of persons in many of his texts. His attraction to the memoir of Pierre Riviere reflects a preoccupation similar to those of ethnomethodologists. The case of Riviere, a man who murdered his family in the nineteenth century, includes accounts by judges, villagers, the mayor, Riviere himself, among others. Foucault (1975: x) sees the memoir as representing "a battle among discourses and through discourses." In other words, he examines the "tactics" used by various institutional actors to establish the memoir's "status as the discourse of either a madman or a criminal" (xii).

Another ethnomethodologically interesting feature of Smith's account of Angela involves its reflexivity and localness. Angela uses the account to construct a world in which she and K are assigned distinct, contrastive, and hierarchical positions and identities. Angela is positively positioned as normal and K as mentally ill. The account is local because its meaning is inextricably linked to the practical circumstances in which it was voiced and interpreted by others. One reason why local circumstances are important to ethnomethodologists is because they stress that social constructions of reality are always potentially open to contest and change. Thus, Angela's description might not always be treated as evidence of K's mental illness. Consider, for example, how the meaning of Angela's description changes if we assume that K is an Olympic swimmer in training or that swimming is part of K's rehabilitation from an accident. In these cases, the contrast between Angela's and K's orientations to swimming might be taken as evidence of K's great (and admirable) commitment to athletic excellence or to recovering from her accident.

Ethnomethodologically informed studies of institutional settings also focus on the social and political contexts within which members use available interpretive methods to construct social realities. These studies analyze how social settings are organized as interpretive hierarchies (Dingwall et al., 1983), local cultures (Gubrium, 1989), or rhetorical domains (Miller and Holstein, 1995, 1996) within which some orientations to practical issues are usually privileged over others. Thus some definitions of social reality are more likely to emerge in institutional settings than others (Gubrium, 1992; Miller, 1991). Similarly, as Foucault (1975) described the significance of Riviere's memoir:

> Documents like those in the Riviere case should provide material for a thorough examination of the way in which a particular kind of knowledge (e.g. medicine, psychiatry, psychology) is formed and acts in relation to institutions and the roles prescribed in them. (xi)

Emerson and Messinger (1977), for example, analyze how troubles are defined and responded to in human service and social control organizations as a micropolitical process. They explain that organizational officials' usual orientation to potential trouble definitions and remedies is hierarchically arrayed along continua, ranging from the most preferred to the least preferred. In these settings, then, all possible definitions of reality (and interpretive methods) are not equally available to organizational officials. As Emerson (1969) shows in his study of decision making by juvenile court officials, dispreferred definitions and remedies may be so devalued in these settings that they are rejected in favor of more typical responses if only one setting member speaks against them.

While they analyze their data from a different standpoint, ethnomethodologists usually observe social settings and interactions in much the same ways as traditional ethnographers. They observe and take notes about the everyday activities and relationships of their research subjects. The difference, as Coulon (1995) notes, does not lie in their field techniques, but in the kinds of questions that conventional and ethnomethodological ethnographers ask about social settings and processes, and the types of data that their questions generate. As the above discussion suggests, ethnomethodologists are more likely than other ethnographers to focus on the interpretive practices of setting members, a focus that requires that they attend to (and record in their field notes) the details of setting members' interactions. A similar concern is central to the methodological strategies of conversation analysis.

CONVERSATION ANALYTIC CONCERNS AND STRATEGIES

Developed simultaneously with ethnomethodology, conversation analysis focuses on the ways in which social realities and relationships are constituted through persons' talk-in-interaction (Sacks et al., 1974). This perspective focuses on the social organization of talk-in-interaction, the interactional and interpretive competencies of the interactants, and how they collaborate to construct social realities. While conversation analysts share ethnomethodologists' interest in interpretive methods, they treat these methods as emergent from the distinctive structure and processes of talk-in-interaction. In its most basic form, talk-in-interaction is organized as sequentially organized turns at

talk through which speakers reflexively construct a context for their interactions as they go about the practical activities that make up the interaction.
These activities include displaying "appropriate" orientations to others' talk
as well as taking and finishing one's speaking turn in "appropriate"
ways.

Consider, for example, the following interaction occurring in a plea-
bargaining meeting, and involving a public defender (PD2) and district
attorney (DA3). Prosecuting and defense attorneys meet to negotiate the
charges to be made against defendants (in this case Delaney) and punishments
that will be given to defendants after they plead guilty to the charges.

1. PD2: Okay uh is there an offer in Delaney?
2. DA3: Yeah plea to Mal Mish and uh uhm modest fine and uh restitution
3. PD2: Okay
4. (0.8)
5. PD2: Fifty dollars?
6. DA3: Yes. (Maynard, 1984: 80)

This exchange displays several of the collaborative skills that we routinely
use in successfully interacting with others. First, notice how PD2 (line 1) opens
the interaction by stating "OK," thus marking off the previous discussion from
that which follows. PD2 then identifies the topic of the subsequent interaction
and invites a plea from DA3 by asking "is there an offer in Delaney?" DA3
accepts the request (line 2) by offering the charge of "Mal Mish" (malicious
mischief) and a punishment ("uhm modest fine and uh restitution"). PD2
continues to collaborate in the interaction by agreeing to the proposed charge
and punishment (line 3). The pause (line 4) might also be understood as
a collaborative act. It signals PD2's and DA3's readiness to move to a new topic
which PD2 raises by suggesting $50 as an appropriate amount for the fine
(line 5). DA3 then closes the interaction on line 6 by agreeing to the suggested
fine.

Conversation analysis is a context-sensitive approach to the study of reality
construction (Rawls, 1987). It focuses on the details and contingencies of social
interactions, and emphasizes how every social interaction is a distinctive
occasion for constructing social reality. But conversation analysts also analyze
social interactions as having elements that are context free because they are
evident in other social interactions. We see both context-sensitive and context-
free aspects of talk-in-interaction in the above exchange between PD2 and
DA3. While each move in the interaction is a local and collaborative accomplishment, PD2 and DA3 also orient to more general conversational practices.
Most obviously, they orient to the interaction as a set of turn-taking sequences
by waiting for, and then taking, their speaking turns in the interaction. They
also display general understandings about how conversational topics are
proposed, negotiated, and terminated through such mundane moves as stating
"Okay" and "Yeah" at the beginning of their speaking turns, and by using
the pause to manage a conversational shift.

Conversation analysts share ethnomethodologists' interest in the distinctive circumstances associated with talk and reality construction in institutional settings. They emphasize how these interactions involve both context-free aspects of ordinary conversations, and how interactants assemble them in distinctive ways to produce social contexts within which some interactional patterns and social relationships are encouraged over others (Atkinson and Drew, 1979; Drew and Heritage, 1992; Jefferson and Lee, 1992; Zimmerman and Boden, 1991). Further, the patterns and relationships associated with institutional settings are unlikely to provide all members with equal opportunities and resources for pursuing their interests in the interactions, thus producing social conditions in which some definitions of social reality are more likely to prevail than others.

For example, this focus is central to Peräkylä and Silverman's (1991) analysis of counseling sessions as communication formats within which setting members take different social roles and positions. The communication formats of most interest to Peräkylä and Silverman (1991) are interviews (in which counselors ask questions and patients answer them) and the information delivery format (in which patients listen to the information and evaluations conveyed by counselors). While different, both formats offer counselors greater opportunities to express and pursue their interests, including their preferred definitions of social reality. Indeed, we might extend this analysis by considering how these communication formats are both contexts of, and sources for, the distinctive professional authority and power exercised by counselors in their interactions with clients.

Conversation analysts usually study social interactions by constructing and analyzing transcripts made from audio and video recordings of social interactions. The transcripts are fine-grained representations of the interactions that often include notations indicating the length and placement of pauses, simultaneous talk by interactants, speakers' intonation, words that are stressed or elongated by speakers, and the direction of interactants' gazes. Because interactants might take any of these aspects of social interactions into account in responding to others' utterances or in moving the interactions in new directions, they are relevant to conversation analysts analyses of how social realities are interactionally constructed, sustained, and changed.

FOUCAULDIAN CONCERNS AND STRATEGIES

Foucault uses the term *discourse* to analyze more than language. It also includes the assumptions, logics, and modes of articulation associated with particular uses of language. Discourses provide persons with coherent interpretive frameworks and discursive practices for constructing different social realities within which particular kinds of people reside, relationships prevail, and opportunities are likely to emerge. We enter into discourses as we go about the practical activities of our lives. The discourses are conditions of possibility that provide us with the resources for constructing a limited array of social realities, and make other possibilities less available to us. Arney and Bergen (1984) elaborate on this point in their discussion of medical discourse as knowledge, power, and truth. They state:

It is more than just a set of facts known by physicians and embodied in a professional, specialized, inaccessible language. The medical discourse is a set of rules that enables facts to become facts for both physicians and patients. It is a set of rules that covers not only what is important to doctors but also what patients can speak about as important. Knowledge is power precisely because the knowledge embedded in the medical discourse supplies rules by which patients ascertain when they are speaking true about the self and when they are speaking about things that are imaginary. Knowledge tells the person what is important and not fanciful about his or her experience of illness and patienthood. (Arney and Bergen, 1984: 5)

In a similar vein, Ainsworth-Vaughn (1998) demonstrates the more micro aspects of negotiation in medical encounters. As opposed to studies that provide evidence of the power over patients that doctors possess and wield, she analyzes the ways that doctors and patients claim power, or struggle over it rhetorically, in exchanges. Certainly, such an inquiry suggests that power is a dominant theme in medical interactions; however, Ainsworth-Vaughn's study examines the small ways that utterances reveal grabs for power in the minutia of talk. Thus, power is produced within the struggle over it.

It matters, then, which discourse we enter into to organize and make sense of the practical issues emergent in our lives. For example, the discourse of law is only one of several discourses available in contemporary Western cultures for making sense of, and responding to, interpersonal and intergroup conflicts. Others include moral, mediative, and therapeutic discourses, each of which involves assumptions, categories, logics, claims, and modes of articulation that differ from those making up legal discourse. While politically consequential, our entrance into discourses is usually experienced as un-remarkable because we associate different discourses with different kinds of settings. Thus, discourses might be said to have their own social settings, although it is uncommon for only one discourse to be available in a social setting.

Conley and O'Barr (1990) show, for example, that while small-claims courts are dominated by legal discourse, judges and litigants occasionally organize disputes within the discourse of relationships. The latter discourse emphasizes the social histories of disputants, and the distinctive (often extenuating) circumstances associated with their disputes. The discourse of relationships also involves a distinctive arrangement of power and authority within the courtroom. That is, the disputants (not judges and lawyers) possess authori-tative knowledge about the social histories and circumstances emphasized in this discourse. Others are restricted to helping the disputants tell their stories, and develop mutually agreeable solutions to their disagreements.

Analyzing the availability of multiple discourses in social settings also raises questions about the discontinuities within, and between, the discourses. This concern is perhaps most evident in Foucault's (1970, 1972) approach to historical change, which he analyzes as filled with radical disjunctures or ruptures that occur when new discourses emerge and replace old ones. While not directly applicable to qualitative studies of social settings involving more limited time spans, this theme in Foucauldian discourse studies is still relevant to qualitative research. At the least, it reminds us of the possibilities for discursive discontinuities in social settings. These discontinuities might be observed, for example, in the ways in which setting members move between different discourses in dealing with the practical issues of everyday life, and when setting members operate within available discourses to produce unanticipated and atypical orientations to practical issues.

While most applications of Foucault's perspective are analyses of historical texts, Merry's (1990) and Conley and O'Barr's (1990) studies show that these issues may also be studied by using interviews, observational techniques, and tape-recorded data. Whatever the form of the data, Foucauldian discourse studies involve treating the data as expressions of culturally standardized discourses that are associated with particular social settings. Foucauldian researchers scrutinize their data, looking for related assumptions, categories, logics, and claims – the constitutive elements of discourses. They also analyze how different (even competing) discourses are present in social settings, how related social settings may involve different discourses, the political positions of setting members within different discourses, and the discursive practices used by setting members to articulate and apply discourses to concrete issues, persons, and events.

ESTABLISHING COMPLEMENTARITY

Despite its limitations, the above discussion of ethnomethodology, conversation analysis, and Foucauldian discourse studies provides us with a beginning for identifying and elaborating on areas of complementarity between the perspectives. These areas are, of course, easier to see in comparing ethnomethodology and conversation analysis because they are informed by the same intellectual traditions, address similar questions, and focus on similar aspects of everyday life. They are similar, for example, in their concern for how social realities are "built up" and sustained. Unlike Foucauldian scholars who focus on the general categories, practices, and logics of historically emergent discourses, conversation analysts emphasize the interpretive and interactional methods (both context sensitive and context free) that people in concrete social situations use to construct realities. The next two sections discuss two related strategies for linking ethnomethodology and conversation analysis, on the one hand, and Foucauldian discourse studies, on the other.

QUALITATIVE METHODS AS ANALYTIC BRIDGES

Ethnomethodologists, conversation analysts, and Foucauldian scholars orient to, and rely upon, empirical data to develop their perspectives. The data analyzed by these theorists are not merely materials for illustrating aspects of their perspectives. The analyses are theory-constructing activities in which data are a central focus. To be sure, the data that these theorists usually analyze are different, but the differences are at least partly matters of choice, not absolute necessities. Indeed, the literature of qualitative sociology includes several examples of how ethnomethodology, conversation analysis, and Foucauldian discourse studies can be done by using "unconventional" methods and data.

Holstein's (1993) study of legal proceedings concerned with the involuntary hospitalization of persons diagnosed as mentally ill, for example, shows how conversation analytic concerns can be successfully addressed by using data collected through observational methods. This analysis was successful because Holstein (1993) brought an appreciation of the significance of talk-in-interaction to his fieldwork. While these data are not so richly detailed as those that might be gleaned from audio and video recordings, they are sufficient for his analytic tasks and include contextual information that is not always present in conversation analytic studies based only on mechanical recordings.

Also, McHoul's (1982) and Silverman's (1975) research illustrates how ethnomethodologists analyze written texts. While he does not cite Foucault, McHoul (1982: x) casts his project in a Foucauldian language when he states,

> The discursive order . . . produces every possible version of 'the social' . . . and that will be so whether it is ethnomethodological discourse that is in question or one of the discourses that ethnomethodology would preferably take as its 'object'.

Conley and O'Barr (1990), Merry (1990), Miller (1991), and Silverman (1987) address Foucauldian issues by using ethnographic and conversational data. While different in their empirical and analytic aims, each of these studies considers how social life is organized within institutional discourses, and how knowledge and power are implicated in them. They advance the Foucauldian project by linking it to qualitative researchers' interests in the social organization of everyday life.

Taken together, these developments in qualitative research suggest that data are not always a problem in creating dialogue between ethnomethodology, conversation analysis, and Foucauldian discourse studies. The analytic concerns of the perspectives can be successfully addressed by analyzing several different kinds of data. Of course, it is easy to take this claim too far, because these perspectives are not compatible with any kind of data. At the very least, conversation analysis requires data that are amenable to sequential analysis, ethnomethodology requires data that might be analyzed as mundane interpretive methods, and Foucauldian analysis requires discursive data. These data can be generated within the same or linked qualitative studies, however, by combining two or more data generating techniques (such as observations, tape recordings of social interactions, and textual analysis). Another promising approach to building bridges linking ethnomethodology, conversation analysis and Foucauldian discourse studies is comparative qualitative research.

There are several recent examples of how qualitative researchers have comparatively analyzed institutional settings, and addressed analytical issues in the process. Gubrium's (1992) ethnographic studies of two family therapy clinics is an example. While presumably dealing with similar problems, Gubrium's (1992) analysis shows how the therapists defined and responded to their clients' troubles in very different ways, in one case treating them as family system problems and in the other as emotional troubles. Further, because Gubrium's (1992) fieldwork was informed by the ethnomethodological perspective, his study provides detailed information about the mundane interpretive and interactional practices through which the therapists entered into, and operated within, these discourses to produce organizationally preferred trouble definitions and remedies.

Miller and Silverman's (1995) comparative study of an AIDS counseling center in London and family therapy clinic in the United States is an example of how a comparative strategy may be implemented to address ethnomethodological, conversation analytic, and Foucauldian concerns. In this case, the researchers collected their data independent of one another, and then collaborated by analyzing the continuities and discontinuities in the data. The study illustrates how conversation analytic and Foucauldian approaches to troubles talk may be bridged through the use of qualitative data. They pursue the latter goal by treating their data as venues for exploring situational and transsituational aspects of counseling discourse, settings, and practices.

Miller and Holstein (1995, 1996) take a different approach to comparative research and analysis in their study of conflict emergence and dispute processing in one human service organization. The study is based on extensive observations of everyday life in the organization and analysis of audio tapes of legal proceedings concerned with dispute resolution. The analysis focuses on the ways in which conflicts and disputes are differently organized as they are considered within different dispute domains which Miller and Holstein (1995, 1996) analyze as made up of the typical assumptions, concerns, vocabularies, and interactional practices associated with different social settings. This study, then, offers a distinctive view of the conditions of possibility associated with the evolution of disputes in one organization.

Miller and Holstein (1995, 1996) consider how organizational settings are linked to form an ecology of knowledge and power, and how outside parties (legal officials associated with a different government agency) sometimes become involved in ongoing disputes. The study considers the ways in which disagreements are changed as they are configured and reconfigured within the conditions of possibility provided by each dispute domain. While maintaining an interest in Foucauldian issues, Miller and Holstein (1995, 1996) also stress ethnomethodological themes. They analyze, for example, how members of these settings use available interpretive and interactional resources to artfully pursue their interests and, based on members' actions, how disputes sometimes move in unanticipated directions.

A final comparative research and analytic strategy involves longer term (even longitudinal) studies of one or a few settings. The focus here is on how discourses and their associated interpretive and interactional practices change over time. This strategy might be useful in observing the disjunctures or ruptures that Foucault emphasizes in his historical studies of social change, but they may also provide qualitative researchers with information about the ways in which discourses, settings, and related interpretive and inter-actional practices evolve over time. While less dramatic than studies of radical disjunctures, studies of the evolution of discourses and their related settings and practices provide insights into the potentially unstable and changing character of language, culture, and institutions (see, for example, Miller, 1997).

In sum, these studies remind us of the complexities of everyday life and how agency and constraint are simultaneously implicated in it. An exclusive focus on either side of this dichotomy is inadequate, since everyday life is lived within culturally standardized discourses and the discourses are changed by the ways in which we use them. While ethnomethodology, conversation analysis, and Foucauldian discourse studies are distinctive approaches to these issues, comparative qualitative research that bridges them provides analysts with conditions of possibility for artfully extending and displaying (in concrete detail) the importance of their insights.

QUESTIONS AND SITES AS ANALYTIC BRIDGES

Qualitative research and analyses are as much about asking questions as providing answers. Thus, asking questions that address themes that are part of, or implied by, two or more perspectives is a form of analytic bridg-ing. The questions allow qualitative researchers to focus on aspects of the perspectives that are – at least potentially – compatible. For example, we might ask, "How do ethnomethodological, conversation analytic and Foucauldian research strategies address aspects of the agency–constraint debate in the social sciences?" The debate focuses on the extent to which social realities and actions are products of individual initiative or are shaped by larger social forces. Ethnomethodologists and conversation analysts might be seen as stressing agency over constraint because they focus on the local and artful ways which setting members assemble and use available interpretive resources in formulating their understandings of, and responses to, practical issues. Foucauldian discourse studies, on the other hand, might be interpreted as stressing constraint over human agency because they focus on the ways in which the assumptions and interpretive procedures used by setting members in constructing social realities are provided by the culturally standardized discourses that predominate in social settings.

This interpretation becomes problematic, however, when we consider ethnomethodologically informed and conversation analytic studies concerned with institutional settings and talk. These studies provide both data and interpretive frameworks for analyzing the practical constraints which institutional actors take into account in pursuing their interests in social settings, and for assessing the micropolitical advantages enjoyed by some setting members in pursuing their interests in institutional settings. Similarly, agency is an aspect of Foucauldian inspired qualitative studies – such as Conley and O'Barr's (1990) – which consider how institutional actors ("artfully") enter into available discourses and shift from one discourse to another in dealing with practical issues. Agency and constraint are not mutually exclusive issues in these studies, then, but coterminous aspects of the settings under study and appropriate topics for study in their own right.

A promising area for reconsidering the agency–constraint debate involves recent qualitative studies of gender, race, and class. The issues are central to Foucauldian studies of discourse, knowledge, and power. Foucauldian scholars treat gender, race, and class as aspects of unequal power relations. Foucault analyzes inequality as a product of people's everyday social practices and activities, that is, as power relations. Within our power relations, we discursively construct realities that justify and sustain gendered, racialized, and class-based inequalities. This approach to discourse and power resonates with Smith's (1987, 1990) institutional ethnography approach to these issues. Smith (1990: 80) states that structures of power and privilege do not exist separate from people's actions. Rather, they are produced and sustained through the "mobilization of people's concerted actions."

Smith's approach to gender, race, and class opens the possibility for building bridges between Foucauldian discourse studies, ethnomethodology, and/or conversation analysis through qualitative research. The studies might focus on the mundane interpretive and conversational practices used by individuals and groups to construct, sustain, and sometimes resist differences in power and privilege. Smith's previously discussed analysis of contrast structures and mental illness is an example of such bridging. For Smith, these contrast structures and related interpretive practices are aspects of larger political relations that express and sustain psychiatric power and patriarchy.

Another example of how such bridges can be built is Miller's (1993) poststructuralist and feminist analysis of part of an interview with Alice Dunn and her husband, Michael Dunn (first published in Brannen and Moss, 1987). Central to Miller's analysis is the Foucauldian assumption that power infuses all talk and therefore all talk is political. The segment under analysis began when the interviewer asked Mrs. and Mr. Dunn about the importance of Mrs. Dunn's earnings for the household budget (Brannen and Moss, 1987: 159). Their interaction turned on whether Mrs. Dunn's earnings were necessary for the household or were used to purchase "luxuries." Mrs. Dunn first stated, "I think it's quite necessary," but in the end, she says, "Yes, I suppose it is for luxuries." (Brannen and Moss, 1987: 89).

Miller draws upon and critiques aspects of ethnomethodology and conversation analysis in analyzing how this interaction depoliticizes Mrs. Dunn's initial portrayal of her earnings as necessary to maintaining the household. Foucault might say that the interaction shows how cultural discourses encourage some portrayals of social reality and discourage other portrayals. Miller (1993: 167) also suggests how ethnomethodologists and conversation analysts might "broaden" their analyses "to include large-scale discourses that influence the ways interaction is accomplished" while not reducing "speakers to the puppets of these macrolevel forces." For Miller, a useful research strategy for extending ethnomethodology and conversation analysis involves noticing and analyzing the "underdog" methods and strategies that marginalized groups and individuals use in countering claims based on dominant discourses, as well as how "top dogs" sometimes use these methods and strategies for their purposes.

A related example of how qualitative researchers might study agency and constraint as coterminous aspects of everyday life is Chase's (1995) analysis of the work narratives of women school superintendents in the United States. Chase displays an ethnomethodological awareness in describing the social contexts of her interviews with the superintendents. She stresses that it is not enough to pay attention to what the superintendents say about their lives and experiences. Chase (1995: x) adds that qualitative researchers must also pay attention to how interviewees tell their life stories "by attending to the cultural, linguistic and interactional contexts and processes of story-telling."

Chase focuses much of her analysis on two major cultural discourses or counternarratives used by the superintendents in telling their life stories. One discourse stressed the many accomplishments achieved by the superintendents in their professional lives. The other discourse consisted of stories about gender, racial, and ethnic discrimination encountered by the superintendents and by other women in pursuing their careers. Chase notes that the women in her study were confident and adept at using both discourses in talking about their lives. This changed, however, when the superintendents were asked to link the discourses. Chase (1995: 11) analyzes this request as creating a discursive disjunction because "talk about professional work and talk about inequality belong to two different discursive realms, two conflicting vocabularies for articulating experience, two different ways of talking about oneself."

Chase further develops this theme by analyzing the various narrative strategies that the superintendents used to manage the disjuncture between the discourses of professional success and social inequality. Her analysis constructs a bridge between Foucauldian discourse studies and ethnomethodology (and perhaps conversation analysis) by displaying the interactional and interpretive skills that the superintendents used in managing this discursive disjunction. These skills are often taken for granted in Foucauldian and other macroscopic studies of power, knowledge, and language. Further, the interviewees' efforts to manage the disjuncture display discursive problems and competencies that sometimes are overlooked in ethnomethodological and conversation analytic studies.

Another example of how analytic bridges may be built by asking questions is Jackson's (2001) recent ethnography of *Harlemworld*. Jackson takes a synthesizing approach to analyzing Harlemworld as a place within New York City and as a symbol of African American history and culture. He draws upon Foucauldian discourse studies in developing his analytic perspective. But his analysis also includes themes that resonate with aspects of ethnomethodology. The themes involve Jackson's analysis of race and class as socially constructed and performed realities. Put differently, Jackson defines race and class as activities that members of Harlemworld do. Jackson (2001: 4) explains that

> many African Americans have decidedly performative notions of social identity. Class position is glimpsed through interpretations of everyday behaviors. Racial identity is predicated on perceptions of particular social actions and is shored up with recourse to specific kinds of activities. Racial "location" is not contingent solely on one-drop rules or degrees of skin pigmentation. Socially meaningful identifications are partially derived from observable behaviors, practices and social performances.

Jackson's study has important implications for the ethnomethodological study of race and class. The study provides a starting point for studying the mundane methods (performances) that people use to cast themselves as members of particular social classes and races, and the methods used by others to "read" the performances as evidence of social class and racial membership. Jackson's ethnography also details the variability of people's social class and racial performances (and claims) across social settings. Finally, Jackson's study might be read as an instruction to ethnomethodologists about how they might analyze mundane reality construction as embodied activity.

Barrett (1996), too, demonstrates the embodiment of reality construction in his study of schizophrenic "cases." Barrett (1996: 19) analyzes how "psychiatric teams" (made up of psychiatrists, social workers, and psychiatric nursing staff) variously construct a single schizophrenic patient differently as a "segmented case," a "fully worked-up case," or a "whole person". Barrett (1996: 19) fuses phenomenology and Foucauldian discourse studies insofar as he analyzes the ways that "psychiatric discourse" characterizes patients as "variously endowed with subjectivity or divested of subjectivity." In contrast to Jackson's study across sites, Barrett looks at the vantage points and positions of actors within a single institution, and how the actors' engagement with the institution and patients frames their interpretation of a case or illness.

CONCLUSION

One advantage of the bridging metaphor is that it avoids the imagery of totalizing synthesis in which the distinctive themes and contributions of two or more perspectives are de-emphasized (even lost) in the interest of developing grand theoretical schemes. The bridging approach offered here seeks to make different perspectives mutually informative, not to obscure or deny their distinctive features. To that end, we conclude by discussing two general implications of our approach to paradigm bridging through qualitative research.

The first implication involves the selection of minimally compatible perspectives. All sociological perspectives are not equally amenable to the sort of linkage that we describe here. Thus, an early task of qualitative researchers involves specifying the conditions of compatibility between the perspectives which they wish to link through their research, such as we have done in noting the complementary emphases in ethnomethodology, conversation analysis, and Foucauldian discourse studies. How they differ on these issues is also relevant, but discussion of the differences is only possible after areas of compatibility have been specified.

Second, qualitative researchers' bridging projects must include the analysis of data about research sites. While the qualitative research tradition includes numerous and significant theoretical contributions, these developments should not be separated from the empirical focus of the tradition. This statement may be a source of controversy for some readers who properly reject past claims by some qualitative researchers that their data are objective facts that "speak for themselves," and should be treated as authoritative adjudicators of theoretical disagreements about the nature of the "real" world. This position neglects the ways in which qualitative data are themselves social constructions that reflect the assumptions and practices of the researchers who produced them.

Acknowledging that qualitative data are social constructions, however, does not render them theoretically useless or irrelevant (see, for example, Miller and Fox, 1999). Rather, acknowledgment recasts them as aspects of a distinctive discourse that treats the practices of everyday life as worthy topics of analysis. It also reminds qualitative sociologists that while theory is – by definition – abstract, it should also speak to issues that are recognizable as features of persons' everyday lives and social worlds.

Recommended reading

Jaber F. Gubrium and James A. Holstein (1997) *The New Language of Qualitative Method*. New York: Oxford University Press.
Gubrium and Holstein discuss many issues raised in this chapter, but they do so in a somewhat different context. Thus, they offer a different standpoint for

thinking about building analytic bridges through qualitative research. We particularly call the reader's attention to Chapter 8 (Conditions of Interpretation).

Amir B. Marvasti (2003) *Being Homeless: Textual and Narrative Constructions*. Lanham, MD: Lexington Books.
Marvasti's study bridges aspects of ethnomethodology and discourse studies by analyzing textual and interactional constructions of homelessness. Marvasti's study also illustrates how analytic bridges may be built by using several different qualitative methods. Specifically, Marvasti uses ethnographic, interviewing, documentary, and historical data in developing his analysis.

Douglas W. Maynard (2003) *Bad News, Good News: Conversational Order in Everyday Talk and Clinical Settings*. Chicago: University of Chicago Press.
Maynard analyzes the social organization of good and bad news delivery in several different social contexts. While stressing conversation analytic concerns and methods, Maynard discusses how conversation analysis relates to other perspectives, including ethnomethodology, phenomenology, and Foucauldian discourse studies.

REFERENCES

Ainsworth-Vaughn, Nancy (1998) *Claiming Power in Doctor-Patient Talk*. New York: Oxford University Press.

Arney, William Ray and Bernard J. Bergen (1984) *Medicine and the Management of Living: Taming the Last Great Beast*. Chicago: University of Chicago Press.

Atkinson, J. Maxwell and Paul Drew (1979) *Order in Court: The Organization of Verbal Interaction in Judicial Settings*. Atlantic Highlands, NJ: Humanities Press.

Atkinson, J. Maxwell and John Heritage, eds. (1984) *Structures of Social Action: Studies in Conversation Analysis*. Cambridge: Cambridge University Press.

Barrett, Rob (1996) *The Psychiatric Team and the Social Definition of Schizophrenia: An Anthropological Study of Person and Illness*. Cambridge: Cambridge University Press.

Best, Steven and Douglas Kellner (1991) *Postmodern Theory: Critical Interrogations*. New York: The Guilford Press.

Boden, Deirdre and Don H. Zimmerman, eds. (1991) *Talk and Social Structure: Studies in Ethnomethodology and Conversation Analysis*. Berkeley, CA: University of California Press.

Brannen, Julia and Peter Moss (1987) "Dual Earner Households: Women's Financial Contribution After the Birth of the First Child," pp. 75–95 in *Give and Take in Families: Studies in Resource Distribution*, eds. J. Brannen and G. Wilson. London: Allen and Unwin.

Button, Graham and John. R. E. Lee, eds. (1987) *Talk and Social Organisation*. Clevedon, UK: Multilingual Matters.

Chase, Susan E. (1995) *Ambiguous Empowerment: The Work Narratives of Women School Superintendents*. Amherst, MA: University of Massachusetts Press.

Conley, John M. and William M. O'Barr (1990) *Rules Versus Relationships: The Ethnography of Legal Discourse*. Chicago: University of Chicago Press.

Coulon, Alain (1995) *Ethnomethodology*. Thousand Oaks, CA: Sage.

Denzin, Norman K. (1978) *Sociological Methods: A Sourcebook*. New York: McGraw-Hill.

Dingwall, Robert, John Eekelaar and Topsy Murray (1983) *The Protection of Children: State Intervention and Family Life*. Oxford: Basil Blackwell.

Drew, Paul and John Heritage. eds. (1992) *Talk at Work: Interaction in Institutional Settings*. Cambridge: Cambridge University Press.

Dreyfus, Hubert L. and Paul Rabinow (1982) *Michel Foucault: Beyond Structuralism and Hermeneutics*. Chicago: University of Chicago Press.

Eagleton, Terry (1983) *Literary Theory: An Introduction*. Minneapolis: University of Minnesota Press.

Emerson, Robert M. (1969) *Judging Delinquents*. Chicago: Aldine.

Emerson, Robert M. and Sheldon L. Messinger (1977) "The Micro-Politics of Trouble," *Social Problems* 25: 121–35.

Foucault, Michel (1970) *The Order of Things: An Archaeology of the Human Sciences*. New York: Vintage Books.

—— (1972) *The Archaeology of Knowledge and the Discourse on Language*, trans. A.M. Sheridan Smith. New York: Harper & Row.

—— ed. (1975) *I, Pierre Riviere, having slaughtered my mother, my sister, and my brother . . . : A Case of Parricide in the 19th Century*, trans. Frank Jellinek. Lincoln, NE: University of Nebraska Press.

—— (1980) *Power/Knowledge: Selected Interviews and Other Writings 1972–1977* ed. Colin Gordon. New York: Pantheon Books.

Garfinkel, Harold (1967) *Studies in Ethnomethodology*. Englewood Cliffs, NJ: Prentice Hall.

Gubrium, Jaber F. (1989) "Local Cultures and Service Policy," pp. 94–112 in *The Politics of Field Research: Sociology Beyond Enlightenment*, eds. J.F. Gubrium and D. Silverman. London: Sage.

—— (1992) *Out of Control: Family Therapy and Domestic Disorder*. Newbury Park, CA: Sage.

Heritage, John (1984) *Garfinkel and Ethnomethodology*. Cambridge: Polity Press.

Hilbert, Richard A. (1992) *The Classical Roots of Ethnomethodology: Durkheim, Weber, and Garfinkel*. Chapel Hill, NC: University of North Carolina Press.

Holstein, James A. (1993) *Court-Ordered Insanity: Interpretive Practice and Involuntary Commitment*. New York: Aldine de Gruyter.

Jackson, John L., Jr. (2001) *Harlemworld: Doing Race and Class in Contemporary Black America*. Chicago: University of Chicago Press.

Jefferson, Gail and John Lee (1992) "The Rejection of Advice: Managing the Problematic Convergence of a 'Troubles-Telling' and a 'Service Encounter'," pp. 521–48 in *Talk at Work: Interaction in Institutional Settings*, eds. Paul Drew and John Heritage. Cambridge: Cambridge University Press.

Lindstrom, Lamont (1990) *Knowledge and Power in a South Pacific Society*. Washington, DC: Smithsonian Institution Press.

Maynard, Douglas W. (1984) *Inside Plea Bargaining: The Language of Negotiation*. New York: Plenum Press.

McHoul, A.W. (1982) *Telling How Texts Talk: Essays on Reading and Ethnomethodology*. London: Routledge & Kegan Paul.

Mehan, Hugh and Houston Wood (1975) *The Reality of Ethnomethodology*. New York: John Wiley & Sons.

Merry, Sally Engle (1990) *Getting Justice and Getting Even: Legal Consciousness Among Working-Class Americans*. Chicago: University of Chicago Press.

Miller, Gale (1991) *Enforcing the Work Ethic: Rhetoric and Everyday Life in a Work Incentive Program*. Albany, NY: SUNY Press.

—— (1994) "Toward Ethnographies of Institutional Discourse: Proposal and Suggestions," *Journal of Contemporary Ethnography* 23(October): 280–306.

—— (1997) *Becoming Miracle Workers: Transformations in the Discourse and Practice of Brief Therapy*. Hawthorne, NY: Aldine de Gruyter.

Miller, Gale and Kathryn J. Fox (1999) "Learning From Sociological Practice: The Case of Applied Constructionism," *The American Sociologist* 30 (Spring): 55–74.

Miller, Gale and James A. Holstein (1995) "Dispute Domains: Organizational Contexts and Dispute Processing," *The Sociological Quarterly* 36(1): 37–59.

—— (1996) *Dispute Domains and Welfare Claims: Conflict and Law in Public Bureaucracies*. Greenwich, CT: JAI Press.

Miller, Gale and David Silverman (1995) "Troubles Talk and Counseling Discourse: A Comparative Study," *The Sociological Quarterly* 36(4): 725–47.

Miller, Leslie J. (1993) "Claims-Making from the Underside: Marginalization and Social Problems Analysis," pp. 153–80 in *Constructionist Controversies: Issues in Social Problems Theory*, eds. G. Miller and J.A. Holstein. Hawthorne, NY: Aldine de Gruyter.

Peräkylä, Anssi and David Silverman (1991) "Reinterpreting Speech-Exchange Systems: Communication Formats in AIDS Counselling," *Sociology* 25(4): 627–51.

Rawls, Anne Warfield (1987) "The Interaction Order Sui Generis: Goffman's Contribution to Social Theory," *Sociological Theory* 5(Fall): 136–49.

Sacks, Harvey (1992) *Lectures on Conversation: Volumes I & II*, ed. Gail Jefferson. Oxford: Blackwell.

Sacks, Harvey, Emmanuel A. Schegloff, and Gail Jefferson (1974) "A Simplest Systematics for the Organization of Turn-Taking for Conversation," *Language* 50: 696–735.

Schutz, Alfred (1970) *Reflections on the Problem of Relevance*, ed. and trans. Richard M. Zaner. New Haven, CT: Yale University Press.

Schwartz, Howard and Jerry Jacobs (1979) *Qualitative Sociology: A Method to the Madness*. New York: The Free Press.

Shumway, David R. (1989) *Michel Foucault*. Boston: Twayne.

Silverman, David (1975) *Reading Castaneda: A Prologue to the Social Sciences*. London: Routledge & Kegan Paul.

—— (1987) *Communication and Medical Practice: Social Relations in the Clinic*. London: Sage.

Smith, Dorothy E. (1978) "'K is Mentally Ill': The Anatomy of a Factual Account," *Sociology* 12(1): 23–53.

—— (1987) *The Everyday World as Problematic: A Feminist Sociology*. Boston: Northeastern University Press.

—— (1990) *The Conceptual Practices of Power: A Feminist Sociology of Knowledge*. Boston: Northeastern University Press.

Unruh, David R. (1983) *Invisible Lives: Social Worlds of the Aged*. Beverly Hills, CA: Sage.

Zimmerman, Don H. (1969) "Record-Keeping and the Intake Process in a Public Welfare Agency," pp. 319–54 in *On Record*, ed. S. Wheeler. New York: Russell Sage Foundation.

Zimmerman, Don H. and Deirdre Boden (1991) "Structure-in-Action: An Introduction," pp. 3–21 in *Talk and Social Structure: Studies in Ethnomethodology and Conversation Analysis*, eds. D. Boden and D.H. Zimmerman. Berkeley, CA: University of California Press.

Part III Texts

---

4 Analysing documentary realities

Paul Atkinson and Amanda Coffey

INTRODUCTION: DOCUMENTARY REALITIES

A significant amount of contemporary ethnographic fieldwork takes place in literate societies, in organizational or other settings in which documents are written, read, stored and circulated. Ethnographic fieldwork was historically conceived and developed for research in essentially oral settings not only in non-literate societies, often studied by social anthropologists, but also in oral cultures or subcultures in more advanced literate societies. In contrast, contemporary fieldwork is often conducted in settings that are themselves documented by the indigenous social actors. While such documentary work is rarely 'ethnographic' in itself, it is important to recognize the extent to which many cultures and settings are self-documenting. In this chapter we consider some of the methodological consequences of studying 'documentary' societies and cultures. We indicate some of the ways in which qualitative field researchers can set about the study of documentary realities and the location of documentary work within the fabric of everyday social life. It is important to do so because many qualitative researchers continue to produce ethnographic accounts of complex, literate social worlds as if they were entirely without writing or texts. Many published studies of, for example, occupational, professional, organizational and even educational or academic settings are implicitly represented as devoid of written documents and other forms of textual recording. Such accounts do not, therefore, always do justice to the settings they purport to describe, and it is necessary to redress the balance if only for the sake of completeness and fidelity to the settings of social research.

Organizations and other research settings have a variety of ways of representing themselves collectively both to themselves and to others. It is, therefore, imperative that our understanding of contemporary societies –

whether our own near-at-hand, or one to which we are strange and distant – incorporates an appreciation of those processes and products of self-description. Consider, for instance, an ideal–typical organization. It goes virtually without saying that this quintessentially modern kind of social formation is thoroughly dependent on paperwork. Administrators, accountants, lawyers, civil servants, managers at all levels, and other experts or specialist functionaries are all routinely, often extensively, involved in the production and consumption of written records and other kinds of document. If we wish to understand how such organizations work and how people work with/in them, then we cannot afford to ignore their various activities as readers and writers. Moreover, if we wish to understand how organizations function on a day-to-day basis, then we also need to take account of these routine tasks and roles of recording, filing, archiving and retrieving information. Indeed, the collective organization of work is dependent on the collective memory that such written and electronic records contain.

In addition to these familiar record-keeping tasks, organizations also produce significant documents of other kinds, including a variety of materials concerned with their self-presentation. These might involve annual reports, prospectuses, financial accounts and the like. Many, though by no means all of those documents, are produced for external, even public, consumption. They may be among the methods whereby organizations publicize themselves, compete with others in the same marketplace or justify themselves to clients, shareholders, boards of governors or employees. In the contemporary world, we should also include electronic and digital resources among the ways in which documentary realities are produced and consumed. Organizations, for example, produce websites, promotional videos and similar artefacts. These are all among the techniques and resources that are employed to create versions of reality and self-presentations. Over and above these institutional documents there are also documentary records that embody individual actions, interactions and encounters. People-processing professions, for example, routinely compile documents and records of professional–client interactions, in the production of medical records, case notes in social work, school records and so on. These written records can be used to inform future action, and are themselves fed into the more formal recording (and documentary) mechanisms of official statistics, performance indicators, efficiency league tables and similar constructs.

The purpose of these introductory paragraphs is not simply to list a few indicative types of documents or to begin to outline what some of their functions might be. Rather, it is to remind us of the pervasive significance of documentary records, written and otherwise, in contemporary social (and hence research) settings. What follows logically from such an observation is that qualitative field research should pay careful attention to the collection and analysis of documentary realities. Such enquiry is not confined just to the inspection of documents themselves (important though a close scrutiny must be). It must also incorporate a clear understanding of how documents are produced, circulated, read, stored and used for a wide variety of purposes.

The production and consumption of documentary data has formed a part of qualitative analyses of a range of settings. Well-cited examples include work that has incorporated analyses of school reports (Woods, 1979), medical records (Rees, 1981), classifications of causes of death (Prior, 1985) and health visitors' case records (Dingwall, 1977). Indeed there are many research questions and research settings that cannot be investigated adequately without reference to the production and use of documentary materials. It would be fruitless to study the everyday work and occupational culture of a profession such as actuaries without addressing the construction and interpretation of artefacts such as the life-table (cf. Prior and Bloor, 1993). Likewise, the ethnographic study of accountants would be jejune without reference to the professional use of accounts, book-keeping techniques and so on. More generally, as Bloomfield and Vurdabakis (1994) point out, textual communicative practices are a vital way in which organizations constitute 'reality' and the forms of knowledge appropriate to it.

In paying due attention to such materials, however, one must be quite clear about what they can and cannot be used for. Documents are 'social facts', in that they are produced, shared and used in socially organized ways. They are not, however, transparent representations of organizational routines, decision-making processes or professional diagnoses. They construct particular kinds of representations using their own conventions. Documentary sources are not surrogates for other kinds of data. We cannot, for instance, learn through written records alone how an organization actually operates day by day. Equally, we cannot treat records – however 'official' – as firm evidence of what they report. This observation has been made repeatedly about data from official sources, such as statistics on crime, suicide, health, death and educational outcomes (Cicourel and Kitsuse, 1963; Sudnow, 1968; Atkinson, 1978; Roberts, 1990; Maguire, 1994). This recognition or reservation does not mean that we should ignore or downgrade documentary data. On the contrary, our recognition of their existence as social facts (or constructions) alerts us to the necessity to treat them very seriously indeed. We have to approach documents for what they are and what they are used to accomplish. We should examine their place in organizational settings, the cultural values attached to them, their distinctive types and forms. The analysis of such evidence should therefore be an important part of ethnographic studies of everyday organizational life and work. Of course documentary work may be the main undertaking of qualitative research in its own right (Prior, 2003). In either event it is important to establish a methodological framework for the analysis of documentary realities. In the remainder of this chapter we outline a number of complementary strategies for approaching this kind of qualitative data analysis. This is not intended as a comprehensive review of all relevant empirical research or analytical strategies. Rather our intention is to introduce some practical approaches to the systematic analysis of documentary data and the contexts of their use.

It is important to recognize throughout our discussion that follows that we are not – as are many of the social actors we observe – trying to use the documents to support or validate other data. It is tempting, when undertaking ethnographic fieldwork or some similar piece of qualitative research, to treat observational and oral data (such as may be derived from interviews or recorded interaction) as the primary data, and any documentary materials as secondary. If used at all, then the latter are often drawn on to cross-check the oral accounts, or to provide some kind of descriptive and historical context. Our view here, on the contrary, is that such attitudes to documentary data are inappropriate and unhelpful. We would urge that documentary materials should be regarded as data in their own right. They often enshrine a distinctively documentary version of social reality. They have their own conventions that inform their production and circulation. They are associated with distinct social occasions and organized activities. This does not mean that there is a documentary level of reality that is divorced from other levels, such as the interactional order. Documents are used and exchanged as part of social interaction, for instance. Nevertheless, it is vital to give documentary data due weight and appropriate analytic attention. There are many ways in which such documentary or textual data can be analysed and it is not our intention to try to describe these in detail (see Silverman, 2001). Rather, we introduce and exemplify a series of related themes and issues that can be brought to bear on documentary sources. Our general perspective is informed by a broadly ethnographic interest, while our specific analytic approaches perhaps derive more from a semiotic perspective. By that we mean an analytic perspective that examines how documents can be examined as systems of conventional signs and modes of representation (cf. Feldman, 1995). Through illustrating such an approach we consider how one needs to take account of the *form* of textual materials, the distinctive uses of language they may display, the relationships between texts and the conventions of genre.

DOCUMENTARY LANGUAGE AND FORM

Documentary reconstructions of social reality depends upon particular uses of language. Certain document types constitute – to use a literary analogy – *genres*, with distinctive styles and conventions. These are often marked by quite distinctive uses of linguistic *registers*: that is, the specialized use of language associated with some particular domain of everyday life. Particular occupations often have distinctive registers, as do particular kinds of organization or cultural activity. One can often recognize what *sort* of document one is dealing with simply through a recognition of its distinctive use of language. One can, for example, probably recognize the register of, say, a theatre review, or a wine appreciation, without seeing more than a random extract from it. Each genre has its characteristic vocabulary, and reviews in general often have characteristic form and tone as well. (The register of wine-talk is richly fascinating in its own right, of course! See Lehrer, 1983.)

At a common-sense level we can recognize that official documents and reports are often couched in language that differs from everyday language use. Indeed, as we shall illustrate, this is one sort of device that is used to construct the distinctive and special mode of documentary representation. It is not necessary to endorse a glib condemnation of 'officialese' or to assume that bureaucracies deliberately confuse or mislead through their special uses of written language. Indeed, it is usually unhelpful to approach the analysis of documentary materials from an initially critical or evaluative stance. It is undoubtedly more helpful to try to adopt – at the outset at least – a more interpretative standpoint. The initial task is to pay close attention to the question of *how* documents are constructed as distinctive kinds of products. It is therefore appropriate to pay close attention to the textual organization of documentary sources.

In order to illustrate our analytic points, and to locate them within a broader cultural context, we shall illustrate our discussion with fragments of text drawn from one highly salient feature of academic life – that is, the UK Research Assessment Exercise (RAE). This is, in turn, an instance of how the 'audit culture' has become prevalent in contemporary 'advanced' societies, not least in the public sector. Audit has become an especially visible aspect of organizational life, as have related processes and pressures, such as quality assurance mechanisms. Indeed, it is arguable that audit in its various guises is characteristic of what has been called reflexive modernity, or modernization. That is, a distinctive mode of modern social organization in which states, corporations, bureaucracies and other agencies are constrained to scrutinize and account for their own activities and their consequences. These processes rely primarily on acts of documentation and the textual artefacts that are generated. Academic life in universities has not escaped these new demands. On the contrary, academics are increasingly called on to account for themselves, and to document what they have done. These accounts are used as evidence by various external bodies that are charged with scrutinizing the 'quality' of research and teaching in academic departments. One of the most high profile of these external audits is the RAE. This is a periodic review of the research of 'units of assessment' (which may or may not be coterminous with 'departments') in all academic disciplines in all UK institutions of higher education. It has taken place at regular intervals since 1985. The most recent RAE results were published in 2001; since then the whole RAE process has been subject to a review and proposed revision (Roberts, 2003) in an exercise that is itself a fascinating exercise in the official reflection on documentary realities. In preparation for each RAE, academic staff and university administrators prepare written submissions. These are then sent to panels of discipline experts, who evaluate the submissions and award grades, ranging from 1 to 2, 3a and 3b, 4, 5 and 5*. (This distinctly odd scale is a very British phenomenon, reflecting past decisions, compromises and additions: it is a seven-point scale that goes up to 5!) The RAE is a very serious exercise for all those who take part in it. It has profound consequences for the esteem in which a given department (and university) is held. More fundamentally still, it drives an important fraction of the state funding that is allocated to universities. Consequently, all universities are involved in competition to gain the highest possible RAE grades. They devote considerable time and effort in long-term preparations for the RAE, and in the shorter term, in preparing the actual documentary submissions.

The RAE is handled by the Higher Education Funding Council for England, on behalf of all the UK funding councils. Each submission has thus far followed a uniform format. For each assessment, the Council issues guidelines and instructions, and also issues standardized electronic forms that have to be used to prepare each assessment. The format of submissions has changed a little since the process began, but there is a basic underlying structure to the returns. This uniformity reflects a very significant thing about documentary realities in the modern world. Documents are often used to create a certain kind of predictability and uniformity out of the great variety of events and social arrangements. This is, after all, one of the most important features of the bureaucratic mode of social organization: persons and courses of action are reconstructed in terms of the categories and rules of the organization itself. Transactions, problems, cases and the like can only be recorded and processed if they can be made to conform to standard formats. It is one of the key functions of organizational documents that they do such work of standardization. When organizations generate documentary records, they transform diverse circumstances and people into documentary forms that can be processed in relatively predictable and standardized ways. It thus becomes possible to apply various kinds of routines to processing them and recording them, to generating statistics that compare and collate cases, problems and outcomes. They can be used to do the sort of work that is currently popular among policy makers: setting achievement targets and measuring outcomes. Such political and organizational work is impossible without the construction of documentary facts and realities. Standardization and categorization through documentary types operates in many domains of modern life. Bowker and Star (1999) provide a particularly telling case study of how classifications of disease actively shape modern medical thought and practice (see also Prior, this volume). Chaney (2002) discusses, from a very different starting point, aspects of the documentary imperative in modern culture and its rationalization.

A great deal of work in modern bureaucracies and other complex organizations would be impossible without the creation of these kinds of documentary reality. Indeed, the development of modern methods of accountancy, marketing, trading and so on has depended completely on the construction of standardized categories and types – largely managed through the creation of standard documentary forms. (The congruence of meaning of the term 'forms' is revealing here – referring as it does to both types and the paper or electronic means through which a typical case is constructed.) Documentary reportage is closely related to the existence of official classificatory systems, such as the international classification of diseases (see Bowker and Star (1999) for a detailed discussion of such classificatory systems). It is important to remember that such official categories and classificatory systems do not simply describe classes and systems – they are active in creating and shaping them.

The author(s) of RAE submissions, for example, had restricted scope in terms of content and form. As well as the written guidelines that were issued, there were also the expectations and understandings about such documents that academics and administrators brought to bear. As drafts are composed, read and commented upon internally, so individuals contribute their shared understandings of such background cultural assumptions.

As part of an RAE unit of assessment submission there are a number of different documents or forms that require preparation. These range from details about research income, research students and staff publications, to discursive reports of, for example, the research structure, environment and activity. Each of these can be considered as representing a particular kind of documentary reality. The submissions for each unit of assessment for the 2001 exercise are now publicly available (see http://www.hero.ac.uk/rae/index.htm). For the purposes of illustration the examples used in this chapter are all taken from the Cardiff University submission to the RAE Education Panel (2001).[1]

Example 4.1 is a reproduction of form RA4, which details research income over the review period. What we are not concerned with here is a detailed analysis of *how much* research income is claimed by the table (though that is not to deny that that may be a significant factor). Rather we can think about the ways in which this form reproduces shared knowledges and assumptions for a particular kind of audience (in this case academic peers and administrators).

Example 4.1

RA4: Research income details

Source of income (Net VAT)	Partial 1995–96	1996–97	1997–98	1998–99	1999–2000	Partial 2000–01
OST research councils et al.	164,014	189,018	209,753	94,210	92,114	23,459
UK-based charities	1,389	2,635	4,767	14,075	12,663	1,201
UK central government bodies	74,447	39,743	54,955	122,038	144,812	25,805
UK industry, commerce and public corporations	1,718	21,786	34,143	33,145	25,755	1,786
EU government bodies	0	6	16,906	0	1,963	0
EU other	0	0	0	11,668	0	0
Other overseas	0	2,984	1,167	0	8,904	4,547
Other	21,015	31,535	17,926	47,022	14,872	10,885

At first glance Example 4.1 is a relatively straightforward table. While it does not textually describe in detail the source or application of research funds, it is set out in a particular way, following some obvious stylistic conventions. It does not contain lengthy descriptive prose or explanation. It is tabulated in an ordered and structured manner. The RA4 statements will look similar in terms of style and layout across all of the submissions. Like the layout, the sources of income detailed in the statement will be familiar to an academic readership, and perhaps less understood by a lay readership. Moreover, funding from the Office of Science and Technology (OST) and the research councils (such as the Economic and Social Research Council) is held in particularly high esteem, and this is perhaps implicit in their position within the table (which, incidentally, constituted for this particular submission the largest source of funding). This positioning at the head of the table hence serves a further purpose in the construction of the research account.

Presented with a file of statements like this one, and others relating to staffing numbers, research studentships, students and so forth, the academic reader or panel member can read a representation of the unit of assessment. This sort of documentary reality might be of limited value to a lay reader. The competent professional reader can, however, read into such documents much more than the lay reader may be able to. The forms also enable all submissions under each unit of assessment to be readily compared, albeit in a particular, coded and highly stylized way. The RAE, in this way, involves the creation and use of particular kinds of documentary artefacts, as a way of constructing and representing academic departments (or parts thereof). Moreover, this codification embodies within it assumptions of 'what counts' as research activity or esteem, as prescribed by the funding councils (and perhaps the academic community at large). Tabular summaries like this can, therefore, provide standardized, shorthand ways in which the relative performance of different organizations can be compared. They thus inscribe implicit assumptions about what is important about organizational life, and what is worth recording. Moreover, such tables provide numerical summaries of a wide range of activities. Obviously, there is much more to academic performance than such summary statistics, but the use of such 'performance indicators' is a very common feature of modern documentation and modern management. It is a representational strategy that is fundamental to the rationalization of modern life (Scott, 1990).

Tabulated data are a particular form of documentary source. Other parts of the RAE submissions by units of assessment relied upon prose text rather than figures. Prose accounts are equally conventional and deserve similar attention to matters of form. This can be illustrated by another example from the RAE submission. Again we use the Cardiff education submission without evaluative intent, but simply as an example of a document of a particular kind, displaying characteristic features. Example 4.2 is an extract from form RA5a, the description of the structure, environment and staffing of the unit of assessment. This extract is part of a broader statement, in which the claims that are made are justified and amplified.

Example 4.2

RA5a: Structure, environment and staffing policy

Educational research at Cardiff has for some time adopted an explicit analytical perspective that views education as a 'cradle-to-grave' process, within which schooling constitutes only one, albeit very important, part. Learning is seen as taking place in a variety of social contexts; in schools, colleges and universities certainly, but also within homes, work-places and wider community settings. The impacts of educational change are understood not simply within the educational system itself, but also in relation to other elements of the social structure, such as families, labour markets and political and cultural institutions. This approach necessitates situating educational research within a strong social scientific framework, which fosters the development of interdisciplinary work. This counters any tendencies for educational research to be both intellectually isolated and dominated by its predominantly teacher education environment. It also facilitates contribution to the improvement of policy and practice in an era of increasingly 'joined-up' government and collaborative initiatives between professional disciplines.

The creation of the School of Social Sciences has boosted capacity to deliver this ambitious research agenda. The School brings together almost 100 research-active staff in education, sociology, social policy, social work and criminology. It therefore provides a highly distinctive environment for educational research. Under the leadership of the Director, the distinguished sociologist, Huw Beynon, it has developed a mission to produce interdisciplinary research which is theoretically informed, methodologically rigorous and contributes to the development of policy and professional practice. Educational researchers have a critical intellectual contribution to make to this wider research agenda, from a disciplinary background in which the relationships between theory, methodology and application to policy and practice are well developed relative to many other social science disciplines. This will be a significant element in the long-term development of the School's research strategy.

How, then, can we begin to make sense of such textual documentary material? We might begin by noting the style in which the report is written. In many ways this follows a conventional narrative format. The reader is reminded that it is educational research at Cardiff that is the focus of the piece. The extract then moves from what appear to be general statements about educational research, to more particular details about the Cardiff School of Social Sciences, its research philosophy and environment. The piece ends again with a more general statement and a look towards the future. On a closer examination, however, many of these general statements are actually providing a canvas onto which educational research at Cardiff is able to locate itself. The views, for example, of education being a 'cradle-to-grave' process, of learning taking place in a variety of contexts, and of interdisciplinarity are 'interpretations' of the educational research environment that particularly suits the kind of educational research that is conducted at Cardiff. Similarly, drawing attention to the view that educational research might have tendencies to be 'intellectually isolated and dominated by its teacher education environment' is purposive given the fact that the Cardiff education unit of assessment is not a centre for initial teacher training, unlike many of its comparative units or schools. Beginning with these kinds of statements is not accidental, therefore, but is designed to 'set the scene' in a very particular way. The text implicitly invites the reader to find a point of contrast that can be used to construct the distinctiveness and special quality of the Cardiff department.

We can also examine the kind of language that is used in the extract. It contains many words and phrases that will seem very familiar to an academic readership. For example, 'a strong social scientific framework', 'the development of interdisciplinary work', 'capacity to deliver', 'research-active staff'. These, and expressions like them, are not necessarily part of everyday talk (even of academics) but they will be familiar to academics charged with authoring and reading such documents. They are among the linguistic building blocks of this particular kind of academic (re)presentation. Indeed it is possible to think of them as resembling verbal/textual formulae and their deployment in documents can be likened to the composition of an oral epic. It is well documented that bards can extemporize the composition of lengthy oral verse, celebrating themes such as heroes or wars. They can 'compose' line after line, usually in strict metre, on stock themes, peopled with stock characters. It has been shown that this capacity for 'improvization' is possible because the bards have at their disposal a repertoire of stock phrases for recurrent actors and actions. The oral bard, therefore, does not actually compose verse from scratch, but rather puts it together from well-established patterns and pre-formed components. These are, in turn, familiar to the audience, who are able to draw upon the same stock of well-understood and well-established phrases and literary conventions. In that sense, such a genre constitutes a kind of restricted code (Bernstein, 1981), with limited possibilities of choice and combination in composition. Such an observation is equally applicable to written language, as the RAE extract demonstrates.

The author(s) of the Cardiff education RAE submission clearly had some leeway in writing the account. (It is worth noting here that the submission is not attributed to named authors, but comes from 'the school', or indeed the university – another feature of official documentation.) Despite this freedom, however, the scope and language of the document will have been restricted in some ways. There were written guidelines that indicated the kinds of things that needed to be covered. Moreover, there are shared understandings and expectations about such documents and their use among academics and higher education administrators. As drafts are composed, read and commented upon internally, so relevant individuals bring to bear these shared meanings and cultural assumptions.

Most importantly, perhaps, we can now see that while this RAE document (or extract thereof) may be 'about' an academic school (or 'unit of assessment' – an RAE category that could be analysed in its own right), it is not a transparent description. One certainly cannot take the document and read off from it a picture of the department and its academic/research programme in any simple sense. That is not because the author(s) set out to deceive in some way. The issue here is not about honesty, or even about accuracy, in any simple sense. It reflects the extent to which documentary realities constitute distinctive levels of representation, with some degree of autonomy from other social constructions. Thus the RAE submission is a particular kind of account of an academic department, in just the same way as a financial audit is a particular kind of account of an organization. The accountants' audit of a company's books and balance sheets is not intended to authenticate every record of every transaction, and the auditor is not forever comparing the 'books' with some independent level of reality. The audit compares records with records, and checks them for features such as consistency. A key auditing process is the referencing of the audit file, a process whereby an auditor (usually a junior accountant) is charged with the task of checking for consistency and order across the range of balances and documents presented to the audit. Like the RAE, it too is conducted primarily within the domain of documentary reality. Such a conclusion does not mean that we cannot learn a great deal from such documentary sources. On the contrary, we have already sketched some ways in which an understanding of the RAE document, and others like it, can start to give us valuable data about organizational life in academic institutions and their characteristic cultures. We can, moreover, learn something about the sort of work, and its associated skills, that goes into the creation and use of such an artefact.

What is at stake here is the construction of a distinctive documentary reality. Our RAE document performs quite distinctive work. It creates a very particular version of reality. It is, moreover, a distinctively documentary one. It draws on the genre of other documents, and their characteristic language. It is constructed so that other kinds of documentary work can be accomplished with it. Such a self-assessment and self-report are eventually used as evidence by a panel who in turn generate yet another documentary reality – their overall report – and perhaps more important than anything else to the participants – the final RAE grading. This brings us, indeed, to our next analytic issue: documents do not exist in isolation. Documentary reality depends on systematic relationships between documents. Analysis must take account of such relationships. We now turn, therefore, to a discussion of the relationships between documents, or the intertextuality of texts.

INTERTEXTUALITY

Documents do not stand alone. They do not construct systems or domains of documentary reality as individual, separate activities. Documents refer –

however tangentially or at one removed – to other realities and domains. They also refer to *other* documents. This is especially, though not exclusively, true of organizational settings and their systems of record keeping. The analysis of documentary reality must, therefore, look beyond separate texts, and ask how they are related. It is important to recognize that, like any system of signs and messages, documents make sense because they have relationships with other documents. In that sense, therefore, we can examine such artefacts and their significance in just the same way we approach the signs of language itself.

Perhaps it is useful here to return to the theme of audit, of which the RAE might be considered an example within UK higher education. If we consider the mechanics of audit, then it starts to become quite easy to grasp the point of systematic relations between documents. One of the root metaphors of an audit is that of the *audit trail*. Traditionally (financially) defined audits of firms and organizations, carried out by accountants, place great emphasis on this audit trail. At the beginning of their training, junior accountants are instructed in how to carry out a detailed audit trail. This involves retracing each document and statement presented in the 'company' accounts to other documents contained in the audit file (the preparation of papers for an audit). There is an inbuilt assumption that reference can and should be made to other documents. An auditor's task is to establish the extent of these relationships and intertextualities. 'Ticking' is a folk term used by accountants to describe this process of retracing links and establishing an audit trail. (It is paralleled by 'bashing', which refers to the action of signing off segments of an audit as consistent and fair.)

Academic auditors follow similar procedures. It therefore ought to be possible for an academic auditor to pick an item, such as a transaction or a decision, and follow a 'paper trail' through the appropriate procedures of meetings, minutes, accounts, and so on, in order to trace an orderly and properly authorized procedure which is in turn correctly accounted for. Such investigative procedures are predicated on the assumption that there are and should be regular, identifiable relationships between documentary records. These relationships are based on elementary – but significant – principles. They include principles of *sequence* and *hierarchy*. These in turn are part of the constitutive machinery whereby organizations produce and reproduce themselves. From a general analytic perspective, therefore, we can see that the realm of documentary reality does not rely on particular documents mirroring and reflecting a social reality. Rather, we can think of a semi-autonomous domain of documentary reality, in which documents reflect and refer (often implicitly) to other documents.

Colleagues in academic life will be perfectly familiar with the application of the audit principle in contemporary universities. All universities and departments find themselves subject to various forms of audit. For example, in recent years in the UK academic departments found themselves subject to assessment by the Quality Assurance Agency (QAA) through the process of Teaching Quality Assessment (TQA). Universities continue to be subject to institutional audit by the QAA. This process of TQA, for example, involved a certain amount of direct evidence gathering, by the observation of teaching and meetings with students and teachers. However, a great deal of the inspection took place through the examination of documentary materials. Academic departments found themselves producing self-assessment documents (not too dissimilar a process from the RAE), as well as providing inspection teams with vast amounts of documentary evidence (such as module outlines and reading lists, minutes of meetings, examples of students' work, and so on). A task of the inspection team was to evaluate the extent to which a department's claims about its teaching was evident through the supporting documentation.

When academic auditors and similar external people use documents to scrutinize organizations of higher education, they examine a range of sources. As we have indicated, they undertake an audit trail. In simple terms, that means following an organizational decision, an innovation or a problem through a sequence of documents. Such a trail might, for instance, examine the minutes of departmental meetings in order to trace the progress of an item from one meeting to the next, and so on. Such organizational records have distinctive characteristics. Again, we can note that such documents have specific, stylized formats. They also have particular functions. Minutes of meetings, for instance, do not record everything that was said and done in a meeting. Indeed, in a sense they precisely are not intended to record what was actually said. They record what was *decided*. In a sense, they constitute what was decided. Unless challenged and corrected with the agreement of the members, the written record takes precedence over members' own recollections and intentions. Moreover, such documents are written in order to refer to other, equivalent documents. They are constructed and read precisely as part of a documentary domain of interlinked documents. If we pursue the hypothetical example of our academic audit, we can see that an audit trail would pick up on documents such as minutes of staff–student meetings, meetings of the academic staff (or subgroups of them). We can analyse such documentary realities in various ways. We have already referred to the notion of *intertextuality*. This term is derived from contemporary literary criticism, in which context it is used to refer to that fact that literary texts (such as novels) are not free standing, and that they do not refer just to a fictional world. Rather, they refer, however implicitly, to other texts. They include other texts of the same genre, or other kinds of textual product (such as journalism, biography, movies). We can therefore analyse texts in terms of these intertextual relationships, tracing the dimensions of similarity and difference.

In analysing the documentary realities of an organizational or work setting, therefore, we can explore the intertextual relationships. We can examine how conventional formats are shared between texts, and thus how they construct a uniform, bureaucratic style. We can note how they are linked as series or sequences of documents. Minutes of meetings refer to previous minutes and things like 'matters arising'. Minutes of different meetings will look remarkably similar in construction, language and tone. They thus construct rational sequences of decisions and their consequences, distributed regularly over time, and reported in uniform formats. We could thus examine how documentary realities have *temporal* dimensions built into them. Note that this is an organizational or documentary time, it does not describe the passage of time as experienced as an everyday phenomenon by the individual actors concerned. In another sense, documentary sources *suppress* time, by lifting events out of the flow of lived experience, and recording them in the de-contextualized language and formats of official records. Intertextuality thus alerts us to the fact that organizational and official documents are part of wider systems of distribution and exchange. Official documents in particular circulate (though often in restricted social spheres) through social networks which in turn help to identify and delineate divisions of labour and official positions. One important analytic theme here is the observation that the systematic relationships between documents actively *construct* the rationality and organization that they purport transparently to record.

Documents can circulate and be exchanged partly because they are used to de-contextualize events. We transform things by incorporating them into texts. By writing something in a documentary format, we translate them from the specific and the local, and make of them 'facts' and 'records' which take on an independent existence. Some texts become 'official', and can become 'proof' of events and identities. This point is made in relation to the production of scientific facts and findings by Latour and Woolgar (1986), who write about the production of scientific papers, and suggest that they achieve an independence of their original site of production – the research group, the laboratory – and take on an independent existence. The accountants' audit of a business organization takes on a similar existence. The audit report becomes the documentary reality, superseding other files, records and memories. Similar observations could be made about the RAE submissions where units of assessments become 'real' and the documentary reality that is presented supersedes other accounts.

Documents are also written and read with reference to other occasions of use. They can be referred to in order to warrant or challenge subsequent actions and decisions – possibly long after they were first constructed. They can also inscribe positions of hierarchy. Documents report discussions, decisions and events to people or bodies that are superior to the originators. The right to construct a document, to challenge it, to receive it and act on it (or not) is part of the formal division of labour within many social settings. One cannot 'read off' such organizational realities from documentary sources, and the attempt to do so would be based on a fundamental misunderstanding. Documentary realities, based on complex inter-linkages between documents, *create* their own versions of hierarchy and legitimate authority. Indeed, the issue of authority raises for us the closely related issue of authorship and readership, to which we now turn.

AUTHORSHIP AND READERSHIP

The kinds of documents we have been discussing may have identifiable, individual authors or they may be anonymous, even collective, products. Equally, they may be addressed to specific individuals or they may appear to address an impersonal world at large. In any event it is important to address authorship (actual or implied) and readership (actual or implied) if one is to understand the overall system of production, exchange and consumption of documentary materials. Documents, like all texts and utterances, are 'recipient designed'. That is, they reflect implicit assumptions about who will be the 'hearer' or reader. The implied reader does not have to be an actual individual person. In many ways the implied recipient corresponds to what George Herbert Mead referred to as the 'generalized other'. It is a basic tenet of interactionist social analysis that social actors monitor and shape their actions in the light of generalized others' imputed responses and evaluations. So when we create a document, we do so in the light of the kind of readership we are expecting or writing for.

In the case of the RAE submissions, for example, the readers are both specific and generalized. The membership of the panels of experts is known to those constructing the submission, as this is public knowledge. But the bureaucratic formats and other conventions governing the preparation of the documents preclude a highly personalized appeal to particular readers. So even if the head of an academic department knows the chair of the expert panel of reviewers, he or she cannot construct the submission as a personal appeal to that specific individual. However much authors might dream of it, they cannot actually write a personal appeal to the panel members. It has to be couched in the appropriate register, suited to the institutional demands and expectations of the exercise itself. Indeed, it is part of the skill in constructing such documents in administrative contexts that one should be able to use the right kinds of phrases, deploy the right kinds of arguments, and generally convey the right sort of tone. In audit exercises like the RAE, this includes the use of distinctive terms and ideas that are intended to reflect the coherence of a department's research strategic thinking and the cogency of its research plans. While the self-assessment part of the document is intended to convey a picture of the research activities of the academic department, in an important sense it *creates* the reality it reports. This report is normally not a highly individual picture, but a highly predictable version, suited to the intentions and the readership created by the RAE itself.

While it is self-evident that a person or a group of people must actually write/author documents (since they do not write themselves) that does not always imply a social recognition of 'authorship'. Indeed, it is part of the facticity of many official and organizational documents that they are not identifiably the work of an individual author. Their very anonymity is part of the official production of documentary reality. There may be an implied 'ownership' of a document – such as the originating administrator or department – but official materials do not normally have visible human agencies expressing opinions, beliefs and so on. We can therefore inspect texts for indications of authorship, or its absence. In that sense, too, we can look for how they claim whatever authority may be attributed to them. To illustrate this point we can return to the RAE, though this time to the overview report prepared by the Education RAE panel (Example 4.3). Each subject panel provided a general overview report on the submissions that it had received, as well as specific feedback for each unit of assessment.

Example 4.3

Education Panel RAE 2001: Overview Report

The strongest research submitted to the Education Panel was characterised by its grounding in high quality methodologies, its underpinning by sound theoretical concerns and its readiness to engage in broad social science debates about enquiry in the field. This was most evident where submissions displayed a breadth and depth of methodological expertise (both qualitative and quantitative), a willingness to associate with broader social science or other disciplinary fields and an engagement with communities of users on the basis of excellent research. These high rated submissions typically published in eminent academic journals, book chapters *and* outlets providing significant interaction with the education community more generally. Some very good work was published in research reports to funding bodies although this was not always easily accessible to the general public.

It is noticeable that these statements are made without explicit reference to the personal agency that was actually responsible for putting together the report. (The entire document is devoid of named authorship, and is identified solely with 'Education Panel'. The membership of the panel is known, but not attributed in this report.) The report is made up of a number of statements that have a similar form to those reproduced above, though some paragraphs/comments are less glowing than these. But the report is not identifiable with an authorial 'voice' as such. We do not read phrases like 'It seemed to us . . . ', or 'we felt . . . '. This lack of a personal author is entirely characteristic of many 'official' documents. In this context it is important to keep in mind a distinction that is taken from literary criticism: the contrast between the author as a person (named or not) and the 'implied author'. The latter expression refers to the textual presence (or absence) of an authorial voice in the text. For instance, a paper in a scientific journal will normally be written in an impersonal manner (using devices such as the passive voice), with no personal implied author, even though an author's name, or a collection of names, may be credited as its 'authors'.

The absence of an implied author is one rhetorical device that is available for the construction of authoritative, 'official' or 'factual' accounts. It implies a reality that exists independently of any individual observer, interpreter or writer. That device is not sufficient in itself to guarantee such status, which also rests on the organizational, professional or bureaucratic contexts in which documents are produced and used. It should also be noted at this point that the overview report we have just quoted is a response to the RAE submission we cited earlier in this chapter (and to other submissions to the Education Panel). This sort of dialogue between the documents is a particular kind of intertextual relationship.

Documentary reality construction also involves *implied readers*. Any literate person may actually pick up and read a document, but texts are often aimed at particular classes of reader, and it may be that only a restricted readership, with specific competencies, will be able fully to decode them. This is especially true of organizational documents, where an understanding of the organization and its working assumptions may be a prerequisite to a thoroughly competent reading. This observation reflects the fact that no text, whether literary or official, can determine or constrain precisely how it shall be read. Reading is an activity, not the passive receipt of information. The reader brings to the text his or her stock of cultural knowledge, a knowledge (or ignorance) of similar texts, and his or her unique biography.

The examples we have already given can be understood quite transparently from this perspective. At one level, any reader of English can make sense of them. On the other hand, it takes somebody who knows about research in higher education, and academic life more generally, to grasp much more of the significance of the phrases that are contained in the documents of the RAE. Moreover, in the examples we have cited, some knowledge of social science in general, and educational research in particular, would make the texts perhaps more meaningful. Such people are among the implied readers. Indeed the members of the Cardiff School of Social Sciences and those specifically included in the education submission are also able to bring to bear their personal knowledge and commitments, and will read the texts differently from readers who are not personally involved.

In some contexts, it takes a highly socialized member of a subculture (such as a professional group) to make any sense at all of a text. The case of the medical record is a classic one that a number of sociologists have focused on. They all conclude that the medical record, or case note, is a partial and cryptic text. Competent medical practitioners can make sense of their own or others' fragmentary notes because they bring to bear a wealth of context-specific, often tacit, knowledge about medical history taking, clinical examination, interpretation of laboratory test results, diagnosis and treatment. The briefest of notes, often in the form of abbreviations, may have a wealth of routine medical work and interpretation read into it.

CONCLUSION

In the course of this brief chapter we have not tried to provide a comprehensive account of how to analyse documents and other kinds of textual materials. Rather, we have tried to indicate, by example, just some of the ways in which documentary reality construction can be approached. The kinds of things we have discussed could well be conducted as exercises in their own right. Equally, and probably more frequently, they could form part of a broader ethnographic examination of organizational settings, work practices, professional cultures and everyday life.

Here, by way of conclusion, we recapitulate some of the key methodological points we have introduced along the way. First, it is important to realize that documentary reality does not consist of descriptions of the social world that can be used directly as evidence about it. One certainly cannot assume that documentary accounts are 'accurate' portrayals in that sense. Rather, they construct their own kinds of reality. It is, therefore, important to approach them as *texts*. Texts are constructed according to conventions that are themselves part of a documentary reality. Hence, rather than ask whether an account is true, or whether it can be used as 'valid' evidence about a research setting, it is more fruitful to ask ourselves questions about the form and function of texts themselves.

Consequently, one can examine texts for some of their formal properties. We have indicated, very briefly, how one might look at the characteristic language used in such texts. Moreover, one can look at them in terms of their *rhetorical* features. Sociologists and others have come to recognize with increasing force that much can be learned from the discipline of rhetoric. Rhetoric is not just about the ornamentation of speeches, or the effects of speakers like politicians. Rhetoric is, fundamentally, about how texts (spoken and written) *persuade* their readers and hearers. We all use rhetorical devices in order to get a particular point of view across to others. We draw on conventions that are widely shared within our culture. We have touched on some of the ways in which documentary sources can be examined from such a perspective.

It is important to think about documents in relation to their production (authorship) and their consumption (readership), but one should note that in textual terms these are not coterminous with the particular individual social actors who write and read. We need to pay close attention to the implied readers, and to the implied claims of authorship. This becomes particularly interesting when we are examining how a text implicitly claims a special kind of status – as factual, authoritative, objective or scientific. Linking this perspective with that of rhetoric, then, we can ask ourselves what claims a text seems to inscribe, and what devices are brought to bear in order to enter that implied claim. The same would be true – though the rhetorical devices would differ – if the document in question had a different function (such as constructing a complaint, a confession or a personal reminiscence).

We have also drawn on another analytic perspective from literary and rhetorical analysis in emphasizing *intertextuality*. We have stressed that texts do not refer transparently to the social world. Their referential value is often to other texts. In literate, bureaucratized settings in particular, one may identify a semi-autonomous domain of texts and documents that refer primarily to one another. A dense network of cross-referencing, and shared textual formats, creates a powerful version of social reality.

In singling out these particular themes, we have implicitly drawn on the ideas and perspectives of literary theory. This is not the only viewpoint from which to examine textual data. You will find others outlined in other chapters in this volume. We do not claim that these are the best – let alone the only – ways of approaching such sociological analysis. It is, none the less, our contention that the ideas we have outlined can be used and developed to provide analytic frameworks for the examination of documents and similar cultural artefacts.

NOTE

1. In the 2001 RAE, Cardiff University was one of two submissions to the Education Panel to be awarded grade 5*.

Recommended reading

L. Prior (2003) *Using Documents in Social Research*. London: Sage.
An excellent and scholarly introduction to the ways in which documentary research can form part of qualitative fieldwork. Considers the ways in which documents are agents of social interaction. Includes a variety of examples of research contexts and analytical strategies. Interesting discussions of authorship and identity.

J. Scott (1990) *A Matter of Record*. Cambridge: Polity Press.
A comprehensive account of the use of documentary sources in social research. A variety of different kinds of documentary evidence available to the social scientist are appraised in terms of authenticity, credibility, representativeness and meaning. Includes discussions of the use of personal documents such as diaries and letters, and 'visual' documents such as photographs.

REFERENCES

Atkinson, J.M. (1978) *Discovering Suicide: Studies in the Social Organization of Sudden Death*. London: Macmillan.

Bernstein, B. (1981) Codes, modalities and the process of cultural reproduction: a model, *Language in Society*, 10 (3): 327–63.

Bloomfield, B.P. and Vurdabakis, T. (1994) Re-presenting technology: IT consultancy reports as textual reality constructions, *Sociology*, 28 (2): 455–78.

Bowker, G.C. and Star, S.L. (1999) *Sorting Things Out: Classification and its Consequences*. Cambridge, MA: MIT Press.

Chaney, D. (2002) *Cultural Change and Everyday Life*. London: Palgrave.

Cicourel, A. and Kitsuse, J. (1963) *The Educational Decision-Makers*. New York: Bobbs-Merrill.

Dingwall, R. (1977) *The Social Organization of Health Visitor Training*. London: Croom Helm.

Feldman, M.S. (1995) *Strategies for Interpreting Qualitative Data*. Thousand Oaks, CA: Sage.

Latour, B. and Woolgar, S. (1986) *Laboratory Life*. Princeton, NJ: Princeton University Press.

Lehrer, A. (1983) *Wine and Conversation*. Bloomington: Indiana University Press.

Maguire, M. (1994) Crime statistics, patterns and trends, in M. Maguire, R. Morgan and R. Reiner (eds), *Oxford Handbook of Criminology*. Oxford: Oxford University Press.

Prior, L. (1985) Making sense of mortality, *Sociology of Health and Illness*, 7 (2): 167–90.

Prior, L. (2003) *Using Documents in Social Research*. London: Sage.

Prior, L. and Bloor, M. (1993) Why people die: social representations of death and its causes, *Science as Culture*, 3 (3): 346–74.

Rees, C. (1981) Records and hospital routine, in P. Atkinson and C. Heath (eds), *Medical Work: Realities and Routines*. Farnborough: Gower.

Roberts, G. (2003) *Review of Research Assessment*. Bristol: Higher Education Funding Council for England.

Roberts, H. (1990) *Women's Health Counts*. London: Routledge.

Scott, J. (1990) *A Matter of Record*. Cambridge: Polity Press.

Silverman, D. (2001) *Interpreting Qualitative Data*, Second Edition. London: Sage.

Sudnow, D. (1968) *Passing On*. Englewood Cliffs, NJ: Prentice Hall.

Woods, P. (1979) *The Divide School*. London: Routledge & Kegan Paul.

5 Doing things with documents

Lindsay Prior

[H]ere I sit and govern [Scotland] with my pen: I write and it is done.
(King James VI (Scotland) and James I (England))[1]

This is an instructive quotation. It demonstrates, above all, how people do things with documents. In the case of the egocentric James, it is clear that he did things with the technology of paper and pen. These days he would more likely have used electronic modes of communication in addition to his inky quill. And as social researchers we could of course decide to concentrate on any number of features associated with the King James quotation. We could focus on the thoughts of the man, and the meaning that James attached to the words on pages that he dispatched from London to Edinburgh. Or we might choose to focus on the meaning of those who read the words (including ourselves, as well as long-dead subordinates). Or, as I have suggested elsewhere (Prior, 2003), we could eschew an interest in meaning altogether and focus, instead, on how the words (and documents that contained them) were used in episodes of social interaction. In this chapter it is the latter rather than the former strategy that will be adopted. As such I shall aim, where possible, to side-step a concern with document content, meaning and interpretation in favour of a focus on the position of text in a network of action.

Normally, when documents are put forward for consideration in schemes of social research they are approached in terms of what they contain. That is, the focus is principally on the language embodied in the document as a medium of thought and expression. Yet it is quite clear that each and every document enters into human projects in a dual relation. First, and as with James's royal commands, they enter the field as a receptacle (of instructions, obligations, contracts, wishes, reports, etc). Second, they enter the field as agents in their own right. Indeed, as agents documents have effects long after their human creators are dead and buried (wills provide a readily available example of such effects). And as agents, documents are always open to manipulation by others: as allies, as resources for further action, as opponents to be destroyed, or suppressed. (We should not forget that people burn and ban documents as well as read them.) It is the examination of this dual role that forms the intellectual backbone of the current chapter.

As I have just stated, in so far as documents have been dealt with as a resource for the social scientific researcher they have hitherto been considered almost exclusively as containers of content. Document content is important and there are numerous routes by means of which such content may be studied. We should not, however, let the presence of content bedazzle us to the exclusion of other qualities. Above all we should recognize the quality of documents as things – as things that can be produced and manipulated, used or consumed, and as things that can act back on their creators – very much as Dr Frankenstein's monster sought to act back on his creator. Indeed, one interesting feature of documents in action is their tendency to exhibit what we might call such 'monster-like' qualities.

In what follows, and for the sake of examples, I intend to emphasize three specific features of documents as a field for social research. They concern, respectively, how documentation is produced in socially organized contexts; how documentation is used in everyday organizational action; and how documentation enters into the manufacture of self and identity.

DOCUMENTS AS PRODUCT

People think with things as well as with words. How they arrange and organize things in the world is important. This, not least because – as was demonstrated during the 1960s by a range of French intellectuals such as Barthes (1985), Foucault (1970) and Lévi-Strauss (1969) – the organization of artefacts provides insight into the most fundamental aspects of human culture. In literate cultures, of course, the organization of things is anchored in writing as well as in three-dimensional space. As a result the social researcher of such cultures has a wealth of data available for analysis that is simply not open to researchers in cultures where writing is absent – though access to other symbolic systems may well be available.

For a panoramic view of the ways in which people arrange things in the world there are few better objects for study than encyclopaedias. Nowadays encyclopaedias are common enough items – accepting that the weighty tomes of the past have been replaced by electronic rather than written media. Yet the world has not always been brimming with encyclopaedias. In fact, it seems fair to assert that a set of volumes that claim to provide a comprehensive overview of the world and the contents within, is essentially a feature of modern Western culture.

There is probably little point in entering into debates about the first instance of any one thing. Yet, it seems fair to suggest that one of the earliest of all encyclopaedias was that published in Paris during the period 1751–72. The editors of the vast work sought, above all, to provide a map of available 'knowledge' and of all the byways within it. In short, to impose an encyclopaedic order on the world. In so doing they used a number of simple ordering devices. Foremost among these was the use of an alphabetic sequence – so the entries in the encyclopaedia were arranged in dictionary order. (Indeed, in the one set of volumes we see the emergence of two rather impressive forms of literality – encyclopaedias and dictionaries.) Alphabetic sequence, was not, however, the only ordering device that was used by the encyclopaedia's editors. They also used an ordering metaphor to organize knowledge. That metaphor was of a tree. The image of a tree of knowledge has, as Darnton (1984) points out, a much older pedigree than that of the *Encyclopédie*. It is also of some interest to note that the only image of evolution provided in Darwin's *Origin of Species* is of a tree, and that the image of a branching tree continues to play an important symbolic role in Western science generally (see Gould, 1989). In the case of Diderot and d'Alembert (the editors of the Paris Encyclopaedia) there were really three trees – named, respectively, Memory, Reason and Imagination. Within each tree there were many branches. So, for example, the tree of Memory had branches leading to 'nature' and its many divisions. Within that there were divisions relating to the 'uniformity of nature', and the 'irregularities of nature'. Among the latter, we find, in turn, articles on monstrous vegetables, unusual meteors, wonders of the earth, and so forth.

Monsters are not to be laughed at, and dividing or segmenting the world into the routine and the monstrous is a serious matter. Above all, it is a form of exercise that provides telling insight into how societies think (see, for example, Douglas, 1966; Ritvo, 1997). Indeed, one might say that the study of taxonomic structure (or forms of classification) is key to the study of any culture precisely because it makes 'thought' visible. That is, in so far as it can reveal a map of concepts and of the links and associations that are made between concepts. With that point in mind it is easy to understand why the authors of the Paris Encyclopaedia often referred to their work as a 'Mappemonde'. Yet, whenever things are divided, much more is implicated than human thought and culture. For, associated with each and every classificatory system is a set of practices. And it is truly in the links between human practices and forms of taxonomy that a space for social research opens up.

In fact, if we re-conceptualize Diderot's *Encyclopédie* as an information storage and retrieval system – rather than as a mere dictionary – we will be led to pose questions not merely about the content of the system, but also ones about how the system was accessed and used and modified and challenged. That is, how the system – as a technology – is nested within a web of activities (Bijker et al. 1987). In recent decades, investigations into the nature of information storage systems and their relationship to organizational life have emerged as a distinct subject area in itself (see, for example, Berg, 1997; Bowker and Star, 1999; Keating and Cambrosio, 2000). And as an introduction to just a few of the issues contained within this newly emergent field it would, perhaps, be useful for us to consider yet another encyclopaedia.

Consider Figure 5.1. It is an extract from a table concerned with the manner in which we classify what, in England, are often referred to as 'toadstools'. The table is to be found in a modern encyclopaedia (Jordan, 1995). It is an encyclopaedia of fungi, and it is designed to enable users to identify specimens found 'in the field'. In an anthropological sense the table facilitates the task of identification in an interesting manner. Thus, one can see that the table is based on little more than a series of binary divisions. So, either something is, or it is not. For example, the fungi either smell distinctly of fish or they do not. They either have rounded caps or they do not. This manner of operating in binary pairs – sometimes referred to as an Aristotelian system of classification – was regarded by Lévi-Strauss (1969) as fundamental to all human cultures. Indeed, Lévi-Strauss tried to decode myths and totems in terms of such logic, pointing out how we should concentrate on how what is said is ordered, rather than with what it 'means'.

Now the content of any classificatory system is important – as is this one. Consequently, the order on the page requires analysis. However, what can be easily overlooked is that order on the page is invariably tied into forms of social order and it is the connection between the two that demands investigation. For example, the use and manipulation of classificatory systems, as tools, invariably serves to mark out the boundaries of social groupings (Keating and Cambrosio, 2000), and in that sense they often function as boundary objects (Star and Griesemer, 1989).

In this light, were we to examine the fungi encyclopaedia a little more closely, it would quickly become evident that the frame within which the classification is embedded marks out a certain kind of user. In fact, it is an encyclopaedia aimed at 'amateurs' (p. 7) – designed for use by the amateur in the field, rather than, say, bench scientists in the laboratory. So, from the outset, it provides the reader with a specific identity for reading (and doing).

Key C Basidiomycotina
(Gill-bearing and pore-bearing forms)

1a Hymenium consisting of gills
1b Hymenium consisting of tubes opening by pores
.
.
.

.
24a Cap campanulate or conical
24b Cap not campanulate or conical
25a Cap greasy or viscid, brightly coloured   Hygrocybe
25b Cap not with this combination
26a Smelling distinctly of fish
26b Not smelling of fish
.
.

.
30a On wood   Micromphale
30b On cones   Baeospora, Strobilurus

FIGURE 5.1 *The Identification of Fungi*

Source: Adapted from M. Jordan, *The Encyclopaedia of Fungi of Britain and Europe*, 1995, Newton Abbot: David and Charles.

At a more detailed level we would also be able to determine that the text urges people to act in specific directions. In particular, it encourages people to 'perform' (Goffman, 1959; Mol, 2000) classification in a defined manner. Thus it suggests that readers smell, taste, look, pick and preserve fungi in order to identify and distinguish one from the other using 'a logical and progressive sequence of checks' (p. 7) – such checks as are outlined in Figure 5.1. So as well as providing the reader with the identity of an 'amateur', the system of classification also provides a script for doing. In that sense, the text orders its readers as much as it orders 'things' (fungi) in the world.

In the same way, the alphabetic ordering of entries in the great Paris Encyclopaedia also orders its readers as much as it orders the entries – it orders them to search the text by letter order rather than by entry size, or date, or author, or topic link. (It is, of course, an ordering process that would be considered by most people to be one that is both efficient and convenient.) In any event, one of the things that is happening with our fungi encyclopaedia (in use) is that it is acting back on its readers and structuring them as amateur field scientists (see Lynch and Woolgar (1990) for similar examples). There are, of course, other ways of ordering fungi, and other classificatory systems. They, however, would be linked into different technological systems and thereby into different social groupings. Thus, a classification of fungi according to, say, the features of the genetic (DNA) code would require a very different group of readers – with different skills, different ways of working and alternative arrays of technological hardware.

How documents place things, how they make things visible, and how such systems of visibility are tied into social practices can form a guiding theme for social research. Indeed, it is particularly instructive to examine how graphical and similar forms of representation can materialize things (phenomena) that would otherwise remain opaque and diffuse. (For an example, see Prior et al., 2002.) Naturally, in order to make things visible, human actors and agents have to translate ideas into images and traces. Such processes of translation are various, and what is supposedly the 'same' object can be translated (Serres, 1995) into a number of alternative forms. How the forms relate one to the other and how they act back on their creators is, however, always a matter open to empirical research.

So far I have discussed issues of representation in a manner that is, perhaps, slightly detached from obvious social scientific concerns. So in the next section I intend to focus specifically on a form of classification/representation that is commonly used to provide a description of social behaviour.

THE NATURE OF NEUROSES

I am looking at a table of research results (Table 5.1). It tells us about the community prevalence rates in Great Britain of certain types of what are sometimes called 'neurotic' disorders, together with some estimates for the 'functional psychoses'. The table represents 'facts' about mental illness. It

TABLE 5.1 **Prevalence of psychiatric disorders in private households by gender. Rates per thousand of population in past week (GB 1995)**

Nature of disorder	Females	Males
Mixed anxiety & depressive disorder (MADD)	99	54
Generalized anxiety disorder (GAD)	34	28
Depressive episode	25	17
All phobias	14	7
Obsessive–compulsive disorder (OCD)	15	9
Panic disorder	9	8
Functional psychoses*	4	4
Alcohol dependence*	21	75
Drug dependence*	15	29

* Rates per thousand of population in past twelve months.

Source: Meltzer et al. (1995)

is intended to be used, together with others related to it, as a resource for researchers. Thus, we can, for example, refer to Table 5.1 as evidence for our statement that, in Great Britain, about 16 per cent of people in any one week show symptoms of a neurotic disorder. But how were this and other facts arrived at? How was the report put together? And what would an answer to such questions tell us about fundamental social processes?

The study of the manner in which social data such as are found in Table 5.1, are produced, has a good sociological pedigree. Some early markers in this particular history are available in the works of Cicourel (1964, 1976), Douglas (1967) and Garfinkel (1967) who tended to focus on crime and suicide statistics. As with the manufacture of crime or suicide or any other form of statistics, the production of psychiatric statistics depends on the existence of at least two foundation stones. The first underpins what we might call a conceptual or theoretical scheme, whilst the second underpins the rules and technical instructions for applying the concepts to a set of events and occurrences. Now, the conceptual scheme in terms of which mental illness is comprehended is that contained in the *Diagnostic and Statistical Manual of the American Psychiatric Association* (the DSM IV, 2000). The latter contains a series of categories relating to the various psychiatric maladies that people might be said to suffer from, and it also contains diagnostic criteria for recognizing the distinct disorders. Some of the disorders are listed in Table 5.1. We will return to the DSM in a moment. For now let us focus on how the figures in Table 5.1 were obtained.

The data in the table are derived from answers to a survey conducted in over 10,000 private households. The appendix to the research report from which these figures are derived provides the detail of the sample frame that was used (Meltzer et al., 1995). It tells us the rules by means of which households and the adults within them were selected. It also provides the questionnaire or instrument by which mental illness was recognized. In this particular case the instrument was called the Clinical Interview Schedule (Revised) or CIS-R. The CIS-R is one of a variety of 'instruments' that produce clinical and other phenomena (see, for example, Bowling, 1997). In many respects documents such as the CIS-R are like machine tools – tools for producing 'things'. Indeed, phenomena such as 'disability', types of psychiatric illness and 'quality of life' are conditions routinely manufactured by instruments of the kind referred to here. In the case of the CIS-R, the tool operates through a system of questions and answers. For example, there are questions about people feeling fatigued or feeling ill. One such question asks, 'During the past month, have you felt that you've been lacking in energy?' Another question asks, 'Have you had any sort of ache or pain in the past month?' Respondents are required to answer 'Yes' or 'No'.

In his *Method and Measurement in Sociology*, Cicourel (1964) discussed the status of questions such as these. The latter raised issues relating to the ways in which the interview process, and the questions and answers provided within the interview, are socially embedded. In particular, he became interested in the process through which the interview – as a social event – can turn conversation into social scientific data, pointing out that the use of instruments (such as, say, the CIS) involved an act of measurement by fiat. That is to say, the instrument imposes a commonality of meaning on questions and answers that are, in all likelihood, variously understood – at different times and by different people (see also Houtkoup-Steenstra, 2000). Indeed, the whole matter of measurement in the social sciences is something of a Pandora's box, raising as it does problems concerning whether or not the CIS-R (or a similar instrument) is valid for measuring such things as depression and anxiety. Rather than concentrate on measurement issues at the level of the interviewing process, however, it would be more useful at this point to turn to an examination of the computer-assisted procedures by means of which psychiatric diagnoses were made. That is to say, to focus on the rules-based procedures by means of which the research managers moved from the 'Yes'/'No' responses on the interview schedule to the categories of 'depressive episode', 'panic attack' and 'obsessive–compulsive disorder' contained in the tables of the report.

The CIS-R depends on the use of 'lay' interviewers. In other words, the people who ask subjects questions about mood and behaviour are not trained psychiatrists. Consequently, it is impossible for them to diagnose the respondents. Instead, on the return of the completed interview schedules to the research team a set of algorithms were put into play. Many of the algorithms involved scoring responses. For example, the questionnaire was divided into sections and points were awarded in each section. On the section relating to anxiety, for example, a respondent would score 1 if they had been 'generally anxious or nervous or tense' for four or more days in the past seven days. They would score another 1 if they felt tense, nervous or anxious for more than three hours in total in any one of the past seven days – and so on. As we move through the questionnaire we add the points, and if they total more than 12 (the cut-off point) then the subject is assumed to display symptoms of a psychiatric disorder. Which disorder it is, is dependent on which sections of the instrument the respondent scores within. So, no mention of the diagnostic conditions is made in the interview schedule and certainly at no stage were subjects asked whether they suffered from obsessive–compulsive neuroses or depression or whatever.

Human beings, of course, rarely pick up disorders singly and sequentially and in an easily labelled fashion. More likely they suffer from many things at once – they are both depressed and psychotic, say. They indulge in substance abuse and suffer from anxiety. So given that many individuals suffer from multiple pathologies at one and the same time, the CIS-R provides precedence rules that enable multiple disorders to be placed in a hierarchical sequence. For example, depressive episodes always rank above phobias. In this respect, the report follows the system prescribed by the DSM.

It was by the posing and coding of questions and answers, then, that diagnoses of psychiatric disorder were arrived at. In fact, there is a sense in which one could argue that the data assembling process – using interview schedules and algorithms – manufactured the disorders. So what does this suggest about our concept of psychiatric disorder? And what would happen if the research managers had set the cut-off point on the schedule to 10 or 18 rather than 12?

Such questions are in many ways related. It is possible, for example, to select a different cut-off point. Moving the point to, say, 10 would increase the prevalence of mental illness in the community. Moving the point to 18 would decrease it. So we can have as much or as little mental illness in the community as we want. (It was once said of Poland that it was a country on wheels seeing how its borders were changed so frequently, and one might be inclined to take the same view about the prevalence of psychiatric disorders.) There are, of course, conventions about where the point should be, but the fact that the point is movable tells us something about what Foucault (1972) would have referred to as a particular type of 'discourse' on mental illness in the late twentieth century. It is a discourse that argues that mental illness is not something that is qualitatively different from sanity, but rather something of the same order that differs only in degree. The implication is, then, that states of health and illness can be arranged along a continuum – a continuum that runs from zero to infinity. Whether or not individuals are to be deemed 'ill' depends not on what they think, feel or do, but on the cut-off point that we use for our classification. The level at which the cut-off is set is important, even in research terms, mainly because the impact of such things as genetic or social factors on psychiatric disorder can be amplified or even 'eradicated' by moving the point upward or downward (see, for example, Brown, 1981).

This vision of psychiatric disorder as a quantitative variation on normal behaviour expresses only one of a number of possible positions on the subject. It was, for example, a vision that used to be contained within the DSM. However, the contents and the theoretical ideas behind the DSM have changed markedly between the appearance of the first (1952) and the fourth (1994) edition. And one consequence of the alteration of the conceptual scheme is that the conditions that we are referring to in the 1990s are not the same conditions as were referred to in the 1952 edition. For example, the word 'depression' occurs in both, but the nature, course and origin of that depression have radically altered (Healy, 1997). Naturally, our table of statistics (Table 5.1) would not highlight this change, but the changes are nevertheless embodied within it. (A table showing trends in the prevalence of 'depression' over the later half of the twentieth century would, however, be affected, in a fundamental way, by these alterations.)

By examining the history of the DSM, then, we can see how it is produced – as with all forms of 'expert' documentation – in a politically structured space (see Rose, 1988; Young, 1995). In fact, the DSM is a document that has been produced by a professional or expert faction. Given the significance of the American Psychiatric Association in the global network of expertise, that faction has the power to decide what is and what is not a psychiatric disorder and how that disorder is to be defined. More importantly, perhaps, we begin to see how the DSM is like a machine tool – a tool that, when assembled with others of the same ilk, can generate new products. Such generative documents set out the boundaries in terms of which experts think and talk and write. In the manufacture of data about psychiatric disorder, they are not, of course, the only machine tools at hand. The CIS-R, the coding frame, the algorithms to which we have referred, also serve in the workshop. Put together such instruments produce, and how the production process unfolds is for ever a matter of legitimate social research. For it is on the basis of such representations that social scientists refer to 'facts' about society.

Naturally, most social researchers tend to use the results of such research as is embodied in Table 5.1 as 'resource'. However, what the above analysis suggests is that it is always worthwhile investigating such data as 'topic' – on this last distinction see Zimmerman and Pollner (1971). That is to say, it is forever beneficial to ask how documents are produced; who, exactly, produced them; and how was the production process socially organized? (For other examples see Prior, 2003.) Having produced documentation, of course, it is inevitable that someone somewhere will use it. It is to issues of use that I shall turn in the next section.

DOCUMENTS IN ACTION

Text and documentation are not only produced, but also, in turn, are productive. For example, in his discussion of a psychiatric record, Hak (1992) provides an illustration of how a professional psychiatrist translates items of patient talk and observed behaviour into a written record. In so doing the psychiatrist – as note taker – highlights the essential details of a patient's conversation, codes them into professional language (of delusions, hallucinations, diagnostic terms, etc.) and makes suggestions for future action (entry into a psychiatric unit or whatever). In Figure 5.2, we can see similar processes at work. Figure 5.2 is a facsimile of a page of nursing assessment notes that I came across in a psychiatric hospital in the late 1980s. It is clear from the notes that the members of the nursing staff were concerned to categorize their patients in a

Patient	Admissions	Diagnosis	Problems/constraints	Medication	Plans	Assets
Name: Dob 11/12/36 **Admin area:** East **Dr:** Yellow **Ward:** Blue	**No. of adm.** = 1 **Date of last adm.** 17/06/1962	Schizophrenia	Long time in hospital Temper tantrums & bad language Activities of daily living poor Recently quarrelsome with ASB	Gaviscon tabs bd Trifluoperazine 2 mg bd Vit BPc 1 tab mane	Maintain	
Name: Dob 23/02/53 North **Dr:** Green **Ward:** Blue	**No. of adm.** = 5 **Date of last adm.** 29/09/1987	Paranoid Schizophrenia	Loner. Poor motivation Wishes to stay in hospital Failed RA (stay in residential accommodation) Injury to right hip	Piroxican 30 mg nocte Ranitidine 150 mg nocte Vit BPC am	Move to community	ADL skills good
Name: Dob 3/07/58 West **Dr:** Green **Ward:** Blue	**No. of adm.** = 3 **Date of last adm.** 17/05/1988	Schizophrenia Low IQ	Poverty of thought Withdrawn ADL skills limited Childish and naive in manner Mother has encouraged dependence over the years but is now opting out Poor road safety	Benxtropine 2 mg mane Thioridizine 75 mg tid Senna 2 tabs nocte	ADL activities	Pleasant & cooperative Hygiene good
Name: Dob 10/08/60 West **Dr:** Green **Ward:** Blue	**No. of adm.** = 6 **Date of last adm.** 10/03/1988	Dependent Personality	Multiple Somatic complaints Resistant to suggestions Poor compliance tends to opt out Poor response to antidepressant therapy Poor attendance at OT unit Poor hearing	Thyroxine 0.1 mg mane Nifedipine 10 mg bd Thioridizine 50 mg bd	Maintain	ADL good

FIGURE 5.2 *Facsimile of a ward-based nursing assessment record (UK psychiatric hospital, 1989)*

variety of ways. The latter included a one-word diagnosis of the patient's condition, an assessment of 'activities of daily living' (ADL) skills, brief notes concerning the level of cooperation and hygiene exhibited by the patient and so forth. These assessments were based on conversations and interchanges between nurses and patients and among nurses alone. It is important to recall that the patients/clients – as with all human beings – commonly indulged in a wide array of activities and behaviours. For example, patients would talk to themselves, watch television, lend each other cigarettes, shout, laugh, go to work in the hospital workshops, and so forth. Yet of such a myriad array of activities only a few are ever highlighted. Thus, in the case of the first named patient, it is their 'schizophrenia', their poor ADL skills, their temper tantrums and quarrelsome behaviour that are highlighted. This selectivity of focus would become even more evident were one to examine other kinds of patient records. Thus, in the hospital to which I am currently referring there were also psychiatric records (called 'charts'), and social work records kept on each patient. The former were maintained by the medically trained psychiatrists and contained other kinds of information, such as data on whether the patients exhibited any 'first rank symptoms' (of schizophrenia), their medication and its effects, their 'history', items about family life, patient delusions, and so forth. In fact the psychiatric records looked very much like those alluded to and reported upon by Hak (1992). Social work records were also made up for each of the patients. These paid relatively little attention to medical diagnoses and the effects of medication and referred more often to the stability and maturity of the patient vis-à-vis relationships with others, the nature and level of their state benefits, and the like. Considerable reference to the whereabouts, behaviours and opinions of other family members was also made within social work files. Access to such records and the 'right' to make entries in such records were more or less restricted to the members of the individual professional groupings. In that respect the 'script' in each document served, in part, to mark out the realm and expertise of the various parties. Social work talk belonged in social work records, psychiatric talk belonged in medical records, and nurse talk belonged in nursing records.

Recorded observations on patients/clients are, then, highly selective. In the case of public service agency files, such records often define the human beings that they refer to in specific and particular ways. In so doing they call upon and activate a whole series of membership categorization devices or MCDs (Silverman, 1998). How a particular device comes to be associated with any individual and how that categorization might be used and called upon to account for and explain an individual's behaviour in specific circumstances can form the occasion for important and fundamental sociological research.

In my work on the psychiatric hospital referred to above, I was primarily interested in how patients came to be classified in different ways through routine procedures (see Prior, 1993). Naturally the use of notes and records forms only one support for the identification system that surrounds patients. Everyday conversation and casual interchanges form another, and in any organization there will always be a constant interchange between talk and text. Thus I provided in my study (Prior, 1993) a short extract of an exchange between nurses in the ward office concerning the issue as to what was wrong with 'X'. Thus:

Nurse 1: Does anyone know what's supposed to be wrong with X?
[*Blank looks and silence meet the question*]
Nurse 2: Schizophrenia, I suppose.
Nurse 1: Hmm. I've never seen any sign of it.
Nurse 3: Well, he's on chlorpromazine, so he must be schizophrenic.

The MCD of 'schizophrenic' recorded in the notes is, then, sustained and underlined in this case by means of a casual conversation – and especially the reference to 'X's' medication. (The use of medication to define a specific psychiatric disorder, rather than the other way around, is not uncommon in psychiatry.) If, however, there were any real doubt about 'what was wrong with X', it would be the notes that would carry the day. So the researcher who wishes to concentrate on the use of documents in action has to be constantly aware as to how the written record is tied into and anchored within other aspects of organizational life such as conversations at the nursing station. Nevertheless, it is only when assessments are written down and can be pointed to that they are used to form a foundation on which routine social actions are built. Thus medical professionals can and do use 'the files' as a warrant for their actions in relation to their patients – showing how what they do to patients is warranted by the information on the record(s). Indeed, in the context of psychiatry Barrett (1996: 107) has underlined how 'clinical writing' not only describes the treatment of patients, but also constitutes the treatment.

In a wider context, Bowker and Star (1999) and Young (1995) have also pointed out how (documented) nomenclatures of disease are routinely tied into the financial accounting mechanisms of hospital life. So, psychiatrists routinely draw down a diagnostic category from the DSM, 'fit' it to a given patient, and then justify what was done for and to the patient/client in the light of the category. (This, in the full knowledge that categories and patients rarely make a 1:1 fit.) Indeed, the naming of diseases and disorders in modern medical systems is often used more for purposes of financial reimbursement (to and from insurance companies), and other accounting and monitoring purposes, than they are for forming accurate descriptions of a given patient's condition.

Arguing along a similar path, Zerubavel (1979: 45) had previously indicated how notes written up by medical and nursing professionals were 'among the main criteria used by their supervisors to evaluate their clinical competence', as well as forming the primary mechanism through which continuous super-vision of patients was maintained. In fact Zerubavel's study highlights the centrality of charts, graphs and records of all kinds in underpinning the routine social organization of hospital life. Thus, printed schedules are used to organize the patient/staff day; printouts of various kinds are routinely used to monitor patients; and notes written so as indicate how the 'hospital' cares for its clients. (In US hospitals, of course, patient records are, as we have already indicated, also used as a hook on which to hang financial costs and transactions.) Above all perhaps, we see in the use of documents to monitor activity an essential component of that self-reflexive capacity that is said by Bauman (1991) to characterize modernity as a whole.

This capacity of medical records to mediate social relationships of all kinds has been further researched by Berg (1996, 1997) who points out how hospital patients are both structured through records and accessed through records. One important feature of patient existence that is emphasized by Berg is the manner in which medical records are used so as to keep the case (and the patient) 'on track'. Such structuring of patient trajectories through records is achieved in numerous ways, planning and monitoring being two of them. In this respect it is of interest to note the column headed 'Plans' in Figure 5.2. In the context of these records the most important plans concerned whether or not the patient was ready for life in the community. (My own hospital study was executed at that rather important cusp where psychiatric patients were being moved out of hospitals and into 'the community'.) In most cases, the patients were to be 'maintained' (kept in the hospital ward). The detail hardly concerns us here. What is important to note is that records of this type always contain some rules for action. Other rules for action are contained in the column relating to medication. Latour (1987) has used the term 'action-at-a-distance' to indicate how decisions written down in one context and setting can carry implications for action in future settings. And it is indeed the case that records often contain instructions for future organizational activity. King James's claim that opened this chapter provides an excellent reflection on the process.

Patient trajectories are not, of course, the only things that are kept 'on track' by the use of records. Patient identities are also constructed through documentation, and in the modern world it is of considerable interest to study how our identities are supported and altered by various forms of identification. In a larger study (Prior, 2003) I have provided some detailed examples as to how self and documentation are interrelated. In the following section I draw upon just some of the attendant insights.

TEXT AND IDENTITY

In a paper published in 1993, Miller and Morgan examined the social nature of the academic c.v. In that paper they indicated how such c.v.s can be understood as a form of autobiographical practice – a form of practice that is centrally concerned with the presentation of self in occupational settings. Using Goffman's (1959) work they seek to demonstrate how the academic c.v. involves matters of presentation of front and manufacture of self. Above all, however, they point out how the academic c.v. is a matter of performance.

Performances of the kind just referred to are, of course, executed solely through writing. In that respect they are of special concern to us. It is also of interest to note that Miller and Morgan indicate how the construction of a c.v. can itself engage the use of generative documents of the kind mentioned in the third section. In this instance the generative document referred to was the *Guidelines for the Presentation of a Curriculum Vitae* of Manchester University. Rather than look at how human actors can use and manufacture documentation for the presentation of the self, however, I propose in this section to look at how documents can structure their readers. That is, to look at how they might guide readers to perform in specific ways.

In this context it is helpful to note Iser's (1989) claims about how the reader's role in the work of English fiction altered between the eighteenth century and the twentieth. We need not attend to the detail, but simply note examples of the manner in which texts provide the reader (and the writer) with specific scripts for performance. For example, Iser points out how fictional texts have structured the reader as passive recipient of a narrative or – as with Thackeray's *Vanity Fair* – as an observer of life's variety and display. With Charles Dickens, on the other hand, the reader is almost invariably structured as a judge of moral character – this, nowhere more so, perhaps, than with *Oliver Twist*. In this text we are inveigled into taking up a moral stance on poverty and exploitation, subservience and domination, whilst the writer remains positioned as a dispassionate teller of a tale. That stance of reader and of writer is, of course, quite different from, say, the one adopted in Dashiel Hammett's *The Maltese Falcon*, a story that features the unforgettably amoral Sam Spade.

Naturally, our concern is not with works of fiction but with routine forms of documentation. In that respect, we have already glimpsed at how a work of non-fiction (the encyclopaedia of fungi) can structure its readers. There we noted how the reader was structured as an amateur and how that amateur was directed to identify fungi in particular ways. But even with everyday documents readers and writers are structured and allocated to specific roles. To that end I intend to refer to a form of documentation that is provided to people in the UK when they collect medicines from a pharmacy. In each case where that happens the client should be provided with a Patient Information Leaflet (appropriately abbreviated to PIL). For each form of medication there is also a 'data sheet' for pharmacists. It will serve our purposes to analyse the text for both forms of document. We will do so with respect to leaflets that relate to one and the same drug.

The PIL to which I am going to refer is that for ziduvodine. The latter is commonly prescribed (under a trademarked name) for people who show symptoms of HIV infection and AIDS. The PIL for ziduvodine opens by highlighting the possibility of the taker of the medication having doubts and worries. Should the 'patient' have any doubts it is suggested that they consult their doctor. And this pattern of the doctor as an expert (with full knowledge, but without doubt and worry), and the consumer as in need of advice, is replicated throughout the leaflet. Consequently, the doctor is presented as someone who will assuage doubt and worry, someone who can provide advice on all aspects of medication, and as someone who will give instructions that ought to be followed.

> If you forget to take a dose, don't worry. . . . If you take a larger dose than prescribed . . . you should let your doctor know as soon as possible if this happens. . . . If someone else takes your medicine by mistake, tell your doctor at once. . . . You should not stop treatment unless your doctor tells you to. (ABPI, 1996)

In line with the structuring of the patient as a non-expert, the leaflet also provides a lay narrative of the manner in which the drug acts on the body. The narrative indicates how the anti-viral agent that is ziduvodine serves to delay the progression of HIV and AIDS but does not provide a 'cure'. Instead it 'fights' against HIV. For, according to the leaflet, HIV – left unchecked – will enter into a group of cells called CD4 cells and turn them into a 'mini-factory' for infection. But in the great struggle against HIV, the anti-viral agent also seeks to invade the CD4 cells and stop the factory producing the viral agent. (It is, if you like, an heroic narrative.)

In the respective data sheet for pharmacists, however, a somewhat different narrative is provided. There one can read of the fact that ziduvodine is 'phosphorylated to the monophosphate derivative by cellular thymidine kinase', that it is 'catalysed', and that it acts as 'an inhibitor of, and substrate for, the viral reverse transcriptase'. Naturally, one would both hope and expect the data sheet for pharmacists to read somewhat differently from that for patients – so as to provide more complex information, for example. But what is important from our standpoint is that in using this complex lexicon of chemistry, rather than metaphors of mini-factories, the texts are also structuring experts and non-experts. And this structuring of expertise is also evident in more direct ways. Thus the pharmacists' data sheet talks, for example, about 'the management of patients', and how patients ought to be cautioned, advised, monitored, and so forth. All in all, then, the PIL structures the reader as an individual subject to the direction of others (who are experts), whilst the data sheet structures the reader as an expert in control of patients.

My main purpose in looking at the examples above has been to indicate how a large part of identity work, as performance, involves documentation. In some cases that documentation may take the form of full-length books – biographies and autobiographies. In ordinary, everyday life it usually takes less notable forms – such as assembling and writing a c.v., or filling out a job application, a census form, an application for a driver's licence or a passport. Yet, exactly how people use and manipulate such routine forms of documentation – to do identity work – is a legitimate field for research in itself, and certainly one that is worthy of exploration by the qualitative researcher.

CONCLUSIONS

The emphasis that social scientists commonly place on human actors manifests itself most clearly in the attention that they give to what such actors say and think and believe and opine. And should we wish to study human actors in a rigorous social scientific manner there are many manuals available to instruct us as to how we should proceed with our research. Most of these texts focus on ways to capture and analyse speech and thought and behaviour. However, few social scientific research manuals concentrate on the written word and, more specifically, on documents that contain words. Indeed, when documents are put forward for consideration they are usually approached in terms of their content rather than their status as 'things'. That is, the focus is usually on the language contained in the document as a medium of thought and action. Yet, as I stated in the introductory section, it is quite clear that each and every document stands in a dual relation to fields of action. Namely, as a receptacle (of instructions, commands, wishes, reports, etc.), as an agent that is open to manipulation by others, and as an ally or resource to be mobilized for further action.

As a receptacle of content, one set of questions that may quite justifiably be asked by the social scientific researcher concern the processes and circumstances in terms of which document 'X' has been produced or manufactured. That is, to treat the document as topic rather than as resource. Yet, documents are not just manufactured, they are consumed, and as with all tools they are manipulated in organized settings for many different ends. They also function in different ways – irrespective of human manipulations. In short, documents have effects. So a further route of analysis for the researcher is to ask questions about how documents function in specific circumstances. Naturally, the way in which a document functions is often affected by its content, but content is not always determinant. Indeed, we need to keep in mind that the content of a document is never fixed and static, not least because documents have always to be read, and reading implies that the content of a document will be situated rather than fixed. In any event, the analysis of content, production and use form three of the corner points around which we can consider the development of a research strategy. In this chapter I have sought to provide some examples as to the kinds of issues that are implicated in such a strategy.

At the risk of seeming to be as egocentric as King James, with whom we opened the chapter, I am going to end this excursus by quoting myself. My aim, of course, is not to hear the sound of my own words, but to argue for a redirection of social scientific interest in documentation as a whole. My argument runs thus:

> It might be objected of course that the most important feature of documentation – content – has been given too low a profile throughout the entire [work]. I might defend such a lack of focus by saying that there are numerous other texts that deal with aspects of content analysis, or discourse analysis, and that there would be little point in duplicating such work here. However, I offer no such defence. There is no need. Instead I offer an analogy. My analogy concerns an operatic libretto (the set of words and phrases that is sung). Taken on its own a libretto rarely adds up to much. The text as narrative is often disjointed, repetitive and lacking in depth. I cannot think of a single one that might hold a person's attention as a gripping tale. Yet, a libretto is not intended to be analysed in isolation. It demands to be analysed in action. How it is integrated into the dramatic action on stage, how it

relates to the melody and rhythm of the music, how it is called upon (recruited) and manipulated by the singers, how it is *performed* – all of these are of primary importance. Its substance as displayed on the inert page is of only secondary concern. (Prior, 2003: 172–3)

NOTE

1. Cited in Lee, M. (1980) Government by pen. *Scotland under James VI and I*. Urbana: University of Illinois Press. p. vii.

Recommended reading

For an overview of issues relating to this chapter, together with a detailed bibliography, see Prior, L. (2003) *Using Documents in Social Research*. London: Sage.

For a somewhat more traditional approach to the issues raised herein, see Scott, J. (1990) *A Matter of Record*. Cambridge: Polity Press.

On the nature and use of diaries, biographies, and other personal documents in social research, see Plummer, K. (2001) *Documents of Life. 2. Invitation to a Critical Humanism*. London: Sage.

For some interesting historical examples of document production and use, see Darnton, R. (1984) *The Great Cat Massacre and other Episodes in French Cultural History*. New York: Basic Books.

On wider issues concerning the impact of writing on social life, see Goody, J. (1968) *Literacy in Traditional Societies*. Cambridge: Cambridge University Press.

REFERENCES

ABPI (1996) *Compendium of patient information leaflets, 1996–97*. London: Datapharm.

American Psychiatric Association (2000) *Diagnostic and Statistical Manual of Mental Disorders. DSM-IV-TR*. Washington, DC: American Psychiatric Association.

Barrett, R. (1996) *The psychiatric team and the social definition of schizophrenia. An anthropological study of person and illness*. Cambridge: Cambridge University Press.

Barthes, R. (1985) *The Fashion System*, trans. M. Ward and R. Howard. London: Jonathan Cape.

Bauman, Z. (1991) *Intimations of Postmodernity*. London: Routledge.

Berg, M. (1996) 'Practices of reading and writing: the constitutive role of the patient record in medical work', *Sociology of Health and Illness*, 18 (4): 499–524.

Berg, M. (1997) *Rationalizing Medical Work. Decision-support techniques and medical practices.* Cambridge, MA: MIT Press.

Bijker, W.E., Pinch, T. and Hughes, T.P. (eds) (1987) *The Social Construction of Technological Systems.* Cambridge, MA: MIT Press.

Bowker, G.C. and Star, S.L. (1999) *Sorting Things Out. Classification and Its Consequences.* Cambridge, MA: MIT Press.

Bowling, A. (1997) *Measuring Health. A Review of Quality of Life Measurement Scales,* Second Edition. Buckingham: Open University Press.

Brown, G. (1981) 'Etiological studies and the definition of a case', in J.K. Wing, P. Bebbington and L.N. Robins (eds), *What is a case? The problem of definition in psychiatric community surveys.* London: Grant McIntyre. pp. 62–9.

Cicourel, A.V. (1964) *Method and Measurement in Sociology.* New York: The Free Press.

Cicourel, A.V. (1976) *The Social Organisation of Juvenile Justice.* London: Heinemann.

Darnton, R. (1984) *The Great Cat Massacre and Other Episodes in French Cultural History.* New York: Basic Books.

Douglas, J.D. (1967) *The Social Meanings of Suicide.* Princeton, NJ: Princeton University Press.

Douglas, M. (1966) *Purity and Danger: An Analysis of the Concepts of Pollution and Taboo.* London: Routledge & Kegan Paul.

Foucault, M. (1970) *The Order of Things.* London: Tavistock.

Foucault, M. (1972) *The Archaeology of Knowledge,* trans. A. Sheridan. New York: Pantheon.

Garfinkel, H. (1967) *Studies in Ethnomethodology.* Englewood Cliffs, NJ: Prentice Hall.

Goffman, E. (1959) *The presentation of the self in everyday life.* New York: Doubleday Anchor Books.

Gould, S.J. (1989) *Wonderful Life. The Burgess Shale and the Nature of History.* New York: W.W. Norton.

Hak, T. (1992) 'Psychiatric records as transformations of other texts', in G. Watson and R.M. Seiler (eds), *Text in Context. Contributions to Ethnomethodology.* London: Sage. pp. 138–55.

Healy, D. (1997) *The Antidepressant Era.* Cambridge, MA: Harvard University Press.

Houtkoup-Steenstra, H. (2000) *Interaction and the standardized survey interview.* Cambridge: Cambridge University Press.

Iser, W. (1989) *Prospecting. From reader response to literary anthropology.* Baltimore, MD: Johns Hopkins University Press.

Jordan, M. (1995) *The Encyclopaedia of Fungi of Britain and Europe.* Newton Abbot: David and Charles.

Keating, P. and Cambrosio, A. (2000) '"Real compared to what?" Diagnosing leukemias and lymphomas', in M. Lock, A. Young and A. Cambrosio (eds), *Living and working with the new medical technologies. Intersections of inquiry.* Cambridge: Cambridge University Press. pp. 103–34.

Latour, B. (1987) *Science in Action. How to follow engineers and scientists through society.* Buckingham: Open University Press.

Lévi-Strauss, C. (1969) *Totemism,* trans. R. Needham. Harmondsworth: Penguin.

Lynch, M. and Woolgar, S. (eds) (1990) *Representation in Scientific Practice.* Cambridge, MA: MIT Press.

Miller, N. and Morgan, D. (1993) 'Called to account. The CV as an autobiographical practice', *Sociology,* 27 (1): 133–43.

Mol, A. (2000) 'Pathology and the clinic: an ethnographic presentation of two atheroscleroses', in M. Lock, A. Young and A. Cambrosio (eds), *Living and working with the new medical technologies. Intersections of inquiry.* Cambridge: Cambridge University Press. pp. 82–102.

Meltzer, H., Gill, B., Petticrew, M. and Hinds, K. (1995) *The prevalence of psychiatric morbidity among adults living in private households. OPCS Surveys of Psychiatric Morbidity in Great Britain. Report 1.* London: HMSO.

Prior, L. (1993) *The Social Organization of Mental Illness.* London and Newbury Park, CA: Sage.

Prior, L. (2003) *Using Documents in Social Research.* London: Sage.

Prior, L., Wood, F., Gray, J., Pill, R. and Hughes, D. (2002) 'Making risk visible: the role of images in the assessment of (cancer) genetic risk', *Health, Risk and Society,* 4 (3): 242–58.

Ritvo, H. (1997) *The Platypus and the Mermaid, and Other Figments of the Classifying Imagination.* Cambridge, MA: MIT Press.

Rose, N. (1988) 'Calculable minds and manageable individuals', *History of the Human Sciences,* 1 (2): 179–200.

Serres, M. (1995) *Conversations on Science, Culture and Time,* with Bruno Latour, trans. R. Lapidus. Ann Arbor: The University of Michigan Press.

Silverman, D. (1998) *Harvey Sacks. Social Science and Conversation Analysis.* Cambridge: Polity Press.

Star, S.L. and Griesemer, J.R. (1989) 'Institutional ecology "translations" and boundary objects: amateurs and professionals in Berkeley's Museum of Vertebrate Zoology, 1907–39', *Social Studies of Science,* 19: 387–420.

Young, A. (1995) *The Harmony of Illusions. Inventing Post-traumatic Stress Disorder.* Princeton, NJ: Princeton University Press.

Zerubavel, E. (1979) *Patterns of Time in Hospital Life: A Sociological Perspective.* London: University of Chicago Press.

Zimmerman, D.H. and Pollner, M. (1971) 'The everyday world as a phenomenon', in J.D. Douglas (ed.), *Understanding Everyday Life.* London: Routledge & Kegan Paul. pp. 80–103.

6 Internet communication as a tool for qualitative research

Annette N. Markham

Qualitative studies of the Internet are diverse. In the early 1990s, Julian Dibbell published an ethnographically informed account and analysis of a rape in cyberspace (1993). In a popular chatroom space of an online community, one member utilized a program that controlled the text-based actions of two females present in the room. He then proceeded to write acts of violation involving these women. While the women were powerless to do anything except turn off their computers, their online characters continued to be violated online in front of many other people. The event had serious repercussions for violated women and the community in general.

In the mid-1990s, Witmer and Katzman (1998) studied computer-mediated communication (CMC) users and the ways they compensated effectively for the absence of non-verbal and para-linguistic elements of conversation. Using emoticons, users convey humor, irony, and other emotions, supplementing the content of the message to enhance interpersonal connectedness.

In the late 1990s, Norwegian scholar Anne Ryen utilized the capacity of the Internet to conduct a long-term and long-distance case study of an Asian businessman in Tanzania. While she began by simply using the Internet as a tool for extending her reach, Ryen ended up also examining how the Internet influenced her personal and professional relationship with the participant (2002).

In 2003, Camille Johnson archived and analyzed nearly 600 web pages promoting anorexia as a lifestyle rather than a disease. She contends that this pro-anorexia network relies on Internet technologies to build and reproduce members' ideologies. Through cutting and pasting images and common texts, such as the "Thin Commandments," these women are actively constructing a global yet anonymous community, which appears to provide solidarity and helps to justify their choice to be anorexic.

These are four brief examples of distinctive Internet studies conducted by qualitative researchers. As a communication medium, a global network of connection, and a scene of social construction, the Internet provides new tools for conducting research, new venues for social research, and new means for understanding the way social realities get constructed and reproduced through discursive behaviors. This chapter seeks to illuminate some of the possibilities as well as limitations of studying the Internet and/or using Internet technologies to augment qualitative inquiry.

DEFINING THE INTERNET

As an umbrella term that includes the associated terms cyberspace and the Web (World Wide Web), the Internet can refer to the actual network and the exchange of data between computers. Many people use the Internet in a seemingly straightforward way: sending and receiving personal email, accessing public information, downloading maps, viewing merchandise and making purchases online, and generally using the technologies for information gathering and transmission. Internet can also refer to social spaces where relationships, communities, and cultures emerge through the exchange of text and images, either in real time or in delayed time sequences. There is a long tradition of social interaction and community development based on the capabilities of the Internet. In short, the Internet can be perceived as a set of technological tools, a complex network of social relations, a language system, a cultural milieu, and so forth. The way one defines and frames the Internet influences how one interacts with Internet-based technologies, as well as how one studies the Internet.

Which of these metaphoric frameworks is most useful for qualitative researchers? What does the Internet contribute to the endeavors of qualitative researchers? The answers depend on the specific phenomena under study, the research questions asked, and the methodological approaches favored.

The following three frameworks can help illustrate how the Internet is typically conceptualized and therefore how the qualitative researcher might use or study it as a context in itself or use it as a tool in a traditional study.

1 As a *medium for communication*, the Internet provides new channels for people to communicate with each other, new channels for researchers to communicate with participants, and new venues for conducting research. Still primarily text-based but increasingly augmented with moving and still images and sound, these tools both parallel and depart from traditional media for interaction. Thus, researchers can tap into emerging discursive forms and practices, either studying the way people use CMC in cultural contexts or utilizing CMC to interact with participants.

2 As a *network of computers*, the Internet collapses physical distances between people, thus creating the potential for collectives and collaborations not heretofore available. This network extends the potential reach of the researcher to a more global scale. The speed of transmission in these worldwide networks, along with the archiving capacity of computers, transforms time into a malleable construct. As individuals gain control over how time structures their interactions with others, researchers gain considerable flexibility in designing and conducting research. Understanding and utilizing time and notions of space in creative ways can significantly

augment research practice, particularly in terms of collecting information for study.

3 As a *context of social construction*, the Internet is a unique discursive milieu that facilitates the researcher's ability to witness and analyze the structure of talk, the negotiation of meaning and identity, the development of relationships and communities, and the construction of social structures as these occur discursively. Whether the researcher participates or simply observes, the linguistic and social structures emerging through CMC provide the opportunity for researchers to track and analyze how language builds and sustains social reality.

Whether conceptualized as a communication medium, a global network of connection, or a scene of social construction, the Internet offers the qualitative researcher many means of observing and/or interacting with participants in order to study the complex interrelation of language, technology, and culture. Regardless of the general framework used, one can utilize the *Internet as a tool* for research topics unrelated to the Internet specifically (e.g., using the Internet as a convenient and anonymous means of gathering information on racial attitudes) and/or study the *Internet as a specific social phenomenon* (e.g., studying the way a special interest group develops and sustains community through the copying and pasting of group-specific images in a network of websites). Put simply, the Internet is both a tool of research and a context worthy of research.

As with any metaphoric framework, these three frameworks guide and naturally restrict the qualitative researcher's general approach and specific practices in using and understanding the Internet, allowing the researcher to focus on certain features or experiences at the expense of other possible views. Understanding the general features of these frameworks can help researchers make wise choices as they investigate potentially unfamiliar research environments or design studies in which Internet technologies augment the collection or analysis of information.

THE INTERNET AS A MEDIUM FOR COMMUNICATION

I begin with the assumption that qualitative researchers analyze discursive practices in naturalistic settings to help build knowledge related to the construction, negotiation, and maintenance of human social practices and structures. Whether exploring culture writ large or a single conversation, we can say that most qualitative inquiry is grounded in information collected from observation, text, talk, and interviews (Silverman, 1997, 2001). At a very basic level, then, qualitative researchers engage in the process of studying communicative practices in context.

Inserting the Internet as a medium for interaction between researcher and participant or studying the Internet as it mediates interactions among subjects in the field changes the research scenario in that the Internet influences communication practices in ways that are simultaneously mundane and profound.[1] Even as one will note similarities between many features of the Internet and earlier media for communication, such as letter writing, telephone, telegraph, Post-it notes, and so forth, certain capacities and uses of Internet communication uniquely shape a user's perceptions and interactions. These influences extend beyond the interpersonal to the social and cultural; outcomes of these communication processes have the potential to shift sensemaking practices at the cultural level. Essentially, the Internet mediates – and in some ways moderates – interactions and the possible outcomes of these interactions at the dyadic, group, and cultural levels. Equally, Internet technologies have the potential to shift the ways in which qualitative researchers collect, make sense of, and represent data.

From "information transmission" to "meaning-making"

The Internet is a medium that transmits information virtually instantaneously between computers, individuals, and groups of people. Because of this, information transmission has become a defining characteristic of the Internet and the term communication is often conflated with the channels or media through which messages are transmitted. However, by shifting their view from this conduit model to a slightly different view of communication as a contextual process of meaning-making, researchers find that other issues become salient. The beauty of the Internet is the way in which it is interwoven with the sensemaking process at various levels. Interfaces on the surface of the screen facilitate certain interpretations of the medium, exerting influence on the way the user perceives the communication process. Below the surface, the content of the information exchanged is made sense of individually within a specific context, adding several variables to the complex relationship among self, other, and technology. Individual negotiation of this relationship interacts with others' negotiation processes.

I have argued elsewhere (Markham, 1998, forthcoming) that people tend to experience the Internet in distinctive ways. Some conceptualize the Internet as only a tool, while others perceive it as a place. Still others experience the Internet as a way of being in the world. These conceptualizations result in very different uses of and interactions with Internet-based technologies. Although not all individuals fall into these neat categories, this heuristic of tool, place, and way of being is a useful starting point for considering how users and, by extension, qualitative researchers tend to (or can) conceptualize and approach the Internet:

1 *As a tool for communicating*: One might naturally or deliberately conceptualize the Internet as a tool for retrieving and transmitting information, extending one's physical reach to connect with others, enteringn and crossing between multiple cultural fields, or performing multiple tasks simultaneously. From this perspective, users tend to perceive CMC in a straightforward way as a convenient addition to traditional media for communication. Email might

be simply a new form of writing letters or leaving short notes for people without the scraps of paper. The Web might be a means of finding and purchasing products and services without leaving one's home. Just as a hammer augments our physical strength, CMC can be perceived as a tool that extends some of our senses out to a global level. For researchers, this tool can be utilized with great benefit. Mann and Stewart (2000) provide an excellent and comprehensive review of methodological and ethical considerations under the umbrella of Internet as Tool.[2] In addition to using these new tools for exchanging information, interacting with participants, or collecting discourse, qualitative research usefully explores the tools themselves as well as social interactions afforded by these tools.

2 *As a place for communicating*: Many users and researchers conceptualize the Internet as a place as well as a tool. From this perspective, the Internet describes not only the network that structures interaction but also the cultural spaces in which meaningful human interactions occur (Jones, 1995). Internet interactions have no literal physical substance, yet they can be perceived as providing a visceral sense of presence (Soja, 1989) and having dimension. Novak (1991) tells us that once we discover space in information, we are freed from the constraints of architectures that occur in standard three dimensions. Internet communication can be seen as "liquid architecture," which "bends, rotates, and mutates in interaction with the person who inhabits it" (Novak, 1991). Interactions in these sensed dimensions are not merely meaningful but can have genuine consequences for participants, as exemplified by the text-based rape mentioned at the beginning of this chapter (Shields, 1996; Dibbell, 1993).

In this frame, the Internet can be a tool but is also a location where one can travel and exist and wherein one's discursive activities can contribute directly to the shape and nature of the place. Researchers can take advantage of these sensed dimensions to create interaction spaces that facilitate particular types of engagement with participants. Alternately, and perhaps more present in the past decade of research in this area, researchers have studied these sensed dimensions as cultural contexts (see, for example, Baym et al., 2000; Jones, 1995; Kendall, 2002; Markham, 1998; Turkle, 1995). Using basic terms, one can study the space itself, the interactions within these places, and the relationships and communities formed through the interactions. In my own work (Markham, 1998), the Internet is an umbrella term for those social spaces constituted and mediated through computer-mediated interactions. In addition, Jones (1995, 1999) provides several volumes in which authors examine Internet as Place.

3 *As a way of being in the world*: One can also conceptualize the Internet as a way of being. In this sense, Internet-based technologies provide a means for reinscribing, reconfiguring, or otherwise redefining identity, body, and self's connection with other. For example, a user might have two online personae with two distinct personalities and gender. Recently, scholars have argued compellingly that the performance of self through CMC has allowed transgendering to flourish, both as a concept and as a way of life,

because users can experience a different gender without the necessity of cross-dressing, makeup, hormones, or surgery (Future of Feminist Internet Studies, 2002). This is a good example of the extent to which users can perceive the Internet as a meaningful way of being, whether completely separate from or inextricably intertwined with their physical lives.

The focus of research from this perspective shifts away from looking at the Internet as a tool or a cultural space and moves toward the ephemeral territory of exploring the ways individuals in a computer-mediated society construct and experience themselves and others because of or through Internet communication. This conceptualization crosses many disciplines and often studies the intersections of social identity, body, and technology (see, for example, Benedikt, 1991; Cherny and Weise, 1996; Featherstone and Burrows, 1995; Sondheim, 1996; Stone, 1996; Turkle, 1995).

It is essential to consider the various ways in which people use and make sense of the Internet as a communication medium, because sensemaking practices differ widely. One might make sense of it as a tool, focusing on the ability of the Internet to make information seeking and retrieval more efficient and effective. Another might perceive the Internet as a place, focusing on the cultural boundaries created by interactions rather than on the channel for communication. These different perceptions can influence greatly the way people utilize and talk about the Internet. As well, the researcher's own perceptions will influence the way he or she observes and interprets discourse in online contexts. Being aware of the distinctions can help one better understand the context.

THE INTERNET AS A GLOBAL, INSTANTANEOUS NETWORK OF INTERACTION

As a tool for connecting with participants and collecting data, the Internet offers many interesting possibilities. So too does the Internet provide a means of understanding better the way that language constructs and maintains particular social realities. The Internet continues to provide environments within which researchers can interact with or gather information from participants. Whether one sets up an environment in which to interact with participants or observes naturally occurring discourse in discussion boards, weblogs, real-time chat environments, email exchanges, and so forth, one must consider the fundamentals of how people are communicating with one another in these environments and how CMC can influence interaction tendencies and outcomes. One can also explore means by which to utilize creatively certain environments to truly augment the way we come to know the subjects of our research and better understand the complexity of language and social reality. Here, I examine three essential aspects of Internet communication to consider in the development of any qualitative research endeavors related to the Internet:

1 Geographic dispersion
2 Temporal malleability
3 Multiple modality

Internet as geographically dispersed

This capacity of the Internet is, for many of us, taken for granted in our everyday communication with others. We can disregard location and distance to communicate instantaneously and inexpensively with people. Logistically, the distance-collapsing capacity of the Internet allows the researcher to connect to participants around the globe. The researcher can include people previously unavailable for study. This not only increases the pool of participants but also provides the potential for cross-cultural comparisons that were not readily available previously for practical and financial reasons. In a world where potential participants are only a keyboard click and fiber optic or wireless connection away, distance becomes almost meaningless as a pragmatic consideration in research design. Ryen (2002), for example, was able to use email to conduct a long-term interview study with an Asian entrepreneur in Tanzania from her home location in Norway. In this case, the Internet served as an extension of the researcher's and participant's bodies.

Research can be designed around questions of interaction and social behavior unbound from the restrictions of proximity or geography. Participants can be selected on the basis of their appropriate fit within the research questions rather than their physical location or convenience to the researcher. Hine (2000) argues that the ethnographer's notion of cultural boundary must be reconsidered given this capacity of the Internet. Rather than relying on traditional, geographically based means of encapsulating the culture under study, such as national boundaries or town limits, ethnographers might find more accuracy in using discourse patterns to find boundaries.

Senft's work (2003) exemplifies this reconsideration of cultural boundary from geographic to discursive. Senft studies the sensemaking practices of "webcam girls," a project that would have been highly unlikely ten years ago for many reasons. In this long-term project, Senft accesses websites wherein women display many – and sometimes all – of their private activities through the use of single or multiple video cameras in their homes. Senft studies the video displays themselves and talks to several women about their use of the Internet to express self or make personal and political statements. Because of the Internet's network of connections, participants are selected because they engage in this activity, regardless of where they live in the world. Not only does Senft have access to archived activities of these women, but also she can sustain contact with these participants over long periods of time, which allows her to study the way their perceptions and displays of self change over time.

The global potential of this medium is often conflated with global reach, an achievement that relies on global access. Popular media accounts have made wildly speculative and promising predictions about free global access to the Internet (see, for example, the many articles written in the 1990s by George Gilder for *Forbes Magazine*). Current statistics fall far short of the predicted mark. Partly this is because the pace of technological development far exceeds the infrastructure required for widespread and inexpensive high-speed access. Even in those countries at the top of the list, diffusion of this technology into the home has not exceeded 67% (ITU, 2002). For qualitative researchers seeking to conduct truly global studies, this medium therefore remains inadequate. More generally, in speaking of the issue of access as a double edge of technology, researchers should remain conservative in their expectations that the general populace accesses and utilizes Internet-mediated communication technologies in the same way and degree as those in academically rich contexts.

As a consequence of geographic distance, the participant can remain anonymous. This has obvious advantages for the qualitative researcher. Anonymous interaction environments may allow participants to speak more freely without restraints brought about by social norms, mores, and conventions. This feature is useful in studies of risky or deviant behaviors or socially unacceptable attitudes. Johnson (2003) explores the way the "pro-anorexia" movement was born and evolved online. Rather than talking face-to-face with participants, she examined their discursive practices in websites they had created. The infrastructure of the Internet allows pro-anorexics to express their ideas and values without censure and without connection to their actual identities. They may have provided this information to the researcher in focus groups or in interviews, but because of the stigmatized nature of this eating disorder, Johnson's task as a researcher would have been much more difficult; in this case, she was able to access over 500 sites (Johnson, 2003).

Bromseth (2002) studied the sensemaking practices of Norwegians exploring lesbianism and bisexuality. Again, although she could have obtained these data in face-to-face settings, it was unlikely that she would have obtained such a rich and diverse sample, partly because the population of Norway is very small and therefore residents may feel less anonymous in general (Bromseth, 2002). Within a culture of heterosexual normativity, the likelihood of involving face-to-face participants in the manner Bromseth achieved via the Internet is low.

Viewed pragmatically, anonymity and geographic distance ease certain ethical considerations: the participant has many ways to withdraw from the study, and the likelihood of maintaining confidentiality is high. The other side of this, of course, is that the researcher does not know who the participant is, at least in any embodied, tangible way, which for some researchers raises concerns about authenticity. The issue of authenticity has been a sticking point for many Internet researchers. On one hand, interacting with participants in anonymous environments results in the loss of many of the interactional qualities taken for granted in face-to-face interviews and observations. This absence of physical non-verbal information may constitute a meaningful gap of information for the researcher who relies on it as a way of knowing.

On the other hand, authenticity is questionable in any setting, online or offline, and the search for authenticity presumes not only that people have real selves to be revealed, but also that the authentic reality of a person is revealed by the person's physical presence (see Silverman, this volume). The Internet appears to engender and highlight the dilemma about authenticity for researchers. First, one's online identity need not correspond to physical markers. If a researcher seeks to understand the physical person yet relies on anonymous CMC as a way of discerning this, authenticity will arise as a problem. Second, it is difficult to "read" participants online. If an interviewer seeks to know the participants in depth but does not spend enough time to get to know them and understand their idiosyncratic discursive tendencies, authenticity may be considered a problematic issue.

Mann and Stewart (2000) take up the question of how researchers have approached the problematic issues of anonymity and authenticity in detail (208–15), noting that solutions must be both pragmatic and case-specific. Regardless of whether one believes authenticity is possible at all, research design must fit well with the questions being raised.

Internet as chrono-malleable

As well as collapsing distance, Internet technologies disrupt the traditional use of time in interaction, with several intriguing results for qualitative researchers conducting interviews or focus groups. Because Internet technologies accommodate both asynchronous and synchronous communication between individuals and groups, the use of time can be individually determined. Though an individual's choice may be somewhat limited by the specific technology used, the Internet marks a significant shift from previous technologies for interaction, which forced simultaneity (telephone), took a long time (letters), or provided only a very limited middle ground (answering machines, facsimile transmission of documents).

This feature of Internet technologies has several pragmatic advantages for the qualitative researcher. Complications regarding venue, commuting, and scheduling conflicts are less restrictive when interactions occur on the Internet. As with the distance-collapsing capacity of the Internet, the elasticity of time is often taken for granted in our everyday interactions. We rely on our ability to send a message at times convenient to us, secure in the knowledge that the recipients will access and read our messages at times convenient to them. Beyond this convenience, Internet communication is persistent; conversations can extend over long periods of time, picking up where they left off with greater ease than in face-to-face settings, where memory instead of archived text aids in the reconstruction of prior events. The ability to archive accurately and trace precisely the history of conversation has been used by researchers to conduct longitudinal studies with individuals (Danet, 2001), to follow the development of groups over time (Bromseth, 2002), and to refocus attention and discourse about certain events that otherwise would degrade in the recesses of organizational memory (Baym, 2000).

In the midst of a conversation, synchronous or asynchronous, users appreciate the opportunity to reflect on a comment or message before responding and, if the communiqué is sensitive or important, to review the message before sending it. In the research setting, these taken-for-granted capabilities can significantly enhance both the scope of a study and the collection of information from participants. In 1997, as I was conducting interviews online, it became clear that the questions asked could be carefully considered and rewritten during the interview. In one interview, I began to write, "Would you describe yourself as an Internet addict?" – Realizing that the outcome of this question was limited by its format, I erased this question and modified it to read: "How would you define an Internet addict?" Whether the latter was an excellent choice is of less importance to this discussion than the fact that it is a better question than the first, which was both leading and close-ended. Even in a synchronous environment, I had the opportunity to reconsider my message and reformat my query.

Backspacing and editing are made possible by stopping time during an interaction. Pauses and gaps are expected in CMC because of speed of connection, interruptions, and the fact that many users are multitasking. In asynchronous media such as email or threaded discussions, these pauses can be quite long, perhaps even weeks or months, yet can still be considered pauses rather than stopping points. Herring discusses this as "persistent conversation," whereby participants understand and work around the disjunctive and fragmented structure of interactions (1996, 1999).[3]

Not only is it useful to consider the way that time can be utilized as a malleable construct in qualitative inquiry, but also it is necessary to consider that as modes of interaction continue to merge, the technologies for communication increasingly saturate our everyday lives (Gergen, 1991). If we take seriously the collapse of time–space distinctions (Giddens, 1991) in the "knowledge age," these become not simply pragmatic but ontological considerations.

Internet as multi-modal

Communication via the Internet occurs in multiple modes, serially or simultaneously. Whether sponsored by software and hardware, a person's individual use, or the emergence of dyadic or group norms over time, these multiple modes operate on the sensemaking practices of users. Consequently, the issue of the Internet as multi-modal becomes meaningful when designing interactions in the research context.

In technical terms, interaction can be synchronous, asynchronous, anonymous or non-anonymous. One can use text, graphic images, sounds, and video, exclusively or in combination. Programs can simulate letter writing or passing notes, display information with few contextual features, or provide a sense of shared space.

In interactional terms, communication via the Internet involves much more than accomplishing the mechanics of these multiple modalities or learning the specific software or hardware: contextual aspects of being with others must be added to the process. We adapt and use technologies to suit our needs, whether or not these uses are those intended. For example, users tend to employ more than one communication technology at once: surfing the Web simultaneously as email is being downloaded; additionally, at any time an Instant Message might pop up onto the screen, occasioning a typed comment within a new or continued conversation. On the surface, this is multitasking; beneath the surface, social reality is both perceived and constituted through the interplay of time, spatiality, technology, information, and the other.

Even in straightforward information transmission environments, which were not designed to facilitate a sense of presence, programs can evolve into shared spaces as the meanings, relationships, and communities created by the interactions transcend the limitations of the programs in which people are interacting. During an online focus-group discussion conducted by me, participants used multiple technologies simultaneously in ways that complicated data collection but facilitated in-depth participation levels. The environment was a synchronous chatroom, which allowed for pseudonymous real-time participation among several people. Each person's comment would be posted as soon as he or she clicked the send or enter button. Messages scrolled up the screen as the conversation progressed. In one session, two participants who had previously been active contributors were not talking as actively as others were. Because of the programmed environment we were using (Internet Relay Chat), I was able to send one of them a request to talk privately, which, when accepted, opened a new screen that appeared only on our two desktops, in which we chatted privately. The participant told me that she and the other non-talkative participant had actually been chatting, as we were, in a private room, discussing one of the group's earlier issues in depth.

My discussion with this participant was similar to whispering during a group conversation, except that exchanges in the larger group were not disrupted. Her private chat with another participant was also an extended side conversation, one that added valuable data and could not have occurred unobtrusively in a physically present focus-group setting. Of course, the data must be captured and archived, which requires that participants be well informed enough to realize this and tell the researcher that they are producing valuable information when they engage in these whispered – and hidden from the researcher – conversations.

In another instance, when a participant appeared to stop participating, I found out, using this same technique, that the participant had been offended by an earlier comment made by another participant. He stated that he was no longer certain that his contributions to the conversation were desired and that perhaps he should withdraw from the study. By talking with him about this in a private, online discussion, I was able to convince him that the offending comment was not directed at him and that his contributions were valuable. Certainly, this could have happened in the course of a physically located focus group, but our private sideline conversation defused the situation, eased the participant's misgivings, and allowed the larger group conversation to continue while we were sorting this out. The participant re-entered the conversation and later told me he talked about the offending comment with the person who wrote it, with positive results. These examples illustrate how a researcher can take advantage of multi-modal features of Internet communication. Allowing multiple conversations to happen at once, when these do not negatively affect the main group discussion, can add depth and texture to the discussion.

Whether the technology provides the multiple modes or the users adapt technologies to a multi-modal way of thinking is less important than the fact that this multi-modal function powerfully influences the way users perceive contexts and interact with one another. For researchers, this has great potential for augmenting traditional approaches and creating previously impossible methods of interacting with participants.

Control over the communication process
Consider the complex combination of oral and written styles, the choice, granted by anonymous software, to create alternate identities online, and the ability to stop time in the middle of any interaction. These means of being in the world with others are associated with a feeling of greater control: control over the content and form of the message, control over the presentation of self, and control over others' perceptions of the self. The issue of control warrants discussion, because it is an inevitable part of doing qualitative Internet-based research.

Internet communication can provide the researcher and participant with the opportunity to reflect on and revise their statements before actually uttering them. Most participants interviewed by me online believe that the ability to edit affords a higher degree of control over the meaning of the message and the presentation of self. Whether or not the producer of the message can actually control the presentation of the self through careful editing is not as relevant as the faith placed in editing.

Jennifer, a participant in an online interview, trusts that careful attention to the construction of her words will give her a higher degree of control over the conversation. When asked how she tends to interact online, Jennifer replies (the programmed environment in use displays the responses as follows):

> Jennifer says, "I would say that I become very attuned to *what* is being said and *how* it is being said — particularly in a synchronous conversation and likewise attuned to how/what I am saying as part of that conversation."

> Jennifer says, "I find myself thinking a lot about what is the "right" thing to say . . . trying to make sense of and interpret the mood/attitude in addition to the words, such that I can be sensitive and focused in what I am saying in reply."

Jennifer says, "Obviously, I have the choice to type in what I want to say to you . . . as well as how I want to say it to you . . . i.e., language choice, depth of explanation, smiling, etc."

Jennifer suggests, "For example, you may or may not have noted that I insert "actions" into what I say- - :) , or things like "X explains" before launching into what I have to say, or emphasis around certain words with asterisks,"

Jennifer continues, "things that I've found tend to humanize the conversation."

Jennifer believes they guide both where she's going and where the listener is going.

Jennifer says, "I think it's very helpful . . . I think it demonstrates more attention to the quality of the inter-action between X# of persons who are participating in the interaction."

Jennifer has always found it helpful to be very descriptive in on-line environments, whether synchronous or asynchro-nous, b/c it gives people more to work with . . . a fuller, more rounded sense of your thoughts, feelings, environment, etc.

To the point of speaking of herself in the third person, Jennifer uses a variety of methods in the text to achieve what she believes to be conversational certainty. This excerpt is instructive in several ways. First, it allows us to see how careful attention to the form of the text can help or hinder comprehension and sponsor certain reactions. Even if one does not grant this level of control by the producer, the keen observations Jennifer makes about the written structure of sentences can remind the researcher that understanding between interviewer and participant (or between participant and participant) is an achievement that might be aided by careful attention to form of the message as well as content.[4]

Second, this excerpt gives us insight into the way people might perceive Internet communication. Some will pay close attention to the use of language in this medium. Others will pay very little attention to form or content. To provide contrast, here is a typical excerpt from a different participant in the same study. Beth, who spends up to fifteen hours a day in her online community, is responding to the question: "Why do you spend so much time online?" We pick up the conversation mid-stream:

Beth says, "yes but I think I like it this way because I can just type what commes to mind and not have to think about it as much thinkgs seem to be communicated better through my fingers then my voice"

> Beth says, "I can type what i'm feeling better then I can voice my;m"
>
> Beth says, "feelings it just comes a little easier seeing things to answer then hearing and having to answer I like to worrk with my hands a lot"
>
> Beth says, "it's just what your typing that counts"
>
> Beth says, "this is a place where you can get to the real person and not have to overcome the obsticle of looks and having people judge you by your appearance insteafd of the real you here your real self comes inside the things your wrte"

Like Jennifer, Beth believes she can better control how others perceive her in this medium. In Beth's case, the control is not in the form of the message but in the meaning "inside the things your wrte [*sic*]." In contrast to Jennifer's typical writing style, Beth's grammar and spelling are, by any standard, terrible and most likely not deliberate. These errors can be a result of typing fast, not editing the text, or being unaware of the errors. Regardless, the example demonstrates an important point for researchers: discursive practices in this medium are wildly different; form can be unnoticeable or glaring; and content cannot be disconnected from form if the form is glaringly disjunctive from traditional writing norms. The researcher cannot help but be influenced by the form of the message, which in turn influences the interpretation of the meaning of Beth's words. Even as Beth believes that she communicates better in this form than through her voice and that people reading her words will see through the form to the real self, the question arises: "How well does she represent her self with this use of language?" These examples are good reminders that participants are likely to have different habits, skill levels, and experience using Internet communication. The same might be said of spoken language, of course, but not with this same degree of difference among speakers one would typically classify in the same category (in this case, native speakers of English, at least high-school educated, self-described heavy users of CMC). The Internet intensifies these issues for researchers.

The text is a fundamentally different space of observation and interaction than sitting next to the participant or observing interactions in natural settings. Careful reflection is necessary to make sense of how we researchers are engaging in or observing these interactions. In most cases, it is recommended to treat each case individually and apply appropriate standards, practices, and procedures to each. Even so, it is impossible to predict how individual participants define, use, and respond to specific computer-mediated media and contexts. Take for example this series of benefits about synchronous, anonymous, text-based CMC, cited by several users participating in a study. These benefits are mentioned in response to the question: "Why do you like using this medium to interact with others?"

"I can write who I truly am clearly and directly by editing."

"I can edit the text and control how I present myself."

"Through editing, I have a lot more control how others perceive me."

"I can be anything and anyone I want to be in the text."

A simple question about benefits of the medium yields multiple interpretations of how text functions in relation to self and self's relation to other. In this set of responses, respondents indicate that they (the writer/sender) control the message, thereby controlling the outcome. As a group, this set of responses tells us these users perceive that they have a high degree of control over the way they are perceived by others because they control the outgoing message. By contrast, consider the statements below, uttered by the exact same participants in response to the question: "What are some of the limitations of this medium for you?"

"In this medium, nobody knows who I really am."

"I can't tell who other people really are if I just have their texts."

"It's difficult to know the reality of somebody if their writing doesn't affect you or speak to you."

"It is a game; everybody wears masks."

The contradictions in these responses are curious. Participants indicate that the benefit of the medium is that the text conveys an accurate or desired sense of self to the other in the interaction (the only message is the message sent). At the same time, however, they also indicate that one of the limitations is that the text cannot convey an accurate or real sense of the other to the self in the interaction (the only message is the message received). Whether this simply means humans operate from an essentially self-centered position is unclear; none the less, this example demonstrates at least two considerations for researchers using the Internet to interact with participants. First, people are still adjusting to Internet media and have distinctive and possibly unknown ways of performing the self through these media. It is hasty to presume all individuals use Internet media in similar ways; information collected from two people using the same medium may yield incomparable results because of the way they perceive the medium, a problem that can go unnoticed because it falls outside the researcher's careful planning and consistency in design. Second, as researchers using these media, we are likely to make these same assumptions about how texts operate in nameless and faceless settings. Does the researcher believe that the only message is the message sent? Conversely, does the researcher believe the only important message is the message received? On the surface, these may seem simple questions with straightforward answers, but even with careful reflection, it is easy to believe that our own utterances are clear and unproblematic. It is valuable practice, whether working in Internet settings or not, to engage in critical self-reflection about how questions are being asked, what presumptions are being made when observing focus groups, and how our own preconceived notions of the communication process shape our interpretation of everyday interactions.

Push versus pull modes

Anyone who markets products on the Web or who teaches courses online can verify the importance of using the right media for the right purpose. Push/pull considerations are vital to whether or not the intended recipient notices or attends to the message. *Push* describes a technology that pushes the information to an individual's computer or handheld device. This term also refers to the extent to which users feel as though the message is pushed toward them, requiring attention to read, trash, file, or otherwise *do* something with. Email is a good example of push technology; messages arrive in a list and, putting filtering programs aside for the moment, require attention and action. Other technologies can collect and push news items from various sources to one's desktop, text messages and weather reports to one's mobile phone, or flight schedule delays to one's PDA.

Pull technologies require a more proactive approach by the user: the idea of the information is so interesting, important, or intriguing that the user will be compelled to seek out, find, and attend to the message. Although distinctions between push and pull technologies are becoming more and more blurred by the evolution of various media and usage patterns, the concept is useful as an initial categorization tool for the researcher.

The following example from a teaching experience illustrates the importance of push/pull considerations in designing an effective communication environment for active group participation (focus group) and collaborative learning. In a recent course focused on hypertext theory and design, students were required in one assignment to redesign the Internet-mediated aspects of the course. I intentionally designed the course to overwhelm the students initially with multiple media choices and requirements for communication. Each week, students were required to log into a password-protected website where they could find links to the syllabus, schedule, and announcements. They were also required to use a threaded discussion board accessed from this site. In addition to this Web-based system, they were expected to check their university-assigned email account, where I sent them both individual and group (listserv) messages. Many students did not use their university-assigned email account, which meant they had to begin to check their university account or notify me to change the default address I used to send email. Finally, each student was required to set up a blog (Web-based journal) to post their responses to readings and other thoughts related to class. They were expected to read and link to other students' online journals in addition to mine.

As planned, too many different modes of communication vied for the students' attention in this configuration, and they quickly realized this problem. The remainder of the course involved solving the problem to meet the goal of building and maintaining a productive learning community. Students examined, among other things, the push versus pull aspects of various communication choices. When some students suggested, "Let's get rid of email and just use the password-protected website for all information," others responded that this would require unsolicited attention to the course, a proactive approach that could not be presumed. In addition, students aptly noted a key usability issue: before the student could even view the front page of the course, the password-protected site required three keyboard events, six clicks, and effective navigation through three screens of information. A public website with easily accessed information would be easier, one bright student said, "but then we would still need to remember to actually go there." After several weeks of lively debate over various issues, the students finally decided on the following elements:

- Public web page, which all students agreed to keep as their browser's default home page for the duration of the semester. Most relevant information appeared on this first page.
- Running chat board on the web page for general student conversation and student announcements (similar to Instant-Messaging software).
- Threaded discussion on the front page of the site for more serious, lengthy, course-content-related discussions.
- Links to all student web journals for those who are interested.
- Links to the course syllabus and schedule (transformed from documents to HTML documents for speed of transmission and ease of reading).

In addition to this single web page serving as the course site, students believed that both the listserv and email should remain active. To a person, they hypothesized (rightly or wrongly) that any information sent from the professor to the student is vital and should be pushed into the student's immediate awareness.

This extended discussion of a single assignment in an academic course underscores the considerations that go into the design of a communication environment. In parallel fashion, research environments utilizing various Internet media must undergo similar evaluation, because each decision concerning participant communication makes a difference. Testing various mediated environments can help one discern which is most suitable for the type of participant. Collecting life histories via email may be satisfactory, but allowing participants to create ongoing life history accounts on websites that they can design with color and images may yield richly textured results. For an interview study, real-time chatrooms may provide anonymous participation and spontaneous conversation, but email interviews may be better suited to participants who have busy schedules and desire time to consider their responses. The key is making a conscious and measured effort to match the mode to the context, the user's preferences, and the research question. If one is studying naturally occurring data, this issue may not be salient to the process of collecting data, but because push/pull variables influence inter-actions within the contexts under study, knowledge of the possibilities and limitations inherent in CMC design can aid in the process of analysis and interpretation.

The overriding message throughout this discussion is that reflection and adaptation are necessary as one integrates Internet communication tech-nologies into qualitative research design. Adapting to the Internet is one level of reflexivity; as we use new media for communication, the interactional challenges and opportunities can teach us about how to use these methods. Adjusting to the individual is another level; as in face-to-face contexts, a skilled researcher will pay close attention to participant conceptualization and utilization of the medium for communication. Without having access to physically embodied non-verbal features of interaction, the researcher may want to deliberately address these concerns with the participants so they may aid in the interpretation of discourse. Alternately, the researcher may want to adjust his or her expectations of these possibly unfamiliar environ-ments. If researchers cannot adjust to the particular features and capacities of Internet technologies, they may miss the opportunity to understand these phenomena as they operate in context. As Gergen (1991) notes: if we are to survive, flexible adaptation and improvization will become our norm.

Along these same lines, Carvajal (2001) reminds us that any decision made about method should derive from a conceptual and epistemological level rather than from a procedural level. In discussing computer-assisted quali-tative data analysis software (CAQDAS) training issues, Carvajal stresses that anyone using computer-assisted programs to analyze data should incorporate "critical thinking instead of mechanical thinking" (section 3.2). "To know a software is to know about the methodological implications its use has for qualitative methodology" (section 3.2). This thinking applies also to the use of the Internet in gathering information for analysis.

THE INTERNET AS SCENE OF SOCIAL CONSTRUCTION

The Internet is a network of computers that allows us to create networks of connection. At a basic level, one can study the connections themselves, or one can use the connections to conduct studies. However, remaining at this simplistic level of binary distinction obscures the complexity with which the cultural and technological aspects of the Internet are interwoven in con-structing possibilities for being with others in everyday social life. Although we might consider the Internet merely a conduit for information transmission, the content and resultant social contexts of these networks and transmis-sions are also fruitfully conceptualized as meaningful phenomena themselves. Through the deceptively simple process of exchanging messages, complex and transformative understandings of self identity, other, and reality are negotiated. As more and more people mediate their social interactions in this confluence of technologies and subjectivity, close attention to the way texts operate is crucial.

The Internet is not novel in that individual use, habitual practice across groups, and technical capacities constitute patterns of temporal interactions, building social structures that may become concrete realities. These processes describe any language system. The Internet is unique, however, in enabling us to view these processes of social construction as solely discursive, primarily textual interactions. Watson reminds us that texts are more than conduits for the transmission of meaning. He critiques a common conceptualization of texts:

> Texts are placed in service of the examination of 'other', separately conceived phenomenon. From this standpoint, the text purportedly comprises a resource for accessing these phenomena—phenomena existing 'beyond' the text, as it were, where the text operates as an essentially unexamined conduit, a kind of neutral 'window' or 'channel' to them. (1997: 81)

Referring to Rose's (1960) notion of the world as a "worded entity," Watson emphasizes that texts mediate social interaction and build social organization. Although we may not be in total agreement as to what comprises text, Watson's point (a point made also by Heritage in this volume) is well taken in considering the centrality of texts in the negotiation and construction of meaning. As a context almost entirely comprised of text, the Internet is an exciting location of social meaning and organization (defining text broadly as discursive practice). One can also usefully recall Prior's discussion of Foucault's approach to the study of culture (this volume), whereby the text becomes the focus of qualitative exploration rather than the always-elusive "knowing subject."

Internet technologies allow qualitative researchers to study the social construction process in a very active way. Because it can constrain, hide, or minimize the visible products of interaction (read: bodies, clothing, accent, mannerisms, and geographically based social structures), the Internet allows focus specifically on the building blocks of culture at the basic level of interaction.

Kendall (2002), for example, spent several years conducting an ethnographic study of an online MUD community called BlueSky, analyzing the discursive foundations and negotiated features of this community. As a consequence of studying the software settings as well as individual conversations, Kendall is able to make interesting arguments about how gender is performed. In MUD environments, for example, gender is a choice one makes by setting a command. One can choose from a variety of genders, including male (he, his), female (she, her), neuter (it, its), spivak (e, er), royal we (we, our), and so forth. After the user makes a choice, certain texts produced for other members show the corresponding pronouns. In BlueSky, some members of this online community use the gender settings for joke purposes, so that, for example, when someone asks the system what gender the other participant is, the preprogrammed response might read, "Not lately," or "No, thank you" (35). BlueSky members might make gender a relevant feature of their persona or not, and those whose gender is typical (male or female, in this case) tend to be responded to in correspondence with their chosen gender, rather than with their embodied gender. In other words, if Mike (offline) has a persona named Susan (online) and declares that Susan is female, people will tend to interact with Susan as a female, even if they know Mike is a male playing the character of Susan and even if they have met Mike offline.

If we accept the basic premise that reality is socially constructed through language, the Internet allows us to study this social construction in progress as a real, enacted process rather than a theoretical premise. Internet technologies allow the researcher to see the visible artifacts of this negotiation process in forms divorced from both the source and the intended or actual audience. Websites and website archives, for example, can give researchers a means of studying the way social realities are displayed or how these might be negotiated over time. In Kendall's ethnographic study (2002), extensive archiving of interactions gave her an immense and enormously rich set of data to work with.

Of course, multiple variables influence the way we make sense of the world and this confronts researchers when making decisions about how to approach the field. In designing the interface with participants, interacting with participants, and analyzing human expressions and experiences in naturally occurring settings, researchers will naturally make assumptions about how the communication process works, taking certain invisible features of interaction for granted, whether or not this is warranted. Certain researchers may naturally rely on non-verbals as well as the content of talk in analyzing both the content and structure of conversation and may unconsciously use socio-economic markers derived from participants' clothing, accent, posture, and other physical features. These are just two factors influencing the way researchers perceive or interpret subjects, particularly in research that relies on researcher interaction with participants, such as case study, focus group, interview, or ethnography. Warranted or not, we use physically embodied features and behaviors to make categorical assessments of conversational partners, which in turn sponsors the creation of a framework for interaction. Researchers trained in analytical methods which do not rely on visual or verbal contact with participants may be less inclined to do this, but a priori assessments based on typical/traditional gendered, ethnic, and socio-economic categories remain a problematic feature of social research.

These statements are not unfamiliar to anyone who pays attention to human interaction. What may be less familiar is the extent to which Internet technologies bring into relief and problematize these working assumptions. Attending to these basic processes of communication not only constitutes healthy practice for social research in general, but also is essential in developing effective, rigorous, and reflexive research practices in Internet-related studies. Depending on any number of factors only discovered during the actual study, the rules, practices, and outcomes of interaction in online contexts may be distinct from or quite similar to face-to-face contexts.

At various levels, some more conscious than others, people interacting in computer-mediated contexts negotiate, rather than simply observe or discover, the identities and social realities of the others with whom they are interacting. Whether interpreting naturally occurring texts or participating in an online interview, researchers can find this quite challenging, perhaps because it is unfamiliar territory for most researchers at this point in time. For example, one may find that some of the typical rules of conversation do not seem applicable in the fragmented structure of online conversation. Sarcasm, irony, or non-obvious humor is extremely difficult to discern in the text. Additionally, many paratextual elements are difficult either to ignore as non-meaningful data or to categorize effectively. The following interview excerpt, taken from an online interview conducted by me, demonstrates the elusion of clear interpretation in the unembodied text.

```
<Annette> Tell me about your most memorable experience
online.
<sherie> gee, i don't know, so many. some are personal. some
aren't.
<Annette> great!
<Annette> choose any--all. talk all you want!
<sherie> well, most seem to have something to do with the
community i belong to. everything from personal relationships
to flesh meets to flame wars . . .
```

Interviewing via CMC requires patience and careful attention to the skills, tendencies, and pacing of the respondent (Markham, forthcoming). The ellipsis at the end of Sherie's last statement above indicated to me that the participant would continue her thought, in accordance with a rule I had devised to help prevent the interruption of a person's story when non-verbal signals are unavailable. Outlined for the participant at the beginning of each interview, this strategy was useful to indicate continuation and – by its absence – the end of a conversational turn. In this case, however, the rule did not work, because even though she used the ellipsis, Sherie's next statement indicates she had completed her thought:

```
<sherie> are you there?
<Annette> oh! yes, I'm here.
<Annette> I'm sorry, I thought you were thinking. . . . I have
a tendency to ask questions too quickly, and always interrupt
people.
```

No response was forthcoming from Sherie at this point, which was surprising given the question I had just asked concerning memorable experiences online. I tried another question to prompt a narrative account:

```
<Annette> if you picked an experience randomly, what would
you tell me about it?
```

After another long pause with no response from Sherie, I changed tactics:

```
<Annette> is it too hard to pick just one experience to talk
about? if you want, we can go in a different direction . . .
<sherie> ok.
```

Throughout this interview, it was difficult to cajole, prod, or compel Sherie to utter more than primarily monosyllabic responses. It is difficult to ascertain whether Sherie did not like the way the questions were being asked, she was not interested in the topic, she was multitasking, she had a migraine, or something else. Perhaps this can be simply dismissed as a non-useful interview. On the other hand, since the study was focused on how people express themselves online and make sense of their experiences through language, the interview has meaning and cannot be immediately dismissed.

Reflecting on that interview, I found the difficulty lay in the fact that there were no non-verbal cues to guide the interpretation of the situation. Questions or conversational direction could not be modified based on embodied signals. To add yet another layer of complexity, in an earlier session, this participant had written that she liked herself better in text because she was eloquent, and that she felt, "more beautiful as text than as flesh." The text above represents Sherie's style throughout the interview process and seems to belie her statement because her responses are a far cry from standard notions of eloquence.

Internet communication gives qualitative researchers an intriguing opportunity to witness the social construction of reality as it occurs textually. This short snippet of Sherie's conversation is one among millions of globally accessible texts, all vying for attention in a cacophony of networks. In this specific case, where the researcher interviews the participant, identity and reality are negotiable during these online interactions in subtle and intriguing ways. Both the participant and researcher send messages that display identity and play into the construction of the context. The researcher makes judgments of the participant and responds with these judgments in mind. The participant makes sense of the researcher in the same way. The structure of interaction is an ongoing accomplishment, drawn from previous interactions and sustained (or adjusted) by adherence to (or the absence of) the rules of conversation.

Another layer of complexity involves the way users perceive the nature of text. The Internet sponsors a casual communication style. It is, however, hasty to assume that because of this, users conceptualize text in a similarly casual manner. Indeed, users frequently conceptualize and respond to the text as a concrete, formal, lasting vessel for truth (Markham, 2000). This is true for both participants and researchers, making this an issue that requires critical self-reflection and careful planning to resolve. Attention to this factor in research design and/or analysis allows the research project to accommodate varying perceptions.

The idea that Internet communication has little value and is, by its nature, fleeting, is made possible by habituated practices as well as the technology. Consider message length: when transmission rates were slower because of bandwidth limitations and storage capacities on servers, short messages, particularly in synchronous environments, were necessary. In email, because the technology did not allow anything beyond plain text and single spacing, simple and short messages were more likely to be read. Though these limitations are being overcome, short messages remain the norm, possibly because the technology evolved in this way and the habit is now a social norm.

Take the issue of informality: informality may be a choice but is also quite often a necessity. Simply put, typing takes longer than talking and errors in typing are frequent even for the most skilled typists. For the average user of CMC, a smooth, flowing conversation may be considered a good tradeoff for simplified phrases, spelling or grammar errors, and unedited messages.

Consider the ephemeral nature of computer-mediated texts. Messages in a bulletin board system are often compared to Post-it notes or notes left on refrigerator doors and counters for one's flatmate to notice. When the message is sent, it seems to disappear, even as much as we know it does not. In these and many other computer-mediated contexts, the notion of the throwaway text is apparent.

In this context of short, informal, and ephemeral communiqués, it would seem likely that users would consistently treat CMC as temporary and casual. However, users simultaneously or alternately privilege the text, giving it a state of considerable concreteness and importance. This is partially because any information transmitted via the Internet may be archived somewhere. Interactions via the Internet can be perceived as having a long-lasting shape or effect, which may result in the participant feeling like he or she is on a public stage as much as it may result in the more commonly believed feeling of being in an informal conversation.

Students often bemoan this very capacity of the Internet. Low participation in online discussion groups during the first few weeks of any school term may be associated with fears of permanent effects: ideas spoken may not be erased and will likely be archived and used later against the student. Second, the only things that should appear in written form for public consumption are good – or at least well-developed – ideas. Not only do students tend to fear that speakers are held accountable for everything they utter, but also they believe that they should be certain of their statements before making them, since they will be written in stone. The pragmatic outcome of this situation is that ideas are less likely to be tested until participants achieve a greater sense of self-efficacy and learn to minimize or demystify the authority of the written text.

Taking this idea to a broader cultural and historical scale, we can see that the tendency to give Internet communication formal and fixed characteristics is in no small measure related to the tradition in most cultures to hold written texts in high regard, giving original documents a near-sacred status. Tearing a page out of a textbook is almost as difficult to imagine as destroying the constitution of the United States or the Magna Carta. We preserve original documents in hermetically sealed containers. We tend to believe what is written more than what is heard. In the United States, witnesses testifying in the judicial system often put their hands on the Bible and swear they will tell the truth in order to verify and solemnize their testimony. These are just a few examples of how we privilege texts. In this context, the Internet falls somewhere between text and nontext, and we are still struggling with the tensions this creates, whether researchers and participants are conscious of it or not.

A student's fear of being judged by his or her texts is well grounded because any comment a person makes operates in conjunction with other factors to represent a person's identity and merit. Likewise, it is not uncommon to judge participants of qualitative studies on the basis of their texts; online, one's typing and writing ability is as much a social marker as one's accent, body type, or skin color. Even though we are trained to know better, textual markers influence our interpretation of participants. A greater appreciation for how users perceive the nature of texts can help researchers make better analytical decisions.

The Internet highlights the influence of non-verbal behaviors on our understanding and interpretation of others. It also illustrates the centrality of the text in negotiating and constructing reality. A fascinating outcome of Internet-based communication has been the revival of focus on basic sensemaking processes. There is great potential in this shift of focus. When geography no longer determines the boundaries of the study's parameters, the researcher can be less constrained by the structure, space, and time within which interactions occur. Observing Internet use as it constructs social reality can be accomplished easily; obtaining access to online groups is a straight-forward process, as is downloading and archiving the interactions of these groups.

At the same time, several ethical concerns arise. For example, although many online discussion groups appear to be public, members may perceive their interaction to be private (Frankel and Siang, 1999; Sharf, 1999) and can be surprised or angered by intruding researchers (Bromseth, 2002). Other groups know their communication is public but none the less do not want to be studied (Gajjala, 2002; Hudson and Bruckman, 2002). Additionally, confidentiality of participants' talk in these groups is almost impossible to preserve with the sophistication of search engines (Mann, 2002). Ongoing discussions and statements about ethical problems and guidelines can provide the researcher with useful background information on how others have approached and dealt with these tricky issues (for good overviews, see Frankel and Siang, 1999; Mann and Stewart, 2000; and the ongoing ethical statements by the ethics committee of the Association of Internet Researchers, 2002).

THE DOUBLE EDGE OF TECHNOLOGY

Social theorists and science fiction writers alike warn us that every technology has a double edge and unforeseen effects. McLuhan (1962) argued that every communication medium extends the capacity of one or more of our cognitive sensibilities. Writing implements and the printing press extended our memory. Radio makes our ears bigger; television allows our eyes to see events around the world. The Internet allows us to connect personally and instantly with countless people around the globe. Wireless technologies allow us to attach technologies to our bodies in much the same manner as physical prostheses. Yet, for each extension there is something removed, dismantled, or constrained. Postman (1985) argues convincingly that as television becomes more and more prominent in our everyday lives, our attention span decreases, so that Americans, for example, have an active attention span of approximately twenty minutes, the average length of the typical sitcom. The premise of this argument is compelling. Few of us in Western cultures can imagine reciting Homer from memory or attending to and analyzing oral arguments for many hours at a time, as early Americans did during the presidential debates between Abraham Lincoln and Steven Douglas.

The sensibilities afforded or limited by the Internet remain unpredictable. As a tool of research it offers many intriguing possibilities; the temptation to insert these as easy solutions to the problems of social research is great. As Mann and Stewart (2000) emphasize, it is vital to consider judiciously how the tool fits the research question and the context, returning always to the core considerations guiding solid, rigorous, systematic, and, above all, deliberate qualitative inquiry.

SUMMARY

This chapter outlines several theoretical and pragmatic issues associated with the use of the Internet in qualitative research. Placed within the fast-growing and swiftly shifting arena of Internet research, this chapter provides general categories for considering both the enabling and constraining aspects of new communication technologies, from which the reader can develop his or her own unique approach. Adopting the Internet as a means of augmenting traditional studies requires attention to the creative possibilities as well as to the foundations of qualitative inquiry, so that one's decisions to use the Internet are both epistemologically and methodologically sound. To review some of the important considerations:

- The Internet is defined variously as a communication medium, a global network of connections, and a scene of social construction.
- The shape and nature of Internet communication is defined in context, negotiated by users that may adapt hardware and software to suit their individual or community needs.

- Internet communication affords qualitative researchers creative potential because of its geographic dispersion, multi-modality, and chrono-malleability.
- The researcher's own conceptualization of the Internet will influence how it is woven into the research project, with significant consequences on the outcomes.
- As social life becomes more saturated with Internet-based media for communication, researchers will be able to creatively design projects that utilize these media to observe culture, interact with participants, or collect artifacts.
- Each new technology bears a double edge for qualitative researchers and users; as it highlights or enables certain aspects and qualities of interaction, it hides or constrains others.

In *Interpreting Qualitative Data*, Silverman (2001) stresses the importance of adhering to sensible and rigorous methods for making sense of data even as we acknowledge that social phenomena are locally and socially constructed through the activities of participants. Similarly, it is clear that although the Internet can fundamentally shift some of our research practices by extending our reach, easing data collection, or providing new grounds for social interaction, application of these methods must remain grounded in the fundamentals of rigorous and systematic qualitative research methods.

NOTES

1. Much debate persists regarding the influence of the Internet on language use and meaning. The vast majority of researchers agree that the structure and content of CMC is distinctive. Language norms and rules are in constant flux and transformation; time and space take on different meaning within interactions, influenced by both technical and normative elements. It is unclear whether this distinctiveness is meaningful at the level of meaning or discursive/relational outcome. Early accounts suggested that the absence of non-verbal cues in CMC would lead to less meaningful, surface interactions among users (Sproull and Kiesler, 1991). Later researchers such as Witmer and Katzman (1998) find that users make necessary changes in their discourse to accommodate technical limitations, replacing non-verbals with emoticons. Gaiser (1997) goes further to contend that there is very little difference between data collected in face-to-face and online interactions. More recently, Thurlow (2003) argues that shortcuts used in SMS (telephone instant messaging) do not significantly influence the meaning of the message, although to an outsider witnessing the interaction, the discourse may seem almost unreadable. Baym et al. (2002) contend that it is not so much the technology that influences interpersonal relationships as it is the interaction itself.
2. See also Sproull and Kiesler (1991) and Chen et al. (in press) for general perspectives.
3. See also the special issue on persistent conversation in the *Journal of Computer-Mediated Communication*, 4(4), 1999.
4. Heritage in this volume provides an excellent overview of conversation analysis, which seeks to examine and illustrate how context is accomplished in and through

talk. Obviously, we do many more skilful things in conversation than we could ever explain to a researcher in an interview. Close examination of texts can help illuminate the building blocks of both individual and institutional contexts.

Recommended reading

For in-depth information on various methodological issues and strategies relating to qualitative Internet research, the most comprehensive book to date is Mann and Stewart's *Internet Communication and Qualitative Research* (Sage, 2000). Also see the edited collection by Chen et al., *Online Social Research: Methods, Issues, and Ethics* (Peter Lang, 2003).

For in-depth case studies that analyze how Internet users interact with technology and frame their experiences, read Sherry Turkle's *Life on the Screen* (Simon and Schuster, 1995); Annette Markham's *Life Online* (AltaMira, 1998); and Stone's *The War of Desire and Technology at the Close of the Mechanical Age* (MIT Press, 1996). For a good introduction to the topic, read Steve Jones's edited collections *Cybersociety* (Sage, 1995) and *Virtual Culture* (Sage, 1997).

For discussions and studies of discourse analysis in CMC contexts, Susan C. Herring's work is the most comprehensive, including her edited collections, *Computer-Mediated Communication: Linguistic, Social and Cross-cultural Perspectives* (John Benjamins, 1996) and *Computer-mediated Conversation* (Hampton Press, in press). Also see the special issue on persistent conversation in the *Journal of Computer-Mediated Communication* (June, 1999, available online).

For ethnographically informed studies of online culture, the following titles are recommended: Nancy Baym's *Tune In, Log On* (Sage, 2000); Lori Kendall's *Hanging Out in the Virtual Pub* (University of California Press, 2002); Christine Hine's *Virtual Ethnography* (Sage, 2001); and Miller and Slater's *Internet Ethnography* (Berg, 2000).

REFERENCES

Association of Internet Researchers (2002) *Ethical decision making and Internet research.* Retrieved December 1, 2002 from http://www.aoir.org/reports/ethics.pdf

Baym, N. (2000) *Tune In, Log On. Soaps, Fandom, and Online Community.* Thousand Oaks, CA: Sage.

Baym, N., Zhang, Y.B., and Lin, M. (2002) The Internet in college social life. Paper presented at the annual conference of the Association of Internet Researchers, Maastricht, The Netherlands, October.

Benedikt, M. (ed.) (1991) *Cyberspace: First steps.* Cambridge, MA: MIT Press.

Bromseth, J. (2002) Public Places . . . Private Activities? In A. Morrison (ed.), *Researching ICTs in Context* (pp. 44–72). Oslo: Intermedia Report 3/2002. Unipub forlag. Retrieved December 1, 2002 from http://www.intermedia.uio.no/publikasjoner/rapport_3/

Carvajal, D. (2002) The Artisan's Tools. Critical Issues When Teaching and Learning CAQDAS. *Forum: Qualitative Social Research*, 3 (2). Retrieved February 2, 2003 from http://www.qualitative-research.net/fqs-texte/2-02/2-02carvajal-e.htm

Chen, S.L.S., Hall, J.G., and Johns, M.D. (eds.) (2003) *Online Social Research: Methods, Issues, and Ethics*. New York: Peter Lang.

Cherny, L. and Weise, E.R. (eds.) (1996) *Wired_women: Gender and new realities in cyberspace*. Seattle, WA: Seal Press.

Danet, B. (2001) *Cyberpl@y: Communicating online*. Oxford: Berg.

Dibbell, J. (1993) A rape in cyberspace or how an evil clown, a Haitian trickster spirit, two wizards, and a cast of dozens turned a database into a society. *The Village Voice*, December 21: 36–42.

Featherstone, M. and Burrows, R. (eds.) (1995) *Cyberspace/cyberbodies/cyberpunk: cultures of technological embodiment*. London: Sage.

Frankel, M.S. and Siang, S. (1999) *Ethical and Legal Aspects of Human Subjects Research on the Internet*. http://www.aaas.org/spp/dspp/sfrl/projects/intres/main.htm

The Future of Feminist Internet Studies (2002) Panel discussion at the annual conference of the Association of Internet Researchers, Maastricht, The Netherlands, 15 October.

Gaiser, T. (1997) Conducting on-line focus groups. *Social Science Computer Review*, (15): 135–44.

Gajjala, R. (2002) An Interrupted Postcolonial/Feminist Cyberethnography: Complicity and Resistance in the "Cyberfield," *Feminist Media Studies*, 2 (2): 177–93.

Gergen, K. (1991) *The Saturated Self*. New York: Basic Books.

Giddens, A. (1991) *Modernity and self-identity: self and society in the Late Modern Age*. Cambridge: Polity Press.

Herring, S.C. (ed.) (1996) *Computer-Mediated Communication: Linguistic, social and cross-cultural perspectives*. Amsterdam: John Benjamins.

Herring, S.C. (1999) Interactional coherence in CMC. *Journal of Computer-Mediated Communication*, 4 (4). Retrieved April 1, 2003 from http://www.ascusc.org/jcmc/vol4/issue4/herring.html

Hine, C. (2000) *Virtual ethnography*. London: Sage.

Hudson, J.M. and Bruckman, A. (2002) IRC Francais: The creation of an Internet based SLA community. *Computer Assisted Language Learning*, 15 (2): 109–34.

ITU (International Telecommunications Union) (2002) *Internet Indicators*. Retrieved April 1, 2003 from http://www.itu.int/ITU-D/ict/statistics/at_glance/Internet01.pdf

Johnson, C. (2003) *Social Interaction and Meaning Construction among Community Websites*. Unpublished Master of Arts thesis, University of Illinois at Chicago.

Jones, S.G. (1995) Understanding community in the information age. In S.G. Jones (ed.), *Cybersociety: Computer-mediated communication and community* (pp. 10–35). Thousand Oaks, CA: Sage.

Jones, S.G. (ed.) (1997) *Virtual Culture: Identity and communication in cybersociety*. London: Sage.

Jones, S.G. (ed.) (1999) *Doing Internet research: Critical issues and methods for examining the Net*. Thousand Oaks, CA: Sage.

Kendall, L. (2002) *Hanging Out in the Virtual Pub: Masculinities and Relationships Online*. Berkeley, CA: University of California Press.

Mann, C. (2002) *Generating data online: Ethical concerns and challenges for the C21 researcher*. Keynote address delivered at Making Common Ground: A Nordic conference on Internet research ethics, Trondheim, Norway, June 1.

Mann, C. and Stewart, F. (2000) *Internet communication and qualitative research: A handbook for researching online*. London: Sage.

Markham, A. (1998) *Life online: Researching real experience in virtual space*. Walnut Creek, CA: AltaMira Press.

Markham, A. (2000) *Losing, Gaining, and Reframing control: Lessons from students of online courses*. Paper presented at the second international conference Learning2000, Roanoke, VA, October.

Markham, A. (forthcoming) The Internet as research context. In C. Seale, J. Gubrium, G. Gobo and D. Silverman (eds), *Qualitative research practice*. London: Sage.

McLuhan, M. (1962) *The Gutenberg galaxy: The making of typographic man*. Toronto: University of Toronto Press.

Miller, D. and Slater, D. (2000) *The Internet: An Ethnographic Approach*. Oxford: Berg.

Novak, M. (1991) Liquid architectures in Cyberspace. In M. Benedikt (ed.), *Cyberspace: First steps* (pp. 225–54). Cambridge, MA: MIT Press. Quote retrieved April 5, 2003 from http://www.centrifuge.org/marcos/

Persistent Conversation. *Journal of Computer-Mediated Communication*, 4 (4), June, 1999. Retrieved April 29, 2003, from http://www.ascusc.org/jcmc/vol4/issue4/

Postman, N. (1985) *Amusing ourselves to death: Public discourse in the age of show business*. New York: Viking Press.

Rose, E. (1960) The English record of a natural sociology. *American Sociological Review*, XXV (April): 193–208.

Ryen, A. (2002) Paper presented at Making Common Ground: A Nordic conference on Internet research ethics, Trondheim, Norway, June 1.

Senft, T. (2003) *Home page heroines: Gender, celebrity and auto-performance on the World Wide Web*. Unpublished working doctoral dissertation, New York University.

Sharf, B. (1999) Beyond netiquette: The ethics of doing naturalistic research on the Internet. In S. Jones (ed.), *Doing Internet Research*. London: Sage.

Shields, R. (ed.) (1996) *Cultures of Internet: virtual spaces, real histories, living bodies*. London: Sage.

Silverman, D. (ed.) (1997) *Qualitative research: Theory, methods and practice*. London: Sage.

Silverman, D. (2001) *Interpreting qualitative data: Methods for analysing talk, text and interaction*. London: Sage.

Soja, E.W. (1989) *Postmodern Geographies: The Reassertion of Space in Critical Social Theory*. London: Verso.

Sondheim, A. (ed.) (1996) *Being Online, net subjectivity*. New York: Lusitania.

Sproull, L. and Kiesler, S. (1991) *Connections: New ways of working in the networked environment*. Cambridge, MA: MIT Press.

Stone, A.R. (1996) *The war of desire and technology at the close of the mechanical age*. Cambridge, MA: MIT Press.

Thurlow, C. (2003) Research talk presented at University of Illinois at Chicago, February.

Turkle, S. (1995) *Life on the screen: identity in the age of the Internet*. New York: Simon and Schuster.

Watson, R. (1997) Ethnomethodology and textual analysis. In D. Silverman (ed.), *Qualitative research: Theory, method and practice* (pp. 80–98). London: Sage.

Witmer, D.F. and Katzman, S.L. (1998) Smile when you say that: Graphic accents as gender markers in computer-mediated communication. In F. Sudweeks, M.L. McLaughlin, and S. Rafaeli (eds.), *Network and Netplay: Virtual Groups on the Internet* (pp. 3–11). Menlo Park, CA: AAAI/MIT Press.

7 The "inside" and the "outside"

Finding realities in interviews

Jody Miller and Barry Glassner

In his *Interpreting Qualitative Data*, Silverman (2001) highlights the dilemmas facing interview researchers concerning what to make of their data. On the one hand, positivists have as a goal the creation of the "pure" interview – enacted in a sterilized context, in such a way that it comes as close as possible to providing a "mirror reflection" of the reality that exists in the social world. This position has been thoroughly critiqued over the years in terms of both its feasibility and its desirability. On the other hand, emotionalists suggest that unstructured, open-ended interviewing can and does elicit "authentic accounts of subjective experience." While, as Silverman points out, this approach is "seductive," a significant problem lies in the question of whether these "authentic accounts" are actually, instead, the repetition of familiar cultural tales. Finally, radical social constructionists suggest that no knowledge about a reality that is "out there" in the social world can be obtained from the interview, because the interview is obviously and exclusively an interaction between the interviewer and interview subject in which both participants create and construct narrative versions of the social world. The problem with looking at these narratives as representative of some "truth" in the world, according to these scholars, is that they are context specific, invented, if you will, to fit the demands of the interactive context of the interview, and representative of nothing more or less.

For those of us who hope to learn about the social world, and, in particular, hope to contribute knowledge that can be beneficial in expanding under-standing and useful for fostering social change, the proposition that our interviews are meaningless beyond the context in which they occur is a daunting one. This is not to say that we accept the positivist view of the possibility of untouched data available through standardized interviewing, nor that we take a romanticized view of seamless authenticity emerging from narrative accounts. Instead, it is to suggest that we are not willing to discount entirely the possibility of learning about the social world beyond the interview in our analyses of interview data.

In this chapter, we try to identify a position that is outside of this objectivist–constructivist continuum yet takes seriously the goals and critiques of researchers at both of its poles. We will argue that information about social worlds is achievable through in-depth interviewing. The position we are attempting to put forward is inspired by authors such as Harding (1987) and Latour (1993), who posit explicitly anti-dualistic options for methodological and theorizing practices in media studies and science studies – options which recognize that both emulation and rejection of dominant discourses such as positivism miss something critically important. Dominant discourses are totalizing only for those who view them as such; they are replete with fissures and uncolonized spaces within which people engage in highly satisfying and even resistant practices of knowledge making.

We concur with Sanders that while

> [w]e would do well to heed the cautions offered by postmodern ethnographers . . . [t]here is a considerable difference between being skeptical about the bases of truth claims while carefully examining the grounds upon with these claims are founded (a conventional interactionist enterprise) and denying that truth – as a utilitarian and liberating orientation – exists at all. (1995: 93, 97)

NARRATIVES AND WORLDS

As Silverman notes, for interviewers in the interactionist tradition, interview subjects construct not just narratives, but social worlds. For researchers in this tradition, "the primary issue is to generate data which give an authentic insight into people's experiences" (Silverman, 2001: 87). While interactionists do not suggest that there is

> "a singular objective or absolute world out-there" . . . [they] do recognize "objectified worlds." Indeed, they contend that some objectification is essential if human conduct is to be accomplished. Objectivity exists, thus, not as an absolute or inherently meaningful condition to which humans react but as an accomplished aspect of human lived experience. (Dawson and Prus, 1995: 113)

Research cannot provide the mirror reflection of the social world that positivists strive for, but it may provide access to the meanings people attribute to their experiences and social worlds. While the interview is itself a symbolic interaction, this does not discount the possibility that knowledge of the social world beyond the interaction can be obtained. In fact, it is only in the context of non-positivistic interviews, which recognize and build on their interactive components (rather than trying to control and reduce them), that "intersubjective depth" and "deep mutual understanding" can be achieved (and, with these, the achievement of knowledge of social worlds).

Those of us who aim to understand and document others' understandings choose qualitative interviewing because it provides us with a means for exploring the points of view of our research subjects, while granting these points of view the culturally honored status of reality. As Charmaz explains:

> We start with the experiencing person and try to share his or her subjective view. Our task is objective in the sense that we try to describe it with depth and detail. In doing so, we try to represent the person's view fairly and to portray it as consistent with his or her meanings. (1995: 54)

Silverman and others accurately suggest that this portrayal of what we do is in some ways romanticized. We will address below some of the problems that make this the case. But the proposition that romanticizing negates, in itself, the objectivity Charmaz defines, or the subjectivities with which we work, does not follow.

We have no trouble acknowledging, for instance, that interviewees sometimes respond to interviewers through the use of familiar narrative constructs, rather than by providing meaningful insights into their subjective view. Indeed, as Denzin notes:

> The subject is more than can be contained in a text, and a text is only a reproduction of what the subject has told us. What the subject tells us is itself something that has been shaped by prior cultural understandings. Most important, language, which is our window into the subject's world (and our world), plays tricks. It displaces the very thing it is supposed to represent, so that what is always given is a trace of other things, not the thing – lived experience – itself. (1991: 68)

In addition to this displacing, the language of interviewing (like all other telling) fractures the stories being told. This occurs inevitably within a story-teller's narrative, which must be partial because it cannot be infinite in length, and all the more partial if it is not to be unbearably boring. In the qualitative interview process, the research commits further fractures as well. The coding, categorization, and typologizing of stories result in telling only parts of stories, rather than presenting them in their "wholeness" (Charmaz, 1995: 60). Numerous levels of representation occur from the moment of "primary experience" to the reading of researchers' textual presentation of findings, including the level of attending to the experience, telling it to the researcher, transcribing and analyzing what is told, and the reading.

Qualitative interviewers recognize these fissures from the ideal text (i.e., interviewees' subjective view as experienced by the interviewees themselves). Interviewers note, for example, that "[t]he story is being told to particular people; it might have taken a different form if someone else were the listener" (Riessman, 1993: 11). The issue of how interviewees respond to us based on who we are – in their lives, as well as the social categories to which we belong, such as age, gender, class, and race – is a practical concern as well as an epistemological or theoretical one. The issue may be exacerbated, for example, when we study groups with whom we do not share membership. Particularly as a result of social distances, interviewees may not trust us, they may not understand our questions, or they may purposely mislead us in their responses. Likewise, given a lack of membership in their primary groups, we may not know enough about the phenomenon under study to ask the right questions.

Studying adolescents, as we have done in our own research, presents unique concerns along these lines. On the one hand, the meaning systems of adolescents are different from those of adults, and adult researchers must exercise caution in assuming they have an understanding of adolescent cultures because they have "been there." On the other hand, adolescents are in a transitional period of life, becoming increasingly oriented to adult worlds, though with "rough edges" (Fine and Sandstrom, 1988: 60). As a consequence, "age begins to decrease in importance as a means of differentiating oneself, and other dimensions of cultural differentiation, such as gender and class [and race], become more crucial" (Fine and Sandstrom, 1988: 66). These dimensions are thus of critical importance in establishing research relationships, rapport, and trust, and in evaluating both the information obtained and the interaction that occurs, within in-depth interviews.

To treat a young person's age as the determinant or predictor of his or her experiences or ways of talking is to neglect another key point about age ordering as well:

> The idea of an ending of childhood is predicated upon a normative system wherein childhood itself is taken for granted. But childhood may also be "ended" by narratives of personal or societal "deviance" or by new stories reconstituting the modelling of childhood itself. (Rogers and Rogers, 1992: 153)

In our experience, much of what adolescents talk about in open-ended interviews is precisely how their acts seem wayward, delinquent, premature, or otherwise not befitting proper youthful behavior. Their discourse toward and with us (and *for* themselves) is much about where and who they are. It is about trying out social locations and identities:

> Our approach is to treat the adolescents' reports as situated elements in social worlds. On the one hand they are ways of making sense to oneself and to another (cf. Mills, 1940). One cannot read the transcripts and fail to recognize that much of what goes on is two persons trying to understand topics that neither would consider in quite this manner or detail except in such special circumstances. The interviewees typically seem to enjoy the chance to "think aloud" about such matters, and often they say this to the interviewer. Much of that thinking is directed at a major project of their present lives – figuring out what type of person they are and what type they want to be. The interview offers an opportunity to try out various possibilities on this older student who is asking questions, and with reference to how it fits with one's self-image or might work out if directed at other audiences. On the other hand, these ways of viewing self and world come from and build into the social

world itself. Ways of thinking and talking derive from daily experiences and are also used in these. (Glassner and Loughlin, 1987: 34–5)

LIFE OUTSIDE THE INTERVIEW

Interactionist research starts from a belief that people create and maintain meaningful worlds. As interactionist research with adolescents illustrates, this belief can be accepted "without assuming the existence of a single, encompassing obdurate reality" (Charmaz, 1995: 62). To assume that realities beyond the interview context cannot be tapped into and explored is to grant narrative omnipotence. The roots of these realities are "more fundamental and pervasive" (Dawson and Prus, 1995: 121; see also Dawson and Prus, 1993; Schmitt, 1993) than such a view can account for. A vivid illustration of this is to be found in Charmaz's work on the chronically ill, who, she notes, experience sickness regardless of whether they participate in her interviews (1995: 50). We note that the adolescents in our studies experience their age-, gender-, and ethnic-based identities and fluidity of identity whether or not we interview them – and within our interviews with them.

Language shapes meanings but also permits intersubjectivity and the ability of willful persons to create and maintain meaningful worlds (Dawson and Prus, 1993: 166). Recognizing this, we cannot accept the proposition that interviews do not yield information about social worlds. Rather, "we take it that two persons can communicate their perceptions to one another. Knowing full well that there are both structures and pollutants in any discussion, we choose to study what is said in that discussion" (Glassner and Loughlin, 1987: 33). While certainly "there is no way to stuff a real-live person between the two covers of a text," as Denzin (in Schmitt, 1993: 130) puts it, we can describe truthfully delimited segments of real-live persons' lives. Indeed, in so delimiting, we may get *closer* to people's lived experience. As Charmaz (1995) notes, many people do not want themselves revealed in their totality. Recognizing this and responding accordingly may result in deeper, fuller conceptualizations of those aspects of our subjects' lives we are most interested in understanding.

Much the same deserves to be said about the interactionist researcher concerning the place and fullness of his or her life within the interview context. On the one hand, scholarship should preserve "in it the presence, concerns, and the experience of the [researcher] as knower and discoverer" (Smith, 1987: 92; see also Harding, 1987) so that the subjectivity that exists in all social research will be a visible part of the project, and thus available to the reader for examination. As Harding (1987: 9) notes, when "the researcher appears to us not as an invisible, anonymous voice of authority, but as a real, historical individual with concrete, specific desires and interests" the research process can be scrutinized.

Yet, on the other hand, these dictates do not necessitate, as some excessively revealing authors have taken them to mean, engaging in confessionals either with one's interviewees or with one's readers, or boring them with excessive details about oneself. It is precisely the "concrete, specific desires and interests" that merit airing, not everything that might be aired.

In our experience, interviewees will tell us, if given the chance, which of our interests and formulations make sense and nonsense to them. Glassner and Loughlin (1987: 36) describe instances in their study in which the interviewer brought up a topic that was seen by the subject as irrelevant or misinterpretation, and they offered correction. Moreover, as Charmaz points out, "creating these observations at all assumes that we share enough experience with our subjects and our readers to define things similarly" (1995: 64).

Of paramount importance regarding how (and how much) we present ourselves is the influence this presentation has on interviewees' ability and willingness to tell various sorts of stories. Richardson notes, "People organize their personal biographies and understand them through the stories they create to explain and justify their life experiences" (1990: 23; see also Lempert, 1994; Mishler, 1986; Riessman, 1993). Highlighting two types of stories of particular relevance, Richardson first describes the "cultural story": "Participation in a culture includes participation in the narratives of that culture, a general understanding of the stock of meanings and their relationships to each other" (Richardson, 1990: 24). These narratives represent the basis on which individuals create cultural stories, or stories about social phenomena that are typically "told from the point of view of the ruling interests and the normative order" (Richardson, 1990: 25). An interviewer who presents him- or herself either as too deeply committed to those interests and that order, or as clearly outside of them, restricts which cultural stories interviewees may tell and how these will be told.

Cultural stories are based in part on stereotypes. Richardson dubs an alternative to these the "collective story." Collective stories take the point of view of the interview subjects, and "give voice to those who are silenced or marginalized in the cultural [story]" (Richardson, 1990: 25). They challenge popular stereotypes by "resist[ing] the cultural narratives about groups of people and tell[ing] alternative stories" (Richardson, 1990: 25). A strength of qualitative interviewing is precisely its capacity to access self-reflexivity among interview subjects, leading to the greater likelihood of the telling of collective stories:

> Respondents may reveal feelings, beliefs, and private doubts that contradict or conflict with "what everyone thinks," including sentiments that break the dominant feeling rules. . . . In other cases, interviewers will discover the anxiety, ambivalence, and uncertainty that lie behind respondents' conformity. (Kleinman et al., 1994: 43)

Here again, to be a candidate for "good listener," the interviewer does best to present him- or herself as someone who is neither firmly entrenched in the mainstream nor too far at any particular margin. Ultimately, though, it is not where the interviewer locates him- or herself that is of greatest relevance to interviewees. In our experience, interviewees' principal concerns focus upon what will become of the interview. Those concerns extend beyond matters such as the protection of confidentiality. Interviewees want to know that what they have to say matters. They want to know what will become of their words. A researcher who interviewed AIDS patients observed:

> Many of my respondents explicitly refer to their interviews as "legacies." They are participating in this project despite the pain it might cause them because they believe I will use their stories to help others. Thus they shoulder me with the responsibility of giving meaning to their lives and their deaths. (Weitz, 1987: 21)

More often, the upshot for both interviewer and interviewee is less monumental, if no less important. In interviews with adolescents we have found, for example, that to be taken seriously and regarded as a teacher by someone whose societal role is that of "teacher" is a defining and highly valued characteristic of the interview situation.

AN ILLUSTRATION

We have suggested that narratives which emerge in interview contexts are situated in social worlds; they come out of worlds that exist outside of the interview itself. We argue not only for the existence of these worlds, but also for our ability as researchers to capture elements of these worlds in our scholarship. To illustrate some of the interactionist strategies for achieving that access we turn to a research effort one of us has recently completed (Miller, 2001).

The study involved in-depth, open-ended interviews with young women (ages 12 to 20) who claim affiliation with youth gangs in their communities. By and large, these gangs were integrated, mixed-gender gangs with both male and female membership. The in-depth interviews followed the completion of a survey interview administered by the same researcher.[1] While the survey interview gathered information about a wide range of topics, including the individual, her school, friends, family, neighborhood, delinquent involvement, arrest history, sexual history, and victimization, in addition to information about the gang, the in-depth interview was concerned exclusively with the roles and activities of young women in youth gangs, and the meanings they describe as emerging from their gang affiliation.

Compared to the interviewees, Miller was ten to fifteen years older (although typically perceived as younger by the interviewees), of the same gender, but often of a different race (Miller is white, the majority of the interviewees were African American) and class background (upper middle versus middle, lower middle, working class, and poor). Some scholars have argued that researchers should be members of the groups they study, in order to have the subjective knowledge necessary to truly understand their life experiences. For example, Collins argues that in order to make legitimate knowledge claims, researchers should "have lived or experienced their material in some fashion" (1990: 232). Likewise, with regard to adolescents specifically, Taylor et al. (1995: 36) point out that "[a]dolescents may choose a form of political resistance—that is, choose not to speak about what they know and feel—to people they see as representing or aligning with unresponsive institutions and authorities." Overcoming these obstacles can only be achieved by building rapport, ensuring and reassuring confidentiality, and establishing trust – facets of the research we describe in greater detail below.

However, we would also suggest that the existence of social differences between the interviewer and interviewees does not mean that the interviews are devoid of information about social worlds. In fact, the interviews can be accomplished in ways that put these social differences to use in providing opportunities for individuals to articulate their feelings about their life experiences. As noted above, one potential benefit of social distances in research of this nature is that the interviewee can recognize him- or herself as an expert on a topic of interest to someone typically in a more powerful position vis-à-vis the social structure (in this case, particularly in terms of age, race, and education). To find oneself placed in this position can be both empowering and illuminating because one can reflect on and speak about one's life in ways not often available. When individuals are members of groups that have been stereotyped and devalued by the larger culture, and whose perspectives have been ignored (as in the case of female gang members), the promise of this approach is all the more apparent. In fact, those interviews conducted by Miller, rather than by her African American male research assistant, often elicited more and different types[2] of detail.

Miller found that her differences from respondents often were beneficial, once trust had been established. Taylor and her colleagues suggest that one advantage of social distance is that it "may elicit explanations that are assumed to be known by someone with insider status" (1995: 36). Reading her transcripts against her research assistant's, Miller found numerous instances in which girls assumed shared understandings with the research assistant, because he was African American and had grown up in the same community as them, while they took more time to explain things to her. The research assistant likewise felt he intuitively knew what girls meant when they used particular words or made note of events, and thus often did not ask for greater explication. In this way, social distances facilitated respondents' recognition of themselves as experts on their social worlds.

In addition, many of the girls were cognizant of the controlling images (Collins, 1990) used to describe aspects of their lives. Consequently, in some instances young women talked to Miller in ways that directly addressed and challenged common stereotypes about adolescents, inner-city youths, and gangs. For instance, one young woman explained:

> Some people stereotype, they just stereotype gang members to be hardcore and to always be shootin' at somebody. They don't stereotype people that that could be a gang member but still they could go to school and get straight A's. That's

stereotyping because I know, I know a few gang-bangers who go to school, get straight A's, hit the books but still when they on the street, you know, they take good care of theirs. They takin' care of theirs in school and they takin' care of theirs on the street and I don't think that's right to stereotype people.

We have suggested that knowledge of social worlds emerges from the achievement of intersubjective depth and mutual understanding. For these to be present, however, there must be a level of trust between the interviewer and interviewee. Social distances that include differences in relative power can result in suspicion and lack of trust, both of which the researcher must actively seek to overcome. Rapport building is a key to this process. Establishing trust and familiarity, showing genuine interest, assuring confidentiality, and not being judgmental are some important elements of building rapport (Glassner and Loughlin, 1987: 35). Miller found that the last of these was particularly important when interviewing adolescent female gang members. These young women were members of a group frequently stigmatized by the social groups to which Miller herself belongs, a reality known to both the interviewees and the interviewer.

Miller's research design proved useful in alleviating tensions that could result from this schism. She began with the administration of a survey interview, which began with relatively innocuous questions (demographics, living arrangements, attitudes toward school), and slowly made the transition from these to more sensitive questions about gang involvement, delinquency, and victimization. In addition, completing the survey interview first allowed her to establish a relationship with each young woman, so that when the in-depth interview was completed, there was a pre-existing level of familiarity. In particular, in the course of the survey when a young woman described participating in serious delinquency – including, in some instances, brutal acts of violence – Miller had the opportunity to respond in a non-judgmental manner. This provided a layer of understanding that facilitated frank discussions when these issues were revisited during the in-depth interviews.

Miller also worked to build trust through efforts to protect youths' confidentiality. The assurance of confidentiality is achieved as much by implicit assurances as by explicit guarantees. There were often opportunities for Miller to convey her concern about protecting the subjects' privacy. For example, when interviewing in open areas (such as the visiting room at a juvenile detention center), she remained aware of the surroundings to ensure against eavesdropping, temporarily stopped the interview when others came within clear hearing range, and moved to more secluded areas when necessary. Likewise, when interviewees accidentally disclosed names, Miller immediately offered to erase these slips from the tape recording and did so in the interviewee's presence before continuing with the interview. Most importantly, she was proactive in reacting to the immediate environment, and did not wait for signs of discomfort from respondents. In fact, she often remained more concerned than they were. Ultimately, she found that these actions helped to engender trust.

Cultural stories

Rapport involves more, however, than provisions of confidentiality, non-judgmental responses, and other offerings from the interviewer. It involves the interviewee feeling comfortable and competent enough in the interaction to "talk back" (Blumer, 1969: 22) – to label particular topics irrelevant, point out misinterpretations, and offer corrections. When respondents talk back they provide insights into the narratives they use to describe the meanings of their social worlds and into their experience of the worlds of which they are a part. One way Miller's interviewees talked back – both to her and to the audiences for her works about them – was in their resistance to her efforts to get them to articulate how gender inequality shaped their experiences in the gang. In doing so, they situated their personal narratives into larger cultural stories about girls in gangs, both by vigilantly challenging these stories, and by embracing them in their discussions of "other" girls.

Scholars have noted "the impact of 'already established cultural standards' on individuals" (Schmitt, 1993: 126). Research participants gain at least part of their understanding, and convey their understanding to the interviewer, by drawing on the narratives that come out of the social worlds around them. For adolescent girls, and gang girls in particular, a primary cultural standard they must contend with is the sexual double standard, in which they receive status from peers for their association with and attractiveness to males, but are denigrated for sexual activities deemed promiscuous. Scholars have noted that a characteristic feature of adolescence is the "shift from the relatively asexual gender systems of childhood to the overtly sexualized gender systems of adolescence and adulthood" (Thorne, 1993: 135), which has different meanings and consequences for girls and boys. It is in this context that girls must negotiate – not just their sexual reputation – but their gender identity as well.

A long-standing cultural stereotype of girls' roles in gangs is that they are peripheral or auxiliary members whose primary function is as a sexual outlet for male members (see Campbell (1984) for a discussion). For the young women in Miller's study, this cultural stereotype was further exacerbated by the practice within some gangs of "sexing in" some female members – requiring the girl to have sex with multiple male members for entry into the group (see Miller, 2001). In tandem with larger stereotypes, this practice challenged the integrity and sexual reputations of girls in gangs. Thus, in Miller's interviews, girls went to great lengths to distance themselves from the practice and to dispute this cultural story when describing their place in the gang. One young woman expressed her frustration that people outside of gangs often assumed that she was sexed in:

> They be showin' these little movies on TV, like, well, the females have to get sexed in and the males have to get jumped in and like that. You know, you've seen 'em on TV. And they, they just figure, well, if you a girl gang member then you got sexed in. And I really didn't. I wasn't even down for nothin' like that.

This young woman was frustrated, not just by TV depictions, but by the perceptions of her non-gang peers. She continued:

> Girls at school . . . was like, "well you probably got sexed in. You probably got sexed in." . . . Like, "oh, you a ho. How'd you get put in?" I was like, "none of your business." They was like, "you probably got sexed in." I was like, "no, I really didn't."

Instead, describing her initiation, she explained:

> I got my respect off the bat because instead of takin' six [punches] from the girls I took six from four guys. I took six hits to the head from four guys. I got my respect off the bat. So the girls, they had nothin' to say about me bein' a punk, neither did the guys.

This type of "talking back" was a direct challenge to one sort of cultural story about girls in gangs – that they are sexually "loose" and function as the sex objects of male gang members. In addition to debunking the stereotype through her denial of being "sexed in," this young woman described her avenue of respect as being willing and able to withstand a beating from male peers.

However, girls also drew from and replicated this cultural story in their analysis and critique of "other" girls, including other female gang members. One way they did so was by labeling and denigrating young women they themselves deemed sexually loose. This was most evident in their discussions of girls who had been sexed in. One young woman commented, "there's really no hope for them. I mean it's just trifling, that's just downgrading yourself." Another concurred: "if you have sex with them, then you a wreck. . . . They don't care about they body, they just let everybody get something off of them." Describing gang members' interactions with girls who had been sexed in, one girl explained: "They know that they was getting' looked at as ho's. We just look at 'em. Sometimes we tell 'em too, we be like, 'ooh y'all look, y'all some little ho's,' or 'why y'all do that?'"

Though extremely judgmental of girls who were sexually abused by male gang members, girls did not negatively evaluate young men's sexual behaviors. In this way, gang girls drew from familiar cultural stories that single out and blame female victims of mistreatment. Women continue to be held responsible for their victimization in both popular discourses about violence against women and legal response: gang girls culled from these cultural traditions when they described and evaluated the exploitation of young women around them.

Collective stories

A proposition of this chapter is that interviews have the capacity to be interactional contexts within which social worlds come to be better understood. One way in which this is achieved is through interviewees' revisions of cultural stories, as we have just suggested. We have proposed that another sort of story can be told as well, one that privileges the social world under discussion and its stories over the stories of the larger society. Miller's interviews illustrate this possibility: young women did more than just challenge prevailing stereotypes in explaining their gang involvement (i.e., "I was not sexed in," "I have respect"). Instead, they also presented a collective story of the gang as a space of gender equality.

The young women Miller interviewed were quite resistant to her attempts to elicit discussions of gender inequality, emphasizing instead that everyone in the gang was "all the same." One young woman explained: "they give every last one of us respect the way they give the males." Another was visibly frustrated with Miller's line of questions, and repeatedly cut her off, or "talked back," in response:

> *Miller*: You said before that the gang was about half girls and half guys? Can you tell me more about that? Like you said you don't think there are any differences in terms of what –
> *Interviewee*: There isn't!
> *Miller*: Ok, can you tell me more –
> *Interviewee*: Like what? There isn't, there isn't like, there's nothing – boy, girl, white, black, Mexican, Chinese.

Another girl noted, "if she consider herself as a gang member, then she gonna be treated like a gang member," and she concluded, "you can't really judge it on the boys or the girls, it ain't based on that." Likewise, another explained: "We just like dudes to them. We just like dudes, they treat us like that 'cause we act so much like dudes they can't do nothing. They respect us as females though, but we just so much like dudes that they just don't trip off of it."

As these comments suggest, part of girls' discussions of their equality within the gang was not so much by suggesting that all women should be treated equally, but by differentiating themselves from young women who were not in gangs. As one girl made explicit:

> A lot of girls get scared. Don't wanna break their nails and stuff like that. So, ain't no need for them to try to be in no gang. And the ones that's in it, most of the girls that's in act like boys. That's why they in, 'cause they like to fight and stuff. They know how to fight and they use guns and stuff.

Thus, the young women Miller spoke to told a collective story that situated their place in the gang as comparable to the male members in terms of activities, toughness, and willingness to fight. According to this collective story, the gang is an arena in which they receive status and esteem from being strong and being willing to stand up for themselves, exhibiting traits that cultural stories commonly associate with males rather than females.

Finding realities in interviews

We have suggested that a strength of qualitative interviewing is the oppor-tunity it provides to collect and rigorously examine narrative accounts of social worlds. In Miller's illustration, both cultural and collective stories provide important insights into how young women understand their place within their gangs and within the broader social world of adolescent peer culture. We have also suggested that it is possible to find realities within interviews – collective stories are a significant aspect of this reality, but so are accounts of events and activities that are ultimately contradictory to these stories. Despite their collective story of equality, without exception the young women Miller interviewed provided evidence to the contrary. For example, they described a distinct gender hierarchy within their gangs that included male leadership, a sexual double standard, the sexual exploitation of some young women, and most girls' exclusion from serious gang crime – specifically those acts that build status and reputation within the group. By juxtaposing girls' collective stories with these incongruous facets of girls' interviews, Miller (2001) built her theoretical discussion around the contradictory operation of gender within gangs.

For example, we noted that the practice of "sexing" girls into gangs was one that challenged the integrity of all girls in mixed-gender gangs. As one non-gang girl told Miller, "I mean, they tell you that [they weren't sexed in], but you don't know how they *really* got in." Because of this, gang girls' vilification of girls who were sexed in was necessary in order to distance themselves from the practice, and maintain an identity as a "true" member – as someone who had not been sexed into the gang. The more vocally girls spoke of these *other* girls as "ho's" and "wrecks," the more successful they were, or hoped to be, in creating a rigid dichotomy between themselves and girls who were sexed in. Ironically, denigrating girls who were sexed in or exploited, rather than holding the young men accountable, was the key to maintaining the tenuous but vital belief that the male gang members viewed them as equals. Creating this dichotomy allowed girls to conclude that the boys in their gang treated and discussed *other* young women in sexually derogatory ways – young women who deserved it because they were "nasty." On the other hand, they could believe that the boys considered them, as one young woman put it, "one of the niggas," or one of the guys.

To challenge the practice, or the general tendency of some gang boys to mistreat girls, would be to risk being ostracized from the group – precisely because of its male-dominated structure. It would also mean having to confront rather than deny that girls were not "equals" in the eyes of their male gang peers. These young women lived in social worlds in which women were devalued; their means of resisting their own devaluation was not to challenge the premise of this treatment, but instead to define themselves as outside of its boundaries. Thus young women appreciated the normative space of "equality" available in gangs, even when it was not always a reality in practice. Identifying with cultural stories about women, and rejecting such

137

images for themselves, allowed gang girls to construct and maintain the collective story that they were "one of the guys."

CONCLUSION

Silverman (2001) argues that, while "open-ended" interviews can be useful, we need to justify departing from the naturally occurring data that surround us and to be cautious about the "romantic" impulse which identifies "experience" with "authenticity." We agree, but with different words in scare quotes.

On the one hand, we have tried to suggest in this chapter some strategies by which interviews can be less-than-problematically open-ended, and that interviewers need not resort to romanticism, or to identifying experience with authenticity, in order to call upon interviewees' experiences and produce authentic accounts of social worlds. On the other hand, we would put in scare quotes "naturally occurring data," because we question the grounds for any neat distinction between the natural and cultural, in sociological data as elsewhere (cf. Douglas, 1986). In making such claims, it is not the case that we are "not too sure whether interviews are purely local events or express underlying external realities," as Silverman (2001: 111) has suggested. Instead, we argue against the dualistic imperative to classify them as one or the other.

All we sociologists have are stories. Some come from other people, some from us, some from our interactions with others. What matters is to understand how and where the stories are produced, which sort of stories they are, and how we can put them to honest and intelligent use in theorizing about social life.

NOTES

1. The project was a comparative study in Columbus, Ohio and St. Louis, Missouri. All of the Columbus interviews were conducted by Miller; many of the interviews in St. Louis were conducted by a research assistant. See Miller (2001) for an in-depth description of the research process.
2. Girls responded to the research assistant as a paternal figure, and felt quite safe disclosing and talking at length with him (and without prompting, as this was not part of the research protocol) about their experiences of victimization. One girl even asked him to adopt her; another tried to fix him up with her aunt.

REFERENCES

Blumer, H. (1969) *Symbolic Interactionism: Perspective and Method*. Berkeley, CA: University of California Press.

Campbell, A. (1984) *The Girls in the Gang*. New York: Basil Blackwell.

Charmaz, K. (1995) "Between positivism and postmodernism: Implications for methods," *Studies in Symbolic Interaction*, 17: 43–72.

Collins, P.H. (1990) *Black Feminist Thought*. Boston: Unwin Hyman.

Dawson, L.L. and Prus, R.C. (1993) "Interactionist ethnography and postmodern discourse: Affinities and disjunctures in approaching human lived experience," *Studies in Symbolic Interaction*, 15: 147–77.

Dawson, L.L. and Prus, R.C. (1995) "Postmodernism and linguistic reality versus symbolic interactionism and obdurate reality," *Studies in Symbolic Interaction*, 17: 105–24.

Denzin, N.K. (1991) "Representing lived experiences in ethnographic texts", *Studies in Symbolic Interaction*, 12: 59–70.

Douglas, M. (1986) *Risk Acceptability According to the Social Sciences*. New York: Russell Sage Foundation.

Fine, G.A. and Sandstrom, K.L. (1988) *Knowing Children: Participant Observation with Minors*. Newbury Park, CA: Sage.

Glassner, B. and Loughlin, J. (1987) *Drugs in Adolescent Worlds: Burnouts to Straights*. New York: St. Martin's Press.

Harding, S. (1987) *Feminism and Methodology*. Bloomington: Indiana University Press.

Kleinman, S., Stenross, B., and McMahon, M. (1994) "Privileging fieldwork over interviews: Consequences for identity and practice," *Symbolic Interaction*, 17 (1): 37–50.

Latour, B. (1993) *We Have Never Been Modern*. Cambridge, MA: Harvard University Press.

Lempert, L.B. (1994) "A narrative analysis of abuse: Connecting the personal, the rhetorical, and the structural," *Journal of Contemporary Ethnography*, 22 (4): 411–41.

Miller, J. (2001) *One of the Guys: Girls, Gangs and Gender*. New York: Oxford University Press.

Mills, C.W. (1940) "Situated actions and vocabularies of motives," *American Sociological Review*, 5: 904–13.

Mishler, E.G. (1986) *Research Interviewing: Context and Narrative*. Cambridge, MA: Harvard University Press.

Richardson, L. (1990) *Writing Strategies: Reaching Diverse Audiences*. Newbury Park, CA: Sage.

Riessman, C.K. (1993) *Narrative Analysis*. Newbury Park, CA: Sage.

Rogers, R.S. and Rogers, W.S. (1992) *Stories of Childhood*. Toronto: University of Toronto Press.

Sanders, C.R. (1995) "Stranger than fiction: Insights and pitfalls in post-modern ethnography," *Studies in Symbolic Interaction*, 17: 89–104.

Schmitt, R.L. (1993) "Cornerville as obdurate reality: Retooling the research act through postmodernism," *Studies in Symbolic Interaction*, 15: 121–45.

Silverman, D. (2001) *Interpreting Qualitative Data: Methods for Analysing Talk, Text and Interaction*. London: Sage.

Smith, D.E. (1987) "Women's perspective as a radical critique of sociology," in S. Harding (ed.), *Feminism and Methodology*. Bloomington: Indiana University Press. pp. 84–96.

Taylor, J.M., Gilligan, C., and Sullivan, A.M. (1995) *Between Voice and Silence: Women and Girls, Race and Relationship*. Cambridge, MA: Harvard University Press.

Thorne, B. (1993) *Gender Play: Girls and Boys in School*. New Brunswick, NJ: Rutgers University Press.

Weitz, R. (1987) "The interview as legacy," *Hastings Center Report*, 17: 21–3.

8 The active interview

James A. Holstein and Jaber F. Gubrium

Thinking about the interview as being "active" is somewhat unconventional. Typically, we approach the interview as a neutral means of extracting information. Interviewers ask questions. Respondents provide answers. The interview process is merely the conduit between the two participants. The standard vision of the interview process keeps the interviewer's involvement to a minimum. The interviewer is supposed to be neutral, inconspicuous, little more than a "fly on the wall," so to speak.

In this chapter, we will look closely at the interview process to see just how active interviewing is in practice – for both the interviewer and the respondent. Indeed, we will argue that it cannot be any other way, no matter how hard interviewers might try to diminish their presence in the interview exchange. Thus, we title the chapter "The Active Interview." This title does not single out a distinctive type of interview, differentiating it from, say, the standardized survey interview or the minimally directive life story interview. Instead we use the title to highlight the fact that interactional, interpretive activity is a hallmark of all interviews. All interviews are active interviews.

FOCUSING ON ACTIVENESS

Today, interviewing is more popular than ever as a means of generating information. In our postmodern "interview society" (see Gubrium and Holstein, 2002a, 2003; Silverman, 2001), the mass media, human service providers, and researchers increasingly generate data by interviewing. The number of television news programs, daytime television talk shows, and newspaper articles that provide us with the results of interviews is growing by leaps and bounds. Regarding more methodical forms of information collection, it has been estimated that 90 percent of all social science investigations use interviews in one way or another (Briggs, 1986). Interviewing is undoubtedly the most widely used technique for conducting systematic social inquiry, as sociologists, psychologists, anthropologists, psychiatrists, clinicians, administrators, politicians, and pollsters treat interviews as their "windows on the world" (Gubrium and Holstein, 2002a; Hyman et al., 1975).

In simple terms, interviewing provides a way of generating empirical data about the social world by asking people to talk about their lives. In this respect, interviews are special forms of conversation. While these conversations may vary from highly structured, standardized, quantitatively oriented survey interviews, to semiformal guided conversations, to free-flowing informational exchanges, all interviews are interactional. The narratives that are produced may be as truncated as forced-choice survey answers or as elaborate as oral life histories, but they are all a product of the talk between interview participants.

While most researchers acknowledge the interactional character of the interview, the technical literature on interviewing stresses the need to keep that interaction in check. Guides to interviewing – especially those oriented to standardized surveys – are primarily concerned with maximizing the flow of valid, reliable information while minimizing distortions of what the respondent knows (Gorden, 1987). The interview conversation is framed as a potential source of bias, error, misunderstanding, or misdirection; it is a persistent set of problems to be minimized. The corrective is simple: if the interviewer asks questions properly and the interview situation is propitious, the respondent will automatically convey the desired information. In this conventional view, the interview conversation is a pipeline for transporting knowledge.

A recently heightened sensitivity to representational matters (see Gubrium and Holstein, 1997) – characteristic of poststructuralist, postmodernist, constructionist, and ethnomethodological inquiry – has raised a number of questions about the very possibility of collecting information in the manner the conventional approach presupposes. Attention has increasingly focused on the activeness of interviews. In varied ways, these alternate perspectives hold that meaning is socially constituted; all knowledge is created from the actions undertaken to obtain it (see, for example, Cicourel, 1964, 1974; Garfinkel, 1967). Treating interviewing as a social encounter in which knowledge is actively constructed suggests the possibility that the interview is not so much a neutral conduit or source of distortion, but rather a site of, and occasion for, producing reportable knowledge.

Sociolinguist Charles Briggs (1986) argues that the social circumstances of interviews are more than obstacles to respondents' articulation of their particular truths. Briggs notes that, like all other speech events, interviews fundamentally, not incidentally, shape the form and content of what is said. Aaron Cicourel (1974) goes farther, maintaining that interviews impose particular ways of understanding reality upon subjects' responses. The general point is that interviewers are deeply and unavoidably implicated in creating meanings that ostensibly reside within respondents (also see Manning, 1967; Mishler, 1986, 1991; Silverman, 2001). Both parties to the interview are necessarily and unavoidably active. Meaning is not merely elicited by apt questioning, nor simply transported through respondent replies; it is actively and communicatively assembled in the interview encounter. Respondents are not so much repositories of knowledge – treasuries of information await- ing excavation – as they are constructors of knowledge in association with interviewers. Interviews are collaborative accomplishments, involving

141

participants in meaning-making work in the process (Alasuutari, 1995; Holstein and Staples, 1992; Holstein and Gubrium, 1995).

Technical attempts to strip interviews of their interactional constituents will be futile. Instead of refining the long list of methodological constraints under which "standardized" interviews should be conducted, we suggest that researchers embrace the view of the interview as unavoidably active and begin to acknowledge, and capitalize upon, interviewers' and respondents' constitutive contributions to the production of interview data. This means consciously and conscientiously attending to both the interview process and the products that interviews generate in ways that are more sensitive to the social construction of knowledge.

Conceiving of the interview as active means attending more to the ways in which knowledge is assembled than is usually the case in traditional approaches. In other words, understanding *how* the meaning-making process unfolds in the interview is as critical as apprehending *what* is substantively asked and conveyed. The *hows* of interviewing refer to the interactional, narrative procedures of knowledge production, not merely to interview techniques. The *whats* pertain to the issues guiding the interview, the content of questions, and the substantive information communicated by the respondent. A dual interest in the *hows* and *whats* of meaning production goes hand in hand, expanding an appreciation of the constitutive activeness of the interview process.

This appreciation derives from ethnomethodologically informed, social constructionist sensibilities (cf. Berger and Luckmann, 1967; Blumer, 1969; Garfinkel, 1967; Heritage, 1984; Pollner, 1987). The process of meaning production is considered to be as important for social research as is the meaning that is produced. In significant ways, this approach also resonates with methodological critiques and formulations offered by feminist scholars (see DeVault, 1990; Harding, 1987; Reinharz, 1992; Smith, 1987). Ethnomethodology, constructionism, poststructuralism, postmodernism, and some versions of feminism point to issues relating to subjectivity, complexity, perspective, and meaning construction. Still, as valuable and insightful as they are, these "linguistically attuned" approaches can emphasize the *hows* of the interview process at the expense of the *whats* of lived experience. We want to strike a balance between these *hows* and *whats* as a way of reappropriating the significance of substance and content to studies of interviewing. While the emphasis on process has sharpened concern with, and debate over, the epistemological status of interview data, it is important to not lose track of what is being asked about in interviews and, in turn, what is being conveyed by respondents. A narrow focus on the *hows* of meaning construction tends to displace the significant *whats* – meanings – that serve as the relevant grounds for asking and answering questions.

KEY POINTS

- In today's interview society, information is increasingly acquired by way of interviews.
- A common view of the interview is that of a one-way pipeline for transporting knowledge.
- Recently, we have come to recognize the interview as a meaning-making conversation – a site and occasion for making meaning. It is more like a two-way informational street than a one-way data pipeline.
- Because it is a two-way conversation, interviewing is always unavoidably interactional and constructive – in a word, the interview is *active*.

IMAGES OF INTERVIEWING

Taking the activity of all interviewing as our point of departure, the following sections discuss how the interview cultivates meaning. We begin by locating this vision of the interview in relation to various conceptions of interviewing, examining alternate images of the subject behind the interview participants (also see Gubrium and Holstein, 2002b).

In order to find out about another person's feelings, thoughts, or experiences we typically believe that we merely have to ask the right questions and the other's reality will be ours. Studs Terkel, the consummate journalist and interviewer, says he simply turns on his tape recorder and asks people to talk. Writing of the interviews he did for his book titled *Working*, Terkel (1972: xxv) notes:

> There were questions, of course. But they were casual in nature . . . the kind you would ask while having a drink with someone; the kind he would ask you. . . . In short, it was a conversation. In time, the sluice gates of dammed up hurts and dreams were open.

As straightforward and unpretentious as it is, Terkel's image of interviewing permeates the social sciences; interviewing is generally likened to "prospecting" for the true facts and feelings residing within the respondent. Of course, there is a highly sophisticated technology that tells researchers how to ask questions, the sorts of questions not to ask, the order in which to ask them, and ways to avoid saying the things that might spoil, contaminate, or otherwise bias the data (Hyman et al., 1975; Fowler and Mangione, 1990). The basic model, however, remains similar to the one Terkel exploits so adroitly.

The image of the social scientific prospector casts the interview as a search and discovery mission, with the interviewer intent on detecting what is already there inside variably cooperative respondents. The challenge lies in extracting information as directly as possible, without contaminating it. Highly refined interview technologies streamline, systematize, and sanitize the process. This can involve varying degrees of standardization (see Gubrium and Holstein, 2002b; Maccoby and Maccoby, 1954), ranging from interviews organized by structured, specifically worded questions and an orientation to measurement (see, for example, Singleton and Straits, 2002), to flexibly organized interviews guided by more general questions aimed at uncovering subjective meanings (e.g., Atkinson, 2002; Fontana and Frey, 2000; Johnson, 2002; Warren, 2002).

John Madge contrasts what he calls "formative" with "mass" interviews, categorizing them according to whether the respondent "is given some sort of freedom to choose the topics to be discussed and the way in which they are discussed" (1965: 165). Formative interviews include the non-directive interviews favored in Rogerian counseling (see Rogers, 1945), informal interviews, and life histories. Most large-scale surveys fall into the mass interview category. By and large, classification centers on the communicative constraints and aims of the interview process, with little attention paid to how interviews differ as occasions for knowledge production.

The subject behind the interview participant

Regardless of the type of interview, there is always a model of the research *subject* lurking behind persons placed in interview roles (Gubrium and Holstein, 2002a; Holstein and Gubrium, 1995). For example, projecting a subject behind the respondent confers a sense of epistemological agency upon the respondent, which bears on our understanding of the relative validity of the information that is reported. In conventional approaches, respondents are subjects basically conceived as passive *vessels of answers* to whom interviewers direct their questions. They are repositories of facts, reflections, opinions, and other traces of experience. Occasionally, such as with especially sensitive interview topics or with recalcitrant respondents, researchers acknowledge that it may be difficult to obtain accurate experiential information. None the less, the information is viewed, in principle, as held uncontaminated by the subject's vessel of answers. The trick is to formulate questions and provide an atmosphere conducive to open and undistorted communication between the interviewer and the respondent.

Much of the methodological literature on interviewing deals with the nuances of these intricate matters. The vessel-of-answers view cautious interviewers to take care in how they ask questions, lest their manner of inquiry bias what lies within the subject. This perspective offers myriad procedures for obtaining unadulterated facts and details, most of which rely upon interviewer and question neutrality. For example, it is assumed that the interviewer who poses questions that acknowledge alternative sides of an issue is being more "neutral" than the interviewer who does not. The successful implementation of neutral practices elicits truths held in the vessel of answers behind the respondent. Validity results if unbiased procedures are successfully applied.

In the vessel-of-answers approach, the image of the subject is passive; this subject is not engaged in the production of knowledge. If the interviewing process goes "by the book" and is non-directional and unbiased, respondents will validly speak out with whatever is presumed to reside inside themselves – the unadulterated facts of experience. Contamination creeps in from the interview setting, its participants, and their interaction; in principle, the subject is "pure," and, under ideal conditions, serves up authentic reports when beckoned to do so.

What happens, however, if we enliven the image of the subject behind the respondent – if we view the subject he or she is as active? From this perspective, the subject behind the respondent not only holds facts and details of experience, but, in the very process of offering them up, constructively adds to, takes away from, and transforms them into artifacts of the occasion. The respondent can hardly "spoil" what he or she is, in effect, subjectively creating.

This activated subject pieces experiences together, before, during, and after assuming the role of respondent. As a member of society, he or she mediates and alters the knowledge that is conveyed to the interviewer; he or she is "always already" an active maker of meaning. Because the respondent's answers are continually being assembled and modified, including his or her sense of what lies within, the answers' truth value cannot be judged simply in terms of whether they match what lies in a vessel of objective answers.

From a more traditional standpoint, the objectivity or truth of interview responses might be assessed in terms of reliability, the extent to which questioning yields the same answers whenever and wherever it is carried out, and validity, the extent to which inquiry yields the "correct" answers (Kirk and Miller, 1986). When the interview is viewed as a dynamic, meaning-making occasion, however, different criteria apply. The focus is on how meaning is constructed, the circumstances of construction, and the meaningful linkages that are assembled for the occasion. While interest in the content of answers persists, it is primarily in how and what the subject/respondent, in collaboration with an equally active interviewer, produces and conveys about the subject/respondent's experience under the interpretive circumstances at hand (see Altheide and Johnson, 1994). One cannot expect answers on one occasion to replicate those on another because they emerge from different circumstances of production. Similarly, the validity of answers derives not from their correspondence to meanings held within the respondent, but from their ability to convey situated experiential realities in terms that are locally comprehensible.

The active image of the interview is best put in perspective by contrasting it with more conventional images. We will focus on two classic exemplars that differ considerably in their orientations to the experiential truths held by the passive subject. The first approach orients to the rational, factual value of what is communicated. It focuses on the substantive statements, explanations, and reasons with which the respondent articulates experience. We use Jean Converse and Howard Schuman's candid book *Conversations at Random* (1974) as an exemplary text. The second approach orients to the purportedly deeper and more authentic value of the subject's feelings. It emphasizes sentiment and emotion, the core of human experience. We use Jack Douglas's book *Creative Interviewing* (1985) to illustrate this perspective.

Survey interviewing

While Converse and Schuman discuss the most standardized of interviewing techniques, their book tries to portray the survey interview "as interviewers see it," richly illustrating how interpretively engaging, and relatedly difficult and exasperating, the survey respondent can be. The book describes the interesting and complex personalities and meanings that interviewers encounter while interviewing, depicting them as "the pleasure of persons" and "connoisseurs of the particular." But the authors caution the reader that, even though it will be evident throughout their discussion that the respondent can be quite interpretively active, this does not work against obtaining objective information. This information, the reader eventually learns, is derived from the repository of knowledge that lies within the basically passive subject behind the respondent. The authors do not believe that the respondent's conduct implicates his or her subject in the construction of meaning. As lively, uninhibited, entertaining, and difficult as the respondent might be at times, his or her passive subject ultimately holds the answers sought in the research.

Converse and Schuman grant that survey interviewing involves experiencing the "pleasure of persons," but the authors hope that interviewers use their clearly designated roles and the rules of standardized interviewing to effectively gain access to the vessel of answers behind the respondent. Their book is replete with anecdotal reminders of what interviewers must learn in order to keep that vessel of answers in view and the respondent on target. In part, it is a matter of controlling oneself as an interviewer so that one does not interfere with what the passive subject is only too willing to put forth. The interviewer must shake off self-consciousness, suppress personal opinion, and avoid stereotyping the respondent. Learning the interviewer role is also a matter of controlling the interview situation to facilitate the candid expression of opinions and sentiments. Ideally, the interview should be conducted in private. This helps assure that respondents will speak directly from their vessels of answers, and not be significantly affected by the presence of others. The seasoned interviewer learns that the so-called pull of conversation, which might have an interpretive dynamic of its own fueled by the active subjects behind both interviewer and respondent, must be managed so that the "push of inquiry" (p. 26) is kept in focus. Ideally, the cross-pressures of conducting inquiry that will produce "good hard data" are managed by means of "soft" conversation (p. 22).

Throughout, Converse and Schuman's book provides glimpses of how problematic the image of the passive subject is in practice. The rich illustrations repeatedly show us that interviews are conversations where meanings are not only conveyed, but cooperatively built up, received, interpreted, and recorded by the interviewer. While the veteran interviewer learns to manage the pressures of trying to standardize conversation for the purposes of inquiry, readers cannot help but feel that they are only a short epistemological step away from encountering the interview as an active, meaning-making occasion.

Creative interviewing

Converse and Schuman's view of survey interviewing contrasts with the approach exemplified in Douglas's book *Creative Interviewing*, but, at bottom, we also see some marked similarities. The word "creative" in Douglas's title refers primarily to the interviewer, not the respondent. His view of interviewing derives from the difficulties he encountered attempting to probe respondents' "deep experience." Douglas writes that in his many empirical studies, he repeatedly discovered how shallow the standard recommendations were for conducting research interviews. Canons of rational neutrality, such as those Converse and Schuman espouse, failed to capture what Douglas calls his respondents' "emotional wellsprings." In response to this shortcoming, Douglas calls for a methodology of deep disclosure.

Most basically, Douglas's difficulties relate as much to his image of the passive subject as they do to shortcomings of standard interviewing technique. Like the image of the subject behind the survey respondent, Douglas also imagines his subjects to be repositories of answers, but in his case, they are viewed as well-guarded vessels of feelings. His model is of a respondent who authentically communicates from an emotional wellspring, at the behest of an interviewer who knows that mere words cannot draw out or convey what experience ultimately is all about. Standard survey questions and answers touch only the surface of experience. Douglas aims deeper by intimately "getting to know" the real subject behind the respondent.

Creative interviewing is a set of techniques for moving beyond the mere words and sentences exchanged in the interview process. To achieve this, the interviewer must establish a climate for *mutual* disclosure. The interview should be an occasion that displays the interviewer's willingness to share his or her own feelings and deepest thoughts. This is done to assure respondents that they can, in turn, share their own intimate thoughts and feelings. The interviewer's deep disclosure both occasions and legitimizes the respondent's reciprocal revelations. This, Douglas suggests, is thoroughly suppressed by the cultivated neutrality of the standard survey interview. As if to state a cardinal rule, he writes:

> Creative interviewing, as we shall see throughout, involves the use of many strategies and tactics of interaction, largely based on an understanding of friendly

feelings and intimacy, to optimize *cooperative, mutual disclosure and a creative search for mutual understanding.* (p. 25, emphasis in the original)

Douglas offers a set of guidelines for creative interviewing. One is to figure that, as he puts it, "genius in creative interviewing involves 99 percent perspiration" (p. 27); getting the respondent to deeply disclose requires much more work than obtaining mere opinions. A second admonition for engaging in "deep-deep probes into the human soul" is "researcher, know thyself" (p. 51). Continuous self-analysis on the part of the interviewer, who usually is also the researcher, is necessary, lest the creative interviewer's own defense mechanisms work against mutual disclosure and understanding. A third rule is to show a commitment to mutual disclosure by expressing an abiding interest in feelings. Referring to a neophyte creative interviewer who "has done some wonderously revealing life studies," Douglas writes that the creative interviewer is "driven by . . . friendly, caring, and adoring feelings, but adds to those an endearing, wide-eyed sense of wonderment at the mysteries unveiled before her" (p. 29).

The wellsprings tapped by creative interviewing are said to be emotional, in distinct contrast to the preferred rational image that permeates Converse and Schuman's book. As Douglas puts it, knowledge and wisdom are *"partially the product of creative interactions—of mutual searches for understanding, of soul communions"* (p. 55, emphasis in original). While Douglas's imagined subject is basically emotional, this subject, in the role of respondent, none the less actively cooperates with the interviewer to create mutually recognizable meanings. In this regard, the mutuality of disclosure – the "creative" thrust of creative interviewing – mediates, adds to, and shapes what is said in its own right.

What Douglas does not recognize is that this admittedly active subject could just as well constitute the wellsprings of experience in rational or other terms, not necessarily emotional ones. By failing to recognize this, the subject behind Douglas's respondent remains an essentially passive, if creatively emotional, fount of experience, not unlike the respondent who "opens up" while having a drink with Studs Terkel. Located deeper inside, perhaps, than the subject behind the survey respondent, the subject behind Douglas's image of the respondent remains a relatively static, inert vessel, in this case, of emotional answers.

KEY POINTS

- All approaches to interviewing presume some image or model of the subject behind the interview participant.
- Traditional approaches envision the subject behind participants as passive.

- A close look at the traditional model of survey interviewing shows that, in practice, interview conversations hint that the respondent is more than a mere vessel of answers. Nevertheless, attempts at standardization help sustain the vision of the passive subject.
- In contrast, *creative interviewing* rests on a model of a deep and emotional subject, but this, too, is a vision of a relatively passive subject or vessel of answers – a wellspring of *feelings*.

ACTIVE INTERVIEWING

Years ago, Ithiel de Sola Pool (1957), a prominent critic of public opinion polling, argued that the dynamic, communicative contingencies of the interview literally activate respondents' opinions. Every interview, he suggested, is an "interpersonal drama with a developing plot" (p. 193). This metaphor conveys a far more active sense of interviewing than we see in traditional models. It is an image of the interview as an occasion for constructing, not merely discovering or conveying, information. As Pool indicated:

> The social milieu in which communication takes place [during interviews] modifies not only what a person dares to say but even what he thinks he chooses to say. And these variations in expression cannot be viewed as mere deviations from some underlying "true" opinion, for there is no neutral, non-social, uninfluenced situation to provide that baseline. (p. 192)

Conceiving of the interview as an interpersonal drama with a developing plot is part of a broader vision of reality as an ongoing, interpretive accomplishment. From this perspective, interview participants are practitioners of everyday life, constantly working to discern and designate the recognizable and orderly features of the experience in question. But meaning-making is not merely artful (Garfinkel, 1967); meaning is not built "from scratch" on each interpretive occasion. Rather, interpretation orients to, and is conditioned by, the substantive resources and contingencies of interaction.

In other words, meaningful reality is constituted at the nexus of the *hows* and the *whats* of experience, by way of *interpretive practice* – the procedures and resources used to apprehend, organize, and represent reality (Holstein, 1993; Holstein and Gubrium, 1994, Gubrium and Holstein, 2000). Interviewing is a form of interpretive practice involving respondents and interviewers as they articulate their orientations and understandings in terms of what Garfinkel (1967) calls "practical reasoning." Reality is continually "under construction." It is assembled using the interpretive resources at hand, in light of the contingencies of the moment. Meaning is not constantly formulated anew, but reflects relatively enduring local contingencies and conditions of possibility (Foucault, 1979), such as the research topics presented by interviewers, participants' biographical particulars, local ways of orienting to those topics, institutionalized ways of understanding and talking about things, and other accountable features of "what everyone knows" about a topic (Gubrium, 1988, 1989; Holstein and Gubrium, 1994, 2000a, 2000b; Gubrium and Holstein, 2000). Those resources are astutely and adroitly crafted to the demands of the occasion, so that meaning is neither predetermined nor absolutely unique.

Active participants

The image of the active interview transforms the view of the subject behind participants. The respondent is transformed from a repository of opinions and reason or a wellspring of emotions into a productive source of either form of knowledge. The subject behind the interviewer is similarly activated. From the time one identifies a research topic, to respondent selection, questioning and answering, and, finally, to the interpretation of responses, interviewing itself is a meaning-making project. The imagined subject behind the participant emerges as part of the project; it is not presumed to exist before or independently of the interview conversation. Within the interview itself, the subject is fleshed out – rationally, emotionally, in combination, or otherwise – in relation to the give-and-take of interviewing and the interview's research purposes. The interview *and* its participants are constantly developing.

Two sets of communicative contingencies enter into the interview's meaning-making activity. As noted earlier, one kind involves the substantive *whats* of the interview enterprise (see Gubrium and Holstein, 1997, 2000). The focus and emerging data of the research project provide interpretive resources for developing both the subject and his or her responses. For example, a project might center on the quality of care and quality of life of nursing home residents (see Gubrium, 1993). This might be part of a study related to the national debate about the proper organization of home and institutional care. If interviews are employed, participants draw out the substantiality of these topics, linking the topics to biographical particulars in the interview process, producing a subject who responds to, or is affected by, the matters under consideration. In one case, a nursing home resident might speak animatedly during an interview about the quality of care in her facility, asserting that, "for a woman, it ultimately gets down to feelings." This brings to mind Douglas's emotional subject, articulating a recognizable linkage between affect and gender. Another resident might coolly and methodically list her facility's qualities of care, never once mentioning her feelings about them. Offering her own take on the matter, the respondent might state that "getting emotional" over "these things" clouds clear judgment, implicating a different kind of subject, more like the rational respondent idealized in Converse and Schuman's text. Particular substantive resources – such as the common cultural link between women and feelings, the traditional cultural opposition of clear thought and emotionality, or institutionalized ways of dealing with emotional problems which are promoted by, say, psychoanalytic or twelve-step therapeutic methods – are used to form the subject.

A second communicative contingency of interviewing directs us to what we called the *hows* of the process. The standpoint from which information is offered is continually developed within ongoing interview interaction. In speaking of the quality of care, for example, nursing home residents, as interview respondents, not only offer substantive thoughts and feelings pertinent to the topic under consideration, but simultaneously and continuously monitor who they are in relation to the person questioning them. For example, prefacing her remarks about the quality of life in her facility with the statement "speaking as a woman," a nursing home resident informs the interviewer that she is to be heard as a woman, not as someone else – not a mere resident, cancer patient, or abandoned mother. If and when she subsequently comments, "If I were a man in this place," the resident frames her thoughts and feelings about the quality of life differently, producing an alternative subject. The respondent is clearly working up the context within which interview answers unfold as she designs her responses to be heard in a particular way (see Holstein and Gubrium, 2004).

Putting the whats *and* hows *to work*

Interviews, of course, hold no monopoly over interpretive practice. Nor are they the only occasions when subjects and their opinions, emotions, and reports are socially constructed. Why, then, is interviewing an especially useful venue for systematic social inquiry? One answer lies in the interview situation's special ability to concertedly incite the production of meanings that address issues relating to particular research concerns. In simple terms, interviews expressly put the *whats* and *hows* of interpretive practice to work. In standardized interviewing, the passive subject ostensibly engages in a "minimalist" version of interpretive practice, participants perceiving, inquiring about, and reporting experience in the interview exchange. Our active conception of the interview, however, invests the subject with a substantial repertoire of interpretive methods and an extensive stock of experiential materials.

On one side, the active view eschews the image of the vessel waiting to be tapped in favor of the notion that the respondent's interpretive capabilities are activated, stimulated, and cultivated in the interview exchange. The interview is also a commonly recognized occasion for formally and systematically provoking the respondent to formulate and talk about experience, opinions, and emotions in particular ways, implicating the interviewer, on the other side. Active interviewers do not merely coax their respondents into preferred responses to their questions. Rather, they converse with respondents in such a way that alternate possibilities and considerations come into play. Interviewers may suggest orientations to, and linkages between, diverse aspects of respondents' experience, hinting at – even inviting – interpretations that make use of specific resources, connections, and outlooks. Interviewers may explore incompletely articulated aspects of experience, encouraging respondents to develop topics in ways relevant to their own experience

(DeVault, 1990). In some interviews, the objective is not to dictate an interpretive frame, as a minimalist standardized survey approach would do, but to provide an environment conducive to the production of the range and complexity of meanings that might occur to all interview participants.

Pool's dramaturgic metaphor is apt because it refers to both the *whats* and the *hows* of the interview. As a drama, the interview conversation is scripted in that it has a topic or topics, distinguishable roles, and a format for conversation. But it also has a *developing* plot, in which topics, roles, and format are fashioned in the give-and-take of the interview. Viewed in this way, the interview is a kind of limited "improvisational" performance. The production is spontaneous, yet structured – focused within the loose parameters provided by the interviewer, who is also an active participant.

While the respondent, for one, actively constructs and assembles answers, he or she does not simply "break out" talking. Neither elaborate narratives nor one-word replies emerge without provocation. The active interviewer's role is to stimulate respondents' answers, working up responses in the process. Where standardized approaches to interviewing attempt to strip the interview of all but the most neutral, impersonal stimuli (but see Holstein and Gubrium, 1995 and Houtkoop-Steenstra, 2000, for a discussion of the inevitable failure of these attempts), an active sense of interviewing turns us to the narrative positions, resources, orientations, and precedents that are brought into play in the process. The interviewer attempts to activate an appropriate stock of knowledge (Schutz, 1967) and bring it to bear on the discussion at hand in ways that fit the research agenda.

Consider, for example, how diverse aspects of a respondent's knowledge, perspectives, roles, and orientations are activated and implicated in an interview involving an adult daughter who is caring for her mother – a victim of senile dementia – at home. The daughter is employed part-time, and shares the household with her employed husband and their two sons, one a part-time college student and the other a full-time security guard. The extract begins when the interviewer (I) asks the adult daughter (R) to describe her feelings about having to juggle so many needs and schedules. This relates to a discussion of the so-called "sandwich generation," which is said to be caught between having to raise their own children and seeing to the needs of frail elderly parents. Note how, after the interviewer asks the respondent what she means by saying that she has mixed feelings, the respondent makes explicit reference to various ways of thinking about the matter, as if to suggest that there is more than one plot to the story. The respondent displays considerable narrative activeness; she not only references possible *whats* of caregiving and family life, but, in the process, informs the interviewer of *how* she could construct her answer.

I: We were talking about, you said you were a member of the, what did you call it?

R: They say that I'm in the sandwich generation. You know, like we're sandwiched between having to care for my mother . . . and my grown kids and my husband. People are living longer now and you've got different generations at home and, I tell ya, it's a mixed blessing.

I: How do you feel about it in your situation?

R: Oh, I don't know. Sometimes I think I'm being a bit selfish because I gripe about having to keep an eye on Mother all the time. If you let down your guard, she wanders off into the back yard or goes out the door and down the street. That's no fun when your hubby wants your attention too. Norm works the second shift and he's home during the day a lot. I manage to get in a few hours of work, but he doesn't like it. I have pretty mixed feelings about it.

I: What do you mean?

R: Well, I'd say that as a daughter, I feel pretty guilty about how I feel sometimes. It can get pretty bad, like wishing that Mother were just gone, you know what I mean? She's been a wonderful mother and I love her very much, but if you ask me how I feel as a wife and mother, that's another matter. I feel like she's [the mother], well, intruding on our lives and just making hell out of raising a family. Sometimes I put myself in my husband's shoes and I just know how he feels. He doesn't say much, but I know that he misses my company, and I miss his of course. [*Pause*] So how do you answer that?

The interviewer then goes on to explain that the respondent should answer in the way she believes best represents her thoughts and feelings. But as the exchange unfolds, it becomes evident that "best" misrepresents the complexity of the respondent's thoughts and feelings. In the following extract, notice how the respondent struggles to sort her responses to accord with categorically distinct identities. At one point, she explains that she now knows how a wife could and should feel because she gathered from the way her husband and sons acted that "men don't feel things in the same way." This suggests that her own thoughts and feelings are drawn from a fund of gendered knowledge as well. Note, too, how at several points the interviewer collaborates with the respondent to define her identity as a respondent. The interviewer, in effect, also puts the *whats* and *hows* of the interview to work. At the very end of the preceding extract, the respondent suggests that other respondents' answers might serve to clarify the way she herself organized her responses, indicating that interpersonal contextualizing might encourage even more interpretations of her experience. She elaborates this position as she continues.

R: I try to put myself in their [husband and sons] shoes, try to look at it from their point of view, you know, from a man's way of thinking. I ask myself how it feels to have a part-time wife and mama. I ask myself how I'd feel. Believe me, I know he [husband] feels pretty rotten about it. Men get that way; they want what they want and the rest of the time, well, they're quiet, like nothing's the matter. I used to think I was going crazy with all the stuff on my mind and having to think about everything all at once and not being able to finish with one thing and get on to the other. You know how it gets – doing one thing and feeling bad about how you did something else and wanting to redo what you did or what you said. The way a woman does, I guess. I think I've learned that about myself. I don't know. It's pretty complicated thinking about it. [*Pause*] Let's see, how do I really feel?

I: Well, I was just wondering, you mentioned being sandwiched earlier and what a woman feels?

R: Yeah, I guess I wasn't all that sure what women like me feel until I figured out how Norm and the boys felt. I figured pretty quick that men are pretty good at sorting things out and that, well, I just couldn't do it, 'cause, well, men don't feel things the same way. I just wouldn't want to do that way anyway. Wouldn't feel right about it as a woman, you know what I mean? So, like they say, live and let live, I guess.

I: But as a daughter?

R: Yeah, that too. So if you ask me how I feel having Mother under foot all the time, I'd say that I remember not so far back that I was under foot a lot when I was a little girl and Mother never complained, and she'd help Dad out in the store, too. So I guess I could tell you that I'm glad I'm healthy and around to take care of her and, honestly, I'd do it all over again if I had to. I don't know. You've talked to other women about it. What do they say?

I: Well, uh

R: Naw, I don't want to put you on the spot. I was just thinking that maybe if I knew how others in my shoes felt, I might be able to sort things out better than I did for ya.

The respondent's comments about both the subject matter under consideration and how one does or should formulate responses show that the respondent, in collaboration with the interviewer, activates diverse communicative resources as an integral part of exchanging questions and answers. Viewing the interview as active, we can acknowledge and appreciate how the interviewer participates with the respondent in shifting positions in the interview so as to explore alternate perspectives and stocks of knowledge. The interviewer sets the general parameters for responses, constraining as well as provoking answers that are germane to the researcher's interest. The pertinence of what is discussed is partly defined by the research topic and partly by the substantive horizons of the ongoing interview exchange.

KEY POINTS

- The interview is an "interpersonal drama with a developing plot."
- The active interview participants in this "interpersonal drama" are constantly engaged in the work of meaning-making – the ongoing production of the recognizable features of everyday experience.
- The versions of meaningful experience that emerge from interviews are constituted in the interplay of the *hows* and the *whats* of interpretive practice.

> * Because all interviews involve the active construction of experiential reality, the traditional model of the respondent as a vessel of answers and the interviewer as a neutral interrogator loses its appeal.

ACTIVE INTERVIEW DATA

Compared to more conventional perspectives on interviewing, the active view might suggest that interviewing merely invites unacceptable forms of bias into the information gathering process. After all, in this view, far more is going on in interviews than simply retrieving information from respondents' repositories of knowledge. "Contamination" would seem to lurk everywhere.

This criticism only holds if one takes a narrow view of interpretive practice. Bias is a meaningful concept only if the subject is seen to possess a preformed, purely informational commodity that the interview process might somehow taint. But if interview responses are seen as products of interpretive practice, they are neither preformed, nor ever pure. Any interview situation – no matter how formalized, restricted, or standardized – relies upon interaction between participants who are constantly engaged in interpretive practice. Because interviewing is unavoidably collaborative (Garfinkel, 1967; Sacks et al., 1974), it is virtually impossible to free any interaction from those factors that could be construed as contaminants. Participants in an interview are inevitably implicated in making meaning. They are involved in meaning *construction*, not contamination.

While naturally occurring talk and interaction may appear to be more spontaneous or less "staged" than an interview, this is true only in the sense that such interaction is staged by persons other than an interviewer. Seemingly spontaneous conversations are not necessarily more "authentic" or bias-free. They simply take place in what have been conventionally recognized as non-interview settings. But these settings, too, play a definite role in the production of experiential knowledge – just like interview situations. Still, with the development of the interview society, and the related increasing deprivatization of personal experience (see Gubrium and Holstein, 1995; Holstein and Gubrium, 2000a), the interview is becoming more and more commonplace, increasingly making it a naturally occurring occasion in its own right for articulating experience.

Given this new, active sense of the interview, how does one make sense of interview data? Once we acknowledge that all interactional and discursive data are products of interpretive practice, analysis may center as much on the *hows* as on the *whats* of interviewing. For example, traditionally, interviews have been used in service to naturalistic research, focusing on *what* social worlds are like (see Gubrium and Holstein, 1997: Chap. 2). They are typically analyzed as more or less accurate descriptions of experience, as reports or representations (literally, re-presentations) of reality. Analysis takes the form of systematically grouping and summarizing the descriptions, and providing a coherent organizing framework that encapsulates and explains aspects of the social world that respondents portray. Respondents' interpretive activity is subordinated to the substance of what they report; the *whats* of experience take precedence over the *hows*.

When the researcher recognizes the activity behind the production of interview data, those data may also be analyzed to describe *how* interview talk is produced, as well as to show the dynamic interrelatedness of the *whats* and the *hows* of interview conversations. Respondents' comments are not viewed as reality reports delivered from a fixed repository. Instead, they are considered for the ways that they construct aspects of experiential reality in collaboration with the interviewer. The focus is as much on the assembly process as on what is assembled.

Using sociologically oriented forms of narrative and discourse analysis, conversational records of interpretive practice are examined to reveal reality-constructing practices as well as the subjective meanings that are circumstantially conveyed (see Baker, 2002; DeVault, 1990; Gubrium and Holstein, 1994, 2000; Holstein and Gubrium, 1994; Riessman, 1993; Silverman, 2001). The goal is to show how interview responses are produced in the interaction between interviewer and respondent, without losing sight of the meanings produced or the circumstances that mediate the meaning-making process. The analytic objective is not merely to describe the situated production of talk, but to show how what is being said relates to the experiences and lives being studied in the circumstances at hand. Viewing the interview as active means analysis must be every bit as rigorous as the analysis of conventionally construed interview data. Analyzing "active" interview data require discipline, methodical procedures, and sensitivity to both process and substance.

Writing up findings from interview data is itself an analytically active enterprise. Rather than viewing the process as a matter of letting the data "speak for themselves," the researcher empirically documents the meaning-making process. With ample illustration and reference to records of talk, the complex discursive activities through which respondents produce meaning are described. The goal is to explicate how meanings, their linkages and horizons, are actively constituted within the interview environment. Reports do not so much summarize and organize what interview participants have said, as they "de-construct" participants' talk to show the reader both the *hows* and the *whats* of narratives of lived experience.

KEY POINTS

- The concept of the active interview casts interview "bias" in a new light. All participants in an interview are implicated in making meaning. They are involved in meaning *construction*, not contamination.
- The leading question should not be whether or not interview procedures contaminate data, but how the interview generates useful information about the phenomenon of interest.
- Because interview data are products of interpretive practice, data analysis demands a new sensitivity to both the interview process and the unfolding substance of responses.

CONCLUDING POINTS

On a final note, we want to emphasize several leading points of this chapter. First, the active interview is *not* a particular type of interview, to be distinguished from other forms of interviewing. We use the term *active interview* to underscore the perspective that all interviews are unavoidably active meaning-making ventures. Even the standardized survey interview itself is active, despite the fact that standardization procedures seek to strictly limit the interviewer's input and restrict the respondent's range of interpretive actions (see, for example, Houtkoop-Steenstra, 2000; Maynard et al., 2002; Schaeffer and Maynard, 2002).

Second, by specifying the vision of an active interview, we are not simply offering an oblique criticism of standardized interviewing methods. In many ways, standardized survey practitioners are intimately aware of the details of interview interaction (see Converse and Schuman, 1974, for example). They deal with them as integral parts of the craft of interviewing. But their vessel-of-answers model provides the basis for problems and methodological challenges that are endemic to that model, not to interviewing in general. By calling attention to the activity inherent in interviewing, we are simply offering a competing epistemological model of the interview in order to expand our ways of understanding how we come to know about inner lives and social worlds. This model, of course, is replete with its own challenges.

Finally, by treating the interview as active, we are not saying that "anything goes" with respect to interviewing technique and analysis. The concept of the active interview provides us with an alternate way of construing the production and collection of information that demands its own set of methodological and analytic principles and guidelines related in the first instance to the distinction between the *whats* and *hows* of the interview process (see Gubrium and Holstein, 1997; Silverman, 2001). Indeed, acknowledging that the interview is active may render interview research even more complicated than conventional approaches already hold it to be. The active view widens the analytic purview of interview research to consider a wider array of questions than are the bailiwick of standardized or naturalistic approaches. The researcher can no longer be content to catalog what was said in an interview. The challenge of the active interview is to carefully consider what is said in relation to how, where, when, and by whom experiential information is conveyed, and to what end. Construing the interview as active, then, provides us with a much wider, more richly variegated field of inquiry than ever before. In an interview society, we must attend to both the *whats* and *hows* of interview practice if we wish to document how experiential data are assembled and produced on the contemporary scene (see Rose, 1998).

Recommended readings

The Active Interview by James A. Holstein and Jaber F. Gubrium (1995) describes the active interview in greater depth. It provides extensive illustration of the interactional, interpretive activity that is part and parcel of all interviewing.

InterViews by Steinar Kvale (1996) is an introduction to qualitative research interviewing. The book frames the issues in terms of the active view presented here.

The *Handbook of Interview Research* edited by Jaber F. Gubrium and James A. Holstein (2002b) is a thematic and encyclopedic collection of state-of-the-art descriptions of different approaches to interviewing. The handbook covers theoretical, technical, analytic, and representational issues relating to interview research.

"Ethnomethodological Analyses of Interviews" by Carolyn D. Baker (2002) describes how one goes about analyzing interview data as conversational interaction. The emphasis is on how interview participants do the work of conversational interaction in an interview situation.

"Interviews," Chapter 4 of *Interpreting Qualitative Data*, by David Silverman (2001) deals with a variety of approaches to interviewing. The chapter considers active interviewing in relation to different approaches, including emotionalism, constructionism, and ethnomethodology.

REFERENCES

Alasuutari, Pertti (1995) *Qualitative Methods and Analysis*. London: Sage.
Altheide, David L. and John M. Johnson (1994) "Criteria for Assessing Interpretive Validity in Qualitative Research," pp. 485–99 in *Handbook of Qualitative Research*, ed. Norman K. Denzin and Yvonna S. Lincoln. Newbury Park, CA: Sage.

Atkinson, Robert (2002) "The Life Story Interview," pp. 121–40 in *Handbook of Interview Research*, ed. Jaber F. Gubrium and James A. Holstein. Thousand Oaks, CA: Sage.

Baker, Carolyn D. (2002) "Ethnomethodological Analyses of Interviews," pp. 777–95 in *Handbook of Interview Research*, ed. Jaber F. Gubrium and James A. Holstein. Thousand Oaks, CA: Sage.

Berger, Peter L. and Thomas Luckmann (1967) *The Social Construction of Reality*. New York: Doubleday.

Blumer, Herbert (1969) *Symbolic Interactionism*. New York: Prentice Hall.

Briggs, Charles (1986) *Learning How to Ask: A Sociolinguistic Appraisal of the Role of the Interviewer in Social Science Research*. Cambridge: Cambridge University Press.

Cicourel, Aaron V. (1964) *Method and Measurement in Sociology*. New York: Free Press.

Cicourel, Aaron V. (1974) *Theory and Method in a Study of Argentine Fertility*. New York: Wiley.

Converse, Jean M. and Howard Schuman (1974) *Conversations at Random: Survey Research as Interviewers See It*. New York: Wiley.

DeVault, Marjorie (1990) "Talking and Listening from Women's Standpoint: Feminist Strategies for Interviewing and Analysis," *Social Problems*, 37: 96–117.

Douglas, Jack D. (1985) *Creative Interviewing*. Beverly Hills, CA: Sage.

Fontana, Andrea and James H. Frey (2000) "Interviewing: The Art of Science," pp. 361–76 in *Handbook of Qualitative Research*, ed. Norman K. Denzin and Yvonna S. Lincoln. Newbury Park, CA: Sage.

Foucault, Michel (1979) *Discipline and Punish*. New York: Vintage.

Fowler, Floyd J. and Thomas W. Mangione (1990) *Standardized Survey Interviewing*. Newbury Park, CA: Sage.

Garfinkel, Harold (1967) *Studies in Ethnomethodology*. Englewood Cliffs, NJ: Prentice Hall.

Gorden, Raymond L. (1987) *Interviewing: Strategy, Techniques, and Tactics*. Homewood, IL: Dorsey.

Gubrium, Jaber F. (1988) *Analyzing Field Reality*. Beverly Hills, CA: Sage.

Gubrium, Jaber F. (1989) "Local Cultures and Service Policy," pp. 94–112 in *The Politics of Field Research*, ed. Jaber F. Gubrium and David Silverman. London: Sage.

Gubrium, Jaber F. (1993) *Speaking of Life: Horizons of Meaning for Nursing Home Residents*. Hawthorne, NY: Aldine de Gruyter.

Gubrium, Jaber F. and James A. Holstein (1994) "Analyzing Talk and Interaction," pp. 173–88 in *Qualitative Methods in Aging Research*, ed. J. Gubrium and A. Sankar. Newbury Park, CA: Sage.

Gubrium, Jaber F. and James A. Holstein (1995) "Biographical Work and New Ethnography," pp. 45–58 in *The Narrative Study of Lives*, Vol. 3, ed. Ruthellen Josselson and Amia Lieblich. Newbury Park, CA: Sage.

Gubrium, Jaber F. and James A. Holstein (1997) *The New Language of Qualitative Method*. New York: Oxford University Press.

Gubrium, Jaber F. and James A. Holstein (2000) "Analyzing Interpretive Practice," pp. 487–508 in *Handbook of Qualitative Research*, Second Edition, ed. Norman K. Denzin and Yvonna S. Lincoln. Thousand Oaks, CA: Sage.

Gubrium, Jaber F. and James A. Holstein (2002a) "From the Individual Interview to the Interview Society," pp. 3–32 in *Handbook of Interview Research*, ed. Jaber F. Gubrium and James A. Holstein. Thousand Oaks, CA: Sage.

Gubrium, Jaber F. and James A. Holstein (eds.) (2002b) *Handbook of Interview Research*. Thousand Oaks, CA: Sage.

Gubrium, Jaber F. and James A. Holstein (2003) *Postmodern Interviewing*. Thousand Oaks, CA: Sage.

Harding, Sandra (ed.) (1987) *Feminism and Methodology*. Bloomington: Indiana University Press.

Heritage, John (1984) *Garfinkel and Ethnomethodology*. Cambridge: Polity.

Holstein, James A. (1993) *Court-Ordered Insanity: Interpretive Practice and Involuntary Commitment*. Hawthorne, NY: Aldine de Gruyter.

Holstein, James A. and Jaber F. Gubrium (1994) "Phenomenology, Ethnomethodology, and Interpretive Practice," pp. 262–72 in *Handbook of Qualitative Research*, ed. Norman K. Denzin and Yvonna Lincoln. Newbury Park, CA: Sage.

Holstein, James A. and Jaber F. Gubrium (1995) *The Active Interview*. Thousand Oaks, CA: Sage.

Holstein, James A. and Jaber F. Gubrium (2000a) *Constructing the Life Course*. Walnut Creek, CA: AltaMira.

Holstein, James A. and Jaber F. Gubrium (2000b) *The Self We Live By: Narrative Identity in a Postmodern World*. New York: Oxford University Press.

Holstein, James A. and Jaber F. Gubrium (2004) "Context: Working It Up, Down, and Across," in *Qualitative Research Practice*, ed. Clive Seale, Giampietro Gobo, Jaber F. Gubrium, and David Silverman. London: Sage.

Holstein, James A. and William G. Staples (1992) "Producing Evaluative Knowledge: The Interactional Bases of Social Science Findings," *Sociological Inquiry*, 62: 11–35.

Houtkoop-Steenstra, Hanneke (2000) *Interaction and the Standardized Survey Interview*. Cambridge: Cambridge University Press.

Hyman, Herbert H., William J. Cobb, Jacob J. Feldman, Clyde W. Hart, and Charles H. Stember (1975) *Interviewing in Social Research*. Chicago: University of Chicago Press.

Johnson, John M. (2002) "In-Depth Interviewing," pp. 121–40 in *Handbook of Interview Research*, ed. Jaber F. Gubrium and James A. Holstein. Thousand Oaks, CA: Sage.

Kirk, Jerome and Marc L. Miller (1986) *Reliability and Validity in Qualitative Research*. Beverly Hills, CA: Sage.

Kvale, Steinar (1996) *InterViews*. London: Sage.

Maccoby, Eleanore E. and Nathan Maccoby (1954) "The Interview: A Tool of Social Science," pp. 449–87 in *Handbook of Social Psychology*, ed. Gardner Lindzey. Reading, MA: Addison-Wesley.

Madge, John (1965) *The Tools of Social Science*. Garden City, NY: Anchor Books.

Manning, Peter L. (1967) "Problems in Interpreting Interview Data," *Sociology and Social Research*, 51: 301–16.

Maynard, Douglas W., H. Houtkoop-Steenstra, J. van der Zouwen, and N.C. Schaeffer (eds.) (2002) *Standardization and Tacit Knowledge: Interaction and Practice in the Survey Interview*. New York: Wiley.

Mishler, Elliot G. (1986) *Research Interviewing*. Cambridge, MA: Harvard University Press.

Mishler, Elliot G. (1991) "Representing Discourse: The Rhetoric of Transcription," *Journal of Narrative and Life History*, 1: 255–80.

Pollner, Melvin (1987) *Mundane Reason*. Cambridge: Cambridge University Press.

Pool, Ithiel de Sola (1957) "A Critique of the Twentieth Anniversary Issue," *Public Opinion Quarterly*, 21: 190–8.

Reinharz, Shulamit (1992) *Feminist Methods of Social Research*. New York: Oxford University Press.

Riessman, Catherine Kohler (1993) *Narrative Analysis*. Newbury Park, CA: Sage.

Rogers, Carl R. (1945) "The Non-Directive Method as a Technique for Social Research," *American Journal of Sociology*, 50: 279–83.

Rose, Nikolas (1998) *Inventing Our Selves*. Cambridge: Cambridge University Press.

Sacks, Harvey, Emanuel Schegloff, and Gail Jefferson (1974) "A Simplest Systematics for the Organization of Turn-Taking in Conversation," *Language*, 50: 696–735.

Schaeffer, Nora Cate and Douglas W. Maynard (2002) "Standardization and Interaction in the Survey Interview," pp. 577–601 in *Handbook of Interview Research*, ed. Jaber F. Gubrium and James A. Holstein. Thousand Oaks, CA: Sage.

Schutz, Alfred (1967) *The Phenomenology of the Social World*. Evanston, IL: Northwestern University Press.

Silverman, David (2001) *Interpreting Qualitative Data*, Second Edition. London: Sage.

Singleton, Royce A. and Bruce C. Straits (2002) "Survey Interviewing," pp. 59–82 in *Handbook of Interview Research*, ed. Jaber F. Gubrium and James A. Holstein. Thousand Oaks, CA: Sage.

Smith, Dorothy E. (1987) *The Everyday World as Problematic: A Feminist Sociology*. Boston: Northeastern University Press.

Terkel, Studs (1972) *Working*. New York: Avon.

Warren, Carol A.B. (2002) "Qualitative Interviewing," pp. 83–102 in *Handbook of Interview Research* ed. Jaber F. Gubrium and James A. Holstein. Thousand Oaks, CA: Sage.

9 Membership categorization and interview accounts

Carolyn Baker

Interviews are among the most widely used methods of data generation in the social sciences (see Gubrium and Holstein, 2002). While a great deal has been written for decades about the procedures for generating such data (how to ask questions, how to relate), rather less attention has been given until relatively recently to the analysis of such data. A focus on *analysis*, a focus on the researcher's expertise in the analysis of the *interactional* data as much as in the generation of it, changes significantly how interviewing may be understood and pursued within the social sciences.

INVESTIGATING INTERIORS AND EXTERIORS

From many conventional social science perspectives, the relevant researcher expertise is in the getting of the data, and criteria of success at interviewing include such matters as whether there was good 'rapport', whether the respondents talked a lot, and what they talked about, whether and how they divulged what the interviewer was after. All such criteria of success rely on the assumption that there is pre-existing information of some sort (e.g. beliefs, attitudes, knowledge, perspectives) to extract from the respondent. The interviewer attempts to position her- or himself as colleague, friend or confessor in order that the respondent speaks openly, authentically or truthfully, to produce valid reporting on some interior or exterior state of affairs. From within this romantic notion of special connection between interviewer and respondent, an interview can be found to be good or not, successful or not.

The analysis which follows from this conventional perspective typically seeks 'themes' in the content of what is said by the respondent. This perspective on interview data might be captured by the phrase 'from thought through language to themes'. That is, the contents of the respondents' thoughts (beliefs etc.) are expressed in the medium of language (the interviewer's task is to encourage this expression) and then this content is rethematized by the analyst, who typically chunks the data, categorizes them, moves them around and rearranges them into a different formation. The words spoken by the respondents and the ideas they are heard to represent are 'the data'. This is a common-sense view of interviewing in which the interviewer, and later the analyst, investigate 'interiors' (states of mind) or 'exteriors' (descriptions of social settings) through a representational view of language.

INVESTIGATING TALK AS SOCIAL ACTION

Another way of approaching the analysis of interview data brackets this common-sense perspective, and brings into play a different set of assumptions about language and social action. Drawing on earlier work in which I analysed interview talk between an adult researcher and adolescent subjects (see Baker, 1984; Silverman, 1993), I will explicate further how the use of 'membership categorization devices' is a key to treating interview data differently. In this perspective, (1) interviewing is understood as an interactional event in which members draw on their cultural knowledge, including their knowledge about how members of categories routinely speak; (2) questions are a central part of the data and cannot be viewed as neutral invitations to speak – rather, they shape how and as a member of which categories the respondents should speak; (3) interview responses are treated as accounts more than reports – that is, they are understood as the work of accounting by a member of a category for activities attached to that category. This accounting work is the core of the analysis of data. In this accounting work, we look for the use of membership categorization devices by the interviewer and respondent, and show how both are involved in the generation of versions of social reality built around categories and activities. Further, in the work done with categories and activities, we see the local production in each case of versions of a moral order.

It is helpful to understand that from this perspective the process of interviewing is better described not as data 'collection', but rather as data 'making' or data 'generation'. The analysis of interview data from talk or transcripts of the talk is organized not to locate interior beliefs or knowledges or to seek actual descriptions of social settings. Rather it is organized to identify the speakers' methods of using categories and activities in accounts. This is a round-about way (but the only one possible) of identifying cultural knowledge and logic *in use*. Cultural knowledge is audible and visible in how people account to one another, whatever might be inside their heads. This approach draws also on Sacks's introduction of the possibilities of using conversational data to do sociology, and on Silverman's many analyses of interview data. It sets up the interviewer and respondent as ordinary competent members of the culture and the analyst as *post hoc* ethnomethodologist, looking for the social–organizational work being done by interviewer and respondent. The speakers are viewed as competent observer–analysts of the interaction they are involved in. It is their artful use of talk we look for in analysis. In this approach, it is not interviews that are good or bad, successful or unsuccessful, in themselves. The criterion of success is the ability of the analyst to explicate the routine grounds of the work that interviewer and respondent do together to assign sense and meaning to the interiors or exteriors they talk about.

MEMBERS' ANALYTIC RESOURCES

Members have analytic resources that they put to work as they engage in any kind of talk, including interview talk. One of those resources is the use of membership categorization devices as introduced by Sacks (1992). Talk, further, is not simply expressive of interior states or contents. Talk is social action: people achieve identities, realities, social order and social relationships through talk. How people describe things and how they reason about them are pragmatic selections from a range of possibilities. Even 'simple' describing is always a social and moral activity (Jayyusi, 1984, 1991; Schegloff, 1988) turning on category identifications. Imagine the differences in being approached to speak as 'a mother of three' and being approached to speak as 'a professor'. Both may be correct identifiers, but the selection made calls on very different domains of knowledge and reason. To account for oneself 'as a mother' calls into play other related categories (such as 'children') and activities or properties associated with those categories (e.g. 'needs' of children, caringness, guilt). Speaking 'as a professor' invokes a different set of category relevances and activities (e.g. 'students', teaching, theorizing or researching). When we are asked to speak in some situation, as in an interview for example, we mobilize the resources of available membership categorization devices. These devices are collections of categories and associated activities (such as mother + father + children = nuclear family).

An anecdote will make more striking the point about members' uses of membership categorizations to assign social identities and achieve social order. Recently I observed the following scene. A woman, a young male child holding a screwdriver, and a man entered a bakery. The woman behind the counter greeted them and then addressed the child as follows: *'Have you been helping Daddy?'* There was a pause that I distinctly remember because, as an observer–analyst of the scene, I had time to consider the gender assumption being made: that *Daddy* was being helped rather than the mother. The woman customer then spoke: *'This is not Daddy.'* What resources had the woman behind the counter used to generate her 'mistake'? Should we take it that the woman customer is the child's mother? *Is this Mommy?* How do we hear her that way?

Category incumbencies are 'made to happen', are produced (and sometimes corrected) in talk. We routinely and pre-reflectively use membership categorization devices to organize our characterizations of what we see or hear. Membership categorization is a pervasive resource for sense-making through utterances. Tracing members' use of these categories and devices in any settings, including interview settings, is a means of showing how identities, social relationships and even institutions are produced.

INTERVIEW TALK AS ACCOUNTING

The first segment from interview talk to be studied here comes from an interview that took place as part of routine institutional practice but was recorded for research purposes. The following interview extract shows the opening turns of an audio-recorded parent–teacher interview (Baker and Keogh, 1995). Right from the beginning, participants immediately go to work with their own and the others' membership categories relevant to this encounter (see the Appendix to this volume for transcription key).

Teacher (T): Ellen
Student: Donna
Parent(s):   Mother (M) and Father (F)

1   T: Ok all right we'll just forget it I should cover it up or something I hate tape recorders! (hh) Right um Donna um I just took over Mister Jay's class um four weeks ago so, I don't really know a lot about Donna's work I've had a quick look at her work in her folder, and from her marks she um, you seem to have, passed in the first part of the year and then really gone down in last two um, pieces of work which was a poetry oral? and a um a novel (2.0) a novel in another form that was putting part of the novel into another style of writing. Now um (2.0) in class (1.0) Donna's a little bit distracted? often? down the back there, with um the girls that she sits with, though she does give in class when she's asked to, she does do all her work, um I'm (1.0) would you like to – do you work with Donna at home with her schoolwork at all? do you see it at all or?

2   F: Not really no=

3   M: =(We very rarely) see her schoolwork

4   F: they generally disappear off to their bedrooms with their homework and um=

5   T: =Ye:es (2.0) Well um

6   F: We don't see much of (it)

7   T: Let me see yes I didn't mark this this was all Mr Jay's (1.0) This is a summary, they had to summarize um this (1.0) um let's see where her, mistakes seem to lie. (3.0) Oh it seems alright. (3.0) Why did she only get four and a half for that. Hmmm.

In the teacher's long first turn, she describes her work in considerable detail and accounts for possible shortcomings in that work prior to turning the talk over to the parents or Donna. The turn combines information segments (how Donna is doing, how she is in class) with apology segments (how the teacher is herself doing in the interview). The combination can be seen as depicting the category of 'teacher' as one who: has first-hand and long-term knowledge of the student; can read other teachers' notations and make sense of them; observes what is going on, where, in the classroom; knows who the student's friends in class are; and knows what the parents want to know. The prefacing of the turn with the information that she is not Donna's long-time teacher and then turning directly to Donna's marks is also a characterization in her talk of the category 'parents' as those who want to know about Donna's academic achievement in the first instance and want to know about her behaviour in class. The teacher's first turn can be heard as an elaborate version of 'who I am/what I know/what my relevancies are, and who you are/what you know/what your relevancies are, and what we want of each other': a way of connecting the two institutional categories, teacher and parents. Donna, the subject of the talk, is present but silent. The teacher's work here can be seen as identifying, colouring in and connecting the two institutional categories of parent and teacher. In Silverman's (1993: 114) terms, she is assembling connections between cultural particulars.

The teacher also calls on unnamed but alluded-to student categories in scenic descriptions such as 'down the back there, with um the girls that she sits with'. These describings are forms of social action done through talk (cf. Schegloff, 1988).

At the end of the first turn the teacher changes the topic to what the parents do at home concerning schoolwork. The teacher's question to the parents, 'would you like to – do you work with Donna at home with her schoolwork at all? do you see it at all or?' begins like a perspective display series (cf. Maynard, 1991) asking for the clients' view of matters but then introduces what looks like an information question. This is information seeking, but in terms of interaction in the interview it is more than that. It is a further elaboration of the category 'parents' – done by adding to 'parenting', as already established, the category-related attribute of possibly working with Donna or seeing what she does at home or something else. The question gives three options of descending involvement for what parents might do: work with Donna's schoolwork (at all = ever? sometimes?), see Donna's schoolwork (at all = ever? sometimes?), or? (hearably, something even less?).

INTERVIEW TALK AS CATEGORY ELABORATION

Before the parents have had a single turn at the formal business of the interview, the teacher has, using her knowledge of category memberships and related activities, presented a complex social landscape that connects the interests, territories and activities of parents and teachers. The landscape is also a moral one now in several respects, including the descending order of parental help to Donna laid out as the teacher asks the parents to speak.

As member–analysts of this scene, the parents can take it that the teacher wants to know what happens at home and where it fits in her descending order. 'Not really no' and 'we very rarely see her schoolwork' are heavily mitigated answers to the information question. The sense these turns produce is that something interferes with this legitimate parental task, and that is that 'they generally disappear off to their bedrooms with their homework'. This is an artfully constructed account. Who 'they' is is not clear, but it is *more than just Donna*. Donna has now been placed in an unnamed category of people who 'disappear off . . . with their homework'. It could be as if Donna cannot wait to get at her homework, she disappears off so fast, and that is why the parents do not see it or work with her. The teacher is called upon to recognize this scenic description of home life.

We now have at least two Donnas produced in this talk: distracted school Donna who sits with the girls at the back (but nevertheless does do her work in class), and keen home Donna who disappears off to do homework. Both are moral constructions of Donna at the same time that they are moral constructions of the speakers themselves as observant parents and teacher.

This analysis suggests a way of beginning a membership categorization device analysis of interview talk. We have in this talk a topic which is 'Donna and her school achievement'. This topic is introduced explicitly, then elaborated through various proposed descriptors of Donna's activities. These descriptors can be seen as 'activities' in terms of the notion of 'category-bound activities' which imply membership in categories. In this case, the descriptors do not all get 'bound' to the category Donna, nor even 'attached' very firmly, since the speakers go on to delve further into Donna's activities. These descriptions of Donna, then, are candidate descriptions, which may or may not turn out to be 'attached' to Donna in the end. The descriptions variously state or imply Donna's membership in possible categories such as distracted student, keen student, and so on. The talk is a display of speakers' knowledge of how such statements and implications might be heard by the other: they use what might be termed social–structural and cultural knowledge. It is certainly at least inter-institutional knowledge that they draw on to do these descriptions of Donna. It is in this sense that the talk provides us with an insight into what they know. What they know is how to do descriptions and how to do accounts in precisely this inter-institutional setting. Remember that their descriptions of Donna are reflexively descriptions of themselves: 'they disappear off to their bedrooms', placed just where it was in the talk, is effectively a scenic description of a parent who could not possibly help with homework, not by his own choice.

In this interview, then, there is much more than the asking for or getting of information or perspectives about Donna and her work. The interview itself is a site for displaying the cultural knowledges that can be used to account for oneself as a competent parent or teacher. These cultural knowledges turn on the naming of or sometimes merely alluding to category, category relations or category-bound activities.

What this recommends for the analysis of interview data is the identification of the category knowledges at work in the talk of the participants. These need not be contained in elaborated turns, but can be sketched – spoken in shorthand – with the same effects. As seen above, a single utterance can call on and convey a great deal of cultural knowledge through its design and placement in talk.

The parent–teacher interviews from which this extract was drawn are thick with accounting on both sides. They are 'inter-views' in the original sense of 'entrevoir' – 'see each other' – perhaps more than are most research interviews.

The talk is not symmetrical but questioning is done by both parties, and there is often a practical outcome in the form of resolutions or advice towards which the participants continue to talk. The interview is often conducted or organized by at least two parties, and three where the student is present and both student and parent(s) are involved in raising topics or responding to them. In one interview with the teacher, father and student present, the interview became an extended speech by the father, with the teacher positioned as audience and the student mostly silent. These parent–teacher interviews have family resemblances to many health, clinical and other institutional encounters and consultations where problems concerning one of the parties to the talk (the client) are discussed. The approach to analysis represented here is interested in the pragmatics of the interactional setting. How people do things with words, and what they do with them, are the focus of interest.

MEMBERSHIP CATEGORIZATION WORK IN RESEARCH INTERVIEWS

Another category of interviews are those which are conducted for research purposes only, which would not have taken place had the research not been undertaken. Unlike the interview described above, research interviews are designed and conducted in order that respondents will speak about some topic of interest to the researcher. In such interviews a more asymmetrical organization of talk is usually seen, with the interviewer asking questions or making probes, while the interviewee talks at more length to supply the information sought.

Such interviews are typically conducted under the traditional social science stand which asks respondents to reveal, describe, report on their interiors or on their external world as they know it. The respondent is positioned essentially as a witness of his or her own interiors and exterior circumstances who gives testimony to his or her experience of events. In this mode of doing social science, the sticky problems of bias (on the interviewer's part) and truth-telling (on the witness's part) come to the fore.

These problems were encountered in analyses of research interviews conducted with 'young adolescents' (Baker, 1984). These interviews were saturated with category talk in the form of powerful assumptions about activities attaching to the category 'adolescent' (see Silverman, 1993: 90–114 for extracts and discussion). These assumptions were lodged right inside the interviewer's questions, for example 'when do you think you'll be an adult?' The resulting talk by the interviewees to questions such as this was rife with talk about responsibilities, the end of carefree living, and other cultural icons of conventional adulthood. The way out of this incestuous relation between interviewer categories and interviewee categories was to treat the interview data as displays of membership categorization work by interviewees as well as interviewer. What this resulted in was in the end not about 'adolescents' or these particular individuals at all, but about how the people positioned as 'adolescents' in the interview used membership categorization analysis in answering the questions. Especially in their use of category-bound or category-implied activities attached to each of the life stages that the interviewer had presented as given, the respondents produced accounts which displayed their cultural knowledge about *adult* constructions of adolescence. If we take this one step further, they displayed their knowledge of culture as framed up through the adult lens of life-stage folk psychology. This is the particular cultural knowledge they activated in order to take part in the interview, on the interviewer's terms. It is cultural knowledge in three senses: first, it is knowledge about the culture; second, it is not specific to individual respondents but reappears in different people's accounts; and third, it demonstrated a 'successful' reading of the particular interview situation: how does this person want me to speak? Which of the many possible ways of characterizing my membership is in play here?

Letting go the presumption that (good) interviews give us some kind of privileged insight into what people really think, believe or do is the first step to seeing interview data as the production of situated 'accountings-for' whatever is the topic the interviewer presents. In Silverman's terms, '[b]y analysing how people talk to one another, one is directly gaining access to a cultural universe and its content of moral assumptions' (1993: 108).

MEMBERSHIP CATEGORIZATION AND CULTURAL LOGICS

A very large proportion of research interviews would be conducted for the purpose of finding out some specific information, perspectives or beliefs. Such interviews are typically characterized by a very asymmetrical organization of talk, in which the interviewer asks the questions but talks much less than the respondent. In such circumstances, the material for analysis is in large part the talk done by the respondent to make available to the interviewer whatever information is asked for.

In a study undertaken of a school's 'welfare system', I was interested to capture the sense and logic behind the system. The system in question was an elaborate system of teacher-assigned 'tickets' to students for good or poor behaviour. Tickets were physically issued to students, either yellow ones for good achievement or behaviour, or white for misbehaviour of some kind.

My knowledge of the system came from visiting the school on several occasions and attending a staff meeting in which changes to the rules were being discussed at considerable length (see Baker (1997) for an analysis of the staff meeting talk).

A talk was later arranged with the Chair of the Welfare Committee. I invited the Chair to give his view of the system, a 'perspective display'.

```
1   I:   Um. What's what's your view (.) of of the system [is it
2   C:   [It's great. It's um (1.0) the good kids it it kind of recognizes what
```

their their efforts ( ) they get. The kids who it is hard for (1.0) who don't get the yellow (.) tickets um ( ) kids who just plod along and they usually don't, mightn't get a yellow ticket for because they haven't done anything extra great (.) but they still go up the system because, if they don't get a ticket, don't get a white ticket for ten weeks they go up anyway. Um (2.0) they're the ones that, you know, you try to encourage (staff), if you look for the plodders who are just plodding along but who are probably putting as much effort in as the (.) people who are getting, you know, the best marks in the class, we try and encourage that.

3   I: It is now possible for the plodders as you say to get up to plus four?

4   C: <u>No</u>. They can still only, still only get to (.) to negative er positive two. ((Sound of paper rustling. 4.0)) Let's see. (10.0) That's basically the state of the nation, that's, the issues. (1.5)

The Chair's view is reported directly and minimally in his first answer: 'It's <u>great</u>'. What follows is an account of how the system is working well, and how it is not. This account turns on the early production of two contrasting categories of students: the 'good kids', whom the system rewards, and the 'plodders'. Thus a membership categorization device of the form [good kids, plodders] is produced, to which further categories could later be added. There are activities attached to the main contrast pair [good kids, plodders] as these categories are produced. The system works well for good kids who have their efforts recognized, but it does not work so well for plodders who 'just plod along' and never get a yellow ticket because they do not do anything 'extra great'. On the other hand, the Chair remarks, the plodders do not get white tickets either and are 'probably putting as much effort in' as the 'people . . . getting . . . the best marks in the class' – a category who may or may not be the same as the 'good kids' he began with.

The interviewer has heard a problem being stated, and asks whether the plodders can now get up to the top of the scale. This question is an acknowledgement of the problem and of the categorization device [good kids, plodders]. It perfectly matches the Chair's concern about how high up the system the plodders can get, and shows the interviewer entering into the problematic. Both interviewer and interviewee characterize the plodders as ambitious in this respect, and the system as autonomously constraining their ascent. This organization of empathy with the plodders confirms their reality in the social world of the school.

The design of the Chair's answer is as important as the contents of it. There may or may not really be good kids and plodders; these may or may not be the same descriptors used elsewhere in discussing the system. The production of the two categories is part of an account which elaborates what we could call a local morality. Looking at the beginning of the Chair's response, we hear that the system is at once 'great', it rewards the efforts of 'good kids', but is hard on 'all the other kids that just plod along'. From this it would appear that a minority of students is benefiting and a majority is not.

As the account proceeds there are some revisions made to the problem and a form of response to the problem is described. The Chair remarks that staff are encouraged to 'look for the plodders', although it is not clear what is supposed to be done differently for plodders except to recognize them. Here 'plodders' are produced as types of students any teacher could recognize. The category device now connects staff and students [good kids, plodders, teachers] – the cast of characters so far – and we can note that they are connected through attributions of empathy and care. Describing plodders now as 'probably putting in as much effort' effects a reorganization of 'plodder' character (earlier, twice, they 'just plod along'). Talk about the distribution of tickets (giving or not giving) seems to refer to an underlying organization of sympathy. Whether or not staff are in fact encouraged to 'look out for plodders', in this interview at least this response to the problem brings forward a version of a duty of care that teachers have towards plodders. This duty of care was not attached to these students when they were (earlier in the answer) 'just plodding along'. At that earlier point they were described as not getting tickets and this was represented as a natural consequence of their (plodding) behaviour, although it was acknowledged that the system is 'hard' for them.

Far from being merely a 'report' about the operation of the ticketing system, this account displays a version of the local practical reasoning that members could use to describe the system. The account is designed to convey the speaker's recognition of the categorizations, motivations and morality that attach to teachers' work with the system. That is, the social world of the school (the 'exterior' being talked about here) is assembled as a complex of categories and motivations which produce a moral order as well as a setting of practical reasoning and action.

Each move in the interview serves to add to and elaborate on the categories and activities proposed in the initial description. Such categories and activities are woven into a set of relationships and values, including justifications and evaluations, in the course of the telling. In effect a moral ordering of this aspect of the work of the school is being done while the Chair provides his views.

The interview continues:

```
 5  I:  Could I get a copy of that?
 6  C:  Yeah you can have that copy.
 7  I:  Thank you.
        (1.0)
 8  C:  Um, we've also got a wel- welfare policy that [principal] a draft
        one that we put together. I'll give you a copy of that too.
 9  I:  Thanks.
        (1.0)
10  C:  Er, we chang- this is different to last year's (.) in that after three
        white tickets they get a warning letter (.) home, and then five white
        tickets they go on to negative one and then another three (1.0)
        they get to er another warning letter, and from here to there is only
```

three so from (.) negative level two to negative level four (.) is going
to be, very quick (.) progression if they continue on (.) on like this.
11 I: Mmm
    (3.0)

In turn 10 the Chair offers the topic of how the system was changed from last
year's. In this turn another category of student is implied through a description
of descent to lower levels of the system. This additional category implied
through talk about tickets and warning letters sent home is the poorly behaved
student who did not appear in the initial description. Such students are ones
who could, hypothetically, 'continue on like this' (getting more and more
white tickets) and who would, in fact, have a quick progression to the bottom
of the levels system. A downward descent is the *only* direction implied in the
organization of the Chair's description, although presumably not everyone
who gets to negative level two does in fact travel down to negative level four,
and the system is elsewhere said to be designed to catch and stop such
descents. The downward descent is accounted for by the possible activity
attached to students in this category, 'if they continue on like this', which
assigns the agency involved to the students persisting in their inappropriate
behaviour. The Chair's concluding formulation 'so from two to four is going
to be a very quick progression if they continue on like this' is first treated as
a description and appears soon after to be heard *as a problem*.

The interviewer, as recipient of the Chair's description, first provides a weak
agreement with the assessment made by the Chair. After a pause, the Chair
starts to speak again, at which point the interviewer provides a stronger
agreement, returning the upshot that progression downward will be quick:

11 I: Mmm
12 (3.0)
13 C: ([ )
14 I: ([Quick, yeah.

The design of the Chair's next turn suggests that the interviewer's appreciation
of the upshot has not been strong enough, that she is still hearing it as a
description rather than as a problem.

14 I: ([Quick, yeah.
15 C: So it's only an extra from negative level two which is ten white
        tickets, it's only another <u>three</u> and then negative level <u>three</u> (.) and
        (.) another another three after that and they can be (.) it's up to
        suspension sort of stage so it's um (2.0) that's where all the kind of
        er (.) er counsellor and er (2.0) all the work with the parents etcetera
        has to be done (.) fairly quickly. Because a kid can get to this stage
        in the matter of a <u>week</u>, you know, well kids <u>have</u>. I- and (.) what we
        also look at is now is (.) that (.) three white tickets if it's within a (.) um
        (1.0) from one teacher we try to kind of counsel the teacher more than
        (2.0) so (.) so <u>one</u> teacher hasn't got that effect on one kid, so one
        one theoretically one teacher can put someone on negative level (.)

two in a matter of a couple of <u>weeks</u> if they're having a run-in with
them. So now we're trying to, looking at, if one teacher's giving out
three or five white tickets we try to kind of (1.0) find out what the
problem <u>is</u> with the teacher as well, more so than (1.0) just the student.
16　I:　Do you cancel the ticket?
17　C:　Well it can be yeah I (mean) we can't <u>cancel</u> them but we <u>can</u>
cancel them we ask the teacher

In turn 15, the Chair embellishes the point he made earlier about quick
descent, that it is 'only' another three tickets that drives the student down the
levels. This was the change from last year's policy introduced in turn 10,
and it is a change that he, and not the interviewer, has made accountable. In
making it accountable in this way, he has underscored its status as a problem. Retrospectively, it seems the interviewer's earlier appreciation of what
it means was not stated strongly enough; she was not grasping the moral
point.

The Chair's turn in 15 can be seen as having three parts, beginning with
the elaboration of the speed of descent and its consequentiality: that is, serious
trouble for those students. At the centre of the turn is a central fact that holds
the whole turn, and the whole logic, together: *'Because a kid can get to this
stage in the matter of a <u>week</u> you know, well kids <u>have</u>'*, of which more below.
In the latter part of the turn, a new category of problem actor in the system
is described: teachers who give out too many white tickets to one kid. This
category is generated as another account of how a kid could get to this stage
so fast. In contrast to the kid 'continuing on like this' in turn 10, now we
have teachers having run-ins with kids and needing counselling themselves.
The description of these teachers appears to be something of a trouble source
for the Chair, given the pauses surrounding the delivery.

Within the third part of this turn, the Chair begins by describing the
Committee's solution ('and (.) what we also look at is now is') before naming
the problem ('three white tickets if it's within a (.) um (.) from one teacher').
What this does is to assign alertness to the Committee, another category of
actors within the school, on whose behalf the Chair is accountably speaking. In the course of this elaboration, a different version of the kid on the decline
has been produced, one who is at least in part possibly a victim of run-ins with
teachers.

There are different possible upshots that could have been produced in
relation to this turn. For example, one could be that run-ins with kids should
not happen and that this problem in teacher–student relations is important
to discuss further. Another upshot could be that the run-ins are taken for
granted but they should not skew the ticketing system. The second hearing
is produced by the interviewer in her question 'do you cancel the ticket?' This
formulation by the interviewer seems to ignore the Chair's description of the
Committee's counselling work and attends to the Committee's moral action
in relation to the practical outcome for the kid understood now as a member
of the category 'victim of teacher run-in'.

It appears that the interviewer has by now heard the central problem as *'Because a kid can get to this stage in the matter of a week, you know, well kids have'*, and not as the problem of teachers and run-ins. The Chair's turn is designed around this central point, first leading up to it, and then moving sideways, producing an account for it. In producing the account for it, what is underscored is the moral issue of 'How can this happen in the matter of a week?', backed up by the adjacent point that it has actually happened. What the Chair is presenting here is an Extreme Case Formulation (Pomerantz, 1986) whose design and placement may achieve up to three things at this point in the interview. First, it may be produced as a correction to the interviewer's failure to appreciate the matter of speeds of descent sufficiently. Second, it underscores the alertness of the Committee to the complexities of the system, the Committee's competence. Finally, it produces the kid/kids in question as the ultimate subjects of the Committee's duty of care.

What we see here is the conversational product of the identity 'Chair of the Welfare Committee', which is the speaking identity he was asked to assume. The interviewer's uptakes and their absences appear to have been oriented to by the Chair in his work of moral description and accounting. By examining the membership categorization and other resources the Chair draws on in his accounts, the cultural particulars he produces for this listener, and by noticing how the interviewer's hearing of the talk itself evidences membership categorization work, we are able to see how deeply interactional this interview is, despite apparently minimal input from the interviewer.

CONCLUSION: ASSEMBLING POSSIBLE WORLDS

In the preceding sections of this chapter I have demonstrated some procedures for beginning a membership categorization device analysis of interview talk. Essentially the search is for how *participants in the interview* make use of the resources of membership categorization. The first step is to locate the central categories (of people, or places, or things) that underpin the talk, including any standard relational pairs such as parents–teacher or contrast pairs such as plodders and good kids. These categories are sometimes named and sometimes implied through the 'activities' that are attached to them. A second step is to work through the activities associated with each of the categories in order to fill out the attributions that are made to each of the categories. The attributions that are hinted at are as important as any stated in so many words: hinted-at categories or activities or connections between them indicate the subtlety and delicacy of much implicit membership categorization work. A third step is to look at the categories + attributions connections that members produce (connections between 'cultural particulars'), to find the courses of social action that are implied: descriptions of how categories of actors do, could or should behave.

As in the examples I have presented here, when speakers 'do describing', they assemble a social world in which their categories have a central place.

These categories are in a sense the speakers' 'puppets', which they can dress up in different ways and make behave in various ways (category-associated activities). These are powerful statements about *what could be the case*, how the social order *might be arranged*, whether or not it really is. The artful production of plausible versions using recognizable membership categorization devices is a profoundly important form of cultural competence. What we hear and attend to in these interview accounts are members' methods for putting together a world that is recognizably familiar, orderly and moral.

Recommended reading

Carolyn Baker develops these arguments in Gubrium and Holstein (2002: 777–96). Anne Ryen deploys a similar approach in the same volume in a chapter on cross-cultural interviewing (335–54). Rapley's (2004) chapter-length treatment of the open-ended interview continues Baker's line of argument.

REFERENCES

Baker, C.D. (1984) 'The search for adultness: Membership work in adolescent—adult talk', *Human Studies*, 7: 301–23.

Baker, C.D. (1997) 'Ticketing rules: Categorization and moral ordering in a school staff meeting', in S. Hester and P. Eglin (eds), *Culture in Action: Studies in Membership Categorization Analysis*. Lanham, MD: University Press of America. pp. 79–102.

Baker, C.D. (2002) 'Ethnomethodological analyses of interviews', in J. Gubrium and J. Holstein, J. (eds), *Handbook of Interview Research*. Thousand Oaks, CA: Sage. pp. 777–96.

Baker, C.D. and Keogh, J. (1995) 'Accounting for achievement in parent–teacher interviews', *Human Studies*, 18 (2): 263–300.

Gubrium, J. and Holstein, J. (2002) 'From the individual interview to the interview society', in J. Gubrium and J. Holstein (eds), *Handbook of Interview Research*. Thousand Oaks, CA: Sage. pp. 3–32.

Jayyusi, L. (1984) *Categorization and the Moral Order*. London: Routledge & Kegan Paul.

Jayyusi, L. (1991) 'Values and moral judgement: Communicative praxis as moral order', in G. Button (ed.), *Ethnomethodology and the Human Sciences*. Cambridge: Cambridge University Press. pp. 227–51.

Maynard, D. (1991) 'The perspective-display series and the delivery of diagnostic news', in D. Boden and D.H. Zimmerman (eds), *Talk and Social Structure: Studies in Ethnomethodology and Conversation Analysis*. Cambridge: Polity. pp. 164–92.

Pomerantz, A. (1986) 'Extreme case formulations: A way of legitimizing claims', *Human Studies*, 9 (2/3): 219–99.

Rapley, T. (2004) 'The open-ended interview', in C. Seale, G. Gobo, J. Gubrium and D. Silverman (eds), *Qualitative Research Practice*. London: Sage.

Ryen, A. (2002) 'Cross-cultural interviewing', in J. Gubrium and J. Holstein (eds), *Handbook of Interview Research*. Thousand Oaks, CA: Sage. pp. 335–54.

Sacks, H. (1992) *Lectures on Conversation*, Vols I and II, ed. G. Jefferson. Oxford: Blackwell.

Schegloff, E.A. (1988) 'Description in the social sciences I: Talk-in-interaction', *IpRA Papers in Pragmatics*, 2 (1/2): 1–24.

Silverman, D. (1993) *Interpreting Qualitative Data: Methods for Analysing Talk, Text and Interaction*. London: Sage.

10 Focus group reseach

Sue Wilkinson

INTRODUCING FOCUS GROUPS

The inclusion of a chapter on focus groups in this second edition of *Qualitative Research* reflects the huge gain in popularity of this method across the social sciences over the past decade or so. Focus groups are now also thoroughly familiar to the general public, particularly in the contexts of 'public opinion' polling (e.g. Elliott, 1998; Kershner, 1998) and consumer affairs (e.g. Aubry, 2003; Knott, 1998). According to the media, politicians hone their images based on focus group assessments (Brooks, 1998), and market research agencies even recruit 3-year-olds to focus groups to tap into their purported 'pester power' (Swain, 2002).

Although the use of focus groups in social science can be traced back as far as the 1920s,[1] prior to the late 1970s their main use was as a market research tool, and most published studies were in the field of business and marketing – still an active area of focus group research today (Greenbaum, 1998). In the 1980s, health researchers pioneered the use of focus groups in social action research, particularly in the field of preventive health education, and the method continues to be widely used in family planning and HIV/AIDS education, as well as in health research more generally (Carey, 1995; Wilkinson, 1998a). From the 1990s on, no doubt partly in consequence of the 'turn to language' in the social sciences (see, for example, Gubrium and Holstein, 1997), there has been a 'resurgence of interest' (Lunt and Livingstone, 1996: 79) in focus groups. This has created a substantial literature on the method across a much broader range of disciplines – including education, communication and media studies, feminist research, sociology, and social psychology (see Morgan, 1996; Wilkinson, 1998b for reviews).

Focus group methodology is, at first sight, deceptively simple. It is a way of collecting qualitative data, which – essentially – involves engaging a small number of people in an informal group discussion (or discussions), 'focused' around a particular topic or set of issues. This could be, for example, young women sharing experiences of dieting, single parents evaluating childcare facilities, or fitness instructors comparing and contrasting training regimes. The informal group discussion is usually based on a series of questions (the focus group 'schedule'), and the researcher generally acts as a 'moderator' for the group: posing the questions, keeping the discussion flowing, and enabling group members to participate fully. Although focus groups are sometimes referred to as 'group interviews', the moderator does *not* ask questions of each focus group participant in turn, but, rather, facilitates group discussion, actively encouraging group members to interact with *each other*. This interaction between research participants – and the potential analytic use of such interaction – has been described as the 'hallmark' of focus group research (Morgan, 1988: 12).

Typically, the focus group discussion is recorded, the data transcribed, and then analyzed using conventional techniques for qualitative data: most commonly content or thematic analysis. Focus groups are distinctive, then, primarily for the method of data *collection* (i.e. informal group discussion), rather than for the method of data *analysis*. It is this, perhaps, which leads most contemporary accounts of the method to emphasize how to run an effective focus group, rather than how to analyze the resulting data. There is a plethora of advice on the methodological and procedural choices entailed in setting up and conducting a focus group (the next section of this chapter provides a brief review), but almost none on the theoretical and epistemological choices entailed in analyzing and interpreting focus group data – an emphasis I will attempt to redress here.

In the sections which follow, I will look, first, at issues related to research design and data collection using focus groups, and then – at greater length – at issues related to data analysis, together with some examples drawn from my own research.

RESEARCH DESIGN AND DATA COLLECTION

The flexibility of focus group research

Undoubtedly, one reason for the contemporary popularity of focus groups in social science research is the flexibility of the method. Focus groups can be used as a stand-alone qualitative method, or combined with quantitative techniques as part of a multi-method project (see Wilkinson, 1999 for a review). They can be used within the classroom/laboratory or in the field, to study the social world, or to attempt to change it, i.e. in action research projects (Johnson, 1996). At almost every stage of a focus group project, there are methodological choices to be made. Some sense of this flexibility and variety can readily be seen by perusing one of the recent edited collections of focus group research: for example, Barbour and Kitzinger (1999) and Morgan (1993a).

A focus group project can involve a single group of participants meeting on a single occasion, or it can involve many groups, with single or repeated meetings. It can involve as few as two, or as many as a dozen or so, participants (the norm is between four and eight). These participants may be pre-existing groups of people (e.g. members of families, clubs, or work teams), or they may be brought together specifically for the research, as representative of a particular population, or simply on the basis of shared characteristics or experiences (e.g. middle-aged men, sales assistants, sufferers of diabetes). In addition to (or instead of) a set of questions, the moderator may present group members with particular stimulus materials (e.g. video clips, advertisements); and in addition to (or instead of) discussing particular questions, they may be asked to engage in a specified activity (e.g. a card-sorting task, a rating exercise). Kitzinger (1990) provides examples of a range of such activities in the context of researching AIDS media messages. The moderator may be relatively directive, or relatively non-directive.

Focus group proceedings may be audio taped or video taped, with or without the use of accompanying field notes. Data transcription may be more or less detailed – ranging from simple orthographic transcription, which preserves just the words spoken, to the 'Jeffersonian' form of transcription used by conversation analysts (see the Appendix to this volume), which also preserves a range of linguistic and para-linguistic features, such as restarts, overlapping talk, pauses, pitch, volume, and intonation. Data management may be undertaken by hand (i.e. involving cutting and pasting sections of transcript) or computer assisted (using programs such as NUD.IST or THE ETHNOGRAPH). A wide variety of different types of data analysis may be undertaken – including content, thematic, ethnographic, phenomenological, narrative, experiential, biographical, discourse, or conversation analysis (several of which are discussed in more detail in other chapters of this volume). I will consider some of the issues involved in data analysis in the second part of this chapter.

Practical aspects of conducting focus groups

The focus group literature includes a substantial number of 'handbooks' which offer detailed information and advice about the process of setting up and running focus groups. The most recent of these include: Bloor et al. (2001); Krueger and Casey (2000); Morgan (1997); and Morgan and Krueger (1998). I have also written elsewhere about such practical matters (Wilkinson, 2003a, 2003b). The handbooks emphasize that obtaining high-quality focus group data depends, at least, upon an effective moderator; and upon a well-prepared session.

Ideally, the moderator should have some basic interviewing skills, some knowledge of group dynamics, and some experience in running group discussions. Although some of the skills involved in moderating a focus group are similar to those involved in one-to-one interviewing (e.g. establishing rapport; effective use of prompts and probes; sensitivity to non-verbal cues), the number of research participants involved in a focus group requires more in terms of active 'people management'. To enable full participation, the moderator may need to encourage quiet participants, to discourage talkative ones, and to handle any 'interactionally difficult' occasions: these matters are covered extensively in the handbooks, particularly Krueger and Casey (2000). Because of the number of participants, ensuring confidentiality is a particular issue. There are also ethical issues specific to the interactional nature of focus groups: for example, group members may collude to silence, intimidate, or harass one particular participant, or even the researcher (Green et al., 1993). The moderator should be prepared to deal appropriately with any such eventualities.

Most of the handbooks provide guidance on planning and implementing the focus group session itself: the six-volume *Focus Group Kit* edited by Morgan and Krueger (1998) is particularly comprehensive. Substantial advance preparation always pays off in focus group research. To ensure attendance on the day, it is necessary to over-recruit by about 50%, and to issue reminders. The venue, refreshments, all necessary materials (from focus group schedule to name badges and pens), and the recording equipment should be prepared and checked. The logistics (particularly arrivals and departures) and the timetable and procedure for the session should be run through. 'Ground rules' and debriefing should be considered. One or more assistants are highly desirable – to act as recording technician(s), to escort participants to and from the room, and to deal with any unforeseen circumstances, thereby allowing the researcher to concentrate on effective moderation of the group discussion.

ADVANTAGES OF FOCUS GROUPS OVER INTERVIEWS

Focus groups have a number of distinct advantages over one-to-one interviews. Most obviously, they provide a way of collecting data relatively quickly from a large number of research participants.[2] More importantly, focus groups are more 'naturalistic' than interviews (i.e. closer to everyday conversation), in that they typically include a range of communicative processes – such as storytelling, joking, arguing, boasting, teasing, persuasion, challenge, and disagreement. The dynamic quality of group interaction, as participants discuss, debate, and (sometimes) disagree about key issues, is generally a striking feature of focus groups, which, at times, may have 'the feel of rap sessions with friends' (Jarrett, 1993: 194). There is a common misconception that people will be inhibited about revealing intimate details in the context of a group discussion. In fact, focus groups are well suited to exploring 'sensitive' topics, and the group context may actually facilitate personal disclosures (Farquhar with Das, 1999; Frith, 2000). According to Kissling (1996), for example, it is easier for young people to talk freely about menstruation in a group context than in a one-to-one interview with an adult researcher: the 'solidarity' among friends seems to decrease their discomfort with the topic.

Focus group interactions also 'allow respondents to react to and build upon the responses of other group members', creating a 'synergistic effect' (Stewart and Shamdasani, 1990: 16). This often leads to the production of more elaborated accounts than are generated in individual interviews. In the context of agreement and support, one or more focus group members may enthusiastically extend, elaborate, or embroider an initially sketchy account: for example, through the consensual piling up of fine detail – the height of shoe heels, the size of buttons, the fastening mechanisms of jewelry, the dangers of beauty appliances – focus group participants with multiple sclerosis provided a cumulative account of the mundane, daily 'hassles' of living with the disease (Lyons et al., 1995: 24–5). However, focus group participants do not always agree: 'they also misunderstand one another, question one another, try to persuade each other of the justice of their point of view and sometimes they vehemently disagree' (Kitzinger, 1994a: 170–1). Disagreements and challenges are also effective in provoking the development and elaboration of accounts. For example, in a project on understandings of HIV/AIDS, which used focus groups based on pre-existing social networks, participants often challenged each other on contradictions between what they *claimed* to believe and how they actually behaved: 'how about that time you didn't use a glove while taking blood from a patient?', 'what about the other night when you went off with that boy at the disco?' (Kitzinger, 1994b: 105). Challenges like these – in forcing people to defend or justify their actions or beliefs – often generate elaborated accounts.

The relatively free flow of discussion and debate between members of a focus group offers researchers an excellent opportunity for hearing 'the language and vernacular used by respondents', particularly respondents 'who may be very different from themselves' (Bers, 1987: 26–7). Listening in on focus group discussions – or 'structured eavesdropping' (Powney, 1988) – promotes familiarity with the way research participants habitually talk, and the particular idioms, terminology, and vocabulary they typically use. This is particularly the case for focus groups conducted within community contexts (see Krueger and King, 1998): indeed, some focus group researchers have argued that the method may be particularly useful in work with severely disadvantaged, hard-to-reach social groups, people who may be 'uncomfortable with individual interviews' but happy to talk with others, particularly others they already know, 'in the safe and familiar context of their own turf' (Plaut et al., 1993: 216). Groups accessed in this way include 'high-risk' families in an inner city (Lengua et al., 1992); black gay men (Mays et al., 1992); and village women in rural counties of China (Wong et al., 1995).

Simply by virtue of the number of participants simultaneously involved, focus groups inevitably reduce the researcher's control over the interaction, making focus groups a relatively 'egalitarian' method. This feature has proved especially attractive to feminist researchers (who have, historically, expressed concern about the power dynamics of the one-to-one interview, e.g. Oakley, 1981; Finch, 1984); focus group research has even sometimes been considered akin to feminist consciousness raising (Herbert, 1989; Fine, 1992). Reduced researcher control enables focus group participants to follow their own agendas, and to 'develop the themes most important to them' (Cooper et al., 1993). One particular benefit of this is to draw researchers' attention to previously neglected or unnoticed phenomena. For example, a focus group with former LSD-using adolescents uncovered the possible use of Robitussin (a strong cough medicine) as a substitute for LSD. In characterizing this discovery as a new piece of the contemporary drug puzzle, the researchers comment:

> this is one place where focus groups shine. Through group interaction, we learn that something we hadn't noticed before is a significant issue for drug-experienced young people. . . . From the way the group takes up the topic, it is clear that something significant is going on, something significant to them. A new piece of territory is revealed. (Agar and MacDonald, 1995: 80)

Focus group research, then, may result in unexpected insights. Many of these are unlikely to have arisen in the context of individual interviews.

I now move on to consider issues relating to focus group data analysis.

DATA ANALYSIS

As indicated, compared with the extensive advice on how to *conduct* focus groups, there is relatively little in the focus group literature on how to *analyze* the resulting data. Data analysis sections of focus group 'handbooks' are typically very brief, and most commentators suggest (or imply) that the techniques suitable for analyzing one-to-one interview data are equally applicable for use with focus group data. In published focus group studies, researchers often omit, or briefly gloss over, the details of exactly how they conducted their analyses.

Further, despite the growing body of literature which considers method – particularly qualitative method – as theory (this volume; see also, for example, Gubrium and Holstein, 1997; Seale et al., 2003; Silverman, 1997, 2000, 2001; Wilkinson, 2000, 2001), social scientists using focus groups often fail to locate their method of choice within a clear theoretical framework. On the rare occasions focus group researchers *have* attempted to justify or explain their choice of method, they have tended to do so in relation to norms of quantitative or positivist research, rather than in relation to alternative qualitative approaches. In particular, in focus group research, as in social scientific research more generally, it is still comparatively rare for data analytic methods to be seen as embodying theoretical choices, rarer still to find explicit discussion of the epistemological status of data. By contrast, my goal in the following discussion of data analytic strategies is to make such theoretical and epistemological assumptions explicit.

'Content' versus 'ethnographic' analysis

I want to make a key distinction between two different approaches to analyzing focus group data: content analysis and ethnographic analysis.[3] Content analysis produces a – relatively systematic and comprehensive – summary or overview of the data set as a whole, sometimes incorporating a quantitative element, whereas ethnographic analysis is more selective, typically addressing the issue of 'what is going on' between the participants in some segment (or segments) of the data, in greater analytic depth and detail. The two different approaches relate, of course, to different types of research question – and the 'results' produced by the two types of analysis look very different. An initial sense of the distinction between them can be gained from a project on heart attack risk factors, which utilizes *both* types of analysis (Morgan and Spanish, 1985). In this project, a content analysis is used to address the question of how *often* different risk factors for heart attacks are mentioned, and what these factors *are*, while an ethnographic analysis is used to address the question of exactly *how* (and could also perhaps address *why*) risk factor information is introduced and discussed, in the context of these particular focus groups.

Content analysis is based on examination of the data for recurrent instances of some kind; these instances are then systematically identified across the data set, and grouped together by means of a coding system. The researcher has first to decide on the unit of analysis: this could be the whole group, the group dynamics, the individual participants, or (as is most commonly the case) the participants' utterances (Carey and Smith, 1994; Morgan, 1995). The unit of analysis provides the basis for developing a coding system, and the codes are then applied systematically across a transcript (or across several transcripts if more than one focus group has been run). Morgan (1997) proposes three distinct ways of coding focus group data: noting whether each group discussion contains a given code; noting whether each participant mentions a given code; and noting all mentions of a given code (i.e. across groups or participants). Once the data have been coded in one (or more) of these ways, the question of whether to quantify them is a further issue – many qualitative researchers would, of course, argue that the most valuable features of qualitative data are thereby lost. Morgan (1993b) argues for the use of simple 'descriptive counts' of codes, i.e. stopping short of using inferential statistical tests, whose assumptions are unlikely to be met in focus groups. These counts are an effective way of providing a summary or overview of the data set as a whole.

By contrast with content analysis, ethnographic analysis is rarely systematic or comprehensive, in the sense of ranging across the full data set; rather, it is much more selective and limited in scope. Its main advantage is to permit a detailed – more or less interpretive – account of mundane features of the social world, whether this relates to processes occurring within the focus group itself, or whether (as is more typical) talk within the focus group is seen as a means of access to participants' lives. Ethnographic analysis aims to be contextual, i.e. to ground interpretation in the particularities of the situation under study, and it aims to represent the social world from the participants' perspective, i.e. to ground interpretation in participants' views of 'what is going on', rather than the analyst's view. Data are generally presented as accounts of social phenomena or social practices, substantiated by means of extensive illustrative quotation from the focus group discussion. Key issues in ethnographic analysis are how to *select* the material to present; how to give due weight to the specific context within which the material was generated, while retaining at least some sense of the group discussion as a whole; and how best to prioritize participants' orientations in presenting an interpretive account.

A particular challenge is substantively to address the *interactive* nature of focus group data: a surprising limitation of focus group research is the rarity with which group interactions are analyzed or reported (Kitzinger, 1994b, Wilkinson, 1999). Extracts from focus group data are typically presented as if they were one-to-one interview data, often with no evidence of more than one research participant being present;[4] still more rarely does interaction per se constitute the analytic focus. This is all the more surprising given that – as noted above – focus group researchers typically emphasize interaction between participants as the most distinctive feature of the method, even cautioning that researchers 'who do not attend to the impact of the group setting will incompletely or inappropriately analyze their data' (Carey and Smith, 1994: 125).

Unpacking content analysis (quantitative and qualitative variants)

The majority of published focus group studies use some type of content analysis. However, given the wide variety of terminology employed in these studies, and their frequent – sometimes extensive – use of illustrative quotation, it may not readily be apparent that this is so. To appreciate the underlying theoretical similarities between most analyses of focus group data, it is necessary to appreciate that content analysis need not employ a formal coding scheme, nor need it be a precursor to any kind of quantification. At its most basic, content analysis simply entails inspection of the data for recurrent instances of some kind, irrespective of the type of instance (e.g. word, phrase, some larger unit of 'meaning'); the preferred label for such instances (e.g. 'items', 'themes', 'discourses'); whether the instances are subsequently grouped into larger units, also variously labeled (e.g. 'categories', 'organizing themes', 'interpretive repertoires'); and whether the instances – or larger units – are counted or not. In the sense, then, that most analyses of focus group data report recurrent instances of some kind, and do so more or less systematically, they are essentially content analyses.

To illustrate this point, I show in Box 10.1 two different content analyses – one quantitative, one qualitative – of the *same* piece of focus group data. The 'results' of the quantitative content analysis are presented as frequency counts, while the 'results' of the qualitative content analysis are presented as illustrative quotations. The data are drawn from a segment of a focus group in which three women who share a breast cancer diagnosis are talking about possible causes of the disease (see Wilkinson (2000) for more information about this focus group, and the larger project of which it is a part). Both analyses take the 'mention' of a cause as the unit of analysis, and organize these 'mentions' using a category scheme derived from Blaxter's (1983) classic study of women's talk about the causes of health and illness.[5] However, the first analysis systematically records the *number* of 'mentions' within each category (including null categories), summarizing what these 'mentions' are, while the second records the *words* in which these 'mentions' are couched, presenting them as quotations under each category heading (excluding null categories).

Box 10.1: Content analyses (causes of breast cancer)

(1) QUANTITATIVE VERSION

1. *Infection*: 0 instances
2. *Hereditary or familial tendencies*: 2 instances
   family history (×2)
3. *Agents in the environment*:

   (a) *'poisons', working condition, climate*: 3 instances
       aluminium pans; exposure to sun; chemicals in food
   (b) *drugs or the contraceptive pill*: 1 instance
       taking the contraceptive pill

4. *Secondary to other diseases*: 0 instances
5. *Stress, strain, and worry*: 0 instances
6. *Caused by childbearing, menopause*: 22 instances
   not breast feeding; late childbearing (×3); having only one child; being single/not having children; hormonal; trouble with breast feeding – unspecified (×4); flattened nipples (×2); inverted nipples (×7); nipple discharge (×2)
7. *Secondary to trauma or to surgery*: 9 instances
   knocks (×4); unspecified injury; air getting inside body (×4)
8. *Neglect, the constraints of poverty*: 0 instances
9. *Inherent susceptibility, individual and not hereditary*: 0 instances
10. *Behavior, own responsibility*: 1 instance
    mixing specific foods
11. *Ageing, natural degeneration*: 0 instances
12. *Other*: 5 instances
    'several things'; 'a lot'; 'multi-factorial'; everybody has a 'dormant' cancer; 'anything' could wake a dormant cancer

(2) QUALITATIVE VERSION

Hereditary or familial tendencies

'I mean there's no family <u>history</u>'

Agents in the environment:

(a) *'poisons', working condition, climate*

'I was once told that if you use them aluminium pans that cause cancer'
'Looking years and years ago, I mean, everybody used to sit about sunning themselves on the beach and now all of a sudden you get cancer from sunshine'

'I don't know (about) all the chemicals in what you're eating and things these days as well, and how cultivated and everything'

(b) drugs or the contraceptive pill

'You know, obviously I took the pill at a younger age'

Caused by childbearing, menopause

'Inverted nipples, they say that that is one thing that you could be wary of'

'Until I came to the point of actually trying to breast feed I didn't realise I had flattened nipples and one of them was nearly inverted or whatever, so I had a lot of trouble breast feeding, and it, and I was several weeks with a breast pump trying to get it right, so that he could suckle on my nipple, I did have that problem'

'Over the years, every, I couldn't say it happened monthly or anything like that, it would just start throbbing, this leakage, nothing to put a dressing on or anything like that, but there it was, it was coming from somewhere and it were just kind of gently crust over'

'I mean, I don't know whether the age at which you have children makes a difference as well because I had my eight-year-old relatively <u>late</u>, I was an old mum'

'They say that if you've only had <u>one</u> that you're more likely to get it than if you have a <u>big</u> family'

Secondary to trauma or to surgery

'Sometimes I've heard that <u>knocks</u> can bring one on'

'I then remembered that I'd <u>banged</u> my breast with this . . . you know these shopping bags with a wooden rod thing, those big trolley bags?'

'I always think that people go into hospital, even for an exploratory, it may be all wrong, but I do think, well the <u>air</u> gets to it, it seems to me that it's not long afterwards before they simply find that there's more to it than they thought, you know, and I often wonder if the <u>air</u> getting to your inside . . . brings on cancer in any form'

Behavior, own responsibility

'I was also told that if you eat tomatoes and plums at the same meal'

Other

'He told them nurses in his lectures that <u>everybody</u> has a cancer, <u>and</u> it's a case of whether it lays dormant'

'I don't think it could be one cause, can it? It must be multi-factorial'

These two content analyses, then, *look* very different, although both are derived from the same underlying theoretical framework. The second type, reporting qualitative data, is often described as a 'thematic' analysis (sometimes as a 'discourse' analysis)[6], and may be presented with the quotations integrated into the text, rather than in tabular form (e.g. Braun and Wilkinson,

2003). We may also note that neither of these analyses has preserved the interactive quality of the focus group data, although it is possible for a thematic analysis to do so (see, for example, Braun and Wilkinson, forthcoming; Ellis, 2002).

Unpacking ethnographic analysis (epistemological distinctions)

So far, we have seen that content analyses which look very *different* (i.e. providing quantitative or qualitative 'results') in fact treat the data in the *same* kind of way (i.e. inspecting them systematically for recurrent instances). We can further note that these various types of content analysis share a *similar underlying epistemology*: one in which research participants' talk is taken as providing a 'means of access' to something that lies behind or beyond it. In my content analyses of women's talk about the causes of breast cancer, the words of focus group participants are taken to provide a 'transparent' window onto what they understand, think, or believe about, say, the role of reproductive factors in the etiology of breast cancer.[7] Similarly, in the AIDS Media Research Project (Kitzinger, 1994b), mentioned earlier, and designed to investigate 'audience understandings' of HIV/AIDS, participants' words are taken as 'revealing' their understandings or beliefs about, say, the mechanisms of HIV transmission. In such studies, self-report is used to infer the relatively stable 'cognitions' (beliefs, attitudes, or opinions) assumed to underlie people's talk (and – at least sometimes – to inform their subsequent behavior), to which the researcher has no independent access.

A similar epistemological status is also commonly afforded to talk in focus group studies which are designedly *ethnographic* (rather than content analytic) in nature, i.e. studies which aim to provide contextual, interpretive accounts of their participants' social worlds. For example, in Lyons et al.'s (1995) study of women with multiple sclerosis, and Agar and MacDonald's (1995) study of ex-users of LSD (both referred to earlier), research participants' talk is taken to provide a 'transparent' window onto the circumstances of their lives outside the focus group (to which the focus group moderator has no independent access), and which are inferred from self-report. What people say in the context of the focus group discussion is seen as 'revealing', for example, the nature of daily life for people with chronic physical illness, or as flagging up a 'significant issue' in the life 'territory' of the drug-experienced young. In other words, talk is used as a 'means of access' to something that lies behind or beyond it, rather than treated as of interest in its own right.

I want to contrast this view of talk (i.e. talk as a means of accessing a pre-given social – or psychological – world) with an alternative one: one which considers talk as *constituting* the social world on a moment-by-moment basis. This is to give talk a very *different* epistemological status from the one presented so far – and one which radically effects both the kind of study undertaken and the kind of 'results' obtained. Affording such a status to talk opens up the possibility of seeing the focus group discussion as a social context *in its own right*, and, further, the possibility of subjecting it to *direct* observation (rather than studying it in order to infer more distal social – or psychological – phenomena).[8] The resulting study will *necessarily* be ethnographic, and will provide a detailed, contextual account of social processes. While this might seem an obvious epistemological move to anyone familiar with theoretical work on language, or with contemporary social scientific debates about essentialism and social constructionism (see, for example, Gubrium and Holstein, 1997; Kitzinger, 1995), it is a radical proposal for most focus group researchers, including those working within an ethnographic tradition. Even though (most) ethnography is predicated upon direct observation, few focus group researchers conducting (broadly) ethnographic analysis have turned their attention to observation of 'what is going on' in the focus group itself; and fewer still have paid detailed attention to talk as constitutive of social – or psychological – life.

In exploring this kind of approach, I have found the theoretical framework offered by ethnomethodology and conversation analysis to be particularly valuable (see Chapter 12, this volume, for a more detailed overview). Conversation analysis assumes that it is fundamentally *through interaction* that participants build social context – indeed, it is often explicitly referred to as the study of 'talk-in-interaction'. It therefore seems extraordinary that focus group researchers looking for a way to analyze the key feature of their data, i.e. interaction between participants, have not more extensively utilized this approach. Central to an ethnomethodological or conversation analytic framework is the notion of talk as *action*, i.e. as designed to *do* particular things within a particular interactional context. Within a focus group we can see how people (for example) tell stories, joke, agree, debate, argue, challenge, or attempt to persuade. We can see the ways in which they present particular 'versions' of themselves (and others) for particular interactional purposes: (for example) to impress, flatter, tease, ridicule, complain, castigate, or condone. Participants build the context of their talk *in* and *through* that talk itself, on a moment-by-moment basis. The talk itself, in its interactional context, can provide the primary data for analysis. Further, it is possible to harness analytic resources intrinsic to that data: by focusing on participants' *own* understanding of the interaction – as displayed *directly* in their talk, through the conversational practices they use. In this way, a conversation analytic approach prioritizes the participants' (rather than the researcher's) analysis of the interaction: a broadly ethnographic goal (if not one achieved in all ethnographic analyses).

The traditions of ethnomethodology and conversation analysis generally rely primarily upon the use of naturally occurring data, i.e. data produced independently of the researcher. These data, however, encompass a range of institutional settings (e.g. classrooms, courtrooms, doctors' surgeries), in which talk has been shown both to follow the conventions of 'everyday' conversation and systematically to depart from these (Drew and Heritage, 1992). Likewise, data from focus groups range across both 'everyday' social actions (e.g. arguing, joking, teasing, complaining) and actions likely to be specific to the particular (research) context, e.g. asking elaborate questions

(Puchta and Potter, 1999); displaying opinions (Myers, 1998). While it may be useful to consider what goes on in focus group *qua* focus group, analysis need not be limited by the specificity of this particular context: it can also address more generic conversational phenomena, ranging across the practices and actions displayed in the talk (Schegloff, 1997).

To illustrate this point, I offer below a sample data analysis which I would characterize as broadly ethnographic, and also as based upon the principles of ethnomethodology and conversation analysis. That is, it seeks to offer a detailed interpretive account of 'what is going on' within the talk which constitutes the focus group; and it theorizes this talk as action oriented, as in pursuit of particular, local interactional goals.

The data on which this analysis is based are presented in Boxes 10.2 and 10.3. These two extracts are drawn from the *same* segment of the *same* focus group as used in the content analyses above, i.e. the part of the discussion in which the three women are talking about possible causes of breast cancer. Here, I have identified myself ('SW') as moderator of the focus group, and I have called the participants 'Freda', 'Doreen' and 'Gertie'. Note that the level of detail presented in the transcript is appropriate to the level of analysis which follows, i.e. it is somewhere between a simple orthographic rendition and a full 'Jeffersonian' (conversation analytic) transcription.

Data extract 1 (Box 10.2) opens with my question (as moderator) about causes, and the responses from Freda and Gertie to this question. Note that a content analysis (of the kind presented earlier) might code Freda's initial response (line 3) as 'I don't know', and Gertie's subsequent response (lines 5–9) as items in the categories 'agents in the environment' (aluminium pans) and 'behavior, own responsibility' (choosing to eat tomatoes and plums at the same meal). A discursive–ethnographic analysis, by contrast, focuses on the immediate interactional context. Talk about causes can be interactionally tricky, particularly when a presumed 'expert' is asking questions, or in settings in which potentially equally knowledgeable others might have different or even conflicting opinions. Conversation analysts (e.g. Sacks, 1992: 340–7) have noted the asymmetry between being the first to express an opinion and being second – in that going first means you have to put your opinion on the line, whereas going second offers an opportunity either for agreement or for potential challenge. Consequently, speakers often try to avoid first position, and this is precisely what Freda does in response to the moderator's question: she declines to give an opinion, and bounces the question right back to the moderator, as a 'counter' (Schegloff, 1995: 7–10). It is not simply then, as a content analysis within an essentialist framework might suggest, that Freda 'doesn't know' what causes breast cancer: from the perspective of a discursive–ethnographic analysis within a social constructionist framework, she is not here reporting a state of mind, but is engaged in a piece of local interactional business.

The moderator (SW) avoids answering Freda's direct question: instead she reformulates it (in the manner typically recommended for interviewers and focus group moderators), making clear she is interested in what the

---

Box 10.2 Data extract 1

SW: BCP12 (Causes extracts 1+2)

```
01 SW:     D'you have any idea what caused your breast
02         cancer[pause] any of you.
03 Fre:    No- What does cause breast cancer do you think.
04 SW:     What do you think it might be?
05 Ger:    [cuts in] There's a lot of stories going
06         about.=I was once told that if you use them
07         aluminium pans that cause cancer. .hh I was also
08         told that if you- if you eat tomatoes and plums
09         at the same meal that-
10 Dor:    [laughs]
11 Ger:    [to Doreen] Have you heard all these those
12         things?
13 Dor:    [laughs] No
14 Ger:    Now that's what I heard and-
15 Dor:    [laughs] Mm
16 Ger:    Oh there's several things that if you listen to
17         people [pause] we::ll-
18 Dor:    Mm
19 SW:     [to Gertie, laughingly] What else have they told
20         you?
21 Ger:    Pardon?
22 SW:     [to Gertie, laughingly] What else have they told
23         you?
24 D/SW:   [laughter]
25 Ger:    I can't think off hand I knew a- I knew a lot
26         that I've heard over the years from people
27         who've passed on 'Oh yeah well that causes
28         cancer'.
29 Dor:    Mm
30 Ger:    But I don't know but-
31 Dor:    [cuts in] I mean uhm-
32 Ger:    Now I've no views on this [To Doreen] have you?
```

---

participants themselves 'think it *might* be' (line 4), rather than in any purported 'actual' (i.e. scientific) causes of breast cancer. It is with this reassurance that Gertie offers some 'stories' (i.e. folk wisdom, labeled as such), thereby putting herself in the vulnerable first speaking position, and attracting just the kind of second speaker disagreement that Freda's counter enabled her to avoid: Doreen, the third member of the group, *laughs* at Gertie's response. Note that within an essentialist framework, Gertie's references to 'stories', and to what she has 'heard over the years', would be taken as transparent reports of the *source* of her ideas about cause, i.e. as indicating a reliance on folk knowledge. Within a social constructionist framework, however, this attribution of ideas about cause to folk knowledge is seen as an *interactional device* seeking to protect the speaker from challenge (although, here, it fails to avert ridicule).

Gertie's candidate causes, then, are presented as 'stories'; however, only moments later, even these 'stories' are retracted. By the end of Doreen and Gertie's subsequent exchange (at line 32), Gertie, like Freda before her, is claiming to have 'no views' on the causes of breast cancer. Again (within this framework), this not simply a straightforward report of a cognitive state: it arises out of the interactional sequence within which it is embedded, in the course of which both Doreen and the moderator have implied, through their laughter, that Gertie's candidate causes are rather implausible; indeed, the moderator's probe (lines 19–20) can be heard as 'positioning' (Wilkinson and Kitzinger, 2003) Gertie as the sort of gullible person who believes anything she is told. Gertie responds first by reminding everyone that she is not reporting her own views, but those of others, and then she flatly refuses to offer further candidate answers, explicitly handing the floor to Doreen at line 32.

When Gertie re-enters the conversation (at line 65,[9] in data extract 2, Box 10.3), with a subsequent suggestion of a candidate cause (the theory that cancer is 'dormant' until woken), she is still attending to the danger of being laughed at. However, here she deals with the risk of ridicule by using a very different kind of footing[10] (Goffman, 1981): the 'dormant cancer' theory is painstakingly constructed as *someone else*'s opinion – that of a specified medical expert, a Dr Patterson, at Springfield General Hospital (the hospital where most of these women will have received treatment). She carefully monitors the reception of this theory, and even though Freda and Doreen affiliate with this view (at lines 73 and 74), she checks to be sure she has their support (line 75), and continues repeatedly to stress that this theory comes from her sister's nursing training: 'she told us that, and that came in her lectures' (lines 77–78); 'according to him' (line 78); 'that's what <u>she</u> was told' (line 84). The effect of all this footing is to emphasize that these ideas are *not* her own, and that she is *not* to be held accountable for believing them. Again, within a social constructionist framework, the attribution of views to others does not offer a 'transparent' window on what Gertie 'believes', nor does it indicate the 'source' of her information. Gertie is not simply repeating what her sister may or may not have told her Dr Patterson had said; rather, she is using footing as a conversational resource, in order to manage the delicate interactional business of presenting an opinion without sounding ignorant or stupid.

Doreen then rejoins the conversation (at line 91) to offer another candidate cause – a 'bang' on her breast. Her story, elaborated in lines 91–113, is apparently 'touched off' by Gertie's mention of 'a knock or whatever in the appropriate place' causing cancer to develop (line 81), followed by Freda's subsequent acknowledgment of the theory that '*knocks* can bring one on' (lines 87–88). Note that just before Doreen begins her story, Gertie and Freda have both placed considerable distance between themselves and the 'knock' theory:

Box 10.3 Data extract 2

SW: BCP12 (Causes extracts 4+5)

```
65 Ger: My sister was a nurse [pause] wa:y back in the
66      1920s she [indistinct]. And she-she was at what is
67      Springfield General now.=She did her training there
68      and there was a doctor Patterson at the time .hh
69      who used to lecture to the nurses .hh and he told
70      them nurses in his lectures that everybody has a
71      cancer[pause] and [pause] it's a case of whether
72      it lays dormant
73 Fre: Yes I've heard that.
74 Dor: Mm
75 Ger: Have you heard that?
76 (F): Mm
77 Ger: Well yes that she told us that and that came in her
78      lectures.hh and [pause] according to him anything
79      could wake it up
80 Dor: Mm
81 Ger: a knock or whatever in the appropriate place.hh
82      and then it would develop but that's what-
83 Dor: Mm
84 Ger: that's what she was told.
85 Dor: Mm
86 Ger: But when I-
87 Fre: [cuts in] Sometimes I've heard that knocks can bring
88      one on but I've never (had any knocks) [indistinct]
89 Ger: No
90 Fre: [cuts in] (I don't think that) [indistinct]
91 Dor: [cuts in] Well I'd heard that from somebody else
92      and so when I- when obviously this was sus-
93      my lump was suspicious I then- I then remembered
94      I'd banged my breast with this .hh uhm [tch] you
95      know these shopping bags with a wooden rod thing
96      .hh those big trolley bags?
97 Fre: Mm
98 Dor: I-I-I >don't ask me how I do these stupid things<
99      but I got it wedged between the car door as I was
100     getting out of the car I got it wedged in the car
101     door so it- so this [pause] appropriately sized
102     rod that was the size of this lump you know went
103     into my breast and I- and I queried that .hh and
104     Mr Fell [consultant surgeon] said you know 'You're
105     always looking for a reason' [laughs] d'you know
106     'You've always got to find something that might be
107     the cause of it' you know.hh but I thought 'Well
```

```
108        I'd just better mention it' in case it turned out
109        to be.hh you know sort of they'll say-, they then
110        come round to me afterwards and say 'Are you sure
111        you haven't d- done some injury to yourself'
112        >or that sort of thing< 'cos you know, it just
113        sprung to mind. .hh 'Cos I-I'd mentioned it to
114        the GP and she'd sort of said 'No no .hh it's
115        nearly always hormonal' so it'd gone out of my
116        head and an- but- but then she was saying 'No
117        it'll be be a cyst' >whatever< and when it wasn't
118        a cyst then I started to think of another cause
119        you see but- .hh
120 (G):   Mm
121 Dor:   uh:m I-I mean I sup- if-if they knew what the cause
122        was they would- they would be able to treat it
123        wouldn't they.
124 Ger:   Well you know I-
125 Dor:   [cuts in]I don't think it could be one cause can
126        it? It must be multi
127 (G):   Mm
128 Dor:   .hh multi-factorial
129 Ger:   [cuts in] You've heard them say-
130 Dor:   whatever the word is
```

Freda saying it is a theory she has 'sometimes heard', but that she has never had any knocks herself (lines 84–5), and Gertie attributing the theory to her sister's nursing training, some seventy years earlier (lines 65–8 and 78–81). In telling a story about her own knock, then, Doreen can be seen to attend to the risk of aligning herself with a belief in knocks, and thereby possibly attracting scorn or censure (see Potter (1996: 142–7) for a detailed discussion of distancing, neutrality, and alignment).

Doreen never actually says directly that she believes her breast cancer to have been caused by a knock to her breast. She simply 'remembered' (line 90) having banged her breast, and reports feeling it necessary to 'mention it' (line 101) to her surgeon – thereby further displaying to her co-conversationalists that she is a rational person who informed a medical professional of the knock in order to check out all possibilities (she has already shown herself to be aware of a range of other possibilities, in her previous discussion of reproductive factors, not reproduced here). The surgeon's reported response, 'You're always looking for a reason' (line 99), is a generalized formulation that does not dismiss the 'knock' theory *specifically*, but that even-handedly dismisses *any* theory (actually or potentially) offered by Doreen – and, by implication, anyone else. Ventriloquizing the surgeon in this way enables Doreen to present the 'knock' theory as no more *or less* plausible than any other theory (to which the 'always looking for a reason' dismissal is equally applicable).

The surgeon's response, with its implicit suggestion that looking for 'reasons' and 'causes' is futile, also provides evidence for Doreen's later claim that 'they' (doctors) do not know the causes of breast cancer (lines 121–122). If they do not, and if looking for causes is pointless, then the 'knock' theory is as plausible as any other. Likewise, the GPs dismissal of Doreen's theory is also reported in such a way that the 'knock' theory is left open as a possible cause: the competing cause offered by the GP ('it's nearly always hormonal', lines 114–115) is explained as having been offered as a cause for a *cyst*, not cancer. The reported misdiagnosis has the added benefit of pointing to the fallibility of the medical profession (re-emphasized in lines 121–122). Within a social constructionist framework, the concern is not with whether Doreen 'really' believes the 'knock' theory, or with whether medical professionals 'actually' dismissed her possible explanation. Rather, it is with how Doreen *designs* her talk to illustrate: (1) her own rationality, both in reporting the knock and in assessing its merits and demerits as a theory; (2) her own willingness to listen to the opinions of expert others; (3) the fallibility of the medical profession; and (4) the plausibility of a knock as a cause for breast cancer. Doreen's final statement – that the causes of breast cancer must be 'multi-factorial' (line 128) – enables her to maintain the possibility that her injury was causally implicated, while not denying the potential relevance of other (more medically approved) causes. In this interaction, then, Doreen designs her talk to display to her co-conversationalists that she is a rational and open-minded person.

IN CONCLUSION

In this chapter, I have outlined what is involved in conducting and – especially – in analyzing a focus group, with particular reference to the theoretical and epistemological issues entailed in different types of analysis. Although I am a keen advocate of focus groups, I would not want to claim that they offer 'a method for all seasons' (Tuck, 1976). Focus groups are a method of choice when the objective of the research is primarily to study *talk*, either conceptualized as a 'window' on participants' lives or their underlying beliefs and opinions, or as constituting a social context in its own right, amenable to direct observation. If, by contrast, the purpose of the research is to categorize or compare types of individuals or social groups, in terms of the lives they lead or the views they hold, then focus groups are less appropriate (although they are not uncommonly used in this way).

Focus group data readily lend themselves to analysis by content analytic or ethnographic methods (both of which I have illustrated here), as well as by other qualitative techniques; and the resulting analyses can be presented in a variety of ways, ranging from numerical tables summarizing a whole data set, through prose accounts containing lengthy illustrative quotations, to detailed interpretive accounts of a relatively circumscribed single data extract. Focus groups offer particular opportunities – although this potential is as yet relatively underdeveloped – for the study of interactions between research participants. I have argued here that ethnomethodological and conversation analytic approaches may prove particularly useful for pursuing such an endeavor.

NOTES

1. Although psychologists Emory Bogardus and Walter Thurstone used focus group techniques to develop survey instruments in the 1920s, the 'invention' of focus groups is more often credited to sociologist Robert Merton and his colleagues, who used them to study audience reaction to radio programs in the 1940s.
2. However, it can be difficult and time consuming to recruit and bring together appropriate participants.
3. Morgan (1988: 64) also uses this terminology, but his two types of analysis are more narrowly defined, mapping (broadly) onto the traditional 'quantitative–qualitative' divide (Bryman, 1988).
4. It is not uncommon to use one-to-one interviews and focus groups in the same study, and to treat the data derived from each method as commensurate, with no discussion of the relationship between them – and often with no indication of which quoted extracts are derived from which source (e.g. Espin, 1995; Press, 1991).
5. With the addition of an 'Other' category.
6. See, for example, Weaver and Ussher (1998). This terminology is potentially confusing, given that the epistemological assumptions of discourse analysis/ discursive psychology are more akin to the 'alternative' ethnographic approach presented in the following section than to content analysis, or even 'traditional' ethnographic analysis (see also Potter, this volume).
7. And elsewhere (Wilkinson, 2000, 2001) I have demonstrated analyses which relate talk about the causes of breast cancer to women's biographies.
8. Viewed in this way, it is not even necessary to address the issue of whether – and in what way – talk may be reflective or representative of something beyond itself.
9. I have omitted a number of lines in the interests of saving space. In this portion of the discussion Doreen offers a range of reproductive factors as possible causes of breast cancer. She ends her turn by suggesting that not having children at all may be a cause, appending the suggestion that 'there's more to it than that, isn't there?'. It is with this encouragement to present additional causes that Gertie comes in again.
10. The term 'footing' refers to the range of relationships between speakers and what they say. It enables distinctions to be made between people making claims on their own behalf, or reporting the claims of others.

Recommended reading

As further reading on focus group research, I would particularly recommend the following:

S. Wilkinson (1998) Focus group methodology: A review. *International Journal of Social Research Methodology*, 1 (3): 181–203.
Good brief introduction to the method and the range of ways in which it has been used in various disciplinary contexts.

R. Barbour and J. Kitzinger (eds) (1999) *Developing Focus Group Research: Politics, Theory and Practice*. London; Sage.
A recent edited collection, issue based, and with a wider range of examples than most anthologies of this type.

R.A. Krueger and M.A. Casey (2000) *Focus Groups: A Practical Guide for Applied Research*, Third Edition. Thousand Oaks, CA: Sage.
One of the two best introductions to doing focus group research, very practical. The second edition of this text (Krueger, 1994) is also very useable.

D.L. Morgan (1997) *Focus Groups as Qualitative Research*, Second Edition. Newbury Park, CA: Sage.
The other best introduction to doing focus group research, covers key issues as well as practical details.

S. Wilkinson (2000) Women with breast cancer talking causes: Comparing content, biographical and discursive analyses. *Feminism & Psychology*, 10 (4): 431–60.
Useful for more examples of different types of data analysis, with extensive discussion of their implications.

REFERENCES

Agar, M. and MacDonald, J. (1995) Focus groups and ethnography. *Human Organization*, 54 (1): 78–86.

Aubry, J. (2003) City of Light in darkness about life in Canada. *The Vancouver Sun*, 24 February: 14.

Barbour, R. and Kitzinger, J. (eds) (1999) *Developing Focus Group Research: Politics, Theory and Practice*. London; Sage.

Bers, T.H. (1987) Exploring institutional images through focus group interviews. In R.S. Lay and J.J. Endo (eds), *Designing and Using Market Research*. San Francisco: Jossey-Bass.

Blaxter, M. (1983) The causes of disease: Women talking. *Social Science & Medicine*, 17: 59–69.

Bloor, M., Frankland, J., Robson, K. and Thomas, M. (2001) *Focus Groups in Social Research*. London: Sage.

Braun, V. and Wilkinson, S. (2003) Liability or asset? Women talk about the vagina. *Psychology of Women Section Review*, 5(2): 28–42.

Braun, V. and Wilkinson, S. (forthcoming) Vagina equals woman? On genitals and gendered identity (submitted)

Brooks, L. (1998) Our Labour ratings. *Guardian*, 27 April: 7.

Bryman, A. (1988) *Quality and Quantity in Social Research*. London: Unwin Hyman.

Carey, M.A. (ed.) (1995) Special issue: Issues and applications of focus groups. *Qualitative Health Research*, 5 (4).

Carey, M.A. and Smith, M.W. (1994) Capturing the group effect in focus groups: A special concern in analysis. *Qualitative Health Research*, 4 (1): 123–7.

Cooper, P., Diamond, I., and High, S. (1993) Choosing and using contraceptives: Integrating qualitative and quantitative methods in family planning. *Journal of the Market Research Society*, 35 (4): 325–39.

Drew, P. and Heritage, J. (1992) Analyzing talk at work: An introduction. In P. Drew and J. Heritage (eds), *Talk at Work: Interaction in Institutional Settings*. Cambridge: Cambridge University Press.

Elliott, L. (1998) Focus groups tested tax plans. *Guardian*, 24 March: 3.

Ellis, S. (2002) Doing being liberal: Implicit prejudice in focus group talk about lesbian and gay human rights issues. *Lesbian and Gay Psychology Review*, 2 (2): 43–9.

Espin, O.M. (1995) 'Race', racism and sexuality in the life narratives of immigrant women. *Feminism & Psychology*, 5: 223–38.

Farquhar, C., with Das, R. (1999) Are focus groups suitable for sensitive topics? In R.S. Barbour and J. Kitzinger (eds), *Developing Focus Group Research: Politics, Theory and Practice*. London: Sage. pp. 47–63.

Finch, J. (1984) 'It's great to have someone to talk to': The ethics and politics of interviewing women. In C. Bell and H. Roberts (eds), *Social Researching: Politics, Problems, Practice*. London: Routledge & Kegan Paul.

Fine, M. (1992) *Disruptive Voices: The Possibilities of Feminist Research*. Ann Arbor, MI: University of Michigan Press.

Frith, H. (2000) Focusing on sex: Using focus groups in sex research. *Sexualities*, 3 (3): 275–97.

Goffman, E. (1981) *Forms of Talk*. Oxford: Basil Blackwell.

Green, G., Barbour, R.S., Bernard, M., and Kitzinger, J. (1993) 'Who wears the trousers?' Sexual harassment in research settings. *Women's Studies International Forum*, 16: 627–37.

Greenbaum, T.L. (1998) *The Handbook for Focus Group Research*. Second Edition. Thousand Oaks, CA: Sage.

Gubrium, J.F. and Holstein, J.A. (1997) *The New Language of Qualitative Method*. New York: Oxford University Press.

Herbert, C.M.H. (1989) *Talking of Silence: The Sexual Harassment of Schoolgirls*. London: Falmer Press.

Jarrett, R.L. (1993) Focus group interviewing with low-income minority populations: A research experience. In D.L. Morgan (ed.), *Successful Focus Groups: Advancing the State of the Art*. Newbury Park, CA: Sage.

Johnson, A. (1996) 'It's good to talk': The focus group and the sociological imagination. *The Sociological Review*, 44 (3): 517–38.

Kershner, V. (1998) Clinton faces nation. *San Francisco Chronicle*, 22 September: A1 and A11.

Kissling, E.A. (1996) Bleeding out loud: Communication about menstruation. *Feminism & Psychology*, 6: 481–504.

Kitzinger, C. (1995) Social constructionism: Implications for lesbian and gay psychology. In A. D'Augelli and C. Patterson (eds), *Lesbian, Gay and Bisexual Identities Over the Lifespan: Psychological Perspectives*. New York: Oxford University Press.

Kitzinger, J. (1990) Audience understanding of AIDS media messages: A discussion of methods. *Sociology of Health and Illness*, 12: 319–55.

Kitzinger, J. (1994a) Focus groups: Method or madness? In M. Boulton (ed.), *Challenge and Innovation: Methodological Advances in Social Research on HIV/AIDS*. London: Taylor & Francis.

Kitzinger, J. (1994b) The methodology of focus groups: The importance of interaction between research participants. *Sociology of Health and Illness*, 16: 103–21.

Knott, B. (1998) Where the focus groups eat. *Weekend Telegraph*, 25 July: 7.

Krueger, R.A. (1994) *Focus Groups: A Practical Guide for Applied Research*, Second Edition. Newbury Park, CA: Sage.

Krueger, R.A. and Casey, M.A. (2000) *Focus Groups: A Practical Guide for Applied Research*, Third Edition. Thousand Oaks, CA: Sage.

Krueger, R.A. and King, J.A. (1998) *Involving Community Members in Focus Groups*. Thousand Oaks, CA: Sage. (*The Focus Group Kit*, Vol. 4)

Lengua, L.J., Roosa, M., Schupak-Neuberg, E., Michaels, M.L., Berg, C.N., and Weschler, L.F. (1992) Using focus groups to guide the development of a parenting program for difficult-to-reach, high-risk families. *Family Relations*, 41: 163–8.

Lunt, P. and Livingstone, S. (1996) Focus groups in communication and media research. *Journal of Communication*, 42: 78–87.

Lyons, R.F., Sullivan, M.J.L., Ritvo, P.G., with Coyne, J.C. (1995) *Relationships in Chronic Illness and Disability*. Thousand Oaks, CA: Sage.

Mays, V.M., Cochran, S.D., Bellinger, G., Smith, R.G., Henley, N., Daniels, M., Tibbits, T., Victorianne, G.D., Osei, O.K., and Birt, D.K. (1992) The language of black gay men's sexual behaviour: Implications for AIDS risk reduction. *Journal of Sex Research*, 29: 425–34.

Morgan, D.L. (1988) *Focus Groups as Qualitative Research*. Newbury Park, CA: Sage.

Morgan, D.L. (1993a) Qualitative content analysis: A guide to paths not taken. *Qualitative Health Research*, 3: 112–21.

Morgan, D.L. (ed.) (1993b) *Successful Focus Groups: Advancing the State of the Art*. Newbury Park, CA: Sage.

Morgan, D.L. (1995) Why things (sometimes) go wrong in focus groups. *Qualitative Health Research*, 5: 515–22.

Morgan, D.L. (1996) Focus groups. *Annual Review of Sociology*, 22: 129–52.

Morgan, D.L. (1997) *Focus Groups as Qualitative Research*, Second Edition. Newbury Park, CA: Sage.

Morgan, D.L. and Krueger, R.A. (1998) *The Focus Group Kit* (6 vols). Newbury Park, CA: Sage.

Morgan, D.L. and Spanish, M.T. (1984) Focus groups: A new tool for qualitative research. *Qualitative Sociology*, 7 (3): 253–70.

Morgan, D.L. and Spanish, M.T. (1985) Social interaction and the cognitive organisation of health-relevant knowledge. *Sociology of Health & Illness*, 7 (3): 401–22.

Myers, G. (1998) Displaying opinions: Topics and disagreement in focus groups. *Language in Society*, 27: 85–111.

Oakley, A. (1981) Interviewing women: A contradiction in terms. In H. Roberts (ed.), *Doing Feminist Research*. London: Routledge & Kegan Paul.

Plaut, T., Landis, S., and Trevor, J. (1993) Focus groups and community mobilization: A case study from rural North Carolina. In D.L. Morgan (ed.), *Successful Focus Groups: Advancing the State of the Art*. Newbury Park, CA: Sage.

Potter, J. (1996) *Representing Reality: Discourse, Rhetoric and Social Construction*. London: Sage.

Powney, J. (1988) Structured eavesdropping. *Research Intelligence*, 28: 10–12.

Press, A.L. (1991) Working-class women in a middle-class world: The impact of television on modes of reasoning about abortion. *Critical Studies in Mass Communication*, 8: 421–41.

Puchta, C. and Potter, J. (1999) Asking elaborate questions: Focus groups and the management of spontaneity. *Journal of Sociolinguistics*, 3: 314–35.

Sacks, H. (1992) *Lectures on Conversation*, ed. G. Jefferson. Oxford: Basil Blackwell.

Schegloff, E.A. (1995) *Sequence organization*. Unpublished MS.

Schegloff, E.A. (1997) Practices and actions: Boundary cases of other-initiated repair. *Discourse Processes*, 23 (3): 499–545.

Seale, C., Gobo, G., Gubrium, J.F., and Silverman, D. (eds) (2003) *Qualitative Research Practice*. London: Sage.

Silverman, D. (1997) *Qualitative Research: Theory, Method and Practice*. London: Sage.

Silverman, D. (2000) *Doing Qualitative Research: A Practical Handbook*. London: Sage.

Silverman, D. (2001) *Interpreting Qualitative Data: Methods for Analysing Talk, Text and Interaction*, Second Edition. London: Sage.

Stewart, D.W. and Shamdasani, P.N. (1990) *Focus Groups: Theory and Practice*. London: Sage.

Swain, G. (2002) Pester power. *The Sunday Times*, 29 December, 'Focus' section: 16.

Tuck, M. (1976) *How Do We Choose?*. London: Methuen.

Weaver, J.J. and Ussher, J.M. (1998) How motherhood changes life: A discourse analytic study with mothers of young children. *Journal of Reproductive and Infant Psychology*, 15: 51–68.

Wilkinson, S. (1998a) Focus groups in health research: Exploring the meanings of health and illness. *Journal of Health Psychology*, 3 (3): 329–48.

Wilkinson, S. (1998b) Focus group methodology: A review. *International Journal of Social Research Methodology*, 1 (3): 181–203.

Wilkinson, S. (1999) Focus groups: A feminist method. *Psychology of Women Quarterly*, 23: 221–44.

Wilkinson, S. (2000) Women with breast cancer talking causes: Comparing content, biographical and discursive analyses. *Feminism & Psychology*, 10 (4): 431–60.

Wilkinson, S. (2001) Theoretical perspectives on women and gender. In R.K. Unger (ed.), *Handbook of the Psychology of Women and Gender*. New York: Wiley.

Wilkinson, S. (2003a) Focus groups. In J.A. Smith (ed.), *Qualitative Psychology: A Practical Guide to Research Methods*. London: Sage.

Wilkinson, S. (2003b) Focus groups. In G.M. Breakwell (ed.), *Doing Social Psychology*. Oxford: Blackwell.

Wilkinson, S. and Kitzinger, C. (2003) Constructing identities: A feminist conversation analytic approach to positioning in action. In R. Harre and F. Moghaddam (eds), *The Self and Others: Positioning Individuals and Groups in Personal, Political and Cultural Contexts*. New York: Praeger/Greenwood.

Wong, G.C., Li, V.C., Burris, M.A., and Xiang, Y. (1995) Seeking women's voices: Setting the context for women's health interventions in two rural counties in Yunnan, China. *Social Science & Medicine*, 41: 1147–57.

Part V Talk

11 Discourse analysis as a way of analysing naturally occurring talk

Jonathan Potter

This chapter will focus on the way discourse analysis can be used to study naturally occurring talk. This may seem to be a straightforward task, and in the course of this chapter I will do my best to make it so. Yet I also want to explore some complexities that may seem like diversions, but if they do not get explored they are likely to remain as traps for analysts to get caught in at later times.

So what complexities are there here? First, and most immediately, a wide range of things have been called discourse analysis. Second, the kind of discourse analysis I will be describing is a broad approach to social life that combines meta-theoretical assumptions, theoretical ideas, analytic orientations and bodies of work. Third, it is quite misleading to think of discourse analysis as a method in the way that social psychologists and many sociologists would conceive of that term. Fourth, the status of naturally occurring talk as a topic is quite complex. Fifth, I will consider the relationship between discourse analysis (DA) and conversation analysis (CA).

In the first part of the chapter I will discuss these five issues as a way of introducing some of the central features of a particular discourse analytic perspective (sometimes called a discursive psychological perspective). I will then move on in the second half of the chapter to discuss an extended example that is intended to illustrate the analytic mentality involved in doing discourse analysis.

ISSUES IN THE DISCOURSE ANALYSIS OF NATURALLY OCCURRING TALK

Stories of discourse

What is discourse analysis? This is a tricky question and its answers are changing rather quickly. The complexity of this question is clearly seen by consulting general introductions and considering the extraordinary variation of what is treated as canonical and peripheral (see, for example, Jaworski and Coupland, 1999; Phillips and Jorgenson, 2002; Schiffrin, 1994; van Dijk, 1997; Wetherell et al., 2001a; Wood and Kroger, 2000). One way of thinking about some of the species of discourse analysis is to consider them as having evolved in the different disciplinary environments of linguistics, cognitive psychology, socio-linguistics and poststructuralism.

In the past, the name discourse analysis has been applied to a range of rather different approaches to social science. In linguistics it has been applied to work on the way sentences or utterances cohere into discourse. For example, it has examined the way words such as 'however' and 'but' operate, along with different kinds of references that occur between sentences. One of the aims of this work was to duplicate on a wider canvas the success of linguistic analyses of units such as sentences (Brown and Yule, 1983). In cognitive psychology the focus has been on the way mental scripts and schemas are used to make sense of narrative. Do people work with story grammars to understand narratives in the way they use sentence grammars to understand sentences (van Dijk and Kintch, 1983)? Again, the hope was to duplicate some of the (perceived) success of work on grammar in the psychological domain.

Another distinctive area of discourse analysis developed in linguistics through work on classroom interaction. Sinclair and Coulthard (1975) attempted to provide a systematic model to describe typical interaction patterns in teaching based around 'initiation–response–feedback' structures. For example,

Teacher:	What is keeping the mercury up?	(*Initiation*)
Pupil:	The vacuum sucking.	(*Response*)
Teacher:	Not really, Peter. Susan?	(*Feedback*)

The goal here was to produce a model that would make sense of discourse structure in a whole range of different settings (Coulthard and Montgomery, 1981).

In poststructuralism and literary theory a very different tradition developed, sometimes called continental discourse analysis to differentiate it from its rather more straight-laced Anglo-Saxon counterparts. This is most associated with Michel Foucault, and is less concerned with discourse in terms of specific interaction as with how a discourse, or a set of 'statements', comes to constitute objects and subjects. For example, medical discourse may come to constitute particular objects as distinct and factual ('vapours', 'HIV+') and the doctor as a particular individual with knowledge and authority. (For an accessible discussion of Foucault's notion of discourse see McHoul and Grace, 1993).

There are, then, at least these four somewhat independent forms of discourse analysis with different disciplinary homes. To make things even more complicated, discourse analysis is sometimes used as an inclusive label for some or all of these approaches combined with speech act work, Gricean pragmatics, linguistic presupposition, critical linguistics and conversation analysis (Stubbs, 1983; van Dijk, 1985). The rough logic of inclusion here is an emphasis on language function and/or a concern with language outside of the restricted categories of grammar, phonetics and phonemics.

The rest of this chapter will concentrate on yet another variant of discourse analysis. This developed initially in the field of sociology and more recently in social psychology and communications (Billig, 1992; Edwards and Potter, 1992; Gilbert and Mulkay, 1984; Potter and Wetherell, 1987). The tradition is now often called discursive psychology to distinguish it from the other varieties. It is distinctive in various ways. Discourse analysts in this tradition reject the cognitivism of the work in linguistics and cognitive psychology because it makes it very difficult properly to address the way discourse is oriented to action (Edwards, 1997). They treat the interactional analysis of Sinclair and Coulthard (1975) as overly based on rather mechanistic linguistic analysis and inattentive to the complex social practices that take place in classrooms and similar locations. They have expressed similar doubts about Foucauldian approaches to discourse, although being impressed by, and influenced by, some of their insights.

Discourse analysis

Discourse analysis of this latter kind (henceforth DA) is characterized by a meta-theoretical emphasis on anti-realism and constructionism. That is, DA emphasizes the way versions of the world, of society, events and inner psychological worlds, are produced in discourse. On the one hand, this leads to a concern with participants' constructions and how they are accomplished and undermined; and, on the other, it leads to a recognition of the constructed and contingent nature of researchers' own versions of the world. Indeed, it treats realism, whether developed by participants or researchers, as a rhetorical production that can itself be decomposed and studied (Edwards et al., 1995; Gergen, 1994; Potter, 1992).

As a complement to this, there is an emphasis on reflexivity: for example, what are the implications from the conclusions of DA research for the practice of DA and for its literary forms, including this very text? Note the way I have introduced this chapter using the conventional homogenizing categorizations of research specialities and the familiar rhetoric of progress. Reflexivity encourages us to consider the way a text such as this is a version, selectively working up coherence and incoherence, telling historical stories, presenting and, indeed, constituting an objective, out-there reality (Ashmore, 1989; Atkinson, 1990; Potter, 1996a).

DA has an analytic commitment to studying discourse as *texts and talk in social practices*. That is, the focus is not on language as an abstract entity such as a lexicon and set of grammatical rules (in linguistics), a system of differences (in structuralism), or a set of rules for transforming statements (in Foucauldian genealogies). Instead, it is the medium for interaction; analysis of discourse becomes, then, analysis of what people do. One theme that is particularly emphasized here is the rhetorical or argumentative organization of talk and texts; claims and versions are constructed to undermine alternatives (Billig, 1987, 1991).

This conception of the focus of DA may make it seem to be pitched at a level of analysis somewhere between studies of individual psychology and studies of structural sociology. On this reading it would be an approach falling within the traditional remit of social psychology or micro-sociology. However, these kinds of distinctions have been made problematic by DA. On the one hand, DA has eaten away at traditional psychological notions by reformulating them in discursive terms. For example, a classic psychological notion such as a cognitive script can be reworked by considering the sorts of business that people do by 'script formulating' descriptions of their own or others' behaviour (Edwards, 1994). The suggestion is that there is a whole field of discursive psychology which is amenable to systematic study and has hardly been touched in mainstream psychology (Edwards, 1997; Edwards and Potter, 1992; Potter and Edwards, 2001).

On the other hand, the micro–macro distinction has also been made problematic. It has been blurred by three kinds of work. First, there are now a range of conversation analytic studies which are concerned with the way in which the institutionally specific properties of a setting such as a news interview, a doctor–patient consultation or an award ceremony are constituted in talk rather than being structurally determined in any simple way (Boden and Zimmerman, 1991; Drew and Heritage, 1992). For example, pedagogic interaction certainly happens in school classrooms, and yet much of what happens in classrooms is not pedagogic (playing around, chatting) while much recognizably pedagogic interaction ('test' questions, encouraging discovery) happens over family breakfast tables or with a partner in front of the television. Second, there is work on the way people produce descriptions or stories of social organization in their talk. For example, Wetherell and Potter (1992) studied the way particular constructions of social groups, processes of conflict and influence, histories, and so on were drawn on as practical resources for blaming minority groups for their own disadvantaged social position. That is, social structure becomes part of interaction as it is worked up, invoked and reworked (Potter, 1996a). Third, there is recent work in discursive psychology that attempts to highlight the way psychological notions are constructed in and for institutions, and how they can constitute some of the characteristic features of organizations (Edwards and Potter, 2001).

Typical DA studies focus on transcripts of talk from everyday or institutional settings, on transcripts of open-ended interviews, or on documents of some kind. Sometimes these different materials are combined together in the same study. DA is overwhelmingly qualitative, although the principled argument is not against quantification per se, but against the way counting and coding often obscures the activities being done with talk and texts (see Heritage, this volume; Peräkylä, this volume; Potter and Wetherell, 1987; Schegloff, 1993).

Discourse analysis and method

In much traditional social research, method is understood as something that can be codified with specific guidelines that, if not guaranteeing good research, are a necessary condition for its conduct. Indeed, it is often the case that the research conclusions are justified by reference to the correct and complete following of procedures such as operationalizing variables, getting high levels of inter-rater reliability for codings, and so on. DA is not like this. The analytic procedure used to arrive at claims is often quite different from the way those claims are justified.

Like most research practices in the natural and social sciences, doing DA has an important element of craft skill; it is sometimes more like sexing a chicken than following the recipe for a mild Chicken Rogan Josh (although, come to think of it, that is rather a craft skill too!). Conversation analysts sometimes talk of developing an *analytic mentality*, which captures what is involved rather nicely (Psathas, 1990). This makes it hard to describe formally and it takes time to learn. But that does not mean that the claims are necessarily hard to evaluate – if you cannot easily say precisely how someone has learned to ride a bike, you do not have so much difficulty saying whether they have fallen off or not. Likewise, there are a range of ways in which the adequacy of discourse analytic studies can be evaluated, including a focus on deviant cases, checking that participants' themselves orient to claimed phenomena, coherence with other discourse analytic studies, and, most importantly, the evaluation that readers themselves can make when they are presented with transcript alongside of its analytic interpretations (Potter, 1996b). Nor does it mean that it cannot be learned – it is dependent on not merely intuitions or imagination, but learning the requisite sets of skills.

In traditional stories of method in social research you have a question and then you search for a method to answer that question. For example, you may be interested in the 'factors' that lead to condom use in sexual encounters, and ponder whether to use an experiment with vignettes, some open-ended interviews or DA to check them out. DA is not like that. Indeed, thinking of it in this way can be positively confusing. Some questions are simply not coherent from a DA perspective. For example, the kinds of assumptions about factors and outcomes that underpin a lot of thinking in traditional social psychology and survey research do not mesh with its rhetorical and normative logic. Rather than conceiving of a world of discrete variables with discrete effects, in DA there are constructions and versions that may be adopted, responded to or undermined. Thus a categorization, say, may be undermined by a particularization, no upshot is guaranteed (Billig, 1991). Norms are *oriented to*; that is, they are not templates for action but provide a way of interpreting deviations. The absence of a return greeting does not disconfirm a regularity, rather it is the basis for inference: the recipient is rude, sad, deaf perhaps (Heritage, 1988).

So what kinds of questions are coherent within DA? Given the general focus is on texts and talk as social practices, there has been a dual focus on the practices themselves and on the resources that are drawn on in those practices. Take gender inequalities, for example. Studies have considered the way in which such inequalities are constructed, made factual and justified in talk, and they have also considered the resources ('interpretative repertoires', identities, category systems, metaphors) that are used to manufacture coherent and persuasive justifications that work to sustain those inequalities (Clarke, et al., in press; Gill, 1993; Marshall and Wetherell, 1989; Wetherell et al., 1987).

Naturally occurring talk as topic

I am going to focus here on DA specifically as applied to naturally occurring talk. However, it is important to note that this topic is not as simple as it might appear. Naturally occurring talk can be relatively straightforwardly defined as spoken language produced entirely independently of the actions of the researcher, whether it is everyday conversation over the telephone, the records of a company board meeting, or the interaction between doctor and patient in a surgery. It is natural in the specific sense that it is not 'got up' by the researcher using an interview schedule, a questionnaire, an experimental protocol or some such social research technology.

Although this is useful in highlighting how far traditional researchers are implicated in the production of 'data', it also suggests a hierarchy moving from somewhat ephemeral interaction in the laboratory to more real inter-action happening naturally out in the world. A better conceptualization treats naturally occurring talk not as a straightforward discovered object, but as a theoretical and analytic stance on conversational interaction. This may seem rather abstruse but it has two advantages. On the one hand, it differentiates DA from other work on records of interaction such as content analysis, which involves the kinds of coding and counting that obscure the subtly contexted nature of conversational interaction as well as the sorts of turn-by-turn displays of understanding and repair that have been effectively used in conversation analysis (Psathas, 1995). On the other hand, it provides a different perspective on research procedures such as interviews. Instead of treating these as machinery for harvesting data from respondents they can be viewed as an arena for interaction in its own right: that is, natural-interaction-in-interview. What I am suggesting, then, is that it is the analytic and theoretical stance that constitutes its object as naturally occurring talk, and we should be wary of accepting too readily assumptions about what kinds of talk are natural and what are not. Some of the quite complex issues at stake here are usefully discussed in an exchange in *Discourse Studies* (Lynch, 2002; ten Have, 2002; Potter, 2002; Speer, 2002).

This point is particularly important for showing what is distinctive about the considerable body of DA work that has used open-ended interviews. When interviews are treated as machinery for harvesting psychologically and linguistically interesting responses, the research is inevitably focused on those elements of interviews contributed by the participant rather than those from the researcher. However, it is possible to conceptualize interviews as arenas for interaction between two or more parties. That is, we can treat them as a form of natural conversational interaction, by analysing them the same way that we might a telephone conversation between friends or a cross-examination in a courtroom. Widdicombe and Wooffitt (1995) provide one of the most thoroughgoing attempts to use interviews in this way, treating materials originally collected for a study of social identity as examples of unfolding conversational interaction where the sense of social categories is refined and reworked. Furthermore, once this perspective on interviews is adopted the standard methodology textbook injunctions to be as neutral and uninvolved as possible become highly problematic. It only makes sense as part of the fiction that the researchers can somehow disappear from the interaction if only they can make themselves passive enough – in DA it has been productive to be actively engaged and even argumentative during interviews (Wetherell and Potter, 1992). Some of the problems with DA work, particularly that on interviews, are discussed in Antaki et al. (2003).

Having resisted a too simple distinction between natural and artificial talk I do not want to diminish the difficulties of working with interview talk. It is contrived; it is subject to powerful expectations about social science research fielded by participants; and there are particular difficulties in extrapolating from interview talk to activities in other settings. Discourse analysts have increasingly turned away from interviews to focus on materials less affected by the formulations and assumptions of the researcher. This move will undoubtedly continue as the power of work on natural conversation becomes more apparent.

How is discourse analysis related to ethnomethodology and conversation analysis?

I have already noted the spread of different approaches that have been called DA. There is some variation in these other approaches. It is common now to distinguish the 'classic' ethnomethodological approach represented by Garfinkel's *Studies in Ethnomethodology* (1967) and the more recent programme of studies of work (Garfinkel, 2002). In the case of Sacks's work there are major differences between the early focus on membership categories and the later work on conversational organization (Sacks, 1992; see Silverman (1998) for an overview). Nevertheless, there is considerable convergence, particularly compared with, say, classic sociological work on institutions or classic experimental social psychological studies of group processes.

To simplify the question six areas of divergence will be highlighted. Hold in mind, though, that these observations are specific to the DA tradition discussed here.

1 *Construction*. DA is constructionist in the sense that it takes a specific focus on the way versions and descriptions are assembled to perform actions. The construction and use of descriptions is a topic of study. Although ethno-methodologists have been critical of the social constructionist tradition in social science, it is not clear that there is so much tension between this take on construction and that in ethnomethodology or conversation analysis (for some arguments, see Button and Sharrock, 1993; Potter, 1996a).

2 *Rhetoric*. Whereas conversation analytic work is focused on sequential organization, DA is also focused on rhetorical organization – the way versions are put together to counter alternatives. Often an understanding of sequential organization is a prerequisite for understanding rhetorical organization.

3 *Cognition*. DP is anti-cognitivist. It rejects the aim of explaining action by reference to underlying cognitive states. The status of cognition in ethnomethodology and CA is a source of some disagreement (see papers in te Molder and Potter, in press). Edwards (1995) has offered an anti-cognitivist reading of Sacks. DP work is often focused on considering the practical work done by cognitivist notions (see, for example, Potter and Hepburn, 2003).

4 *Interviews and texts*. Although CA and ethnomethodological work have eschewed interviews, studies in DA have often used interview material (Billig, 1992; Wetherell and Potter, 1992). However, more recently discourse analysts have increasingly worked with naturalistic data. DA research has also worked more with texts than conversation analysts – although, texts have been an important topic for ethnomethodologists.

5 *Resources*. DA has focused on the resources drawn on in practices as well as the practices themselves. This is especially so with earlier work on 'interpretative repertoires' (Potter and Wetherell, 1987). Live issues remain as to how far one thing can be studied independently of the other, as the continuing debate over the status of membership categorization analysis attests (Hester and Eglin, 1997).

6 *Epistemology*. An important influence on DA has been the sociology of scientific knowledge. This has led to a more sceptical position on issues of truth and knowledge than is common in CA. These differences show themselves most clearly at the level of theory and the justification of research procedures than in the actual procedures themselves.

In the opening parts of the chapter I have addressed a number of background issues for discourse analytic research. There are a range of other concerns to do with transcription, interview conduct, coding, forms of validation, writing up discourse research that there is no space to discuss. For a more detailed coverage of these see Hepburn and Potter (2003), Potter (2003a, 2003b), Potter and Wetherell (1987), Wetherell et al. (2001b), Widdicombe and Wooffitt (1995), Willig (2003) and Wood and Kroger (2000). For the rest of this chapter I will focus on a particular example, with the aim of illustrating the analytic mentality involved in discourse analytic research on talk. In addition, I hope to highlight some of the recurring themes in such work as well as exploring some of the similarities and differences between CA and DA.

DISCOURSE ANALYSIS OF NATURALLY OCCURRING TALK

There is a wide range of different ways of analysing discourse. It is useful to make a distinction between studies that focus on the kinds of resources drawn on in discourse and the practices in which those resources are used. The emphasis here will be on the latter kind of study. What I will do is highlight some of the concerns that analysis works with, and one of the best ways of doing this is to work with some specific materials. It will try to avoid the common goal in writing about method that is to provide justifications to other academics rather than assist in the conduct of analysis itself.

Princess Diana and 'I dunno'

I have chosen to start with a piece of talk that is interesting, and probably familiar, at least in its broad outline, to many readers. It comes from a BBC television interview; the interviewer is Martin Bashir and the interviewee is the late Princess Diana.

```
1 Bashir:     The Queen described nineteen ninety two as
              her (.) annus horribilis, .hh and it was in that year that
              Andrew Morton's book about you was published.
  Princess:   Um hm. (nods)
  Bashir:     .hh Did you ↑ever (.) meet Andrew Morton or
              personally (.) help him with the book?
  Princess:   In never- I never met him, no.
              (1.0)
  Bashir:     Did you ever (.) personally assist him with
              the writing of his book.
              (0.8)
  Princess:   A lot of people .hhh (clears throat)
              saw the distress that my life was in. (.)
              And they felt (.) felt it was a supportive thing
              to help (0.2) in the way that they did.
  Bashir:     Did you (.) allow your ↑friends, >your close friends,<
              to speak to Andrew °Morton°?
  Princess:   Yes I did. Y [es, I did
  Bashir:                  [°Why°?
  Princess:   I was (.) at the end of my tether (.)
              I was (.) desperate (.)
              >I think I was so fed up with being< (.)
              seen as someone who was a ba:sket case (.)
              because I am a very strong person (.)
              and I know (.) that causes complications, (.)
```

```
                    in the system (.) that I live in.
                    (1.0) ((smiles and purses lips))
Bashir:             How would a book change that.
Princess:           I [↑] dunno. ((raises eyebrows, looks away)) ←
                    Maybe people have a better understanding (.)
                    maybe there's a lot of women out there
                    who suffer (.) on the same level
                    but in a different environment (.)
                    who are unable to: (.) stand up for themselves (.)
                    because (.) their self-esteem is (.) cut into two.
                    I dunno ((shakes head))                    ←
Bashir:             .hh What effect do you think the book had on (.)
                    your husband and the Royal Family?
Princess:           I think they were (.) shocked,
                    and horrified,
                    and very disappointed.
                    (0.8)
Bashir:             Can you understand why?
Princess:           (Well) I think Mr Dimbleby's book (0.2)
                    was a shock to a lot of people,
                    and disappointment as well.
```

(from *Panorama*, BBC1, 20 November 1995 –
see Appendix for transcription conventions)

The first thing to note here is that even a short sequence of interaction of this kind is enormously rich, and could be the starting point for a wide range of different studies. For example, conversation analysts have considered the way the different interactional roles of interviewer and interviewee are interactionally produced, and the way issues such as neutrality and evasiveness are managed (Clayman and Heritage, 2002). I am going to pick up a theme more characteristic of DA, and discursive psychology in particular. I am going to focus principally on just the two lines that have been arrowed – the two 'I dunno's'. Why these? There are three reasons, all of which illustrate different facets of doing work of this kind.

First, these fragments of talk relate to broader and established analytic concerns with fact construction and the role of descriptions in interaction. The point, then, is that although I have not come to this material with a pre-set hypothesis of the kind that a social psychologist might have when designing an experiment, my way into it is related to a wide range of prior interests, knowledge and concerns. However, there is nothing particularly special about the topic of fact construction; a range of different established interests could be bought to bear on this same material.

Second, these fragments are easily treated as the trivial details of interaction. If we were to make a précis of the interaction we would probably not draw attention to them. On the video they sound almost throwaway. However, one of the features of talk that has been strongly emphasized by Sacks (1992) and other conversation analysts is that what seem to be its details are fundamental. Social scientists often treat talk as a conduit for information between speakers: there is a message and it is passed from one person to another. When we use this picture it is easy to imagine that what is important is some basic package of information, and then there is a lot of rather unimportant noise added to the signal: hesitations, pauses, overlaps, choice of specific words, and so on. For conversation analysts this view is fundamentally misguided. Rather than treating these features of talk as simply a blurred edge on the pure message these features are treated as determining precisely what action is being performed as well as providing a rich analytic resource for understanding what that activity is.

It is for this reason that talk is carefully transcribed as it is delivered rather than being rendered into the conventional 'playscript' that is common in some kinds of qualitative work. Note that it is sometimes complained that such transcription is unnecessary, unhelpful or even – sin of sins – positivistic! However, it is important to remember that the potential playscript that often passes for transcript is itself highly conventionalized and buys into a whole set of more or less explicit assumptions about interaction.

The third reason for focusing on 'I dunno' is that it provides a neat way of contrasting DA with a cognitive psychological approach to talk. What might a cognitive psychologist make of 'I dunno's'? There are all sorts of possibilities, but one approach that might be taken is to treat such utterances as 'uncertainty tokens': that is, words or expressions that people use to report states of uncertainty. This would be in line with the general cognitive psychological approach of relating language use to an individual's cognitive processes and representations (Edwards, 1997). Considering 'I dunno's' therefore has the virtue of allowing us to compare and contrast a cognitive and discursive approach to talk.

One of the notable features of discourse analytic work is that the best way into some materials like this may be to consider *other* materials or *other* sorts of findings. At its most basic, a good feel for some of the standard features of everyday and institutional talk is particularly useful for producing high-quality analyses (Hutchby and Wooffitt (1998) provide a basic introduction and overview). In this case, I suggest that one of the ways into Princess Diana's 'I dunno's' is to consider the way issues of stake and interest have been conceptualized in discursive psychology.

Stake as a participants' concern

Work in the ethnomethodological and conversation analytic tradition has highlighted the centrality of accountability in interaction. More recently, discourse analysts dealing with psychological issues have emphasized the significance that participants place on issues of stake and interest (Edwards and Potter, 1992). People treat each other as entities with desires, motives, institutional allegiances, and so on, as having a stake in their actions. Referencing stake is one principal way of discounting the significance of an action or reworking its nature. For example, a blaming can be discounted as merely a product of spite; an offer may be discounted as an attempt to influence.

Here is an explicit and familiar example where the speaker invokes an interest to undercut a (reported) claim. The extract is from a current affairs programme in which the author Salman Rushdie is being interviewed by David Frost. Frost is asking about the fatwa – the religious death sentence on Rushdie.

> 2   **Frost**:   And how could they cancel it now? Can they cancel it
>   – they say they can't.
> → **Rushdie**:   Yeah, but you know, they would, wouldn't they,
>   as somebody once said. The thing is, without going
>   into the kind of arcana of theology, there is no technical
>   problem. The problem is not technical. The problem
>   is that they don't want to.
>   (Public Broadcasting Service, 26 November 1993)

Rushdie's response to the claim that the fatwa cannot be cancelled is to discount the claim as obviously motivated. The familiar phrase 'they would, wouldn't they' treats the Iranians' claim as something to be expected: it is the sort of thing that people with that background, those interests, that set of attitudes *would* say; and it formulates that predictability as shared knowledge. This extract illustrates the potential for invoking stake and interest to discount claims.

Both discourse and conversation analysts have stressed that where some difficulty or issue is widespread there are likely to be some well-developed procedures for dealing with it. For example, given the established procedures that exist for managing turn taking we would expect there to be some procedures to exist for terminating conversations, and this is what is found (Levinson, 1983; Schegloff and Sacks, 1973). Or, to take a more discourse analytic example, given that scientists tend to keep separate the inconsistent repertoires of terms they use for justifying their own claims and undermining those of opponents, we would expect that some devices would be developed for dealing with situations where those repertoires come together; and this is what is found (Gilbert and Mulkay, 1984). Following this logic, we might expect to find procedures that people use to resist the kind of discounting seen in Extract 2.

Here is a candidate discursive technique for undermining discounting. It was not the product of a systematic search; rather I came across it while reading the newspaper and thinking about this issue. It comes from an article in the *Guardian* newspaper headlined 'Psychiatrist reveals the agony and the lunacy of great artists'.

> 3   The stereotype of the tortured genius suffering for his art and losing his
>   mind in a sea of depression, sexual problems and drink turns out to be
>   largely true, a psychiatrist says today.
>   While scientists, philosophers and politicians can all suffer from the
>   odd personality defect, for real mental instability you need to look at
>   writers and painters, says Felix Post.

→ Dr Post was initially sceptical, but having looked at the lives of nearly 300 famous men he believes exceptional creativity and psychiatric problems are intertwined. In some way, mental ill health may fuel some forms of creativity, he concludes. (*Guardian*, 30 June 1994)

The feature of the article that struck me was: 'Dr Post was initially sceptical . . .'. Following the idea that all features of talk and texts are potentially there to do some kind of business, we can ask why this particular feature is there. What it seems to do is counter the potential criticism that Dr Post is perpetrating stereotypes about madness and creativity. His initial scepticism encourages us to treat his conclusions as factual because they are counter to his original interests.

I have suggested that such features of discourse can be understood by a medical analogy. People can avoid catching a disease such as tuberculosis by being inoculated against it. Perhaps in the same way conversationalists and writers can limit the ease with which their talk and texts can be undermined by doing a *stake inoculation* (Potter, 1996a). Just as you have a jab to prevent the disease, perhaps you can inject a piece of discourse to present undermining.

Let me now stand back and highlight two features of the kind of analytic mentality I am working with. First, in common with conversation analysts, discourse analysts are concerned to use evidence from the materials as far as possible rather than basing interpretations on their own prior assumptions about people, mind, society or whatever. In this case, note that the idea that there is a stereotype about madness and creativity is not my own, it is introduced in the text itself. Moreover, the analysis does not depend on this stereotype actually existing, merely that it is invoked as an issue in this text. Note that this does not mean that the analysts expects to be able to free themselves of all their preconceptions, rather it is that analysis is, to an important extent, an interrogation of those expectations.

Second, note the way I have moved in this analysis between conversational and textual material. Discourse analysts have been much more willing than conversation analysts to combine such materials and have tried to avoid making a priori assumptions about differences between the two. Both talk and texts are treated as oriented to action; *both* orient to issues of stake and may be inoculated against discounting.

'I dunno' as a stake inoculation

So far, then, I have emphasized some background considerations that might help us understand what Princess Diana's 'I dunno's' in Extract 1 are doing. One helpful way to continue the analysis is to collect some more examples of a similar kind. More formally, we might think of this as building a corpus for study or even coding of a set of data. Whatever we call it, the goal is to help the analyst see patterns and to highlight different properties of particular constructions. Although some of the initial procedures are superficially similar, the goal is not the content analytic one of providing counts of occurrences of particular kinds of talk within categories.

A search for 'I don't know's' through a set of materials taken from relation-ship counselling sessions provided Extract 4. The extract comes from the start of a long story in which the speaker, Jimmy, is describing a difficult evening in a pub with his wife, Connie. As well as Connie and Jimmy there is a counsellor present. One of the themes in the session is a series of complaints by Jimmy that Connie flirts with other men. At the same time Connie has made a number of suggestions that he is pathologically jealous and prone to seeing harmless sociability as sexual suggestion (Edwards, 1995).

```
4        Jimmy:   This ↑one particular night, (0.2)
                  anyway (0.2) there was uh: (1.2) I didn't-
                  Connie had made arrangements to ↑ meet people.
                  (1.8)
                  And I didn't want to. (0.6)
                  It wasn't any other thing.
                  (1.6)
                  A:nd (0.8) we sat in the pub and
                  we (.) started to discuss=
                  =>we had a little bit of a row.< (2.0)
                  In the pub. (0.6)
                  And arguing about the time. (0.8)
                  U:m (.) whe:n these people came in. (.)
                  >It was:< (.) John and Caroline. (1.0)
                  And then they had- (.)
                  this other fella Dave.
                  °With them as well.°
                  [6 lines omitted]
                  they all came in the pub anyway. (1.0)
                  Well (.) Connie sat beside (0.6) Caroline.
                  And I sat (further back).
                  So you was (.) you was split between us.
                  They sat in- on the other side.
                  (1.0)
                  [16 lines omitted]
                  And uh:: (1.0)
1→                Connie had a short skirt on
2→                I don't know. (1.0)
                  And I knew this- (0.6)
                  uh ah- maybe I had met him. (1.0) Ye:h. (.)
                  I musta met Da:ve before. (0.8)
                  But I'd heard he was a bit of a la:d ( ).
                  He didn't care: (1.0) who he (0.2) chatted up or (.)
                  who was in Ireland (.) y'know
                  those were (unavailable) to chat up with.
                  (1.0)
                  So Connie stood up (0.8)
```

> pulled her skirt right up her side (0.6)
> and she was looking <u>straight</u> at Da:ve (.)
> >°like that°< (0.6)
>
> (DE:C2:S1:10–11)

Let us start by considering Jimmy's description of Connie's skirt length (arrow 1). For Jimmy this description does some important business related to why they are here for counselling, and who has the problems that need fixing. The short skirt exemplifies something about Connie's character. It is a building block in the construction of Connie as 'flirty', an objective particular rather than just an opinion. He is merely reporting something that she chose to wear rather than engaging in psychological judgement. However, the description is an especially delicate one, where Jimmy's stake in it is likely to be a particular concern. The problem for Jimmy is that the description could be turned round and used as evidence that he is *precisely* the sort of pathologically jealous guy who obsessively remembers every detail of his partner's skirt length. That is, his description might generate problems for him as much as for Connie. How can he manage this delicacy?

It is immediately after the description of the skirt length that Jimmy says 'I don't know' (arrow 2). Why might he be saying just this just here? Let us consider the possibility that it attempts to head off the potential counter that Jimmy was jealously inspecting Connie's clothing: that he was *already* concerned about it even before the evening was under way? This interpretation is consistent with the detail of the sequence. Jimmy provides a description of Connie's skirt length that is part of his picture of *her* flirtatious behaviour, which, in turn, makes *his* own strong reaction more accountable. At the same time the expression of uncertainty works against the idea that *he* is saying this, noticing this, because *he* is pathologically jealous.

Why not treat the 'I don't know' as Jimmy straightforwardly reporting his uncertainty about this feature of the narrative? This would be in line with the cognitive psychological account of such utterances as 'uncertainty markers'. Can we adjudicate between these different interpretations of 'I don't know'? There are various ways we might go about this. One approach that discourse analysts have found particularly fruitful has been to look for variability between different versions. Variability is to be expected where people are constructing their talk in different ways to perform different actions – variability in and between versions can be an important clue to understanding what action is being done. In this case, for example, we can search the materials for other references to Connie's skirt length. We do not have to look very hard! The very first thing Connie says after Jimmy's long narrative is the following.

> 5 **Connie:** My skirt <u>prob</u>ably went up to about there. ((gestures))
> **Jimmy:** ((a sharp intake of breath))
> **Connie:** <u>May</u>be a bit <u>short</u>er. It was <u>done</u> for <u>no</u>- I never <u>look</u>ed at
> that particular bloke when I did it it was my friend commented
> Oh you're <u>show</u>ing o:ff a lot o' leg tonight.
>
> (DE:C2:S1:11)

Two things are particularly worth highlighting here. First, note that despite the various dramatic events in Jimmy's long narrative (including a suicide attempt) the very first thing that Connie picks out to contest is the description of the skirt length. In doing this she is displaying a skilled awareness of the relationship of descriptions to moral categories. This is a display that we can use to help support our own understanding of the working of this description.

Second, note that *here* Jimmy does not seem to be in any doubt about the precise length of Connie's skirt. His sharp, highly audible, inbreath is a display of disagreement with Connie's claim about her skirt length that occasions a grudging modification by Connie. The point, then, is that there is no evidence of Jimmy's cloudy memory – no 'I dunnoness' – here; precision in skirt length now seems to be the order of the day. This variability supports the interpretation of this 'I dunno' as a stake inoculation and is hard to fit with the plain vanilla cognitive account in which the speaker merely reports his or her lack of certainty.

Let us return now to Martin Bashir's interview with Princess Diana. We are now in a better position to make some systematic suggestions about the 'I dunno's' in this passage of talk. We can start to make sense of their role in the management of stake and interest, and in particular their operation as stake inoculations.

The first thing we need to be confident of is that there is an orientation to issues of stake in this material. It is not hard to find. Bashir opens the sequence by formulating the relation between Andrew Morton's book and a hard year for the Queen (her well-known 'annus horribilis'). He then pursues a line of questioning to the Princess about her involvement with this book. He attempts to tease out for the viewing audience how responsible she is for this (negatively constructed) book.

Princess Diana responds to these questions with a series of denials, evasions, accounts and implicit versions of the role of the book (in that order to the first three questions). However, having accepted that she had some involvement with the book, if only via her friends, she is now faced with a tricky question about how the book can be a positive thing (how would a book change that?). This question is so tricky because of its potential for suggesting that Princess Diana has acted as a spurned and vindictive ex-wife, getting her revenge for a book that Prince Charles had an involvement with (as she makes at the end of the extract). The category 'spurned and vindictive ex-wife' is perhaps not fully available in this sequence – but it is a commonplace in tabloid newspaper reporting, and helps make sense of both the persistence of the questioning and the strength of the resistance. We can certainly identify an orientation to stake.

Given this issue of stake, we can understand the placement of the two 'I dunno's'. The uncertainty displayed in the answer to 'how would a book change all of that?' precisely manages the danger she will be seen as calculating and malevolent, a woman who has carefully planned her revenge. The 'I dunno's' help break the connection between her action of helping with the book and the potentially noxious identity implied. Note the coordination of verbal and non-verbal here. Her first 'I dunno' is accompanied by what might be called a display of wondering – she looks into the distance as if never having been asked this before or had to think about it before. It is a lovely exhibition of visual psychology closely coordinated with the business at hand.

This is by no means a definitive account of the role of 'I dunno' in Extract 1. And, of course, it does not address the very many other live and relevant features of the extract. However, what I have tried to do is show some of the procedures that can help build an interpretation of a piece of discourse, and the mentality that goes with such analysis. Let me list some of these features.

Themes in the analysis of discourse

This chapter has attempted to overview some of the issues that arise when analysing discourse. Developing analytic skills is best characterized as developing a particular mentality. DA is more inductive than hypothetico-deductive; generally work starts with a setting or particular discursive phenomenon rather than a preformulated hypothesis. The focus is on texts and talk as social practices in their own right. Part of DA may involve coding a set of materials, but this is an analytic preliminary used to make the quantity of materials more manageable rather than a procedure that performs the analysis itself. There is nothing sacred about such codings and extracts are often freely excluded and included in the course of some research.

DA follows the conversation analytic assumption that any order of detail in talk and text is potentially consequential for interaction, and for that reason high-quality transcripts are used in conjunction with tape recordings. In addition, DA research generally avoids trading on analysts' prior assumptions about what might be called ethnographic particulars (e.g. participants' status, the nature of the context, the goals of the participants), preferring to see these as things that are worked up, attended to and made relevant in interaction rather than being external determinants. (Although it is worth noting that this issue has become a source of not always illuminating dispute – Billig, 1999; Schegloff, 1997, 1999; Wetherell, 1998).

DA does not use talk and texts as a pathway to underlying cognitions; indeed, DA resolutely steers clear of cognitive reduction, instead treating purportedly cognitive phenomena as parts of social practices. Such discursive psychology has focused on the way participants invoke stake and interest to understand and undercut accounts, and how such undercutting may be resisted by performing actions via accounts that are constructed as factual.

In this chapter I attempted to illustrate these themes by way of a discussion of 'I dunno' and 'I don't know'. I have considered only a small number of examples. However, I hope that the insights are more general (see Potter (1996a, 1998) for further analysis). Let me end with an extract from the US sitcom *Friends*. Even with my minimal, cleaned-up transcription I think we can start to see the way the humour in the sequence depends on the sorts of features of 'I don't know' discussed above. The sequence starts with Ross talking to a psychologist, Rodge, about his ex-wife.

6 **Ross**: You see that's where you're wrong! Why would I marry her if I thought on any level that she was a lesbian?

   Rodge: I don't know. ((shrugs)) Maybe you wanted your   ←
marriage to fail. ((laughs))

   Ross: Why, why, why would I, why, why, why.

   Rodge: I don't know. Maybe . . . Maybe low self esteem,   ←
maybe to compensate for overshadowing a sibling. Maybe you w-

   Monica: W- w- wait. Go back to that sibling thing.

   Rodge: I don't know. ((shrugs)) It's conceivable that   ←
you wanted to sabotage your marriage so the sibling would feel less like a failure in the eyes of the parents.

   Ross: Tchow! That's, that's ridiculous. I don't feel guilty for her failures.

('The One with the Boobies', 27 June 1996 –
Ross is Monica's brother, Rodge is a psychologist
boyfriend of Ross and Monica's friend.
Note, each 'I don't know' is heavily emphasized)

Recommended reading

D. Edwards (1997) *Discourse and cognition*. London and Beverly Hills, CA: Sage.
Highlights the interplay of discursive psychology, ethnomethodology and conversation analysis with a range of analyses of psychological matters. Rewards close study.

J. Potter (1996) *Representing Reality: Discourse, Rhetoric and Social Construction*. London: Sage.
An overview of constructionism from a discourse analytic perspective. Introduces a range of relevant approaches and develops specific analyses of fact construction.

J. Potter (2003a). Discourse analysis. In M. Hardy and A. Bryman (eds), *Handbook of Data Analysis* (pp. 607–24). London: Sage.
This takes further some of the themes introduced in the current chapter, including further discussion of technology and transcription and illustrative examples of particular styles of work.

M. Wetherell, S. Taylor and S. Yates (eds) (2001) *Discourse as data: A guide for analysis*. London: Sage.
This (and its companion volume *Discourse theory and practice*) cover a range of different approaches and cover different approaches to analysis.

REFERENCES

Antaki, C., Billig, M., Edwards, D. and Potter, J. (2003) Discourse analysis means doing analysis: A critique of six analytic shortcomings, *Discourse Analysis Online*, 1. http://www.shu.ac.uk/daol/previous/v1/n1/index.htm

Ashmore, M. (1989) *The reflexive thesis: Wrighting sociology of scientific knowledge*. Chicago: University of Chicago Press.

Atkinson, P. (1990) *The ethnographic imagination: The textual construction of reality*. London: Routledge.

Billig, M. (1987) *Arguing and thinking: A rhetorical approach to social psychology*. Cambridge: Cambridge University Press.

Billig, M. (1991) *Ideologies and beliefs*. London: Sage.

Billig, M. (1992) *Talking of the royal family*. London: Routledge.

Billig, M. (1999) Whose terms? Whose ordinariness? Rhetoric and ideology in conversation analysis, *Discourse & Society*, 10: 543–58.

Boden, D. and Zimmerman, D. (eds) (1991) *Talk and social structure: Studies in ethnomethodology and conversation analysis*. Cambridge: Polity.

Button, G. and Sharrock, W. (1993) A disagreement over agreement and consensus in constructionist sociology, *Journal for the Theory of Social Behaviour*, 23 (1): 1–25.

Brown, G. and Yule, G. (1983) *Discourse analysis*. Cambridge: Cambridge University Press.

Clarke, V., Kitzinger, C. and Potter, J. (in press) Kids are just cruel anyway: Lesbian and gay parents talk about homophobic bullying, *British Journal of Social Psychology*.

Clayman, S.E. and Heritage, J. (2002) *The news interview: Journalists and public figures on the air*. Cambridge: Cambridge University Press.

Coulthard, M. and Montgomery, M. (eds) (1981) *Studies in discourse analysis*. London: Routledge.

Drew, P. and Heritage, J.C. (eds) (1992) *Talk at work: Interaction in institutional settings*. Cambridge: Cambridge University Press.

Edwards, D. (1994) Script formulations: A study of event descriptions in conversation, *Journal of Language and Social Psychology*, 13 (3): 211–47.

Edwards, D. (1995) Two to tango: Script formulations, dispositions, and rhetorical symmetry in relationship troubles talk. *Research on Language and Social Interaction*, 28: 319–50.

Edwards, D. (1997) *Discourse and cognition*. London and Beverly Hills, CA: Sage.

Edwards, D. and Potter, J. (1992) *Discursive psychology*. London: Sage.

Edwards, D. and Potter, J. (2001) Discursive psychology. In A.W. McHoul and M. Rapley (eds), *How to analyse talk in institutional settings: A casebook of methods* (pp. 12–24). London: Continuum International.

Edwards, D., Ashmore, M. and Potter, J. (1995) Death and furniture: The rhetoric, politics and theology of bottom line arguments against relativism, *History of the Human Sciences*, 8: 25–49.

Garfinkel, H. (1967) *Studies in Ethnomethodology*. Englewood Cliffs, NJ: Prentice Hall.

Garfinkel, H. (2002) *Ethnomethodology's program: Working out Durkheim's aphorism*. New York: Rowman and Littlefield.

Gergen, K.J. (1994) *Realities and relationships: Soundings in social construction*. Cambridge, MA: Harvard University Press.

Gilbert, G.N. and Mulkay, M. (1984) *Opening Pandora's box: A sociological analysis of scientists' discourse*. Cambridge: Cambridge University Press.

Gill, R. (1993) Justifying injustice: Broadcasters' accounts on inequality in radio. In E. Burman and I. Parker (eds), *Discourse analytic research: Repertoires and readings of texts in action*. London: Routledge.

ten Have, P. (2002) Ontology or methodology: Comments on Speer's 'natural' and 'contrived' data: A sustainable distinction, *Discourse Studies*, 4: 527–30.

Hepburn, A. and Potter, J. (2003) Discourse analytic practice. In C. Seale, D. Silverman, J. Gubrium and G. Gobo (eds), *Qualitative Research Practice* (pp. 180–96). London: Sage.

Heritage, J.C. (1988) Explanations as accounts: A conversation analytic perspective. In C. Antaki (ed.), *Analysing everyday explanation: A casebook of methods*. London: Sage.

Hester, S. and Eglin, P. (eds) (1997) *Culture in action: Studies in membership categorization analysis*. Washington, DC: International Institute for Ethnomethodology and Conversation Analysis and University Press of America.

Hutchby, I. and Wooffitt, R. (1998) *Conversation analysis: Principles, practices and applications*. Cambridge: Polity.

Jaworski, A. and Coupland, N. (eds) (1999) *The Discourse Reader*. London: Routledge.

Levinson, S.C. (1983) *Pragmatics*. Cambridge: Cambridge University Press.

Lynch, M. (2002) From naturally occurring data to naturally organized ordinary activities: Comment on Speer, *Discourse Studies*, 4: 531–7.

Marshall, H. and Wetherell, M. (1989) Talking about career and gender identities: A discourse analysis perspective. In Skevington, S. and Baker, D. (eds), *The social identity of women* (pp. 106–29). London: Sage.

McHoul, A.W. and Grace, A. (1993) *A Foucault primer: Discourse, power, and the subject*. Melbourne: Melbourne University Press.

Phillips, L.J. and Jorgenson, M.W. (2002) *Discourse analysis as theory and method*. London: Sage.

Potter, J. (1992) Constructing realism: Seven moves (plus or minus a couple), *Theory & Psychology*, 2: 167–73.

Potter, J. (1996a) *Representing Reality: Discourse, Rhetoric and Social Construction*. London: Sage.

Potter, J. (1996b) Discourse analysis and constructionist approaches: Theoretical background. In J.E. Richardson (ed.), *Handbook of qualitative research methods for psychology and the social sciences* (pp. 125–40). Leicester: British Psychological Society.

Potter, J. (1998) Cognition as context (whose cognition?), *Research on Language and Social Interaction*, 31: 29–44.

Potter, J. (2002) Two kinds of natural, *Discourse Studies*, 4: 539–42.

Potter, J. (2003a) Discourse analysis and discursive psychology. In P.M. Camic, J.E. Rhodes and L. Yardley (eds), *Qualitative research in psychology: Expanding perspectives in methodology and design* (pp. 73–94). Washington, DC: American Psychological Association.

Potter, J. (2003b) Discourse analysis. In M. Hardy and A. Bryman (eds), *Handbook of data analysis* (pp. 607–24). London: Sage.

Potter, J. and Edwards, D. (2001) Discursive social psychology. In W.P. Robinson and H. Giles (eds), *The new handbook of language and social psychology* (pp. 103–18). London: John Wiley & Sons.

Potter, J. and Hepburn, A. (2003) I'm a bit concerned – Early actions and psychological constructions in a child protection helpline, *Research on Language and Social Interaction*, 36: 197–240.

Potter, J. and Wetherell, M. (1987) *Discourse and social psychology: Beyond attitudes and behaviour*. London: Sage.

Psathas, G. (1990) Introduction. In Psathas, G. (ed.), *Interactional competence*. Washington, DC: University Press of America.

Psathas, G. (1995) *Conversation analysis: The study of talk-in-interaction*. London: Sage.

Sacks, H. (1992) *Lectures on conversation, Vols I and II*, ed. G. Jefferson. Oxford: Basil Blackwell.

Schegloff, E.A. (1993) Reflections on quantification in the study of conversation, *Research on Language and Social Interaction*, 26: 99–128.

Schegloff, E.A. (1997) Whose text? Whose context?, *Discourse & Society*, 8: 165–87.

Schegloff, E.A. (1999) 'Schegloff's texts' as 'Billig's data': A critical reply, *Discourse and Society*, 10: 558–72.

Schegloff, E.A. and Sacks, H. (1973) Opening up closings. *Semiotica*, 7: 289–327.

Schiffrin, D. (1994) *Approaches to Discourse*. Oxford: Blackwell.

Silverman, D. (1998) *Harvey Sacks: Social science and conversation analysis*. Oxford: Polity.

Sinclair, J. McH. and Coulthard, R.M. (1975) *Towards an analysis of discourse: The English used by teachers and pupils*. London: Oxford University Press.

Speer, S. (2002) 'Natural' and 'contrived' data: A sustainable distinction, *Discourse Studies*, 4: 511–25.

Stubbs, M. (1983) *Discourse analysis*. Oxford: Blackwell.

te Molder, H. and Potter, J. (eds) (in press) *Talk and cognition: Discourse, mind and social interaction*. Cambridge: Cambridge University Press.

van Dijk, T.A. (ed.) (1985) *Handbook of discourse analysis. Vols 1–4*. London: Academic Press.

van Dijk, T.A. (1997) *Discourse Studies: A multidisciplinary introduction (2 vols)*. London: Sage.

van Dijk, T.A. and Kintch, W. (1983) *Strategies of discourse comprehension*. London: Academic Press.

Wetherell, M. (1998) Positioning and interpretative repertoires: Conversation analysis and post-structuralism in dialogue, *Discourse & Society*, 9: 387–412.

Wetherell, M. and Potter, J. (1992) *Mapping the language of racism: Discourse and the legitimation of exploitation*. London: Harvester, New York: Columbia University Press.

Wetherell, M., Stiven, H. and Potter, J. (1987) Unequal egalitarianism: A preliminary study of discourses concerning gender and employment opportunities, *British Journal of Social Psychology*, 26: 59–71.

Wetherell, M., Taylor, S. and Yates, S. (eds) (2001a) *Discourse theory and practice: A reader*. London: Sage.

Wetherell, M., Taylor, S. and Yates, S. (eds) (2001b) *Discourse as data: A guide for analysis*. London: Sage.

Widdicombe, S. and Wooffitt, R. (1995) *The language of youth subcultures: Social identity in action*. London: Harvester Wheatsheaf.

Willig, C. (2003) Discourse analysis. In J.A. Smith (ed.), *Qualitative psychology: A practical guide to research methods* (pp. 159–83). London: Sage.

Wood, L.A. and Kroger, R.O. (2000) *Doing discourse analysis: Methods for studying action in talk and text*. London: Sage.

12 Conversation analysis and institutional talk

Analyzing data

John Heritage

INTRODUCTION

In a long series of writings, Erving Goffman (1955, 1983) established that social interaction embodies a distinct moral and institutional order that can be treated like other social institutions, such as the family, education, religion, etc. This "interaction order," he argued, comprises a complex set of interactional rights and obligations which are linked both to face and personal identity, and also to large-scale macro social institutions. Further, the institutional order of interaction has a particular social significance. It underlies the operations of all the other institutions in society, and it mediates the business that they transact. The political, economic, educational, and legal conduct of societies is all unavoidably transacted by means of the practices that make up the institution of social interaction.

Goffman's idea of an "institutional order *of* interaction" was pursued by conversation analysts who study the practices that make up this institution as a topic in its own right. Conversation analysis (CA) has established that these practices – which are complex and intricate and, in many cases, acquired early in life – make social action and interaction, mutual sense-making, and social reality construction possible. These practices are special and significant because they are basic to human sociality (Schegloff, 1992). CA studies of these practices describe how people take turns at talk in ordinary conversation and negotiate overlaps and interruptions; how various kinds of basic action sequences are organized and different options are activated inside those sequences; how various kinds of failures in interaction – for example, of hearing and understanding – are dealt with; how conversations are opened and closed; how gaze and body posture are related to talk; how laughter is organized; how grammatical form and discourse particles are related to turn-taking and other interactional issues; and so on.

However, there are also social and institutional orders *in* interaction. The social worlds of the corporation and the classroom, of medicine, law, etc., are evoked and made actionable in and through talk. But though their reality is invoked in talk – "talked into being" (Heritage, 1984) in interaction – their reality is not confined to talk. These institutional realities also exist in and as documents, buildings, legal arrangements, and so on. The conversation analytic study of institutional talk is concerned with how these institutional realities are evoked, manipulated, and even transformed in interaction.

There are, therefore, at least two kinds of conversation analytic research going on today and, though they overlap in various ways, they are distinct in focus. The first examines the social institution *of* interaction as an entity in its own right; the second studies the management of social institutions *in* interaction. The aim of this chapter is to describe some ways to go about the second task, and specifically to identify ways of cutting into the data to gain access for analysis. To keep things simple, I will illustrate the chapter mainly with observations about a single "institutional" conversation which is typical of the "professional–lay" interaction that many sociologists are interested in. But the relevance of the entry points I describe is not confined to this interaction. In fact, I believe that there is a reasonable chance that they are useful in gaining access to most kinds of "institutional" data, including the new "workplace" studies (Goodwin, 1996; Goodwin and Goodwin, 1997; Heath and Luff, 2000) that have recently emerged.

CONVERSATION ANALYSIS AND INTERACTIONAL SEQUENCES

CA is a field that focuses heavily on issues of meaning and context in interaction. It does so by linking both meaning and context to the idea of sequence. In fact, CA embodies a theory which argues that sequences of actions are a major part of what we mean by context, that the meaning of an action is heavily shaped by the sequence of previous actions from which it emerges, and that social context is a dynamically created thing that is expressed in and through the sequential organization of interaction.

Underlying this approach is a fundamental theory about how participants orient to interaction. This theory involves three interrelated claims:

1 In constructing their talk, participants normally address themselves to preceding talk and, most commonly, the immediately preceding talk (Sacks, 1987 [1973], 1992 [1964–72]; Schegloff and Sacks, 1973; Schegloff, 1984). In this simple and direct sense, their talk is *context-shaped*.
2 In doing some current action, participants normally project (empirically) and require (normatively) that some "next action" (or one of a range of possible "next actions") should be done by a subsequent participant (Schegloff, 1992). They thus *create* (or *maintain* or *renew*) a context for the next person's talk.
3 By producing their next actions, participants show an understanding of a prior action and do so at a multiplicity of levels – for example, by an "acceptance," someone can show an understanding that the prior turn was complete, that it was addressed to them, that it was an action of a particular

type (e.g., an invitation), and so on. These understandings are (tacitly) confirmed or can become the objects of repair at any third turn in an ongoing sequence (Schegloff, 1992). Through this process they become "mutual understandings" created through a sequential *"architecture of inter-subjectivity"* (Heritage, 1984).

CA starts from the view that all three of these features – the responsiveness to context by producing a "next" action that a prior action projected, the creation of context by the production of that next action, and the showing of understanding by these means – are the products of a common set of socially shared and structured procedures. CA analyses are thus simultaneously analyses of action, context management, and intersubjectivity because all three of these features are simultaneously, but not always consciously, the objects of the participants' actions. Finally, the procedures that inform these activities are normative in that participants can be held morally accountable both for departures from their use and for the inferences which their use, or departures from their use, may engender.

CONVERSATION ANALYSIS AND INSTITUTIONAL INTERACTION

As CA turned to the study of talk in institutions, it began with the same assumptions that had proved successful in studying ordinary conversation. Rather than starting with a "bucket" theory of context (Heritage, 1987) in which pre-existing institutional circumstances are seen as enclosing inter-action, CA starts with the view that "context" is both a project and a product of the participants' actions. The assumption is that it is fundamentally through interaction that context is built, invoked, and managed, and that it is through interaction that institutional imperatives originating from outside the interaction are evidenced and made real and enforceable for the participants. We want to find out how that works. Empirically, this means showing that the participants build the context of their talk *in and through* their talk. For example, if we analyze emergency calls to the police, we want to be able to show the ways in which the participants are managing their inter-action *as* an "emergency call" on a "policeable matter." We want to see how the participants co-construct it as an emergency call, incrementally advance it turn by turn as an emergency call, and finally bring it off as having been an emergency call.

Now how are we going to go about this business of digging into institutional talk to see the ways in which participants are addressing themselves to these specialized and particular tasks? In general, we can look at three main types of features (Drew and Heritage, 1992):

1 Institutional interaction normally involves the participants in specific goal orientations which are tied to their institution-relevant identities: doctor and patient, teacher and pupil, etc.

2 Institutional interaction involves special constraints on what will be treated as allowable contributions to the business at hand.
3 Institutional talk is associated with inferential frameworks and procedures that are particular to specific institutional contexts.

These special features create a unique "fingerprint" (Heritage and Greatbatch, 1991: 95–6) for each kind of institutional interaction, the fingerprint being made up of specific tasks, identities, constraints on conduct, and relevant inferential procedures that the participants deploy and are oriented to in their interactions with one another.

Implicit in this way of thinking is the idea that, relative to ordinary conversation, institutional interaction generally involves a reduction in the range of interactional practices deployed by the participants, and a specialization and respecification of the practices that remain (Drew and Heritage, 1992). These reductions and respecifications are often experienced as constraining and irksome – especially by the lay participants (Atkinson, 1982). And underlying these ideas is the further assumption that, again relative to the institution of conversation, the law courts, schools, news interviews, doctor–patient interactions, etc., are relatively recent inventions that have undergone a great deal of social change. The institution of conversation by contrast exists, and is experienced as, prior to institutional interaction both in the life of the individual and in the life of the society.

Where would someone go in the data to look for these and other related features of institutional interaction? The short answer to this question, of course, is "everywhere." But we need to start somewhere, and I will describe six basic places to probe the "institutionality" of interaction. These are:

1 Turn-taking organization
2 Overall structural organization of the interaction
3 Sequence organization
4 Turn design
5 Lexical choice
6 Epistemological and other forms of asymmetry

I will deal with each one in turn.

Turn-taking organization

A first thing to consider is whether the interaction you are looking at involves the use of a special turn-taking organization. All interactions involve the use of some kind of turn-taking organization (Sacks et al., 1974), and many kinds of institutional interaction use the same turn-taking organization as ordinary conversation. Some, however, involve very specific and systematic transformations in conversational turn-taking procedures. These special turn-taking systems can be very important in studying institutional interaction because they have the potential to alter the parties' opportunities for action, and to recalibrate the interpretation of almost every aspect of the activities that they structure. Think, for example, of how the opportunities for action, what the actions mean, and how they will be interpreted can be shaped by the turn-taking rules for interaction in a "formal" classroom (McHoul, 1978).

In conversation, very little of what we say, the actions we perform, or the order in which we do things is determined in advance (Sacks et al., 1974). In this sense, conversations are unpredictable. In some forms of interaction – debates, ceremonies, and many kinds of meetings – the topics, contributions, and order of speakership are organized from the outset in an explicit and predictable way. This kind of organization involves special turn-taking procedures.

The decisive feature of a special turn-taking organization is that departures from it – for example, departures from the order of speakership, or the types of contributions individuals are expected to make – can be explicitly sanctioned. This happens in meetings when speakers are ruled "out of order," in the courts when persons are sanctioned for answering when they should not, or failing to answer appropriately, or when children in classrooms are punished for "shouting out" answers, or talking when the teacher is talking. These explicit sanctions are very important analytically. They tell us that the turn-taking organization is being oriented to normatively *in its own right*. Many of these turn-taking organizations work by specifically restricting one party to asking questions and another to answering them. Interactions organized by this kind of Q–A turn-taking organization are distinct from those, like many professional–client interactions, in which one party tends to do most of the question asking and the other does most of the answering. Here the imbalance between the two parties is normally a product of the task the parties are engaged in or some other feature of the interaction, and is *not* the result of a special – and sanctionable – turn-taking organization (Heritage and Greatbatch, 1991).

The most intensively studied institutional turn-taking organizations have been those that obtain in the courts (Atkinson and Drew, 1979), news interviews (Greatbatch, 1988; Clayman and Heritage, 2002a), and classrooms (McHoul, 1978; Mehan, 1985). As these examples – courts, news interviews, classrooms – suggest, special turn-taking organizations tend to be present in large-scale "formal" environments when (1) there are a large number of potential participants in the interaction, whose contributions must be "rationed" in some kind of formal way, and/or (2) when the talk is designed for an "overhearing" audience. However, special turn-taking systems can be found in other contexts. For example, Peräkylä (1995: Chap. 2) has described turn-taking practices within counseling contexts that are designed to implement special therapeutic processes. Similarly Garcia (1991) has shown that mediation can involve special turn-taking practices as a means of limiting conflict between the participants. Finally, there are other turn-taking organizations that order speakership by age, rank, or other criteria of seniority (Albert, 1964; Duranti, 1994) though, perhaps because European and North American societies are less hierarchical than others in the world, these systems have so far been less studied.

Overall structural organization

Once you have determined whether (or not) some special turn-taking organization is in operation in your data, the next thing to do is to build an overall "map" of the interaction in terms of its typical "phases" or "sections." This will help you to look at the task orientation which is normally central in the kinds of interaction we are looking at. While institutional interactions cannot always successfully be described in terms of a phase structure, it is always worth making an attempt to do so.

This is a convenient moment to introduce the piece of data that we will look at during the rest of this chapter. It is a short telephone conversation in which a school employee telephones a mother whose son may be a truant from school. This conversation is drawn from a small collection, and many of the observations I will make are confirmed by other cases in the set. In general, the more conversations you collect, the more sure you can be that what you are studying is representative (see Peräkylä, this volume). As we turn to the data, you will see right away that this conversation is very "institutional" in the sense of being task-focused, but it will also be obvious that no special turn-taking organization is involved in the conversation. To preserve the participants' anonymity, all names in this conversation have been changed. The Appendix to this volume outlines the transcription conventions.

```
Arroyo
 1  Mom:  Hello.
 2        (0.5)
 3  Sch:  Hello Mister Wilson?
 4        (0.8)
 5  Mom:  Uh: this is Missus Wilson.
 6  Sch:  Uh Missus Wilson I'm sorry. This is Miss Matalin
 7        from Arroyo High School calling?
 8  Mom:  Mm⌈hm
```

End of Section 1

```
 9  Sch:       ⌊.hhhhh Was Martin home from school ill today?=
10  Mom:  =U:::h yes he was in fact I'm sorry I- I didn' ca:ll
11        because uh::h I slept in late I (.) haven' been feeling
12        well either. .hhhh And uh .hhh (0.5) u::h he had uh yih
13        know, uh fever:
14        (0.2)
15  Mom:  this morning.
16  Sch:  U::h hu:h,
17  ( ):  .hhh=
18  Mom:  =And uh I don' know y'know if he'll be (.) in
19        tomorrow fer sure er no:t, He's kinna j'st bin laying
20        arou:nd j(hh)uhkno:w,=
```

End of Section 2

```
21  Sch:   =Okay well I'll ⌈go ahead en:' u:hm
22  Mom:              ⌊( )
23  Sch:   I won' call you tomorrow night if we don' see 'im
24         tomorrow we'll just assume he was home ill.
25         (.)
26  Mom:   nnRig[ht ( )
27  Sch:        [A:n-
28  Sch:   Send a note with him when he does return.
29  Mom:   I will.
```

End of Section 3

```
30  Sch:   O:kay.
31  Mom:   Okay=
32  Sch:   =Thank you
33  Mom:   Uh huh Bye [bye
34  Sch:              [B'bye
```

- End Call -

In this phone call Ms. Matalin, who has been notified by teachers that Martin did not attend school on the day of this call, calls Martin's home to check on his whereabouts. Martin's mother picks up the phone (it could have been another relative or even Martin himself) and the call proceeds. I have divided this phone call into four sections because, although Ms. Matalin has only one piece of business to transact with this mother, it takes four distinct clusters of activity to achieve:

1 *Opening*: The first section (lines 1–8) is an "opening" section in which the parties enter into a state of interaction and establish their identities for one another (Schegloff, 1986).
2 *Problem initiation*: In the second section (lines 9–20), Ms. Matalin gets to the "business" of the call by raising the question of Martin's absence and the mother explains it. I have termed this the "problem initiation" section, because although Martin's mother resolves the problem in this call, simple resolutions of this kind do not always happen.
3 *Disposal*: In the "disposal" section (lines 21–9), Ms. Matalin details the bureaucratic action she will take toward Martin's absence in the light of the mother's account, and describes the action that the mother should take. In other calls, she describes what the child should do as well.
4 *Closing*: The final section of the call (lines 30–4) is devoted to managing a coordinated exit from the conversation (Schegloff and Sacks, 1973).

Now that we have identified these four sections, we can see that each of them involves the pursuit of a specific sub-goal. Each section is *jointly* oriented to – indeed co-*constructed* – by both participants as involving a task to be achieved. In this call, all tasks are fulfilled to the apparent satisfaction of both parties, but this does not always happen and it is not essential to identifying sections of institutional talk. What we are identifying here are goal- or task-oriented sections, which the parties co-construct and identify as somehow relevant to the completion of their business together.

Identifying these main sections of the call allows us to notice other features as well:

1 Doing the sectional analysis forces us to see that the call is focused on a single topic – "dealing with Martin's absence from school." Other interactions may have more than one "item" of business to transact: a patient, for example, may have several ailments to be dealt with, or a family may have several difficulties that require social worker support. This distinction can be important in analyzing institutional interaction.

2 The sectional analysis allows us to see significant stages in the *parties'* co-construction of the tasks and goals of the conversations, and that for the parties, these are incremental moves toward the completion of the business of the call. This is significant: there are institutional interactions where the goals and tasks of the encounter can be unclear, opaque, or even suspicious to one or both of the participants (Baldock and Prior, 1981; Heritage and Sefi, 1992). In these interactions, the "sections" are shapeless or non-existent for the parties and, correspondingly, difficult or impossible to identify analytically.

3 Within each section, we can examine how the parties progressively develop (or not) a joint sense of the task that is to be accomplished and look at the roles each party plays in this process.

4 We can look at whether the parties agree about "where the boundaries are" as they shift from one section to another (Robinson and Stivers, 2001). In this call, the parties make very "clean" transitions from one section (and one component of their "business") to the "next." But confusion and foot-dragging are also possible: one party may want to move on to the next issue while the other party is reluctant to quit the current one. Or one party may not recognize that a "next issue" is now relevant, while another is trying to press on with it. Different interests (and clear conflicts of interest) may be involved in these clashes.

Using this four-section framework, it is relatively easy to identify the same sections, occurring in the same order, in most of the phone calls Ms. Matalin makes. However, the purpose of identifying these sections is not to exhaustively classify every piece of every one of Ms. Matalin's interactions in these terms. Still less is it to assert that these sections will always occur in her conversations in this order, or even that they will always occur (cf. Byrne and Long, 1984 [1976]; Robinson, 2003). In other cases of these school calls, we can find the participants *reopening* sections and *reinstating* task orientations that they had previously treated as complete. So we are not trying to find invariance or even statistical regularity in the presence or ordering of these sections. The purpose of describing these sections is to identify task orientations which the *participants* routinely co-construct in routine ways. *Overall structural organization, in short, is not a framework -fixed once and for all – to fit data into. Rather it is something that we are looking for and looking at only to the extent that the parties orient to it in organizing their talk.*

Sequence organization

With the third level of analysis – sequence organization – we come to a very central aspect of CA work. It is by means of specific actions that are organized in sequences that the participants initiate, develop, and conclude the business they have together, and generally manage their encounters. In analyzing sequences, we essentially look at how particular courses of action are initiated and progressed and, as part of this, how particular action opportunities are opened up and activated, or withheld from and occluded. All of these possibilities, while explicitly analyzed by us, are also implicitly grasped – to a greater or lesser extent – by the participants who may use what transpires as a basis for inferences about the character and situation of their co-interactants.

Ms. Matalin's phone call is a rich source for sequence analysis, but here we will just focus on one aspect of the conversation: the fact that after Ms. Matalin's question at line 9, the mother's reply seems to go on and on and on. This is an accomplishment. If we look at the structure of the reply, we can see right away that the mother answers Ms. Matalin's question in the very first line of her response with "U:::h yes he was":

```
 9  Sch:      [.hhhhh Was Martin home from school ill today?=
10  Mom:  =U:::h yes he was * in fact * I'm sorry I- I didn' ca:ll *
11              because uh::h I slept in late * I (.) haven' been feeling
12              well either. .hhhh And uh .hhh (0.5) u::h he had uh yih
13              know, uh fever:
14              (0.2)
15  Mom:  this morning.
16  Sch:   U::h hu:h,
17  ():     .hhh=
18  Mom:  =And uh I don' know y'know if he'll be (.) in
19              tomorrow fer sure er no:t, He's kinna j'st bin laying
20              arou:nd j(hh)uhkno:w,=
```

However, the mother then continues with an apology for not "calling" (to notify the school), and then with an elaborate series of explanations for the situation. A noticeable feature of her turn from line 10 to line 12 is that she is careful to avoid pausing at sentence boundaries. At all the other points where her sentences are grammatically complete (marked with an asterisk in this transcript), she (1) is careful to avoid a falling ("final") intonation (which would be marked with a period – see the transcript conventions in the Appendix), and (2) moves straight to the next sentence without a break. It is also noticeable, looking at line 11, that she only pauses at grammatical places where she is unlikely to be interrupted – after the word "because" in line 11, and also *after* she starts a new sentence with the word "I" (also in line 11). All of this is significant because, given the turn-taking system for conversation (which is in play in this interaction), a sentence boundary is a place where Ms. Matalin could intervene with a question or a new observation, and thus disrupt the explanation that the mother is piecing together. It seems clear that the mother talks in the way she does so as to avoid creating these opportunities, and that she does this so that she can conclude her explanation for why she has not called the school without being interrupted. Thus it is only *after* she has completed her explanation that she has not been feeling well "either," that she takes a breath at a sentence boundary (and it is a big breath as indicated by the four h's!).

If the mother's talk to this point is managed so as to retain the turn in progress, her subsequent elaboration seems to emerge because she is unable to relinquish it. Extending her turn at lines 12–13 with a description of the child's illness, she pauses at line 14, only to find no uptake from Ms. Matalin. In response to this, she recompletes her turn with an incremental (and redundant) time specification ("this morning"), and then encounters a response from Ms. Matalin ("uh huh") that is prototypically used to indicate an understanding that the previous speaker (in this case, the mother) is not yet finished. In the face of this response, the mother continues with a prognosis of her son's condition (lines 18–20), finally coming to a halt at line 20.

Thus in this exchange of question and answer-plus-elaboration, we can see that the mother treats Ms. Matalin's question as implicitly pointing to a fault in her conduct, a fault for which she is accountable, and for which she is at pains to supply an explanation (for some parallels in medical encounters, see Silverman, 1987: 233–64, Heritage and Sefi, 1992, and Heritage and Lindström, 1998). Her treatment of the question is not as a "casual inquiry," but rather embodies a particular – and specifically "institutional" – understanding of its relevance. Subsequently we can see the further extension of her account as the product of an implicit sequential negotiation over who will make the conversational running. The detailed internal structure of the mother's rather lengthy turn is thus the product of a complex sequential negotiation. There are many other aspects of the sequences making up this exchange that merit analysis of the "institutional" relevances that inform their production. We will catch some of these aspects as we move on to the fourth area where initial analysis might proceed: turn design.

Turn design

Turn design is an important place to examine the "institutionality" of interaction. When we talk about a turn being "designed," we are pointing to two distinct selections that a person's speech embodies: (1) the action that the talk is designed to perform and (2) the means that are selected to perform the action (Drew and Heritage, 1992).

One sense in which a turn is "designed" concerns the selection of the action which someone wants to accomplish in a turn at talk. In work with Sue Sefi on health visitors' home visits to mothers of newborns, I came across the following sequence in the health visitor's opening visit. The father and mother respond to what looks like a casual observation by the health visitor by performing quite different actions:

```
1  HV:        He's enjoying that [isn't he.
2  F:    →                     [°Yes, he certainly is=°
3  M:    →                     =He's not hungry 'cuz (h)he's ju(h)st (h)had
4                              'iz bo:ttle .hhh
5                              (0.5)
6  HV:        You're feeding him on (.) Cow and Gate Premium.=
                              (HV:4A1:1) (Heritage and Sefi, 1992: 367)
```

The health visitor's remark "He's enjoying that" notices the baby sucking or chewing on something. (Unfortunately, we do not have a video tape, but certainly this is how the mother understands the word "enjoy" when she responds "He's not hungry . . ." (lines 3–4).) In replying that way, the mother treats the health visitor's remark as implying that the baby is "enjoying" whatever he is sucking or chewing because he is hungry – an implication which she rejects by observing that the baby has just been fed. The mother's response, then, is "defensive" in rejecting an unstated implication which she treats the health visitor's remark as having conveyed. The father, by contrast, simply agrees with the health visitor.

Thus in "constructing" their responses (quite apart from the particular designs of their turns), the mother and father have elected to perform alternative activities. Both activities, of course, have a "logic" as relevant next actions. The father treats the health visitor's remark as innocent while the mother finds in it an implied criticism regarding the proper care of her baby. They thus construct their responses differently by selecting different "next" actions. These two actions may well reflect a "division of labor" in the family, in which the mother is treated as having the primary responsibility for her baby (reflected in her defensiveness), while the father, with less responsibility, can take a more relaxed and "innocent" view of things.

The second aspect of turn design is that speakers also select among alternative ways of saying something or performing the same action. The following extract – from the same health visitor interaction as the previous one – illustrates this clearly. In this extract, the mother and father each perform a broadly similar activity – agreeing with the health visitor's suggestion that they will be "amazed" at the child's progress (in physical development), and they do so nearly simultaneously (lines 5 and 6). But they design their agreements rather differently. While the mother's agreement refers to the development of children in general ("They learn so quick don't they"), the father refers to their experience of their own child's progress ("We have noticed hav'n't w-"). While the father's utterance exhibits a commitment to noticing their own child's behavior and development, the mother's response does not.

```
1  HV:   →   It's amazing, there's no stopping him now, you'll be
2                  amazed at all the di[fferent things he'll start doing.
3  F:                                  [(hnh hn)
```

```
 4              (1.0)
 5  M:    →   Yeh. They [learn so quick don't they.
 6  F:    →              [We have noticed hav'n't w-
 7  HV:       That's right.
 8  F:    →   We have noticed (0.8) making a grab for your bottles.
 9              (1.0)
10  F:         Hm[::.
11  HV            [Does he: (.) How often does he go between his feeds?
                              (HV:4A1:2) (Drew and Heritage, 1992: 34)
```

Significantly, the mother's response avoids the "expert–novice" stance that the health visitor's remark might be seen as expressing, while the father's agreement(s) (at lines 6 and 8) seem designed to prove to the health visitor that they are observant and alert about their new baby. The different ways in which they design their actions may also point to the same underlying division of labor in the family that we suggested earlier. The father, who is putatively the junior partner in the family's childcare arrangements, appears eager to prove their competence in noticing the details of their child's behavior. The mother's agreement, by contrast, seems to avoid taking the "inferior" and "inexpert" position of "proving" anything to the health visitor, but rather asserts an agreement in bland and general terms.

The alternatives that may be involved in turn design are rarely as explicitly contrasted as they are here where different speakers employ different designs in the same responsive position. More usually, we analyze turn design by looking at the details of a turn's component features, and by determining their interactional purpose or significance.

To illustrate this, I want to go back to Ms. Matalin's telephone call and look at line 9: "Was Martin home from school ill today?=". Ms. Matalin very frequently begins her inquiries to the families she calls with this question. In an important sense, it is a "highly designed" turn that is repeated exactly (or nearly exactly) over and over again.

One way of analyzing a highly designed turn of this kind is to think of the interactional contingencies it might be addressing. In the context of Ms. Matalin's calls, there are two main possibilities that her question might turn up:

1 The child is away from school sick and the parent knows it. Sickness, of course, is bad news in its own right for the child (who may be in pain) and the parent (who may be worried and losing pay by being away from work). But Ms. Matalin's call is also bad news for the parent at another level. The parent of a sick child is normally supposed to call in to notify the school of the situation. There is, if you like, a kind of informal contract between home and school such that the school tells the parent if they have reason to believe the child is missing, but the parents equally have the obligation to tell the school if they suppose that the child will not be coming to school. The fact that Ms. Matalin has had to call in the first place may be the product of a little "breach of contract" on the parent's part. It is just that breach of

contract which the mother's defensive explanation, which we looked at earlier, seems designed to address.

2   The child is away from school and the parent does not know it, i.e., the child is truant. For this possibility, Ms. Matalin's call may involve a very serious piece of information for parents who, up to now, may have no idea that their child is not attending school.

It is in this context that we can begin to see that how Ms. Matalin opens up the topic of this call matters a lot, and that her opening utterance involves quite a bit of caution.

Consider the turn itself: (1) it indicates that the child has not been at school "today" (i.e., on the day of the call), but does not assert it as a fact: that the child has not been at the school is presupposed in the design of the question rather than stated as such (Pomerantz, 1988). (2) It offers as an account for the child's presupposed absence the most *commonplace* and the most *legitimate* reason for the child to be away from school – sickness. (3) The question is designed so that the easiest response for the parent will be an affirmative "yes" response to the possibility of sickness. In CA terminology, the question "prefers" a "yes" response. (4) Even if the child is, in fact, a truant, the inquiry avoids any implication of this and particularly avoids any accusation of truancy. (5) The question does not in any way directly thematize the parent's responsibility to inform the school. Instead, it leaves it open for the parent, where relevant, to *assume* that responsibility – as our mother in fact does. This, then, is a highly judicious, cautious, and "institutional" piece of question design (see the next section but one).

Now in recognizing that this is so, you do not have to assume that Ms. Matalin is a very tricky, Machiavellian type of person. You just have to remember that she makes dozens, even hundreds, of these calls every week. She has learned the range of possible responses that mothers make to her question, and she has also learned that certain ways of asking this question can attract resistance or cause arguments. So, for Ms. Matalin, recurrently raising this topic is like a "wind tunnel" experiment: the "wind tunnel" of repetition leads her to a question design that evokes the least resistance. You can see this wind tunnel effect in many other kinds of institutional talk – in medicine, social security offices, emergency calls to the police and fire departments, and others – where the institutional representative has a repetitive set of tasks to be worked through.

Thus, the second sense in which one can say that a turn is "designed" is that there are always alternative ways of saying something from which speakers, unavoidably, make a selection. The syntactic, lexical, and other (e.g., prosodic) selections by a speaker are aspects of a turn that articulate with the performance of organizational tasks and, very often, are shaped into "least resistant" forms by the repetition of those tasks. An important component of turn design is our next topic: lexical choice.

Lexical choice

A clear way in which speakers orient to institutional tasks and contexts is through their selection of descriptive terms. For instance, while someone might use "cop" in ordinary conversation, when giving evidence in court they are likely to select "police officer" instead (Sacks, 1979). The fact that this can involve selection is evident when speakers – as in Jefferson's (1974) data – cut off the beginning of "cop" ("kuh-") in favour of the word "police." Many studies that have dealt with the context-sensitivity of descriptions show that speakers select descriptive terms which are fitted to the institutional setting, or their role within it (Drew and Heritage, 1992). A dramatically clear illustration – first noted by Sacks (1992 [1964–72]) – is the way that, when speaking as a member of an organization, persons may refer to themselves as "we", not "I" (Drew and Heritage, 1992). There is a clear case in our data (lines 23–4). Here Ms. Matalin initially describes a course of action as her own decision ("I won' call you tomorrow night"), but then adds the inference that will be made if Martin is not at school tomorrow: "if we don' see 'im tomorrow we'll just assume he was home ill.". Here the "we" referred to as making this inference is evidently the school as an institution.

Another systematic type of lexical selection involves what might be termed "institutional euphemism." Here issues that may be problematic for the institution's representatives to address for some reason are downplayed. In the *New York Times* (November 5, 1995) it is reported that Microsoft – the giant software corporation – no longer likes to talk of "industry dominance" but rather of "industry leadership." In medicine, references to pain are often euphemistic – a patient will be asked "Is it sore?" rather than "Is it painful?" (Heritage and Sorjonen, 1994). In other phone calls like the one we are looking at, when Ms. Matalin does not get an adequate explanation for a child's absence, she often says "We need him/her to come into the office to clear this up." While this seems to indicate just a matter of bureaucratic record keeping, it leaves open the broader question of the child's accountability for the absence and what kind of punishment might be involved in "clearing up" his or her record.

Lexical selections can shape whole sequences and, with them, the overall pattern of the interaction. For example, the beginning of Ms. Matalin's phone call runs as follows:

```
1 Mom:  Hello
2       (0.5)
3 Sch:  Hello Mister Wilson?
4       (0.8)
5 Mom:  Uh: this is Missus Wilson.
6 Sch:  Uh Missus Wilson I'm sorry. This is Miss Matalin
7       from Arroyo High School calling?
8 Mom:  Mm hm
```

At line 8, the mother, rather than greeting Ms. Matalin by saying "hello" – which is the kind of action that normally occurs at this point (Schegloff, 1986), just says "mm hm" – a prototypically non-committal "continuer" (Schegloff, 1982) that invites Ms. Matalin to proceed with the conversation. Now one could imagine that this is an unfriendly, even a hostile, action from someone who does not like talking to school officials. But if we look back up the sequence, we can see an alternative basis for the mother's action. In particular, we can see that Ms. Matalin identifies herself using a particular lexical choice – a formal "last name plus organizational id" identification. By using this identification, rather than, for example, "Nancy Matalin" or just "Nancy," she identifies the phone call as a "business call" and, specifically, a "call about school business." (In fact, that process begins to emerge even earlier when, trying to identify who she is talking to, Ms. Matalin names the mother using "Mister Wilson" rather than a more informal identification – the mistaken identification (Mister for Missus) seems to arise because the mother's voice sounds rather deep on the phone.) So, when the mother responds to Ms. Matalin's formal, business-oriented self-identification with "mm hm" at line 8, she is in fact inviting Ms. Matalin to proceed with the business-based "reason for the call" that Ms. Matalin has clearly projected right from the start. That clear projection – and, because of it, the very brevity and economy of this opening sequence – arises from the lexical selections made at the earliest stages of this telephone call.

Interactional asymmetries

Finally, interactional asymmetries are a place at which to begin examining the specific institutionality of interactions. Here, I will briefly mention four types of asymmetry that involve: (1) participation; (2) "knowhow" about the interaction and the institution in which it is embedded; (3) knowledge; and (4) rights to knowledge.

Asymmetries of participation

Many studies of institutional interaction document asymmetries of participation in institutional interactions, and in particular that institutional participants in lay–professional encounters – for example, involving doctors, teachers, social workers, etc. – take and retain the initiative in these interactions (Linell et al., 1988; Mishler, 1984; Frankel, 1990). Underlying these observations is an implicit contrast with a standard of "equal participation" between speakers in ordinary conversation. As Linell and Luckmann (1991) have commented, we need to be cautious about this. This dichotomy between the symmetries of conversation and the asymmetries of institutional discourse can oversimplify the nature of asymmetry and overlook the ways in which talking in ordinary conversation can be asymmetric. As they observe: "if there were no asymmetries at all between people, i.e. if communicatively relevant inequalities of knowledge were non-existing, there would be little or no need for most kinds of communication!" (Linell and Luckmann, 1991: 4). Viewed from a perspective that asks which persons participate in talk and to what effect, it is apparent that ordinary conversation can embody several kinds of asymmetry – between the speaker and the hearer of a turn at talk; between the initiator and the respondent in a sequence of interaction; between those who, more broadly, are active in shaping topics and those who are not; and between those whose interventions are decisive for the outcomes of conversations and those whose interventions are not (Linell, 1990; Linell and Luckmann, 1991). From this standpoint, the contrast between the symmetry of ordinary conversation and the asymmetry of institutional discourse is indeed oversimplified (Robinson, 2001; Stivers and Heritage, 2001): all social interaction must inevitably be asymmetric on a moment-to-moment basis and many interactions are likely to embody substantial asymmetry when moment-to-moment participation is aggregated over the course of one or more encounters.

Yet at a more general level, it is clear that there is a fundamental distinction between the symmetry of ordinary conversation and the asymmetries of institutional interaction. The general operation of ordinary conversation is not tied to any particular set of social roles, identities, or tasks. If it were, conversation would be a much less flexible and sophisticated institution. In many forms of institutional discourse, by contrast, there is a direct relationship between institutional roles and tasks on the one hand and discursive rights and obligations on the other. For example, institutional representatives commonly ask questions and require of lay participants that they answer them. In this way, they may secure the initiative in determining (1) when a topic is satisfactorily concluded, (2) what the next topic will be, and, (3) through the design of their questions, how that new topic will be shaped (Mishler, 1984; Drew and Heritage, 1992). Thus institutional representatives can often direct the interaction in ways that are not found in ordinary conversation.

Asymmetries of interactional and institutional "knowhow"

An important dimension of asymmetry between the participants in institutional interaction arises from the difference, and often tension, between the organizational perspective that treats the individual as a "routine case" and the client for whom the case is personal and unique. Ms. Matalin's phone call to the mother in our data was one of around a dozen she made that day and, for her, it was absolutely routine. For the mother, however, it was an unusual and morally threatening occasion. The parties, therefore, brought asymmetric experience and reasoning to the encounter. All agencies have procedures for the routine management of multiple cases, for "processing" cases by assigning them to routine categories, and so on. However, the clients – whose inquiries, troubles, illnesses, claims, and the like constitute an organization's routine cases – may not be really aware of, or concerned with, the pattern into which their individual cases fit. The client's perspective often arises out of the particular circumstances which bring him or her into contact with the organization, perhaps for the first or only time, or at least not frequently enough to have developed a self-conception as a routine case. In doctor–patient encounters, this gap between routine institutional "knowhow" and singular experience can be extraordinarily stressful (Zola, 1987; Whalen and Zimmerman, 1998) and can emerge in behavior that can be experienced as very callous (Maynard, 1996). This gap can exist, and be significant, in all forms of institutional talk. In some psychiatric and social service encounters, the "client" may have only a dim awareness of the professional objectives being pursued across the entire encounter (Baldock and Prior, 1981; Heritage and Sefi, 1992; Peräkylä, 1995). In others, the lay caller may have an exact idea of the purpose of the conversation, but may be unable to grasp the point of a particular action. For example, in a notorious call for emergency assistance (Whalen et al., 1988), the following episode occurs. The caller (B) has just given his address and then is asked, using a "fixed choice" question design, whether the address is a house or an apartment. As the data show, he responds with a lexical selection drawn not from the choices he is given, but rather from the language of real estate. He replies: "it is a home":

> A: Okay iz this uh <u>hou</u>se or n' a<u>part</u>men'?
> B: It- it <u>is</u> a <u>ho:me</u>

Here, probably under the pressure of the emergency (the caller's mother is dying), the caller simply fails to grasp the relevance of the distinction between a house and an apartment to an ambulance crew looking for an address and a way to enter the location.

Routine organizational contingencies, which are taken for granted by one party but are unknown to the other, can be the source of many other kinds of difficulty and confusion. In the case of "911" emergency calls, Whalen (1995) has argued that such contingencies as the current position of the cursor on a menu-driven computer screen can influence the order in which questions are asked, and sometimes make them seem confusing or irrelevant to callers. Similar asymmetries in organizational and interactional "knowhow" often strongly influence police and courtroom interrogations, and other interactions in which organizational resources and routines are used to evaluate the truth of lay claims (Boyd, 1998; Drew, 1992; Heritage et al., 2001; Watson, 1990).

Epistemological caution and asymmetries of knowledge

A notable feature of many kinds of institutional interaction is a kind of epistemological "cautiousness" in which the professionals avoid committing themselves to taking firm positions. This cautiousness is mandatory in certain institutional interactions such as the news interview (Heritage, 1985; Clayman, 1988, 1992; Heritage and Greatbatch, 1991) or the courts (Atkinson and Drew, 1979; Atkinson, 1992). In other contexts, such as medical diagnosis, it is quite common. Even in Ms. Matalin's calls a kind of epistemological caution is evident. For example, when a parent seems unaware that their child is away from school, Ms. Matalin normally tells them about the absence in this way:

> 1 Sch: Was William home from school <u>ill</u> today?
> 2   . . . ((conversation off the phone in which Mom asks another person
> 3   . . . if William was home))
> 4 Mom: No he wasn't

5   Sch: .hhh Well he was reported absent from his <u>thir</u>:d and
6   his fifth period cla:sses today.

Here Ms. Matalin does not say "he was absent from . . ."; instead she says "<u>he</u> wz reported absent from. . . ." By including "reported," Ms. Matalin invokes an (unnamed) source for the information and thus portrays herself as *relaying* the information she is giving. She thus avoids underwriting the information as a *fact* and, because "reports" need to be confirmed before becoming "facts," she also avoids committing the school to an "official" position on the issue.

At the same time as professionals and institutional representatives are often cautious about making claims, they also deploy distinctive, functionally specialized, and superior knowledge bases that can impart a specific expert authority to claims made within the relevant knowledge domain. The epistemological superiority of expert knowledge is something that is recurrently renewed in talk and in many different ways (Silverman, 1987; Gill, 1998; Jacoby and Gonzales, 1991; Peräkylä, 1998, 2002; Raymond, 2000). Medicine provides numerous examples. Patients may orient to the authority of medical knowledge by their lexical choices, for example, the tentative or uncertain use of medical terminology (Silverman, 1987; Drew, 1991; Maynard, 1991), or by failing to raise questions about important problems and concerns (Frankel, 1990; Todd, 1993), or by permitting "medical" definitions of their problems to prevail over their lifeworld concerns (Mishler, 1984). Moreover, lack of medical knowledge may mean that patients may not know or understand the purposes lying behind particular questions, and they may not grasp the line of inquiry which the doctor is pursuing in questions on what seem to be unconnected topics. This lack of access to the "hidden agenda" of doctors' questioning represents another avenue of analysis into asymmetry in medical interaction (Fisher, 1983; Silverman, 1987).

Rights of access to knowledge

Asymmetry of knowledge arises when people – usually lay people – have limited resources with which to answer the questions "what do I know?" and "how do I know it?" But these same people may also have limited resources with which to answer the questions "what am I entitled to know?" and "how am I entitled to know it?" Limitation in this regard is an asymmetry in rights of access to knowledge. Here lay persons are sometimes in a position analogous to the gossips described by Bergmann (1993): they have information that is relevant or significant, but they do not have *rights* to know it or they have come to know it in a "morally contaminated" way. Thus a person calling to inform the emergency services about an incident may be at pains to show that they are calling from a sense of duty about an event that imposed itself on them, and not because they are "nosey" or "looking for trouble" (Whalen and Zimmerman, 1990). A patient who is concerned about a possible illness may be similarly at pains to show that he or she is not excessively preoccupied with minor bodily changes (Halkowski, 2004). Patients are similarly reluctant to voice diagnostic hunches about their illnesses except under relatively defined circumstances (Heath, 1992; Peräkylä, 1998; Gill, 1998; Stivers, 2002;

Heritage and Robinson, 2004), and Strong (1979) documents the fact that doctors accompanying their children on pediatric consultations suspend their medical expertise and act "like parents" when dealing with the attending physician. In this last case, persons with every "right" to medical expertise voluntarily suspend those rights in the limited environment of a medical consultation with another person qualified as expert. In institutional interaction then, knowledge may not be enough; one must also be entitled to the knowledge, and have come to it in an appropriate way.

FROM QUALITATIVE TO QUANTITATIVE RESEARCH: A NOTE

As many readers will have inferred, if the kinds of qualitative observations made in this chapter are true, then they should have an impact and significance that is quantitatively measurable as well. For example, questions that are designed to favor a "no" response, e.g., negatively polarized questions such as "Any questions?" (Heritage, 2002; Boyd and Heritage, 2004), should result in less questioning overall than positively polarized questions, e.g., "Do you have questions you would like to ask?" Most of the work that has explored quantitative aspects of institutional interaction has focused on this level of *turn design*. For example, Boyd (1998) distinguished between "bureaucratic" and "collegial" opening questions in interactions in which physicians were questioned about patients' need for surgery and found a systematic relationship between the "collegial" opening questions and the likelihood that the patient would be approved for surgery. This research can also have an historical dimension: for example, Clayman and Heritage (2002a, 2002b) showed that question designs that are more hostile and assertive have become very much more frequent in presidential press conferences over the past fifty years.

This quantitative work can have significant "applied" value. Stivers (2002) distinguished between medical problem presentations that simply describe symptoms ("sore throat, scratchy cough, phlegm") and those that suggest a diagnosis ("strep throat"), and found that physicians were more likely to believe that the latter problem presentations reflected a desire for antibiotics (and prescribed accordingly) even though the differences did not reflect actual patient desires as revealed in pre-visit surveys (Stivers et al., 2003). Similarly conversation analytic research that suggested that "online commentary" (e.g., "Your throat's a little red") produced during patients' physical examination might be a means of forecasting "no problem" diagnostic outcomes and avoiding unnecessary prescribing also turned out to have quantitative support (Heritage and Stivers, 1999; Mangione-Smith et al., 2003).

These are relatively straightforward linkages that focus centrally on turn design – the easiest dimension of interaction to quantify. They suggest that the study of institutional talk can support an important "applied" dimension in the future, though considerable work will be needed to achieve this objective.

CONCLUSION

By now, readers will have seen that many of the different dimensions or levels of "institutionality" in talk are thoroughly interrelated. Rather like Russian dolls that fit inside one another, each of these elements is a part of the next higher level: lexical choice is a part of turn design; turn design is a part of sequence organization; sequence organization is a part of overall structural organization.

There are two "wild cards" in the pack. Turn taking is one because where a distinct turn-taking system is in place, it has major effects at many levels of an interaction's organization. Asymmetry is the other because it is embodied at all other levels of the organization of interaction in institutional settings – lexical choice, turn design, sequence organization, overall structure organization, and turn taking. Indeed CA may end up with an affinity with a rather Foucauldian conception of power, advocated by other contributors to this volume. The view that power inheres in institutional knowledge, classifications, knowhow, and normative arrangements is compatible with the CA view that it is created, renewed, and operationalized in many disparate but interlocking facets of the organization of interaction. Both perspectives converge in the idea that this power inheres both in the knowledge, classificatory, and interactional practices of institutions and their incumbents, and in the discretionary freedoms which those practices permit for the incumbents of institutional roles.

Recommended readings

For a range of studies of talk in institutions, two collections from the early 1990s are still relevant:

Paul Drew and John Heritage (eds.) (2002), *Talk at Work*, Cambridge University Press, contains chapters dealing with a wide range of settings, together with an Introduction that sets the contents within a sociolinguistic context.

Dierdre Boden and Don Zimmerman (eds.) (1991), *Talk and Social Structure*, University of California Press, contains several chapters that situate conversation analytic approaches to talk in institutions within sociology.

John Heritage and Douglas Maynard (eds.) (2004), *Practicing Medicine*, Cambridge University Press, contains state of the art chapters on primary care.

REFERENCES

Albert, E. (1964). "Rhetoric," "logic," and "poetics" in Burundi: culture patterning of speech behavior. *American Anthropologist* 66, pt 2 (6): 35–54.
Atkinson, J.M. (1982). Understanding formality: notes on the categorisation and production of "formal" interaction. *British Journal of Sociology* 33: 86–117.

Atkinson, J.M. (1992). Displaying neutrality: formal aspects of informal court proceedings. In P. Drew and J. Heritage (eds.), *Talk at Work*. Cambridge: Cambridge University Press, pp. 199–211.

Atkinson, J.M. and Drew, P. (1979). *Order in Court: The Organisation of Verbal Interaction in Judicial Settings*. London: Macmillan.

Atkinson, J.M. and Heritage, J. (eds.) (1984). *Structures of Social Action: Studies in Conversation Analysis*. Cambridge: Cambridge University Press.

Baldock, J. and Prior, D. (1981). Social workers talking to clients: a study of verbal behaviour. *British Journal of Social Work* 11: 19–38.

Bergmann, Jörg R. (1993). *Discreet Indiscretions: The Social Organization of Gossip*. Chicago: Aldine.

Boyd, Elizabeth (1998). Bureaucratic authority in the "company of equals": the interactional management of medical peer review. *American Sociological Review* 63 (2): 200–24.

Boyd, Elizabeth and Heritage, John (2004). Taking the Patient's Medical History: Questioning During Comprehensive History Taking. In John Heritage and Douglas Maynard (eds.), *Practicing Medicine: Structure and Process in Primary Care Encounters*. Cambridge: Cambridge University Press.

Byrne, P.S. and Long, B.E.L. (1984 [1976]). *Doctors Talking to Patients: A Study of the Verbal Behaviours of Doctors in the Consultation*. Exeter: Royal College of General Practitioners.

Clayman, S. (1988). Displaying neutrality in television news interviews. *Social Problems* 35 (4): 474–92.

Clayman, S. (1992). Footing in the achievement of neutrality: the case of news interview discourse. In P. Drew and J. Heritage (eds.), *Talk at Work*. Cambridge: Cambridge University Press, pp. 163–98.

Clayman, S. and Heritage, J. (2002a). *The News Interview: Journalists and Public Figures on the Air*. Cambridge: Cambridge University Press.

Clayman, S. and Heritage, J. (2002b). Questioning Presidents: Journalistic deference and adversarialness in the press conferences of Eisenhower and Reagan. *Journal of Communication* 52 (4): 749–75.

Drew, P. (1991). Asymmetries of knowledge in conversational interactions. In I. Markova and K. Foppa (eds.), *Asymmetries in Dialogue*. Hemel Hempstead: Harvester Wheatsheaf, pp. 29–48.

Drew, P. (1992). Contested evidence in a courtroom cross-examination: the case of a trial for rape. In P. Drew and J. Heritage (eds.), *Talk at Work*. Cambridge: Cambridge University Press, pp. 470–520.

Drew, Paul and Heritage, John (1992). Analyzing Talk at Work: An Introduction. In P. Drew and J. Heritage (eds.), *Talk at Work*. Cambridge: Cambridge University Press, pp. 3–65.

Duranti, Alesandro (1994). *From Grammar to Politics*. Berkeley, CA: University of California Press.

Fisher, Sue (1983). Doctor talk/patient talk: how treatment decisions are negotiated in doctor/patient communication. In S. Fisher and A. Todd (eds.), *The Social Organization of Doctor-Patient Communication*. Washington, DC: Center for Applied Linguistics, pp. 135–57.

Frankel, Richard (1990). Talking in interviews: a dispreference for patient initiated questions in physician-patient encounters. In G. Psathas (ed.), *Interaction Competence*. Lanham, MD: University Press of America, pp. 231–62.

Garcia, Angela (1991). Dispute resolution without disputing: how the interactional organization of mediation hearings minimizes argumentative talk. *American Sociological Review* 56: 818–35.

Gill, Virginia (1998). Doing attributions in medical interaction: patients' explanations for illness and doctors' responses. *Social Psychology Quarterly* 61 (4): 342–60.

Goffman, Erving (1955). On face work. *Psychiatry* 18: 213–31.

Goffman, Erving (1983). The Interaction Order. *American Sociological Review* 48: 1–17.

Goodwin, Charles and Goodwin, Marjorie Harness (1997). Seeing as a Situated Activity: Formulating Planes. In David Middleton and Yrjö Engestrom (eds.), *Cognition and communication at work*. Cambridge: Cambridge University Press.

Goodwin, Marjorie Harness (1996). Informings and Announcements in Their Environment: Prosody within a Multi-Activity Work Setting. In Elizabeth Couper-Kuhlen and Margret Selting (eds.), *Prosody in Conversation: Interactional Studies*. Cambridge: Cambridge University Press, pp. 436–61.

Greatbatch, David (1988). A Turn-Taking System for British News Interviews. *Language in Society* 17 (3): 401–30.

Halkowski, Timothy (2004). Realizing the illness: patients' narratives of symptom discovery. In John Heritage and Douglas Maynard (eds.), *Practicing Medicine: Structure and Process in Primary Care Consultations*. Cambridge: Cambridge University Press.

Heath, Christian (1992). The delivery and reception of diagnosis and assessment in the general practice consultation. In P. Drew and J. Heritage (eds.), *Talk at Work*. Cambridge: Cambridge University Press, pp. 235–67.

Heath, Christian and Luff, Paul (2000). *Technology in Action*. Cambridge: Cambridge University Press.

Heritage, John (1984). *Garfinkel and Ethnomethodology*. Cambridge: Polity Press.

Heritage, John (1985). Analyzing News Interviews: Aspects of the Production of Talk for an Overhearing Audience. In Teun A. Dijk (ed.), *Handbook of Discourse Analysis Volume 3*. New York: Academic Press, pp. 95–119.

Heritage, John (1987). Ethnomethodology. In Anthony Giddens and Jonathan Turner (eds.) *Social Theory Today*. Cambridge: Polity Press, pp. 224–72.

Heritage, John (2002). Ad hoc inquiries: two preferences in the design of "routine" questions in an open context. In D. Maynard, H. Houtkoop-Steenstra, N.K. Schaeffer, and H. van der Zouwen (eds.), *Standardization and Tacit Knowledge: Interaction and Practice in the Survey Interview*. New York, Wiley Interscience, pp. 313–33.

Heritage, John and Greatbatch, David (1991). On the Institutional Character of Institutional Talk: The Case of News Interviews. In Dierdre Boden and Don H. Zimmerman (eds.), *Talk and Social Structure*. Berkeley, CA: University of California Press, pp. 93–137.

Heritage, John and Lindström, Anna (1998). Motherhood, medicine and morality: scenes from a medical encounter. *Research on Language and Social Interaction* 31 (3/4): 397–438.

Heritage, John and Robinson, Jeffrey (2004). Accounting for the visit: giving reasons for seeking medical care. In John Heritage and Douglas Maynard (eds.), *Practicing Medicine: Structure and Process in Primary Care Consultations*. Cambridge: Cambridge University Press.

Heritage, John and Sefi, Sue (1992). Dilemmas of Advice: Aspects of the Delivery and Reception of Advice in Interactions Between Health Visitors and First Time Mothers. In P. Drew and J. Heritage (eds.), *Talk at Work*. Cambridge: Cambridge University Press, pp. 359–417.

Heritage, John and Sorjonen, Marja-Leena (1994). Constituting and maintaining activities across sequences: and-prefacing as a feature of question design. *Language in Society* 23: 1–29.

Heritage, John and Stivers, Tanya (1999). Online Commentary in Acute Medical Visits: A Method of Shaping Patient Expectations. *Social Science and Medicine* 49 (11): 1501–17.

Heritage, John, Boyd, Elizabeth, and Kleinman, Lawrence (2001). Subverting Criteria: The role of precedent in decisions to finance surgery. *Sociology of Health and Illness* 23 (5): 701–28.

Jacoby, Sally and Gonzales, Patrick (1991). The Constitution of Expert-Novice in Scientific Discourse. *Issues in Applied Linguistics* 2 (2): 149–81.

Jefferson, Gail (1974). Error Correction as an Interactional Resource. *Language in Society* 2: 181–99.

Linell, P. (1990). The power of dialogue dynamics. In I. Markova and K. Foppa (eds.), *The Dynamics of Dialogue*. Hemel Hempstead: Harvester Wheatsheaf, pp. 147–77.

Linell, P. and Luckmann, T. (1991). Asymmetries in dialogue: some conceptual preliminaries. In I. Markova and K. Foppa (eds.), *Asymmetries in Dialogue*. Hemel Hempstead: Harvester Wheatsheaf, pp. 1–20.

Linell, P., Gustavsson, L., and Juvonen, P. (1988). Interactional dominance in dyadic communication: a presentation of initiative-response analysis. *Linguistics* 26: 415–42.

Mangione-Smith, Rita, Stivers, Tanya, Elliott, Marc, McDonald, Laurie, and Heritage, John (2003). Online commentary on physical exam findings: a communication tool for avoiding inappropriate antibiotic prescribing? *Social Science and Medicine* 56 (2): 313–20.

Maynard, D. (1991). On the interactional and institutional bases of asymmetry in clinical discourse. *American Journal of Sociology* 92 (2): 448–95.

Maynard, Douglas (1996). On "realization" in everyday life. *American Sociological Review* 60 (1): 109–32.

McHoul, A. (1978). The Organization of Turns at Formal Talk in the Classroom. *Language in Society* 7: 183–213.

Mehan, Hugh (1985). The Structure of Classroom Discourse. In Teun A. Dijk (ed.), *Handbook of Discourse Analysis Volume 3*. New York: Academic Press, pp. 120–31.

Mishler, E. (1984). *The Discourse of Medicine: Dialectics of Medical Interviews*. Norwood, NJ: Ablex.

Peräkylä, Anssi (1995). *AIDS Counselling; Institutional Interaction and Clinical Practice*. Cambridge: Cambridge University Press.

Peräkylä, A. (1998). Authority and accountability: the delivery of diagnosis in primary health care. *Social Psychology Quarterly* 61 (4): 301–20.

Peräkylä, A. (2002). Agency and authority: extended responses to diagnostic statements in primary care encounters. *Research on Language and Social Interaction* 35 (2): 219–47.

Pomerantz, Anita (1988). Offering a Candidate Answer: An Information Seeking Strategy. *Communication Monographs* 55: 360–73.

Raymond, Geoffrey (2000). The voice of authority: the local accomplishment of authoritative discourse in live news broadcasts'. *Discourse Studies* 2(3): 354–79.

Robinson, Jeffrey D. (2001). Asymmetry in action: sequential resources in the negotiation of a prescription request. *Text* 21 (1/2): 19–54.

Robinson, Jeffrey D. (2003). An Interactional Structure of Medical Activities During Acute Visits and its Implications for Patients' Participation. *Health Communication* 15 (1): 27–59.

Robinson, Jeffrey D. and Stivers, Tanya (2001). Achieving activity transitions in primary-care consultations: from history taking to physicial examination. *Human Communication Research* 27 (2): 253–98.

Sacks, Harvey (1979). Hotrodder: A Revolutionary Category. In George Psathas (ed.), *Everyday Language: Studies in Ethnomethodology*. New York: Irvington, pp. 7–14.

Sacks, Harvey (1987 [1973]). On the Preferences for Agreement and Contiguity in Sequences in Conversation. In Graham Button and John R.E. Lee (eds.), *Talk and Social Organisation*. Clevedon, England: Multilingual Matters, pp. 54–69.

Sacks, Harvey (1992 [1964–72]). *Lectures on Conversation* (2 Vols.). Oxford: Basil Blackwell.

Sacks, Harvey, Schegloff, Emanuel A., and Jefferson, Gail (1974). A Simplest Systematics for the Organization of Turn-Taking for Conversation. *Language* 50: 696–735.

Schegloff, Emanuel A. (1982). Discourse as an interactional achievement: some uses of "uh huh" and other things that come between sentences. In D. Tannen (ed.), *Analyzing Discourse* (Georgetown University Roundtable on Languages and Linguistics 1981). Washington, DC: Georgetown University Press, pp. 71–93.

Schegloff, Emanuel A. (1984). On Some Questions and Ambiguities in Conversation. In J. Maxwell Atkinson and John Heritage (eds.), *Structures of Social Action*. Cambridge: Cambridge University Press, pp. 28–52.

Schegloff, Emanuel A. (1986). The Routine as Achievement. *Human Studies* 9: 111–51.

Schegloff, Emanuel A. (1992). Repair after next turn: the last structurally provided defense of intersubjectivity in conversation. *American Journal of Sociology* 95 (5): 1295–345.

Schegloff, Emanuel A. and Sacks, Harvey (1973). Opening Up Closings. *Semiotica* 8: 289–327.

Silverman, D. (1987). *Communication and Medical Practice*. London: Sage.

Stivers, Tanya (2002). "Symptoms only" and "Candidate diagnoses": Presenting the problem in pediatric encounters. *Health Communication* 14 (3): 299–338.

Stivers, Tanya and Heritage, John (2001). Breaking the sequential mold: answering "more than the question" during medical history taking. *Text* 21 (1/2): 151–85.

Stivers, Tanya, Mangione-Smith, Rita, Elliott, Marc, McDonald, Laurie, and Heritage, John (2003). What Leads Physicians to Believe that Parents Expect Antibiotics? A Study of Parent Communication Behaviors and Physicians' Perceptions. *Journal of Family Practice* 52 (2): 140–8.

Strong, P. (1979). *The Ceremonial Order of the Clinic*. London: Routledge.

Todd, Alexandra (1993). Exploring women's experiences: power and resistance in medical discourse. In Sue Fisher and Alexandra Todd (eds.), *The Social Organization of Doctor-Patient Communication* (2nd Edition). Norwood, NJ: Ablex, pp. 267–86.

Watson, D.R. (1990). Some features of the elicitation of confessions in murder interrogations. In G. Psathas (ed.), *Interactional Competence*. Lanham, MD: University Press of America, pp. 263–96.

Whalen, Jack (1995). A technology of order production: computer-aided dispatch in public safety communications. In Paul ten Have and George Psathas (eds.), *Situated Order: Studies in the Social Organization of Talk and Embodied Activities*. Washington, DC: University Press of America, pp. 187–230.

Whalen, J. and Zimmerman, D.H. (1998). Observations on the display and management of emotions in naturally occurring activities: the case of "hysteria" in calls to 9-1-1. *Social Psychology Quarterly* 61 (2): 141–59.

Whalen, Marilyn and Zimmerman, Don H. (1990). Describing trouble: practical epistemology in citizen calls to the police. *Language in Society* 19: 465–92.

Whalen, Jack, Zimmerman, Don H., and Whalen, Marilyn R. (1988). When Words Fail: A Single Case Analysis. *Social Problems* 35 (4): 335–62.

Zola, Irving K. (1987). Structural constraints in the doctor-patient relationship: the case of non-compliance. In Howard Schwartz (ed.), *Dominant Issues in Medical Sociology*. New York: Random House, pp. 203–9.

Part IV Visual data

---

13 The conceptualization and analysis of visual data

Michael Emmison

INTRODUCTION

Pick up almost any of the existing textbooks dealing with 'visual research' and it is a safe bet that the discussion will focus in some way on the use of photographic images. Dramatically oversimplifying, one branch of visual research, that stemming from the Anglo-Saxon tradition of ethnography and social anthropology, advocates the use of the camera in the generation of a visual record of the research setting; a second branch, one with closer affinities to the continental schools of semiotics and cultural studies, favours the investigation of commercially produced images and an analysis of their implicit ideological and cultural messages. Equating the study of 'the visual' with either the collection or analysis of images seems, on the face of it, so self-evident that to suggest things could be otherwise might be construed as perverse or even provocative. And yet this is precisely what I hope to achieve in this chapter. In what follows I mount an argument for social researchers interested in embracing visual material in their work to rethink both the empirical and analytical possibilities which accompany this domain. In summary from the case I develop is to think of the visual in terms of not only what the camera can record but what the eye can see. One useful way to begin to unpack this claim is to examine a concrete instance of image-based visual enquiry.

DOES A PICTURE SPEAK FOR ITSELF?

Page 383 of *Sociology: exploring the architecture of everyday life* (Newman, 2000) is occupied by three black and white photographs. At the top, to the right, is a picture of an adult and child of indeterminate sex, both dressed identically in jodhpurs, riding jackets and hats, astride white horses on a deserted beach. Underneath, offset to the left, a balding man in his forties dressed in casual attire is shown scooping the leaves from the surface of a backyard swimming pool. Below this a third photograph depicts a smiling bikini clad woman in her late twenties. Cradled in her left arm is a toddler whilst her right arm is hooked round a fallen tree stump. The pair are seated in a shallow free-flowing mountain stream. A single, three word, caption accompanies the images: 'Water and Class'.

What is going on here? What are these images trying to tell us? Equally importantly, how do they tacitly trade upon the viewers' commonsense reasoning to achieve this goal? We quickly learn that the photographs are part of a 'visual essay' designed to accompany Chapter 11 of the book *The Architecture of Disadvantage: Poverty and Wealth*. Similar 'visual essays' can be found at the end of the majority of each of the chapters. Somehow, then, the images are purporting to present us with scenes and information relevant to these sociological concepts.

Visual researchers frequently allude to the popular maxim that their photographs 'speak for themselves'. But in 'Water and Class' – and many others like this – it is not the photographs which generate whatever sociological insight is claimed on their behalf, but the viewer. That is, it is *we* who make the images speak, we who do the work of 'class analysis' not the photographs. One key component here is our commonsense understanding of the conventions of textual layout and what they signify. That is, we make the assumption that the first photograph is a depiction of an 'upper class' scene on account of its location at the *top* of the page; conversely the representation at the bottom *must* be that of the 'working' or 'lower' class. Moreover, we provide additional narrative material locatable in the images which serves to reinforce this interpretation: only the upper class can afford the ownership of horses; the deserted beach must be part of the riders' private estate and so on.

In making sense of these images in the way I have suggested, something very similar to what Schegloff (1988), in another context, has referred to as 'sociology by epitome' can be detected. Schegloff's target in this instance was Erving Goffman and the widely held view that his (Goffman's) work was densely empirical. In Schegloff's view this was misplaced; Goffman's observations of social life, he argued,

> achieve their sense of typicality, by using but a stroke or two, . . . a detail or two, to indicate the scene which we as readers are to call up from memory, personal experience or imagination. If he succeeds, that is if *we* succeed in calling such a scene to mind, our ability to do so from his detail or two is proof of its typicality. The typicality of the scene or action has not only been 'shown' but has been enlisted and exploited, and the adequacy of his description . . . has *ipso facto* been demonstrated. (Schegloff, 1988: 101)

Much of conventional image-based visual enquiry operates, I argue, according to the same method of epitome. The photographs which provide the illustrative material for the field's ethnographic essays, research reports and monographs serve a purpose only to the extent that *we* can supply the theoretical or conceptual point *they* purport to deliver. 'Water and Class' may be an extreme example of this genre but it is not atypical. To press the point further for a moment, what if the order of the images on the page has been reversed? Would this have led to confusion on the part of the viewer? Most likely not. As Garfinkel (1967) famously showed, humans have the capacity to find sense and purpose even in settings where these features have been violated. In this case the two horse riders – now relegated to the bottom of the page – might well have been construed as apprentice working class jockeys or strappers out exercising their charges at dawn. Conversely the bikini-clad female, now occupying the top billing, could well have been seen as a wealthy heiress luxuriating in the clear waters of her private mountain retreat. It would be difficult to identify the balding, casually dressed man as anything other than middle class.[1]

Paradoxically, the very problems of indeterminacy, or 'polysemy' to use cultural studies jargon, which I have identified in the use of photographic images have been turned to advantage by some researchers. As Mason (2002) has noted, photographs and other forms of visual or documentary material have been used as methods of data generation in conjunction with other methods such as interviewing or focus groups. In the method of 'photo-elicitation' (Schwartz, 1989) the researcher trades upon the task of interpreting existing photographs of family or local community to generate extensive verbal commentary which might not be otherwise forthcoming during the interview process. Alternatively, subjects can be asked to take their own photographs which can then be the basis of subsequent discussion and analysis by the researcher. Generally referred to as 'autophotography', this method has been used to investigate such phenomena as sex role differences (Clancy and Dollinger, 1993) or cross-cultural perceptions of national identity (Ziller, 1990).

THE FIELD OF VISUAL RESEARCH: SOME PRELIMINARY CONSIDERATIONS

These possibilities notwithstanding, it remains the case that until relatively recently, the vast majority of qualitative researchers in the social sciences have had only minimal interest in visual enquiry or visual methodologies. In the last few years, however, this has begun to change and there has been a burgeoning interest in all aspects of 'the visual' – in visual communication, in practices of visualization and visual culture more broadly. 'The visual' has become not only a focus of concern in its traditional homelands of anthropology, sociology and cultural studies, but something which has engaged the interests of scholars in disciplines as diverse as architecture and design, geography and urban studies, material culture, new technology and multimedia, and science and museum studies. The plethora of new books and journals[2] – what one contributor has referred to as a 'deluge' (Pink, 2001b) – which have recently made their appearance, testifies to the legitimacy, if not unqualified acceptance, of the field in the eyes of social and cultural researchers.

At the same time, however, and partly as a consequence of this increasing interest, questions remain about the viability of visual research as a coherent intellectual endeavour. The multi-disciplinary nature of the field is such that it is no longer possible – if it ever were – to speak of *the* method of visual enquiry, not least because there is no obvious agreement about what this term should embrace. Significant fault lines can be detected on the basis of even a cursory inspection of the literature. For example, as we have noted above, there is no consensus as to whether visual researchers should generate the material they seek to analyse or alternatively confine their attention to the analysis of pre-existing cultural images and representations. Both practices are widely advocated but both draw upon divergent theoretical traditions and demand correspondingly different analytic stances. Tensions dating back to the realist and artistic traditions from the foundation period of photography have resurfaced in new guises. There are those who insist that visual images are inherently interpretive: a domain of genres, narratives and codes. For others photographic information is a faithful record of what occurred and which might even be quantified. Traditional and experimental ethnographers alike who have added video to their repertoire of research techniques ply their trade in apparent ignorance of the use of the video record in the ethnomethod-ologically influenced analysis of naturally occurring forms of interaction (see Heath, this volume). It is not putting too fine a point on it to state that the field of visual research stands as one of the most disorganized and theoretically inchoate in the social science academy.

The principal message I want to convey in this chapter is the need to think of visual enquiry as embracing *more* than the photographic image. There are several strands in this argument which require unravelling. The first, and less contentious, is to think of images not simply as a realm of representation but also as containing information or data which can be bought to bear on the investigation of social and cultural processes. It is this theme – that the visual is a realm of 'data', not simply a domain amenable to 'cultural' or 'interpretive' modes of inquiry – which is intended to be conveyed by the chapter title. In part, thinking of the visual as data may require going beyond the reliance on the photograph and considering the possibilities inherent in other forms of visual material of the kind I shall refer to later as two-dimensional. For example, newspaper cartoons or comic strips can tell us a good deal about the wider political, economic and gender systems in which they are embedded. Other forms of two-dimensional visual data such as directional signs, diagrams and maps can be used to explicate the claims of ethnomethod-ology about the role of commonsense reasoning. Here the focus is not so much on the discovery of cultural meanings by the academic analyst but rather the ways in which ordinary actors use or make sense of such visual information in the course of their everyday practical routines.

But the equating of 'the visual' only with such two-dimensional images is also curiously short-sighted and unduly restrictive. Social life is visual in diverse and counter-intuitive ways. Consequently, I shall argue, there are many more forms of visual data other than the photograph, the advertisement or the cartoon. Objects, places and locales carry meanings through visual means just like images. Clothing and body language are significant signs which we use to establish identity and negotiate public situations. Eye contact – Simmel's 'mutual glance' – plays a role in regulating social life among strangers. The material ecology of the built environment – shopping malls, museums and public spaces more generally – has been argued to exert a determining influence on the movement and mutual coordination of people. Tensions between surveillance, visibility and privacy regulate our uses of such spaces. In all of these areas there are rich supplies of material for the visual researcher. In giving up the idea that visual research is only the study of photographs or advertisements, then a far broader range of data becomes available for investigation. From this vantage point visual enquiry is no longer just the study of the image, but rather the study of the seen and observable. Photographs may be helpful sometimes in recording the seen dimensions of social life. Usually they are not necessary.

In the remainder of this chapter I develop these arguments in more detail. I begin by looking at some further examples of photographically based visual research as image-based work remains the most recognized variant. My verdict on this material is mixed. There have been some deservedly famous examples of researchers who have used this form of visual material to make important theoretical arguments. However, a great deal – perhaps the majority – of such visual enquiry can only be described as questionable. I then turn to the more inclusive conception of visual data outlined above and explore the possibilities for research which this provides.

PHOTOGRAPHS AS DATA: DOCUMENTARY AND REPRESENTATIONAL CONSIDERATIONS

At its best visual enquiry utilizing photographic images has produced some sophisticated studies which clearly demonstrate the viability of using visual material critically and reflexively. At its worst, however, image-based visual enquiry has incorporated photographs in ways which are purely illustrative and where it is sometimes even difficult to find a rationale for their inclusion.

A cursory acquaintance with the history of photographic visual enquiry suggests that these concerns are not new as the case of the *American Journal of Sociology* reveals. Photographic illustrations were a conspicuous part of articles published in the journal's early years between 1896 and 1916 but almost overnight they disappeared. The then editor of the journal, Albion Small, argued that the elimination of such images was necessary if sociology was to move 'out of amateurishness, not to say quackery, and advance toward responsible scientific procedure' (Small, 1905: 637, quoted in Stasz, 1979: 132).

Even contemporary luminaries such as Howard Becker, who pioneered the modern developments of visual sociology in the 1970s, have voiced suspicions as to the appropriateness or adequacy of photographic techniques. Commenting on the work of social documentary photographers and their relevance to sociological enquiry, Becker noted a 'double reaction':

> At first, you find that they call attention to a wealth of detail from which an interested sociologist could develop useful ideas about whose meaning he could spin interesting speculation. . . . Greater familiarity leads to a scaling down of admiration. While the photographs do have these virtues, they also tend to restrict themselves to a few reiterated simple statements. Rhetorically important as a strategy of proof, the repetition leads to work that is intellectually and analytically thin. (Becker, 1974: 11)

Elsewhere (Emmison and Smith, 2000) I have argued that it is this reliance on the photographic image – with all its attendant problems – that has been the major impediment to a robust or vibrant tradition of visual enquiry. Visual researchers frequently claim that their field has been marginalized from the core concerns of the social sciences. In the case of sociology, where this tendency is probably the most pronounced, visual researchers consequently have been ghettoized and reduced to communicating with each other about a narrow range of specialist issues. My argument is that this marginalization is, to a large extent, self-inflicted on account both of the inability of visual researchers to use photographs in anything other than a questionable illustrative fashion but also – a point to be developed in more detail shortly – to see beyond the use of photography.

Notwithstanding my comments above about the unexplicated common-sense reasoning which underpins much photographic work, my reservations about an image-based visual sociology also turn on the point that photographs have been misunderstood as constituting forms of data in their own right when in fact they should be considered in the first instance as means of preserving, storing or representing information. In this sense photographs should be seen as analogous to code-sheets, the responses to interview schedules, ethnographic field notes, tape recordings of verbal interaction or any one of the numerous ways in which the social researchers seek to capture data for subsequent analysis and investigation. Mainstream social researchers capture their data with surveys, questionnaires and interviews amongst other methods; visual researchers have traditionally captured images. But unlike the former who can readily appreciate the difference between the reality they investigate and their means of apprehending this reality, amongst the latter this distinction has become confounded.

Consider, by way of example, one of the most influential works of visual sociology, Wagner's (1979) edited collection *Images of Information*. The book includes, *inter alia*, photographically illustrated research reports on the social life of tramps or vagrants, the work practices and clientele of a beauty parlour, an inner-city ethnic community in decline, and pedestrians negotiating their passage on wind-swept streets. Collecting these disparate phenomena together in this way suggests they have something in common: that in some way each cumulatively advances our understanding of social life. But this is not the case: the only unifying theme in each of these essays is the reliance on photography as a means of recording and displaying information. The apparent unity these phenomena have as a consequence of being collected is thus entirely spurious. Whatever utility they might have as data for social science does not stem from their appearance in photographs but from their characteristics as objects in their own right.

Where the use of photographs, *qua* photographs, appears most suited to play a part in visual enquiry is in the more critical or reflexive forms of analysis that have characterized the best of the representational and documentary approaches. Commentators on visual methodology invariably cite the well-known but now relatively dated work of Bateson and Mead (1942) or Goffman (1979) as exemplary illustrations of what can be achieved, but a number of more recent studies display an equivalent sensitivity towards the use of visual materials. One of the most intriguing is Born's (1998) analysis of an exhibition of museum photography: 'Camera Obscured: Photographic Documentation and the Public Museum'. The photographs Born analyses are part of the archival record of the in-house photographic studios of several major European and North American public museums which had been collected between 1865 and 1960. The photographers' task had been to record the varied activities integral to the running of these institutions – essentially the construction, renovation, transportation of the displays. The images she examined offered a fascinating insight into the 'labour' of the museum as a working institution, its social relations and hierarchies, as well as its wider social and cultural significance. But the photographic images of the museum practices also engendered some epistemological puzzles. As Born notes, there was a 'baffling, endless regress' to her analysis:

> to interpret/represent a representation (the exhibition) of a representation (the museum photographers' texts) of a representation (the institutionalised representations of the museum). (Born, 1998: 224)

Born argues that in their exhibited form the museum photographs clearly exceed their original documentary function. Collectively, the images present a 'realist meditation' on the infrastructure of the museum's own 'heroic realism' – a 'realism squared'. One way in which this was manifest lay in the appropriation of surrealist codes – a play with scale, camera angle or incongruous juxtaposition – in many of the images. One photograph from the 1920s depicts an 'elephant being removed for renovation'. The stuffed elephant, its trunk raised skyward, is shown on the back of a horse-drawn cart being slowly wheeled through the inner-city streets of London. Themes from natural history feature in a number of other archival images:

> A museum worker nestling among giant leaves composes a giant millipede on a staged set while arms reach up from below and out of frame. An 'artist' puts the

finishing touches to a model man in a 'Neolithic Sun Worship diorama'; the artist has a white lab coat, dark suit and tie, and stiffly pokes with his brush the 'Neolithic man' who is slightly larger, naked and somehow more human than the 'artist'. (Born, 1998: 235)

Born concludes her analysis by suggesting that museum photographic records need to be rescued from their current liminal or ambiguous status and should form part of the museum's permanent display. Making the museum's hidden representational labour publicly available in this way would be consistent with a move towards 'the post-modern museum' and the rejection of the museum as a mausoleum 'dedicated to the piecing together from fragmentary objects and narratives from a totalising history' (Born, 1998: 239).

The documentary and representational dimensions of photography are also raised by Stuart Hall in his discussion of the problems of interpretation attending the photographic record of the history of black settlement in the UK during the 1950s. Hall's argument is that many of the photographs which could serve as documentary evidence of post-war migration have already 'made a public appearance in the field of representation' and as a consequence will have already acquired meanings and inflections through their earlier positioning within the discourses of the news-photo agency, the photographic studio or magazine colour supplement. For Hall this means that:

It is difficult, if not by now impossible, to recapture the earlier meanings of these photographs. In any event, the search for their 'essential Truth' – an original founding moment of meaning – is an illusion. The photographs are essentially multiaccentual in meaning. No such previously natural moment of true meaning, untouched by the codes and social relations of production and reading, and transcending historical time, exists. . . . Black historians, especially, handling these explosive little 'documents', will have to steer their way through the increasingly narrow passage which separates the old Scylla of 'documentary realism as Truth' from the new Charybdis of a too-simplistic 'avant-gardism'. (Hall, 1991: 152–3)

Whereas Born and Hall both deal with issues of representation in images generated by largely anonymous or unknown photographers, Peter Hamilton (1997) focuses his energies on the much more familiar photographic work of members of the French humanist school, men such as Robert Doisneau and Henri Cartier-Bresson who were active from the end of the Second World War until the late 1950s. For Hamilton the essence of this work was its attempt to capture a quintessential 'Frenchness'. The images produced by the French humanists – pictures of street life, families, children, lovers, the 'classes populaire' – served to celebrate everyday life and promote themes of community, solidarity. The French humanist photographers employed a variety of techniques to achieve these goals. Perhaps the most important was the device of positioning the viewer of the scenes as a self-same member of the ordinary classes who had chanced upon the activity as part of their own daily routines. In 'post-structuralist' language the photographs created particular 'subject-positions' for their viewers from which their preferred readings could be derived. Hamilton's overall argument is that such images, which were initially widely distributed and promoted as documentary photo-journalism in magazines such as *Life or Paris Match*, served as an integrating force to reunify the French nation which had been traumatized by the experience of wartime occupation and collaboration.

The work of Born, Hall and Hamilton provides exemplary case studies of the potential of image-based visual enquiry. Unlike 'Water and Class' each writer moves beyond a dubious illustrative use of photography to make important theoretical points about meaning and representation in their cultural and historical manifestations which are only available through visual means. Collectively they demonstrate what can be achieved when the photographic record is harnessed to a powerful theoretical imagination. Nevertheless, some final comments about this 'representational' mode of visual enquiry are in order. The first is that these studies are invariably idio-syncratic to the extent that there is no obvious cumulative methodological or conceptual lessons to be drawn. Such studies appear to be 'one-offs', self-contained reports, fascinating or illuminating in their own right but offering no guide to the neophyte researcher as to how to proceed. The second is that they still serve to perpetuate the narrow assumption that visual research is equivalent to the use of the photographic image. In the remainder of the chapter I return to my earlier argument about the need to move beyond the representational analysis of the image and to embrace not only alternative forms of two-dimensional data, but a wider, more inclusive, conception of visual enquiry.

RETHINKING THE VISUAL: SPACE, PLACE AND DIMENSIONALITY

In *Researching the Visual* (2000) Philip Smith and I introduced the idea of 'dimensionality' as a core organizing principle for thinking about the different forms of visual information. Underpinning this argument is the point that visual is also spatial. That is, spatial considerations influence the various categories or types of visual data that are available for analysis, and spatial considerations also enter into the ways we think about the meaning, or the relevance, of these items as data. The objects, people and events, which constitute the raw materials for visual analysis, are not encountered in isolation but rather in specific contexts. For the most part we observe the myriad features of our environment as also having a spatial existence and it is this which serves as the means whereby much of their socio-cultural significance is imparted. Visual data, in short, must be understood as having more than just the two-dimensional component which its representation in the photographic image suggests.

Thinking of visual research in this more inclusive form does not, of course, mean that photographs play no part. Two-dimensional images – a category which includes photographs and also billboards, cartoons, advertisements, directional signs, maps, instructional diagrams and so on – are a constituent feature of social life. But rather than imposing a spurious unity upon them – as visual researchers have tended to do – it is necessary to look specifically at how each of these forms operate in everyday life and the analytical techniques they demand. The addition of spatial considerations in the conceptualization of visual data, however, opens up new vistas whilst simultaneously allowing more fruitful theoretical connections to be established.

One of these would be to point to closer affinities between traditional ethnography and 'visual enquiry'. Nearly twenty years ago Stimson (1986) noted that questions of place and space had been virtually ignored in most qualitative research, to such an extent that any talk of participant *observation* is misleading: most ethnography is about listening rather than looking. Stimson developed his call for a visual ethnography by describing in detail the room in which the General Medical Council (GMC) in the UK holds its disciplinary hearings. Most of us will never have occasion to attend the regulatory activities of professional groups like the GMC but we can readily appreciate from Stimson's description how the room can be viewed, not simply as a place where the hearings are conducted, but a constituent element of the hearing itself. All aspects of the room – the oak panelling, leather chairs, high ceilings, the glass-fronted bookcases, the spatial arrangements of the tables, the presence of a uniformed commissionaire – he argues, convey the formality and solemnity of the occasion:

> This is a room in which serious matters are discussed: the room has a presence that is forced upon our consciousness. This is a room that, even when unoccupied, impresses on the visitor a solemn demeanour and subdued speech. When occupied, it retains its solemnity, and speech is now formal, carefully spoken, and a matter for the public record. (Stimson, 1986: 643)

Stimson concludes his discussion of the GMC disciplinary tribunal by rhetorically posing the question of how successful the hearings would be if they were conducted in a radically different architectural space such as a McDonald's restaurant. In contrast to the tradition and permanence of the disciplinary setting everything about the fast-food restaurant signifies transience and informality. Furnishings and equipment are plastic, vinyl and polystyrene; lengthy stays are discouraged through uncomfortable seating, noise and proximity to the kitchen areas. 'Conversation here, for customers, is informal. For staff it is rehearsed and repetitive. . . . Speech here will not make history. It would be difficult to conduct a disciplinary hearing in this setting' (p. 650).

Stimson's analysis of the GMC room illustrates perfectly how visual enquiry which is not dependent upon the photograph can be conducted. By not including photographs in his article two important consequences have followed. The first is that his work has not been seen as a contribution to 'the field' by self-proclaimed visual researchers. But, second, their absence also eliminates the epistemological confusions over the status of data in visual enquiry referred to earlier. Stimson's data are the actual objects encountered in the room and its overall spatial configuration. It is the inferences that he draws from encountering these as phenomena in their own right, not via their representation in an image, which are central to his methodology. In terms of the framework being proposed here, Stimson is analysing both 'three-dimensional' and 'lived' visual data. I look shortly in more detail at these concepts and offer further examples of research that could be conducted on these topics.

TWO-DIMENSIONAL VISUAL DATA

But let us return first to two-dimensional material for there is a need here to think of additional possibilities for investigation. Although visual researchers have paid a great deal of attention to cultural and semiotic analyses of texts such as newspaper and magazine photographs and advertisements, there has been a general neglect of other equally available media material such as cartoons or comic strips. One advantage of these latter materials is that it is generally possible to obtain lengthy historical records which can be mined for evidence of changing social and cultural norms. For example, elsewhere (Emmison, 1986; Emmison and McHoul, 1987) I have demonstrated that cartoons which represent economic categories and themes can yield insights into the changing assumptions about the workings of the economy or the relation between the economic and political realms which are not available through the conventional print record of the business pages. Prior to the 1940s there was no idea of 'the economy' as an aggregate entity either linguistically or visually. Cartoons featuring economic messages were confined to an older notion of 'economy' as wise or prudent expenditure. But once the modern conception of 'the economy' appears – a process which is bound up with the Keynesian 'revolution' in economic thinking – cartoons invariably feature the economic system and its constituent components as an entity, thing or even a person. Inflation becomes a 'dragon' to be conquered by the would-be St George treasurer or chancellor. Anthropomorphic representations of sick or ailing currency or the entire economy become commonplace. Importantly, even when monetarist economic doctrine gained ascendancy and the role of the government in economic affairs was downgraded, cartoonists still persisted with these 'Keynesian' representational forms, turning them to humorous or ironic advantage in their satirical endeavours.

A great deal of 'two-dimensional' visual data we encounter in everyday life – maps, directional signs, assembly guides, traffic regulations and the like – provide us with not simply information, but information which is to be incorporated into practical routines. That is, this is material which, unlike texts such as advertisements or cartoons, is specifically designed to be used by actors in the accomplishment of their goals. For these data a different set of theoretical coordinates, those offered by ethnomethodology, provide the most appropriate analytical tools. For example, Sharrock and Anderson (1979) demonstrate the value of this perspective in their examination of directional signs in a medical school complex. Signs in themselves, they declare, are of no sociological interest: rather it is the ways in which they are interpreted and the ways these interpretations occasion practical courses of action which deserve attention. Sharrock and Anderson illustrate their analytic interest in directional signs by showing how 'an ordinary user' of the premises in which they were located might conceivably use these signs in negotiating their way around. Sharrock and Anderson argue that the interpretation of signs is an irremediably practical and local matter. Signs are not observed in isolation but in particular contexts and in particular sequences. Finding our way around a building is, quite literally, a procedural affair. Visitors to the medical school may need to follow the directions of several information signs before arriving at their desired destinations. In this process, although signs are encountered 'one at a time', the sequences in which these occur are equally important in conveying information about places or locales.

One important lesson to be drawn from Sharrock and Anderson's analysis is the tacit 'work' that readers – or more precisely users – of sign systems must perform in way-finding. Pedestrian signs, that is, can never provide every detail of the journey that must be taken but instead rely upon the common-sense reasoning of the sign user to supply the 'missing' information. But it is interesting to compare the format of pedestrian direction signs with those which are erected for motorists. Pedestrians may misinterpret signs and be forced to retrace their steps as matters of course, but it is a different matter to rectify a missed turn when one is at the wheel of a car on a freeway. Pedestrians can readily modify their routes, make abrupt turns, or stop dead in their tracks generally without any fear that such activities will occasion collisions with their fellows, but these are not options which are available to drivers. What we find, then, is that these contrasting 'logics of navigation' – finding one's way around on foot as opposed to finding one's way around by car – are reflected in different sign systems. Whereas pedestrians are given only general outlines of where to proceed and must 'work out' the details en route, motorists are invariably given much more explicit visual information as to how to proceed, presumably with the intention of avoiding the kind of recoverable errors that pedestrians routinely engage in. The result is that key traffic directional signs tend to be iconic in that the physical layout of an up-coming road system is reproduced as a constituent feature of the sign itself.

THREE-DIMENSIONAL VISUAL DATA

The ethnomethodological investigation of two-dimensional texts, to the extent that it draws attention to their practical uses in particular environments, has, strictly speaking, foreshadowed one of the analytical possibilities in what I shall refer to as 'three-dimensional' visual data. Under this broad heading we can locate the objects of material culture which operate as signifiers in social life. These range from those of everyday life encountered in the home and which carry personal meanings to those in public spaces, such as statues or monuments, which represent official public discourses. Although such forms of data can be analysed in traditional semiotic terms, they are also implicated in human actions. Stimson was making much the same point in his discussion of the GMC room, although his analysis of how the activities constitutive of the disciplinary hearing were shaped by its material and spatial configuration did not make these methodological differences explicit. Barthes, however, does just this in his famous essay on the Citroen DS. We have become so accustomed to the cultural studies' semiotic interpretation of advertising texts that it is easy to forget that the objects or artefacts which figure in these texts also carry meanings. Much of Barthes' achievement was to spell out that myth-ologies were not only located in the representational practices of advertising campaigns but actually embodied in objects and activities. In the case of the Citroen DS, Barthes likens the car to 'the great Gothic cathedrals'; he empha-sizes the smoothness and shape of the car, and suggests its curvaceous glass contributes to a light, spiritual quality: 'Here the glass surfaces are not windows, openings pierced in a dark shell; they are vast walls of air and space, with the curvature, the spread and the brilliance of soap bubbles' (1973: 89). But Barthes also demonstrates the value in going beyond the object itself to look at the responses that people make when they encounter it in its pristine state:

> In the exhibition halls, the car on show is explored with an intense, amorous studiousness: it is the great tactile phase of discovery. . . . The bodywork, the lines of union are touched, the upholstery palpated, the seats tried, the doors caressed, the cushions fondled; before the wheel, one pretends to drive with one's whole body. The object here is totally prostituted, appropriated. . . . (1973: 90)

Generalizing, we can suggest that one of the primary advantages of objects or artefacts for visual enquiry is that they offer a greater range of possibilities than two-dimensional data for inference making about social and cultural behaviour and processes. There is not a great deal we can learn about 'behav-iour' from observing people reading or watching television (but see Morley, 1986) but observing what people do with objects is much more promising. Often the twin strategies of 'decoding' and behavioural inference making can be utilized in the same research site. For example, simply noting the placement and the gender, racial or other demographic characteristics of the statues or monuments which are located in the urban environment can tell us some-thing about the values or priorities associated with men and women in the official civic culture or national narratives (Bulbeck, 1992; Inglis, 1987). But observing what people actually do when in the presence of such monuments may give us a clearer idea about the attitudes or values of ordinary people (see, for example, Wagner-Pacifici and Schwartz, 1991). Indicators of the cultural significance of particular monuments can be gauged by the simple task of recording the degree or intensity of contact which people make when encountering these objects. Do they stop to read information plaques, do they discuss the item's aesthetic or historical significance, do they photograph it, perhaps even to the point of placing themselves in the frame? Informal research in Brisbane, the state capital of Queensland, suggests that it is not the predominantly masculine politicians, explorers and generals which the official culture recognizes which are of most relevance to visitors to the city, but the assorted animal figures which have been erected.

Object-centred visual enquiry has obvious methodological affinities with an older – and these days somewhat neglected and unfashionable – branch of social research, the use of unobtrusive or non-reactive measures (e.g. Webb et al., 1966). The sheer visibility of many kinds of objects means that it is possible to explore social life covertly. Because respondents are not required for many kinds of object-based research we can circumvent the usual problem of normative responding – providing the researcher a socially acceptable answer. This may be particularly useful in researching fields such as crime and deviance or urban disorder. There is a well-established branch of unobtrusive research which has utilized visual information in these fields in the form of 'traces' and 'accretions': rubbish, litter, graffiti, visible signs of vandalism, and so on. Perhaps the most well known is the 'broken-windows' thesis (Wilson and Kelling, 1982) which argues that signs of public incivilities – such as the existence of unrepaired windows, abandoned cars or drinking in streets – tend to attract further crime because potential offenders assume that police and residents alike do not care about the character of these neighbourhoods. Studies on these topics do not need to be small scale or impressionistic. For example, Sampson and Raudenbush (1999) recently undertook a study of the sources and consequences of public disorder which involved collecting information from over 23,000 street segments in Chicago. Using what they referred to as the 'method of systematic social observation' and 'taking seriously the idea that visual cues matter' (p. 605), Sampson and Raudenbush devised a project which involved driving a utility vehicle slowly down every street in 196 Chicago census tracts and video recording the social activities and physical features of each side of the street simultaneously. From this voluminous – and permanent – visual record they were able to devise complicated scales to capture the presence or absence of both physical and social disorder. The items they coded included garbage, graffiti, abandoned cars, condoms, syringes, public intoxication, street fighting or arguing, and drug selling. The theoretical underpinnings and statistical details of the project are not relevant in this context; it is mentioned only to provide some indication of the enormous potential – both qualitative and quantitative – which can be associated with visual enquiry.[3]

LIVED VISUAL DATA

It nevertheless remains the case that most research which utilizes the visual record has employed interpretive or qualitative techniques. This is evident as we turn to consider the concept of 'lived visual data'. From exploring the possibilities in the use of three-dimensional data it is a short step to the next 'higher' analytical level, which is the places and settings – the actual environments or locales – in which humans conduct their lives. In thinking of this as 'lived visual data' we turn our attention to such matters as the observable movements of people in time and space, to questions of visibility and invisibility and the patterning of zones and activities. A good deal of the contemporary research on these topics has revisited the classic discussions of the *flâneur* – the detached or reflexive urban spectator – first introduced by the French poet Baudelaire, or the writings of Simmel on the blasé attitude through which the metropolitan dweller copes with the sensory overload of urban life. However, this work has also benefited from the inclusion of more contemporary analytical frameworks. Some of the most interesting and innovative research in these fields has been carried out in locales such as museums and art galleries. Museum planners and designers (e.g. Dean, 1994) have long been aware of the ability of the physical layout to influence both the flow of 'traffic' and the nature of the learning experience. To date, however, the majority of findings from this research have been relatively 'broad-brush'. For example, other things being equal, people will invariably turn to the right on entering the museum; people spend more time at displays at the start of an exhibition than the end; people generally dislike entering areas without visible exits.

More recently a much more 'fine-grained' appreciation of museum visitor behaviour has emerged in the work of researchers drawing upon ethno-methodology and conversation analysis. Using video recordings of naturally occurring visitor behaviour in galleries and museums, vom Lehn et al. (2001; see also Heath et al., 2002) have looked specifically at how exhibits are encountered and experienced and the mutual conduct and collaboration on the part of both companions and strangers which this entails. Such research draws upon the long-standing symbolic interactionist interest in behaviour in public places, but it adds the complicating factor of how conduct is inextricably embedded in the immediate ecology and the material realities at hand. The research questions being posed here concern precisely how the objects and artefacts – the exhibits, paintings and installations – are both given sense by people in interaction and how, in turn, such objects reflexively inform the production of intelligible conduct. Like a great deal of ethnomethod-ological enquiry into naturally occurring behaviour, this research defies easy summary and requires for its full explication detailed consideration of the actual sequences of behaviour that are recorded (see also Heath, this volume). These considerations notwithstanding, a brief summary of some of the principal findings to emerge from this research is as follows:

- Visitors to galleries and museums in pairs or family groups appear not to encounter exhibits as 'individuals'; rather the experience is a consequence of the interactional dynamic of being a member of a pair.
- Social interaction also determines the length of time parties spend at each exhibit as well as their decision to move on.

- Visitors are sensitive to the presence of others, both adjacently and peripherally, and monitor each other's actions so that an ordered temporal use of the available space around exhibits is maintained.
- Exhibits do not appear to have a 'uniform stopping power'; rather the attractiveness or novelty of a given exhibit is often determined by the activities and conduct of others.

Collectively, what this research is pointing to is the crucial importance of factors such as co-presence, peripheral awareness and the like in shaping the conduct of visitors to such locales. Visual communication, in all its richness and between both companions and strangers, appears to be as significant as the actual architectural layout and design in shaping precisely how exhibits are encountered, experienced and appreciated.

CONCLUSION

If we move away from the commonsense equation of visual research as purely an image-based activity and embrace the claims being advanced here it is possible to regard many aspects of twentieth-century social science, and many of the major figures in this discipline, as contributing to the development of visual research. Visual research, in short, need no longer remain the marginalized speciality that it appears to be in the minds of most social scientists. Thinking of visual research as the study of the seen and the observable can facilitate important conceptual connections to be made between 'the visual' as a domain of enquiry and the work of many classical and contemporary theorists alike who might not otherwise be regarded as contributing to this field. Several examples have already been alluded to in the foregoing discussion. Simmel is one the most obvious candidates for inclusion: indeed Simmel explicitly addressed the issue such as the observability of social interaction and the significance of mutual glances in a famous essay (Simmel, 1921) first published in 1908. But there are many other figures in the history of social and cultural enquiry who, it can be argued, have been thinking about the visual or using visual methodologies in their work, although not necessarily as explicitly or self-consciously as Simmel. For example, to the extent that it has been concerned with reading the urban landscape then much of the tradition of urban research can be construed as a form of visual research. But other approaches to the social organization of the built environment come to mind. As Prior has demonstrated, a case can be made for 'a sociology of space rather than a sociological geography' (1988: 87) through focusing not so much on the spatial relationships which exist between buildings, settlement patterns and the like characteristic of urban landscapes, but on the internal features of buildings – upon their architectural configurations. Prior's own research in this field offers a fascinating account of how the design of hospitals and asylums can be used to illustrate changing institutional assumptions concerning disease, insanity and the most appropriate forms of treatment and control.

Last, but not least, there are those contemporary schools and writers who, in various ways, have focussed more upon the issue of the visibility of human conduct and the opportunities this provides. Here we can mention the tradition inspired by Foucault's example of surveillance, the panopticon and the gaze, and how the visual can be linked to themes of power and control (see for example Shearing and Stenning, 1995). Finally, of course, there is the tradition of naturalist observation of social life which connects Simmel with Goffman, his intellectual heir. Many of Goffman's most important concepts are specifically designed to illustrate observable aspects of social conduct. Indeed it is something of a puzzle why Goffman relied on purely verbal accounts of the interactions he so painstakingly documented. From Goffman it is but a short step to the field of proxemics and the work of Hall (1966), who did employ photographic illustrations and diagrams to visualize his work. A longer, and possibly more contentious, route also connects Goffman to the ethnomethodological and conversation analysis tradition where, as we have seen, the video recording of naturally occurring interaction is emerging as an increasingly required empirical component.

Photographic images – in either their representational or informational form – will no doubt continue to figure in visual enquiry, but only when researchers come to appreciate the value of direct observation of the social world, harnessed with a powerful theoretical imagination, will visual research come to enjoy the centrality throughout the social and cultural fields which it deserves.

NOTES

1. We cannot, of course, let the example pass without a comment on the caption. Without this the images – regardless of the order in which they appear – are almost indecipherable. Barthes' (1977: 39) point about the need for a verbal text (a caption) 'to counter the terror of uncertain signs' has never been more effectively illustrated.

2. The list continues to expand almost monthly and the following guide to the field will almost certainly have been superseded by the time of this chapter's publication. Books devoted to these themes which have recently appeared include Banks (2001), Barnard (2001), Evans and Hall (1999), Heywood and Sandywell (1999), van Leeuwen and Jewitt (2000), Mirzoeff (1998), Pink (2001a), Prosser (1998), Sturken and Cartwright (2001) and Walker and Chaplin (1997). In addition at least two new journals catering specifically for this field have also made their appearance, *Visual Communication* and *Journal of Visual Culture*, whilst a number of other existing journals now carry illustrative material on a more regular basis.

3. In this sense Sampson and Raudenbush's research can be seen as a continuation – albeit one with added technical complexity – of an important tradition in visual enquiry which has draw upon quantitative methods and large-scale samples to make important and often unexpected empirical findings. See for example Richardson and Kroeber (1940); Robinson (1976); and Alexander (1994).

Recommended reading

The broad parameters of the field of visual research as I have conceptualized it in this chapter inevitably makes the selection of additional recommended reading somewhat difficult. However the following cover much of the territory to which I have directly or indirectly referred:

Prosser, J. (ed) (1998) *Image-based Research: A Sourcebook for Qualitative Researchers*. London: Routledge/Falmer.
Prosser's edited collection provides a comprehensive coverage of the use of photographic images as research devices.

Barthes, R. (1977) 'The rhetoric of the image' in his *Image, Music, Text*. London: Fontana.
This remains one of the most sophisticated examples of a semiotic or cultural studies interpretation of a commercially-produced image.

Banks, M. and Morphy H. (eds) (1997) *Rethinking Visual Anthropology*. New Haven, CT: Yale University Press.
Banks and Morphy's collection offers a way of thinking about the anthropological possibilities and significance of visual data which has some similarities with the position advanced in this chapter.

Pink, S. (2001) *Doing Visual Ethnography: Images, Media and Representation in Research*. London: Sage.
Pink gives a useful example of how the use of video-recording technology can enhance more conventional written ethnography.

REFERENCES

Alexander, V.D. (1994) 'The Image of Children in Magazine Advertisements From 1905 to 1990', *Communication Research*, 21 (6): 742–65.

Banks, M. (2001) *Visual Methods in Social Research*. London: Sage.

Barnard, M. (2001) *Approaches to Understanding Visual Culture*. Basingstoke: Palgrave.

Barthes, R. (1973) *Mythologies*. St Albans: Paladin.

Barthes, R. (1977) 'The Photographic Message', in *Image, Music Text*. London: Fontana.

Bateson, G. and Mead, M. (1942) *Balinese Character: a photographic analysis*. New York: New York Academy of Sciences.

Becker, H. (1974) 'Photography and Sociology', *Studies in the Anthropology of Visual Communication*, (1): 3–26.

Born, G. (1998) 'Public Museums, Museum Photography and the Limits of Reflexivity', *Journal of Material Culture*, 3 (2): 223–54.

Bulbeck, C. (1992) 'Women of Substance: the depiction of women in Australian monuments', *Hecate*, 18 (2): 8–22.

Clancy, S. and Dollinger, S.J. (1993) 'Photographic Depictions of the Self: gender and age differences in social connectedness', *Sex Roles*, 7/8: 477–508.

Dean, D. (1994) *Museum Exhibition: theory and practice*. London: Routledge.

Emmison, M. (1986) 'Visualising the Economy: fetishism and the legitimation of economic life', *Theory, Culture & Society*, 3 (2): 81–97.

Emmison, M. and McHoul, A. (1987) 'Drawing on the Economy: cartoon discourse and the production of a category', *Cultural Studies*, 1 (1): 93–112.

Emmison, M. and Smith, P. (2000) *Researching the Visual: images, objects, contexts and interactions in social and cultural inquiry*. London: Sage.

Evans, J. and Hall, S. (eds) (1999) *Visual Culture: The Reader*. London: Sage/Open University Press.

Garfinkel, H. (1967) *Studies in Ethnomethodology*. Englewood Cliffs, NJ: Prentice Hall.

Goffman, E. (1979) *Gender Advertisements*. London and Basingstoke: Macmillan.

Hall, E.T. (1966) *The Hidden Dimension*. New York: Doubleday.

Hall, S. (1991) 'Reconstruction Work: images of post-war black settlement', in J. Spence and P. Holland (eds) *The Meanings of Domestic Photography*, London: Virago.

Hamilton, P. (1997) 'Representing the Social: France and Frenchness in post-war humanist photography', in S. Hall (ed.) *Representation: Cultural Representation and Signifying Practice*. London: Sage.

Heath, C., Luff, P., vom Lehn, D., Hindmarsh, J. and Cleverly, J. (2002) 'Crafting Participation: designing ecologies, configuring experience', *Visual Communication*, 1 (1): 9–33

Heywood, I. and Sandywell, B. (1999) *Interpreting Visual Culture: explorations in the hermeneutics of the visual*. London: Routledge.

Inglis, K. (1987) 'Men, Women and War memorials: Anzac Australia', *Daedalus*, 116 (3): 35–58.

Mason, J. (2002) *Qualitative Researching*, 2nd Edition. London: Sage.

Mirzoeff, N. (ed.) (1998) *The Visual Culture Reader*. London: Routledge.

Morley, D. (1986) *Family Television: cultural power and domestic leisure*. London: Comedia.

Newman, D. (2000) *Sociology: exploring the architecture of everyday life*, 3rd Edition. Thousand Oaks, CA: Pine Forge Press.

Pink, S. (2001a) *Doing Visual Ethnography: images, media and representation in research*. London: Sage.

Pink, S. (2001b) 'More Visualising, More Methodologies: on video, reflexivity and qualitative research', *Sociological Review*, 49: 586–99.

Prior, L. (1988) 'The Architecture of the Hospital: a study of spatial organization and medical knowledge', *British Journal of Sociology*, 39 (1): 86–113.

Prosser, J. (1998) *Image-Based Research: a sourcebook for qualitative researchers*. London: RoutledgeFalmer.

Richardson, J. and Kroeber, A.L. (1940) 'Three Centuries of Women's Dress Fashions: a quantitative analysis', *Anthropological Records*, 5 (2): 111–53.

Robinson, D. (1976) 'Fashions in Shaving and Trimming of the Beard: the men of the Illustrated London News, 1842–1972', *American Journal of Sociology*, 81 (5): 1133–41.

Sampson, R. and Raudenbush, S. (1999) 'Systematic Social Observation of Public Spaces: a new look at disorder in urban neighborhoods', *American Journal of Sociology*, 105 (3): 603–51.

Schegloff, E.A. (1988) 'Goffman and the Analysis of Conversation', in P. Drew and T. Wootton (eds) *Erving Goffman: exploring the interaction order*. Oxford: Polity Press.

Schwartz, D. (1989) 'Visual Ethnography: using photography in qualitative research', *Qualitative Sociology*, 12 (2): 119–54.

Sharrock, W.W. and Anderson, D.C. (1979) 'Directional Hospital Signs as Sociological Data', *Information Design Journal*, 1 (2): 81–94.

Shearing, C. and Stenning, P. (1995) 'From the Panopticon to Disney World: the development of discipline', in J. Muncie, E. McLaughlin and M. Langan (eds) *Criminological Perspectives: a reader*, London: Sage.

Simmel, G. (1921) [1908] 'Sociology of the Senses: visual interaction', in R. Park and E. Burgess (eds) *Introduction to the Science of Sociology*. Chicago: University of Chicago Press. pp. 356–61.

Small, A. (1905) 'A Decade of Sociology', *American Journal of Sociology*, 9: 1–10.

Stasz, C. (1979) 'The Early History of Visual Sociology', in J. Wagner (ed.) *Images of Information: Still Photography in the Social Sciences*. Beverly Hills, CA: Sage. pp. 119–36.

Stimson, G. (1986) 'Place and Space in Sociological Fieldwork', *Sociological Review*, 34: 641–56.

Sturken, M. and Cartwright, L. (2001) *Practices of Looking: an introduction to visual culture*. Oxford: Oxford University Press.

van Leeuwen, T. and Jewitt, C. (2000) *Handbook of Visual Analysis*. London: Sage.

vom Lehn, D., Heath, C. and Hindmarsh, J. (2001) 'Exhibiting Interaction: conduct and collaboration in museums and galleries', *Symbolic Interaction*, 24 (2): 189–216.

Wagner, J. (ed.) (1979) *Images of Information: Still Photography in the Social Sciences*. Beverly Hills, CA: Sage.

Wagner-Pacifici, R. and Schwartz, B. (1991) 'The Vietnam Veterans' Memorial', *American Journal of Sociology*, 97: 376–420.

Walker, J. and Chaplin, S. (1997) *Visual Culture: an introduction*. Manchester: Manchester University Press.

Webb, E.J., Campbell, D.T., Schwartz, R.D. and Sechrest, L. (1966) *Unobtrusive Measures: non-reactive research in the social sciences*. Chicago: Rand McNally.

Wilson, J. and Kelling, G. (1982) 'Broken Windows', *The Atlantic Monthly*, 249 (3): 29–38.

Ziller, R.C. (1990) *Photographing the self: methods for observing personal orientations*. Newbury Park, CA: Sage.

14 Analysing face-to-face interaction

Video, the visual and material

Christian Heath

INTRODUCTION

One of the most impressive developments in sociology over the past couple of decades has been the burgeoning body of empirical research concerned with talk in interaction. Ethnomethodology and conversation analysis have made a profound contribution to our understanding of the social organization of language use and talk and the ways in which they feature in the accomplishment of social actions and activities. The visual and material aspects of social interaction have received less attention and yet it is increasingly recognized that bodily conduct, objects and artefacts are critical to the practical accomplishment of social action and activity. The increasing availability of cheap and reliable video equipment, coupled with the emergence of relevant methodological resources, is leading to a growing interest in the naturalistic analysis of social interaction and the ways in which it is accomplished through talk, bodily conduct and the material resources at hand.

This chapter considers the ways in which we can use video recordings of everyday conduct and interaction to examine the ways in which participants accomplish particular activities in collaboration with others. In particular it suggests that analytic developments within the social sciences, namely, ethno-methodology and conversation analysis, provide resources through which we can examine the situated production of social action and address the visual, material as well as spoken features of an activity's accomplishment. The focus of the chapter is social interaction, and the ways in which we can begin to analyse the practices and procedures through which participants themselves in ordinary, everyday environments produce their own actions and make sense of the conduct of others. In this way, the chapter suggests that sociology can develop a distinctive approach to the ways in which bodily comportment and physical artefacts feature in everyday activities and contribute to our understanding of a range of analytic and substantive issues.

The chapter begins by providing a sketch of one or two more general methodological considerations which inform the analysis of video data, that is audio-visual recordings of 'naturally occurring' activities and events. We then take an example drawn from a medical consultation and discuss the ways in which we can begin to examine aspects of the participants' conduct.

Before considering some basic methodological issues, it is worth briefly mentioning that whilst sociology has been relatively slow to exploit the opportunities afforded by video, there is a long-standing, though largely disregarded, tradition in social anthropology of 'interaction analysis' using recorded data of naturalistic activities. It emerged in the early 1950s in Palo Alto through the pioneering work of Bateson and Mead and others including McQuown, Hockett and Ruesch, and led to extraordinary studies undertaken by Birdwhistell (1970), Scheflen (1964) and others. Coupled with the wide-ranging essays by Goffman (1959, 1963, 1967,) the tradition also influenced Kendon's (1991) impressive work on gesture and bodily comportment in interaction and the more ethological studies by Cosnier (1978) and others.

These studies have some parallels with a very different tradition which has led to the emergence of a distinctive body of sociological research concerned with the ways in which talk and bodily conduct feature in social interaction. In particular, ethnomethodology and conversation analysis have provided the methodological resources which have informed the development of a growing body of sociological research which uses video recordings to examine the *in situ* organization of social actions and activities in face-to-face interaction. For example, in a pioneering series of essays, C. Goodwin (1979, 1980, 1981) examined the ways in which the production of turn at talk, a speaker's utterance, is coordinated with the gaze of the recipient, and went on to identify various devices employed by speakers to establish mutual orientation. Related research examined the organization of gesture, and in particular the ways in which various forms of bodily conduct are used by speakers to shape the co-participation of the person(s) with whom they are speaking (see for example C. Goodwin, 1980, 1981; M.H. Goodwin, 1980; Heath, 1986). Since these beginnings we have witnessed the emergence of a wide-ranging body of research which has used video recordings of 'naturally occurring events' to examine visual, vocal and material aspects of a range of activities in both conversational and institutional environments (see for example Goodwin 1987, 1994, 1996; Goodwin and Goodwin, 1996a; LeBaron and Streeck, 2000; Streeck, 1988, 1996; Hindmarsh and Pilnick, 2002; Whalen, 1995; vom Lehn et al., 2001; Hindmarsh and Heath, 2000; Heath, 2002; Heath and Luff, 2000).

ANALYTIC CONSIDERATIONS

Conversation analysis and ethnomethodology provide the resources through which it has been possible to exploit video for sociological purposes. Before presenting an example, it might be helpful to provide a brief overview of the analytic issues which informed the research. In general, analysis has been informed by three principal issues. Firstly, it has been concerned with the detailed analysis of the local, situated accomplishment of social actions and activities. Secondly, it has been directed towards the investigation of the methodological resources, the practices and reasoning, through which participants themselves produce social actions and make sense of the actions and activities of others. Thirdly, conversation analysis has drawn on the emergent and sequential character of talk in interaction to examine the ways in which participants orient to and make sense of each other's conduct and engender locally relevant action and activities.

Ethnomethodology emerged through the pioneering studies of Harold Garfinkel and rapidly led to the development of conversation analysis through the innovative research of Sacks and his colleagues, Schegloff and Jefferson. Unlike other forms of social science enquiry, ethnomethodology and conversation analysis do not provide a 'method', in the sense of a clear-cut set of procedures that if followed will generate scientifically valid results or findings. However, they do involve a number of critical analytic commitments which have provided a foundation to a substantial body of empirical studies.

In *Studies in Ethnomethodology* Garfinkel (1967) develops a radical approach to the analysis of human practical activity. He argues that we place the situated production of social actions and activities at the forefront of the analytic agenda and treat mundane events, even physical and biological phenomena, as the 'artful accomplishment' of the participants in the settings in which they arise. Garfinkel suggests that we 'bracket' events and ask of any phenomenon what the methodological resources are which inform the production and intelligibility of the event or activity in question. At one point, he contrasts his analytic recommendations to those recommended by Durkheim:

> Thereby, in contrast to certain versions of Durkheim that teach that the objective reality of social facts is sociology's fundamental principle, the lesson is taken instead and used as a study policy, that the objective reality of social facts as on ongoing accomplishment of the concerted activities of daily life, with the ordinary artful ways of that accomplishment being by members known, used, and taken for granted, is for members doing sociology, a fundamental phenomena. (Garfinkel, 1967: vii)

So, for example, in their different studies of 'suicide problem', both Garfinkel (1967) and Atkinson (1978) do not take the official category 'suicide' for granted and examine the variables which explain patterns in the rates of suicide amongst particular classes of individuals. Rather, they examine the practices and practical reasoning on which those responsible for the investigation of equivocal deaths rely, in warrantably ascribing the category 'suicide' in a particular case. In this way, analytic attention is directed towards the *in situ* accomplishment of particular events and activities, and in particular the resources on which individuals rely in the production of social actions and activities. Moreover, it is argued that we take for granted or gloss the systematic ways in which we accomplish social actions and activities, the 'objective order to social facts', so as to encounter the 'normal appearances' of everyday life, whilst we concertedly accomplish the very scenes and events we confront.

It can be argued that conversation analysis shares these analytic commitments and in particular treats 'conversation' and its methodological foundations as a realm of sociological enquiry. Whilst his *Lectures on Conversation* embodies a diverse range of observations and analytic insights, it is perhaps the work of Sacks (1992) and his colleagues Schegloff and Jefferson on the sequential organization of talk which has provided one of the most wide-ranging and fruitful contributions to ethnomethodological studies. It is certainly these studies, reflected perhaps most explicitly in a classic paper on the organization of turn taking in conversation (Sacks et al., 1974), which has had a profound influence on the analysis of talk in both sociology and a range of other disciplines. It should be said, however, that conversation analysis is not concerned with language per se, but rather derives from the recognition that talk is a principal means through which we produce and recognize social actions and activities. Schegloff and Sacks (1974) argued for example that their original interest in talk derived from the recognition that it provided the possibility of developing a 'naturalistic discipline which could deal with the details of social action(s) rigorously, empirically and formally'. Using audio recordings and transcriptions of naturally occurring talk, conversation analysis has developed a substantial corpus of empirical studies which delineate the practices and reasoning, the competencies, which inform the accomplishment of a diverse range of conversation activities. In recent years, the original focus on conversation has been increasingly replaced by a growing interest in institutional talk and a rich body of work has emerged concerned with the interactional organization of events such as news interviews, medical consultations and political speeches (see for example Boden and Zimmerman, 1991; Heritage and Maynard, 2004).

For Garfinkel the 'indexicality of practical actions' is a fundamental concern. Indexicality points to the uniqueness of any activity or event, and draws our attention towards the ways in which participants accomplish the rational, routine and mundane character of practical action. The uniqueness of practical activities which informs ethnomethodology and conversation analysis is more radical than the notion of context that is found elsewhere in social sciences. All too often 'context' is treated as the realm of local variables which can be invoked to explain the specific character of practical activity within some particular occasion or circumstance. Indeed, even more radical forms of sociological enquiry, such as symbolic interactionism and certain developments in cognitive science such as distributed cognition, retain a model of human conduct that, whilst emphasizing the temporal organization of practical action, presupposes that shared meanings or definitions, common frames of reference and the like remain stable, if only for brief moments of interaction within social life. In contrast, in ethnomethodology and conversation analysis, social actions and activities are inseparable from, or, better, part and parcel of, the 'context at hand'. The intelligibility of a scene, the character of the event, the 'objective order of social facts', is ongoingly accomplished in and through the practical and concerted actions of the participants themselves; there is 'no time out' from the moment-by-moment production of the 'objective order of social facts'. The reflexive character of practical action therefore is a central concern and directs analytic attention to the methodological foundations of practical actions and activities and the achieved character of ordinary events.

For conversation analysis, with its principal focus on interaction, the turn-by-turn, sequential organization of talk has provided an important resource for the analytic depiction of context and the 'indexical properties of practical action'. Heritage (1984) for example suggests that 'communicative action is both context shaped and context renewing'; 'a speaker's contribution is both designed with regard to the local configuration of activity and in particular the immediately preceding actions, and itself inevitably contributes to the framework in terms of which the next action will be understood' (1984: 242). This step-by-step, sequential organization of talk in interaction, whereby each subsequent turn both displays an understanding of prior and is recognized with regard to the immediately preceding action(s) (unless otherwise indicated), provides an important analytic resource. Rather than simply stipulate the meaning or significance of particular utterances in the light of their own personal intuition, researchers can inspect subsequent actions in order to determine how the participants themselves are responding to and displaying their understanding of each others' conduct.

The double-edged feature of interaction whereby sequential organization is both an integral feature of the social organization of talk and a methodological resource for its analysis remains a central and powerful feature of conversation analytic research. As Sacks et al. suggest, for example:

> [It] is a systematic consequence of the turn taking organisation of conversation that it obliges its participants to display to each other, in a turn's talk, their understanding of the other turn's talk. More generally, a turn's talk will be heard as directed to a prior turn's talk, unless special techniques are used to locate some other talk to which it is directed. . . . But while understandings of other turns' talk are displayed to co-participants, they are available as well to professional analysts, who are thereby provided a proof criterion (and a search procedure) for the analysis of what a turn's talk is occupied with. Since it is the parties' understandings of prior turns' talk that is relevant to their construction of next turns, it is their understandings that are wanted for analysis. The display of those understandings in the talk in subsequent turns affords a resource for the analysis of prior turns, and a proof procedure for professional analyses of prior turns, resources intrinsic to the data themselves. (1974: 728–9)

The emergent and sequential organization of interaction is also relevant to how we might consider the contextual or *in situ* significance of visual conduct and the physical properties of human environments. Gestures and other forms of bodily conduct arise in interaction, people not infrequently use artefacts when talking to each other, and it is not usual for aspects of the physical environment to become relevant within the course of social activities.

Unfortunately, however, there has been a widespread tendency amongst research on non-verbal communication to assume that the meaning of a gesture is inextricably tied to its physical form rather than the context in which it arises, an assumption which is not unlike the idea that an utterance gains its meaning solely by virtue of its lexicon or syntax, rather than sequential location. We might also suggest that the physical environment in which actions and activities take place does not have a stable and overarching influence on interaction, but rather its relevance and sense is accomplished by participants within the interaction as it emerges moment by moment. In consequence, we need to consider the ways in which visual conduct features in interaction, with and within talk, and to draw on the sequential organization of conduct as a resource for the analysis of *in situ* social actions and activities.

Visual and tactile elements of human conduct, features of the local environment and the like, do not reflect the turn-by-turn, speaker-by-speaker organization, characteristic of talk in interaction. Whilst it is speakers who ordinarily gesticulate, even a single turn at talk may involve a complex array of actions produced by various participants, both speaker and listeners and others, which may stand 'within some perceptual range of the event' (cf. Goffman, 1981). For example, as suggested earlier, a single utterance may be coordinated in the course of its production with the visual actions of the person(s) to whom it is addressed, and the speaker may employ various gestures and the like to shape the forms of co-participation he or she requires at different junctures within the turn's development. The utterance, and the way in which it is understood, is the outcome of a complex interaction that includes both visual and vocal contributions by the participants during the very course of its production. When considering the visual, vocal and material features of activities in interaction therefore, it is important to consider the sequential organization of the participants' conduct even though next actions may occur prior to next turn. As in the example above, it is found that the reorientation by a potential recipient within the emerging utterance or turn at talk is engendered through the speaker's gestures and bodily conduct. Or, for example, a co-participant will examine some feature of the local environment, such as picture on a wall, a line of text in a document, or a diagram on a computer screen, by virtue of the actions of a co-participant – a participant who, through bodily comportment, momentarily renders the object relevant. So while visual conduct with and within talk is not necessarily organized on a turn-by-turn basis, we can consider the ways in which participants respond to each others' conduct as a way of investigating how their activities are organized with regard to the actions of the other. The sequential and interactional organization of the conduct remains a critical resource for the analysis of how participants themselves orient to each other's action, make sense of each other's contributions, and produce their own conduct.

OBSERVING CASES

The situated character of practical action, and the interest in the method-ological resources used by the participants themselves, inevitably drives analytic attention towards the investigation of activities and events within the contexts in which they occur. Detailed and repeated inspection of the accomplishment of actual activities, coupled with the analytic orientations briefly discussed above, provide the resources through which researchers can begin to identify the practices and reasoning through which particular events are produced and rendered intelligible.

As some ethnomethodological and conversation analysis researchers become increasingly concerned with talk and interaction, it has been found that audio and audio-visual recordings provide useful resources with which to subject *in situ* practical actions and activities to detailed analysis. Originally the use of recorded data primarily consisted principally of telephone con-versations (see for example Sacks, 1992, or Sacks et al., 1974); however, with the increasing interest in the visual material as well as vocal aspects of human activity the use of video has become increasingly common (see for example Goodwin, 1994, 1996; Goodwin and Goodwin, 1996b; LeBaron and Streeck, 2000, Streeck, 1988, 1996; Whalen, 1995; Hindmarsh and Heath, 2000, 2003; Heath and Luff, 2000). It has been recognized that recordings of human activities and interaction, despite their limitations, provide researchers with unparalleled access to social action, allowing the aspects of the complexity of particular events to be subjected to detailed and repeated scrutiny. Unlike other forms of qualitative and quantitative 'data', recordings of naturally occurring human activities not only provide colleagues and the 'scientific community' at large with access to the raw materials on which the investi-gations are based, but also provide a corpus of data which can serve a range of theoretical and analytic interests. As Heritage and Atkinson suggest:

> In sum, the use of recorded data serves as a control on the limitations and fallibilities of intuition and recollection; it exposes the observer to a wide range of interactional materials and circumstances and also provides some guarantee that analytic considerations will not arise as artefacts of intuitive idiosyncrasy, selective attention or recollection, or experimental design. (1984: 4)

Notwithstanding the limitations and constraints of video, it is surprising that there has been such relatively little interest within sociology, and in particular perhaps field studies and ethnography, in exploiting the possibilities it provides. In anthropology, film, and more recently video, has received more attention, and yet even there, it has been increasingly used as a medium of representation and documentation rather than a resource for the analysis of social actions and activities. Marks (1995) suggests that ethnographic film has been influenced by successive shifts in anthropological theory since the beginning of the century, and that the absence of a suitable methodological and conceptual framework undermined the early attempts to examine the details of human conduct and locomotion originally initiated by Meybridge and others in the late nineteenth century. Similarly, in sociology the conceptual and theoretical resources which have informed a substantial corpus of rich ethnographic work since the 1950s, for example Hughes (1958), do not readily lend themselves to an analysis of the details of social actions and activities captured on video. In contrast, however, ethnomethodology and conversation analysis, with their commitment to the local *in situ* organization of human conduct, and their interest in taking talk and interaction seriously, as topics in their own right, provide an analytic orientation which can take advantage of the opportunities afforded through video.

As studies of talk and interaction have become increasingly concerned with more specialized forms of social activity, often arising within particular organizational or institutional domains, it has been recognized that it is necessary to augment recorded materials with fieldwork. So for example our own studies of general practice involved a long period of non-participant observation before any recording took place in order to begin to assemble a sense of the organization of certain specialized tasks such as diagnosis, treatment and using medical records (Heath, 1984; Heath and Luff, 2000). With the emergence of more wide-ranging studies of the workplace interaction, especially those concerned with the use of tools and artefacts in complex technological environments such as control rooms and emergency centres, we have witnessed an increasing commitment to undertaking wide-ranging fieldwork alongside more focused interaction analyses (Goodwin and Goodwin, 1996b; Hindmarsh and Pilnick, 2002; Suchman, 1993; Whalen, 1995; Luff et al., 2000; Heath and Luff, 2000). The necessity to undertake observation and even interviews derives not simply from the complexity of the specialized forms of activities under scrutiny, but as a consequence of the range of often distributed activities which feature, if only momentarily, in the accomplishment of the work and tasks in question. It is not unusual in such studies to delay gathering recorded materials until researchers have a passing understanding of the activities in question and the various tools and technologies which feature in the accomplishment of even the more mundane activities in such settings.

THE BODY IN ACTION

As a way of illustrating how we might begin to unpack aspects of the organization of an activity, it is perhaps useful to consider the following fragment. It is drawn from a medical consultation and arises towards the end of the consultation as the doctor begins to prepare a prescription. As he begins to write, the patient, who is still standing following the physical examination, begins to tell a story, a story that gives an example of the difficulties she has walking. (Details of the transcription systems can be found in the Appendix to this volume.)

Fragment 1

Dr: {Begins to write a prescription}
    (1.4)
P: When I went <u>down</u> into Debenhams I an I felt <u>so</u> <u>aw::ful</u> (eh) I wen
    (.) I was coming up the steps li:ke this all the way up I felt, (0.4)
    terribly
    (0.3)
P: terrib⌈ly (.) really you know
Dr: ⌊yeh   yes
             (0.2)
Dr: No::: (.) it's the knee itself (.) you've go some rheumatism there.

The patient's story provides an example of the complaint with which she has contacted the doctor. It recounts the events that occurred as she walked up the steps at Debenhams, a local department store, and in particular describes the suffering she incurred. It is interesting to note how the doctor responds to the story. He acknowledges the suffering the patient experienced with 'yeh' and the 'yes' in overlap with the word 'terribleness'. However, rather than encourage further discussion concerning the patient's difficulties, the doctor's subsequent turn, 'No::: (.) it's the knee itself (.) you've got some rheumatism there', simply pinpoints the area of difficulty and provides a diagnostic assessment. In this way the doctor discourages further discussion of the difficulties and suffering incurred by the patient and (re)aligns the consultation towards the management of the problem (see Heath, 2002).

As the patient describes the difficulties she had walking up the stairs at Debenhams, she walks up and down on the spot, illustrating the problems she experienced. She places here hand on the doctor's desk and, balancing her weight, demonstrates the way in which she distorted her hip and leg movement to actually climb the stairs. The movements give sense to the talk they accompany. They lucidly reveal the problems she experienced and provide a vivid picture of the suffering she incurred. The story points to the difficulties and provides a framework in which the movements embody, literally, the patient's difficulties and suffering.

To make sense of the story, and for the story to achieve its local sequential and interactional significance, therefore the doctor needs both to hear as well as to see what the patient says and does.

A transcript which includes some details concerning the visual conduct of the participants might be helpful. The participants' conduct is transcribed across the page with aspects of the visual conduct indicated above and below the talk. The accompanying images are taken from the original. The images have been degraded to conceal the identity of the participants.

Fragment 1. Transcript 2 and Figure 14.1

walks
up   down   up   down   up   down   up   down

P: I was coming up the steps li:ke this all the way up I felt,

^

Dr: *writes*
      prescription

The patient assembles an activity, a story which illustrates the problems she has suffered. The patient foregrounds aspects of her bodily conduct, and attempts to have the body itself feature, then and there, as an interactionally relevant and regarded feature of the participants' activities. Talk and bodily activity are mutually and reflexively constituted to give a sense of the event and her suffering.

What is curious perhaps is that the patient tells a story that requires the potential recipient both to listen and to look when he shows little interest in temporarily abandoning the activity in which he is engaged. The doctor does not look up during the first part of the story where the patient sets the scene and indeed even as she begins to walk up and down leaning on his desk, he continues doggedly to write the prescription. Unless the patient can encourage the doctor not only to listen, but also to look and watch her performance, then the gist of the story and its potential sequential significance is lost. In the way in which the story is told, the patient's activity requires the doctor to transform that way in which he participates in the interaction.

There are aspects of the earlier part of the patient's story which may well reveal her sensitivity to the activity in which the doctor is engaged and her determination to establish a more involved co-participant. For example, the restart and repair 'I wen (.) I was' may itself be an attempt to encourage the practitioner to turn towards the patient (cf. Goodwin, 1981) and the sentence 'I an I felt <u>so aw::ful</u>' coupled with the restart and emphasis on 'so awful' may well be an attempt to delay the gist of the story, while encouraging the doctor temporarily to abandon the prescription. If so they fail, and deep into the turn, the patient constructs the story so that it demands a visually attentive as well as listening recipient. Despite the risk, however, the patient not only illustrates her experience and suffering but successfully encourages the doctor to abandon writing the prescription and watch the significant part of the performance. In this way the story achieves its local interaction significance: an appreciation and response from the doctor.

Fragment 1. Transcript 3 and Figure 14.2

```
       walks
       up    down   up    down   up    down   up    down
       ⌄      ⌄      ⌄      ⌄      ⌄      ⌄      ⌄      ⌄
P:     I was coming up the steps li:ke this all the way up I felt,

       ∧                    ∧      ∧              ∧
Dr:    writes               turns to   turns to   nods &
       prescription         P's face   P's legs   smiles
```

The patient's success in encouraging the doctor to watch the performance and thereby achieve the sequential relevance of the story derives from the ways in which she designs her bodily comportment. As she begins to step up for the second time, she swings her hips towards the doctor. In particular, she swings her hips towards his visual field, an area midway between the prescription pad and his face. Just as her hips near the doctor, he looks up, turning to the face of the patient. The patient's movement, a component of the overall demonstration, engenders the reorientation by the doctor, encouraging him to abandon the prescription temporarily and transform the ways in which he is participating in the delivery of the story.

On turning to the patient's face, the doctor finds her looking at her own legs as she utters 'like this'. He looks down and watches her dramatic performance as she steps up and down. And, as she brings the performance to completion with 'terribly' and the doctor utters 'yeh', 'yes' and nods, the patient successfully transforms the participation of the doctor and has him temporarily abandon his current activity to witness the difficulties that she experienced walking up the steps at Debenhams.

The story, its impact and the doctor's ability to respond are the outcome of a complex negotiation between patient and doctor. The story itself involves and invokes the bodily portrayal of an event which illustrates the patient's difficulties and to which the doctor responds with an appreciation and a diagnostic assessment. In this way the doctor's professional assessment serves to discourage perhaps any further elaboration by the patient concerning her experience of her problems. But even before the patient begins to describe the events, she is sensitive to the concurrent conduct of the doctor and appears to make various attempts to encourage him to transform the way in which he is participating in the talk. Indeed, it may even be the case that the very enactment of the events arises in the light of the patient facing a potentially recalcitrant recipient; a recipient, who is looking at a note pad and writing as she begins to tell of her 'awful' suffering.

The patient's actions are highly complex and contingent. They not only serve to illustrate the difficulties she once experienced, but simultaneously establish an audience for their performance and thereby achieve the sense and sequential significance of the story. The patient's bodily conduct creates different, but interrelated, sequential trajectories. It forms an integral part of the story to which the doctor responds following its completion. It also, as part of the story, encourages the doctor to transform the ways in which he is participating in the talk and in particular to watch the performance. In a sense therefore, we might speak of the bodily comportment as a 'double duty' activity, sequentially implicating specific actions from the recipient at different locations during the course of the movements' articulation (see Heath, 1986). And yet such a characterization hardly catches the complexity of the activity; not only is the relevance of the story as an illustration as a whole contingent on establishing within its course a visually oriented recipient, but also the activity is accomplished in and through both talk and bodily conduct.

In this way therefore we can begin to disassemble aspects of the social and interactional organization which feature in the accomplishment of a particular event and provide for its character and uniqueness. Even this cursory glance at the fragment reveals the complexity of the participants' activity and the remarkable resources which are brought to bear in the production and intelligibility of the story. In particular it shows the emergent and contingent character of the participants' actions and the ways in which they are interactionally organized and accomplished. We can see that while the visual aspects of the participants' conduct is not organized on the turn-by-turn basis characteristic of talk, none the less the sequential organization is a critical feature of the activity's production and intelligibility. The elicitation of the doctor's gaze is sequentially responsive to an action by the patient, and the doctor's reorientation forms the foundation to the sense of the story and the sequentially appropriate reply. The methodological resources used by participants themselves in the activity's production and intelligibility drive analytic attention towards the ways in which their conduct is interactionally accomplished within the emerging course of the event.

ACTIVITIES IN INTERACTION

The growing body of video-based research within ethnomethodology and conversation analysis concerned with the visual as well as vocal aspects of human conduct stands in marked contrast to more traditional contributions to the understanding of non-verbal behaviour. Non-verbal behaviour is no longer treated as a distinct channel of communication, in isolation from talk and other aspects of human interaction. Rather attention is directed towards the various resources that participants bring to bear on the accomplishment of social actions and activities. Given the 'situated' character of human activity and the uniqueness of particular events, studies are naturalistic rather than experimental and deliberately avoid the a priori theorizing and the development of hypotheses characteristic of the more variable centred approaches found within many psychological and social–psychological studies of non-verbal communication. Most importantly perhaps, analysis is directed towards developing observations which characterize aspects of the indigenous reasoning and practices that participants themselves use in the production and intelligibility of particular social actions and activities. So, for example, in the data at hand, the analysis is concerned with building a characterization of the resources on which the participants rely in accomplishment of the activity, with regard to the ways in which they produce and coordinate their actions with each other during the developing course of their articulation. The interactional and sequential foundations of the activity's accomplishment provide an important resource in the identification and description of the actions, and the practices and reasoning upon which the participants rely in their production and intelligibility.

The analytic commitment to describing the resources on which participants rely in the accomplishment of social action and activities has led to a growing interest in exploring the ways in which objects, artefacts and other features of the physical environment feature in conduct and interaction. In part, these studies are concerned with readdressing the dematerialized conception of action found within certain areas of social science and with placing the object in action at the heart of agenda. A motivation of these studies is to explore the ways in which material resources are used and constituted within social action and to consider how the sense and significance of objects, artefacts and the like arise in and through interaction. So, for example, studies have explored the ways in which conversationalists over the dinner table orient to and manipulate objects within talk during the developing course of particular activities (Goodwin, 1984), how doctors use particular artefacts such as medical records in the interaction with patients (Greatbatch et al., 1993; Heath and Luff, 2000), how participants mutually constitute features of complex scenes (Goodwin, 1994), and the ways in which students embody gestures in objects to enable others to gain a sense of their imaginary function and purpose (Hindmarsh and Heath, 2003). More generally, these studies have explored ways in which objects are found, handled, manipulated, examined, referenced, discussed and how the talk is embedded in, and constituted through, occasioned features of the material environment.

The growing interest in objects and artefacts in interaction has also arisen through a burgeoning body of research which is commonly known as 'workplace studies'. These studies have a curious provenance, emerging in part through a wide-ranging critique of artificial intelligence and traditional cognitive models of human–computer interaction (Suchman, 1987). Some of these workplace studies draw from ethnomethodology and conversation analysis and are concerned with the highly variable and contingent forms of interaction and participation which arise within complex organizational environments, environments which encompass a range of activities accomplished through an array of tools and technologies. Many of these studies have focused on 'centres of coordination', in such areas as transport, medicine and the news media, and explored the ways in which personnel with differing roles and responsibilities coordinate the actions with each other and those located elsewhere when engaged in interdependent but interrelated activities. So, for example, in their wide-ranging study of ground operations in an airport Suchman (1993) and Goodwin and Goodwin (1996b) examine the ways in which personnel identify particular problems and events through interaction and develop a coordinated response. In our own studies of operations on the London Underground, we have addressed the ways in which personnel configure activities to enable others, both within the same location and those located elsewhere, to have sense of action and to produce sequentially appropriate activities (Heath and Luff, 1996, 2000). These and an array of related studies not only demonstrate the ways in which ethnomethodology and conversation analysis can inform the analysis of visual, vocal as well as material aspects of conduct and action, but also point to the ways in which we can begin to consider highly complex forms of interaction and co-participation beyond the dyadic, mutually focused encounter which has formed the mainstay of studies of talk. Video recording, coupled with extensive fieldwork, provides the resources through which we can build upon the methodological initiatives developed within ethnomethodology and conversation analysis.

SUMMARY

Ethnomethodology and conversation analysis provide an analytic resource through which we can begin to exploit the opportunities provided through video. The possibility of capturing aspects of the audible and visual elements of *in situ* human conduct as it arises within its natural habitats provides researchers with unprecedented access to social actions and activities. With ethnomethodology and conversation analysis, the technology opens up the possibility of developing a sociology which takes the visual, material as well as vocal aspects of human interaction seriously, as a topic for investigation and analysis. Such studies will not replace or supersede the extraordinarily rich body of work concerned with talk in interaction, but further enhance our understanding of how the body and physical objects feature with talk in the production and intelligibility of everyday social actions and activities. In order to develop a sociology which addresses the detail of the body and objects in interaction, it is important that we abandon some of the traditional distinctions which have informed our understanding of non-verbal behaviour and consider the ways in which visual, material and vocal conduct features in the *in situ* accomplishment of particular social actions and activities. In this way we can begin to move away from the psychological and cognitive characterization of visual conduct and the use of artefacts, and begin to develop insights into the social and interactional organization of activities and the range of resources on which participants rely in their practical, situated accomplishment. By turning analytic attention towards the methodological and reflexive foundations of social action, we can develop a distinctive understanding of the organization of human activity in all its intelligence and momentary glory.

Recommended reading

Goodwin, C. and Goodwin, M.H. (1996) Seeing as a situated activity: formulating planes. In Y. Engeström and D. Middleton (eds) *Cognition and Communication at Work*, (pp. 61–95). Cambridge: Cambridge University Press.

Goodwin, C. (1995) Seeing in depth. *Social Studies of Science*, 25 (2), 237–74.

Heath, C.C. and Luff, P. (2000) *Technology in Action*. Cambridge: Cambridge University Press.

Heath, C.C. (2002) Demonstrative suffering: the gestural (re)embodiment of symptoms. *Journal of Communication*, 52 (3): 597–617.

REFERENCES

Atkinson, J.M. (1978) *Discovering Suicide: the Social Organisation of Sudden Death*. London: Macmillan.
Birdwhistell, R. (1970) *Kinesics in Context: Essays on Body Motion Communication*. Philadelphia: University of Philadelphia Press.
Boden, D. and Zimmerman, D.H. (eds) (1991) *Talk and Social Structure*. Oxford: Polity Press.
Cosnier, J. (1978) Specificité de l'attitude ethologique dans l'étude du comportement humain. *Psychologie Française*, 23 (1): 19–26.

Garfinkel, H. (1967) *Studies in Ethnomethodology*. Englewood Cliffs, NJ: Prentice Hall.

Goffman, E. (1959) *The Presentation of Self in Everyday*. New York: Doubleday Anchor.

Goffman, E. (1963) *Behaviour in Public Places: Notes on the Social Organization of Gatherings*. New York: Free Press.

Goffman, E. (1967) *Interaction Ritual*. New York: Doubleday.

Goffman, E. (1981) *Forms of Talk*. Oxford: Basil Blackwell.

Goodwin, C. (1979) An interactional construction of turn at talk in natural conversation. In G. Psathas (ed.) *Everyday Language: Studies in Ethnomethodology*. New York: Irvington.

Goodwin, C. (1980) Restarts, pauses and the achievement of mutual gaze at turn-beginning. *Sociological Inquiry*, 50: 272–302.

Goodwin, C. (1981) *Conversational Organisation: Interaction between a Speaker and Hearer*. London: Academic Press.

Goodwin, C. (1984) Notes on Story Structure and the Organisation of Participation. In J.M. Atkinson and J.C. Heritage (eds) *Structures of Social Action*. Cambridge: Cambridge University Press.

Goodwin, C. (1987) Forgetfulness as an interactive resource. *Social Psychology Quarterly*, 50 (2): 115–30.

Goodwin, C. (1994) Professional Vision. *American Anthropologist*, 96 (3): 606–33.

Goodwin, C. (1996) Transparent Vision. In E. Ochs, E.A. Schegloff and S. Thompson (eds) *Interaction and Grammar*. Cambridge: Cambridge University Press. pp. 370–404.

Goodwin, C. and Goodwin, M.H. (1996a) Formulating Planes: Seeing as a Situated Activity. In D. Middleton and Y. Engeström (eds) *Cognition and Communication at Work: Distributed Cognition in the Workplace*. Cambridge: Cambridge University Press.

Goodwin, C. and Goodwin, M.H. (1996b) Seeing as a Situated Activity: Formulating Planes. In Y. Engeström and D. Middleton (eds) *Cognition and Communication at Work*. Cambridge: Cambridge University Press. pp. 61–95.

Goodwin, M.H. (1980) Processes of mutual monitoring implicated in the production of description sequences. *Sociological Inquiry*, 50: 303–17.

Greatbatch, D., Luff, P., Heath, C.C. and Campion, P. (1993) Interpersonal Communication and Human-Computer Interaction: an examination of the use of computers in medical consultations. *Interacting With Computers*, 5 (2): 193–216.

Heath, C.C. (1984) Participation in the medical consultation: the coordination of verbal and nonverbal behaviour. *Journal of the Sociology of Health and Illness*, 6 (3): 311–38.

Heath, C.C. (1986) *Body Movement and Speech in Medical Interaction*. Cambridge: Cambridge University Press.

Heath, C.C. (2002) Demonstrative suffering: the gestural (re)embodiment of symptoms. *Journal of Communication*, 52 (3): 597–617.

Heath, C.C. and Luff, P.K. (1996) Convergent activities: collaborative work and multimedia technology in London Underground Line Control Rooms. In D. Middleton and Y. Engeström (eds) *Cognition and Communication at Work: Distributed Cognition in the Workplace*. Cambridge: Cambridge University Press. pp. 94–130.

Heath, C.C. and Luff, P.K. (2000) *Technology in action*. Cambridge: Cambridge University Press.

Heritage, J.C. (1984) *Garfinkel and Ethnomethodology*. Cambridge: Polity Press.

Heritage, J.C. and Atkinson, J.M. (1984) Introduction. In J.M. Atkinson and J.C. Heritage (eds) *Structures of Social Action: Studies in Conversational Analysis*. Cambridge: Cambridge University Press.

Heritage, J.C. and Maynard, D. (2004) *Practicing Medicine: Talk and Action in Primary Care Encounters*. Cambridge: Cambridge University Press.

Hindmarsh, J. and Heath, C.C. (2000) Embodied Reference: a study of deixis in workplace interaction. *Journal of Pragmatics*, 32 (12): 1855–78.

Hindmarsh, J. and Heath, C.C. (2003) Transcending the Object in Embodied Interaction. In J. Coupland and R. Gwyn (eds) *Discourse, the Body and Identity*. London: Palgrave.

Hindmarsh, J. and Pilnick, A. (2002) The Tacit Order of Teamwork: collaboration and embodied conduct in anaesthesia. *Sociological Quarterly*, 43 (2): 139–64.

Hughes, E.C. (1958) *Men and Their Work*. Glencoe, NJ: Free Press.

Kendon, A. (1991) *Conducting Interaction: Patterns of Behaviour in Focussed Encounters*. Cambridge: Cambridge University Press.

LeBaron, C. and Streeck, J. (2000) Gestures, knowledge and the world. In McNeil, (ed.) *Language and Gesture*. Cambridge: Cambridge University Press.

Luff, P., Hindmarsh, J. and Heath, C. (eds) (2000) *Workplace studies: recovering work practice and informing system design*. Cambridge: Cambridge University Press.

Marks, D. (1995) Ethnographic film: from Flaberty to Asch and after. *American Anthropologist*, 97 (2): 337–47.

Sacks, H. (1992) *Lectures in Conversation, Volumes I and II*. Oxford: Blackwell.

Sacks, H., Schegloff, E.A. and Jefferson, G. (1974) A simplest systematics for the organization of turn taking in conversation. *Language*, 50: 696–735.

Scheflen, A.E. (1964) The Significance of Posture in Communication Systems. *Psychiatry*, 27: 316–31.

Schegloff, E.A. and Sacks, H. (1974) Opening up closings. In R. Turner (ed.) *Ethnomethodology: Selected Writings*. Harmondsworth: Penguin.

Streeck, J. (1988) The Significance of Gesture: How it is Established. In *Papers in Pragmatics*, 2 (1/2): 60–83.

Streeck, J. (1996) How to do things with things: *objects trouvés* and symbolization. *Human Studies*, 19: 365–84.

Suchman, L. (1987) *Plans and Situated Actions: the Problem of Human Machine Interaction*. Cambridge: Cambridge University Press.

Suchman, L. (1993) Technologies of Accountability: On Lizards and Aeroplanes. In G. Button (ed.) *Technology and the Working Order*. London: Routledge. pp. 113–26.

vom Lehn, D., Heath, C.C. and Hindmarsh, J. (2001) Exhibiting Interaction: Conduct and Collaboration in Museums and Galleries Interaction. *Symbolic Interaction*, 24 (2): 189–217.

Whalen, J. (1995) Expert Systems vs. Systems for Experts: Computer-Aided Dispatch as a Support System in Real-world Environments. In P. Thomas (ed.) *The Social and Interactional Dimensions of Human-Computer Interfaces*. Cambridge: Cambridge University Press. pp. 161–83.

Part VII Validity

15 Reliability and validity in research based on naturally occurring social interaction*

Anssi Peräkylä

As Kirk and Miller (1986: 11) and Silverman (2001: 219) point out, the issues of reliability and validity are important, because in them the *objectivity* and *credibility* of (social scientific) research is at stake. The aim of social science is to produce descriptions of a social world – not just any descriptions, but descriptions that in some controllable way correspond to the social world that is being described. Even though all descriptions are bound to a particular perspective and therefore represent the reality rather than reproduce it (Hammersley, 1992), it is possible to describe social interaction in ways that can be subjected to empirical testing.

There is no single, coherent set of 'qualitative methods' applicable in all analysis of texts, talk and interaction. Rather, there are a number of different sets of methods: different ways of recording and analysing human activity and the use of symbols. In so far as these various methods claim an epistemic status different from mere common sense, in so far they claim to report more than the research subjects' own descriptions of their circumstances, the question of objectivity is relevant for all these methods.

In research practice, enhancing objectivity is a very concrete activity. It involves efforts to assure the accuracy and inclusiveness of recordings that the research is based on as well as efforts to test the truthfulness of the analytic claims that are being made about those recordings. These concrete efforts, however, take different shapes according to the type of recordings on which the research is based. Questions that arise in the context of ethnographic field notes, for example, are different from questions that arise in the context of written texts. Field notes can be produced so as to be focused on particular issues or, alternatively, they can be produced so as to include as wide a range of events as possible (Hammersley and Atkinson, 1983: 150–1). In the analysis of written texts such a question does not arise: the researcher cannot control the focus of a given text that is used as data. (But the researcher can, of course, select the range of texts that he or she uses.)

This chapter will deal with issues of reliability and validity in research based on audio or video recordings and transcripts, and, in particular, in conversation analysis. I will focus this discussion on one specific type of qualitative research only mainly because, as was just pointed out, the questions of reliability and validity take a different form in different qualitative methods. The second reason for focusing on this specific variant of qualitative research is the fact that there are no accessible discussions available on issues of validity and reliability in conversation analytic studies.[1] This does not mean, however, that questions of validity and reliability have been addressed in conversation analytic research practice. In fact they are addressed more there than in many other types of qualitative research. But what has been lacking is a general student-oriented discussion about validity and reliability in conversation analytic research. The purpose of this chapter is to make a contribution in that direction.

Although the discussion in this chapter focuses on a specific type of qualitative research (conversation analysis), the basic issues raised here are relevant in the context of any qualitative method. Therefore, readers who are not primarily interested in conversation analysis are encouraged to treat this chapter as an *example* of the kinds of considerations that need to be addressed by any qualitative researcher. Even though the specific questions and answers concerning validity and reliability are different in other qualitative methods, the basic concerns are the same.

The argumentation presented in this chapter concerns primarily conversation analytic research *on institutional interaction* (Drew and Heritage, 1992; Drew and Sorjonen, 1997). As John Heritage points out in his contribution to this volume, there are two different kinds of conversation analysis going on today: 'The first examines the social institution *of* interaction as an entity in its own right; the second studies the management of social institutions [such as corporation, classroom, medicine, etc.] *in* interaction' (p. 223). The first type of conversation analysis focuses on what is called 'ordinary conversation': informal talking among friends, family members, or the like. The latter one focuses on verbal interaction between professionals and clients or amongst professionals.

The methodological constraints facing these two types of conversation analysis are partially overlapping and partially different. In this chapter, the primary focus is on the latter type of conversation analysis. Hence, I will discuss issues such as the use of written documents along with the conversational data, and the criteria for validating claims about the relevance of an institutional context of interaction. These issues concern the analysis of institutional interaction, not the study of ordinary conversation. Some other issues that I will discuss, however (such as deviant case analysis), are also applicable to the analysis of ordinary conversations.

The aim of all conversation analytic studies (both on ordinary conversation and on institutional interaction) is to produce descriptions of recurrent patterns of social interaction and language use. Conversation analysis (CA) is particularly rigorous in its requirement of an empirical grounding for any descriptions to be accepted as valid. In this respect, CA differs from some other forms of discourse analysis (Fairclough, 1999; Parker, 1992) and social constructionism (Gergen, 1994) which emphasize more the 'openness' of any language use to different interpretations and hence underline more the active contribution of the researcher in 'constructing' the descriptions that he or she produces about language use. Nevertheless, these issues are complex; other forms of discourse analysis and notably discursive psychology (see Potter, this volume) draw directly on conversation analytic thinking.

RELIABILITY

Kirk and Miller define reliability as 'the degree to which the finding is independent of accidental circumstances of the research' (1986: 20). In ethnographic research, the reliability of research results entails 'whether or not (or under what conditions) the ethnographer would expect to obtain the same finding if he or she tried again in the same way' (1986: 69).

In the context of ethnography, as Silverman (2001: 227–8) also points out, checking the reliability is closely related to assuring the quality of field notes and guaranteeing the public access to the process of their production (cf. also Hammersley and Atkinson, 1983: 144–61). In conversation analytic research, recordings and transcripts are the 'raw material' comparable to ethnographers' field notes. Accordingly, the quality of recordings and transcripts has important implications for the reliability of conversation analytic research.

Concerns of reliability as a reason for working with recordings and transcripts

Working with audio and video recordings and transcripts eliminates at one stroke many of the problems that ethnographers have with the unspecified accuracy of field notes and with the limited public access to them. According to Harvey Sacks, realizing the potential of audio- or video-recorded materials actually gave a crucial impetus to the creation of CA:

> It was not from any large interest in language or from some theoretical formulation of what should be studied that I started with tape-recorded conversation, but simply because I could get my hands on it and I could study it again and again, and also, consequentially, because others could look at what I had studied and make of it what they could, if, for example, they wanted to be able to disagree with me. (Sacks, 1984: 26)

Recordings and transcripts based on them can provide for highly detailed and publicly accessible representations of social interaction. Therefore, Kirk and Miller's suggestion that in qualitative research 'issues of reliability have received little attention' (1986: 42) does not apply to conversation analytic research. CA claims part of its justification on the basis of being free of many shortcomings in reliability characteristic of other forms of qualitative research, especially ethnography.

Securing maximum inclusiveness of recorded data

-Although audio- or video-recorded data have intrinsic strength in terms of accuracy and public access, special attention needs to be paid to the *inclusiveness* of such data. Video or audio recordings of specific events (such as telephone conversations, medical consultations or public meetings) may entail a loss of some aspects of social interaction, including (a) medium- and long-span temporal processes, (b) ambulatory events and (c) impact of texts and other 'non-conversational' modalities of action. The potential loss can be prevented with appropriate arrangements in the data collection.

Temporal processes

Conversation analytic research has brought a new kind of temporality into the central focus of sociological analysis: sequential organization of interaction operates in and through the relative timing of actions. As ethnographic research has repeatedly shown, however, local social worlds are also organized in terms of longer temporal spans (let alone the historical time focused on in the classical macro-sociological works of Durkheim, Weber and Marx). In hospitals, for example, management of chronically ill or dying patients involves complex trajectories shaped in and through the evolving daily actions of staff and patients (Glaser and Strauss, 1968; Strauss et al., 1985; Sudnow, 1967). Similarly, in social services, the recognition of events such as child mistreatment involves long-span processes with a multitude of agents and their negotiations at different sites (see Dingwall et al., 1983).

In the research based on recordings of single encounters, there is a risk that some of these longer-term temporal processes will be lost from sight. To prevent this from happening, longitudinal study designs can be used. Heritage and Lindström (1998), for example, report research based on recordings of six consecutive visits by a health visitor to a mother who had recently given birth. Their analysis focuses on the ways in which the mother progressively discloses morally problematic material, and the ways in which the health visitor manages these disclosures.[2]

Ambulatory events

People move about in doing things. In Goffman's terms, the participants in any face-to-face interaction are 'vehicular entities, that is, human ambulatory units' (1983: 7). For anyone who has acted as a participant or as an observer in a hospital setting, this must be obvious. The ward round, for example, is, from the professionals' point of view, a single event with a number of alternating subgroups of patient participants; this event moves about in patients' rooms and in the corridors of the ward.

The whole richness of ambulatory interaction can hardly be encapsulated using a stationary video camera, say, in one patient room. By collecting ethnographic data along with the audio or video recordings, the researcher can capture some aspects of ambulatory events. A good example of the fruitful combination of ethnographic and audio- or video-recorded data is provided by Goodwin (1994, 1995). Moreover, by the use of multiple cameras, recordings can be made that are both comprehensive and accurate. Multiple cameras also need to be used when the interaction involves multiple sites which are connected using technical means, such as monitors or telephones. Charles and Marjorie Goodwin, for example, have used multiple cameras in recording the work of the crew on an oceanic research vessel (Goodwin, 1995) and the activities of air-traffic controllers (Goodwin and Goodwin, 1997). Similarly, Heath and Luff (2000); Luff and Heath, 2002) have analysed convergent activities in various technological working environments.

Documentary realities
Written documents (and their production and use) are important for social life, as a domain of signification of its own, or, as Smith (1974, 1990) puts it, as a 'textual reality'. Written documents also constitute a domain which is in contact with the domain of spoken interaction and which in some events organizes some aspects of it. As Firth (1995: 205–11) has shown, in international business communication, written messages (communicated through telex and fax) relate in many ways to the organization of the telephone conversations between the trade partners. Therefore, full understanding of some of the institutional activities conducted by telephone is not possible without the analysis of the prior written messages that inform their production. Similarly, in medical settings the content and the ordering of some of the questions that the professionals pose to the clients can be strongly influenced by clinical forms that the professionals need to fill in. Thus, even though every question has its local interactional management which can be observed in the recording, the logic of the questioning as a whole may not be derivable from the vocal events only. Therefore, it is important that the conversation analyst carefully collects and uses all the relevant written documents, along with the collection of recordings (for further examples of this, see Maynard, 1996; Whalen, 1995).

Different aspects of social organization
In sum, by appropriate research design, conversation analytic studies of institutional interaction can be made more inclusive in terms of different layers of the organization of action. However, it also needs to be pointed out that *conversation analytic studies do not aim at describing all aspects of social organization.* (This is, of course, true concerning any other methodology as well.) The organization of verbal interaction in face-to-face encounters and telephone conversations is the domain in which adequate conversation analytic studies can rightly claim superior reliability, and this is indeed the home base of CA methodology. In studies that focus primarily on other aspects of social

organization (such as textual, pictorial or technological realities) other methods may be more suitable.

Improving the reliability of CA in its own field

The claim of superior reliability in studies of face-to-face interaction needs to be justified, however, in each single piece of conversation analytic research. The key aspects of reliability involve *selection of what is recorded, the technical quality of recordings* and *the adequacy of transcripts*.

Basic *selection of what is recorded* arises, of course, from the research problem. But after this has been done (i.e. when the researcher has decided to record encounters in a specific setting such as classroom, doctor's surgery, educational counsellor's office, or the like) the researcher still has to make some very consequential choices. The most important choice is *how much to record*.

There is a limit to how much data a single researcher or a research team can transcribe and analyse. But on the other hand, a large database has definite advantages. As the analysis of data in conversation analytic studies usually progresses inductively, the researcher normally does not know at the outset of the research what exactly the phenomena are that he or she is going to focus on. Therefore, it may turn out that he or she wants to analyse events that do not occur very many times in each single recording. For example, delivery of the diagnosis in medical consultations is such an event: there are consultations where no diagnosis is delivered, and in many consultations, it is done only once (cf. Heath, 1992; Peräkylä, 1998). In order to be able to achieve a position where he or she can observe *the variation of the phenomenon* (such as the delivery of the diagnosis) in any reliable way, the researcher needs a large enough collection of cases. Therefore, he or she may need to have access to a relatively large database. In practice, a large portion of the data can be kept as a resource that is used only when the analysis has progressed so far that the phenomena under study have been specified. At that later stage, short sections from the data in reserve can be transcribed, and, thereby, the full variation of the phenomenon can be observed.

The technical quality of recordings is a decisive issue: if something is lost from sight or remains inaudible in the recording, there is no way of recovering it. It may be extremely frustrating to have some badly recorded sections of events that at a later stage of the research turn out to be of primary importance for the analysis. This kind of frustration can be minimized already at the planning stage of the research by paying enough attention both to the quality of the equipment and to the arrangements of recording. The crucial aspects of quality include the sound (quality and location of microphones) and the inclusiveness of the video picture (the location and the type of the lens of the camera(s)) (cf. Goodwin, 1992; ten Have, 1999: 71–3). The recording technology is developing quickly; digital recordings offer many advantages in comparison with older analogue technology.

The adequacy of transcripts is equally important: even though in a proper analysis of data the recording needs to be listened to and watched, at least the selection of what is analysed in detail is usually done on the basis of the transcripts only (cf. ten Have, 1999: 77–8). The quality of transcripts in research on naturally occurring interaction seems to vary greatly. Not only are the details of intonation and prosody sometimes omitted, but, what is more problematic, whole utterances (especially in multi-party situations) can be missing from transcripts in studies that otherwise have been seriously and adequately designed and conducted.

Transcription is a skill that can only be acquired through long enough training. It is extremely useful if an experienced transcriber can supervise a beginner. This is most easily done by the more experienced one correcting some of the beginner's transcripts. In fact, the correction of transcripts is useful for anybody preparing them: another researcher can always hear some of the things that one has not noticed. Correction by colleagues also enhances a culture of shared practices in measuring pauses, intonation, and so on.

It is advisable to include many aspects of vocal expression in the initial transcripts (for the conversation analytic transcription conventions developed by Gail Jefferson, see the Appendix to this volume and Atkinson and Heritage, 1984: ix–xvi). A rich transcript is a resource of analysis; at the time of transcribing, the researcher cannot know which of the details will turn out to be important for the analysis. After the analysis has been accomplished and the results are published, however, some of the special notation not used in the analysis can be left out. 'Simplified' transcripts can make the reception of the analysis easier, especially if the audience is not specialized in CA.

In sum, the reliability of observations in conversation analytic research (as in any other empirical method) can only be achieved through serious effort. The method itself does not guarantee reliability. In conversation analytic studies, proper attention needs to be paid to the selection and technical quality of recordings as well as to the adequacy of the transcripts.

VALIDITY IN CONVERSATION ANALYTIC RESEARCH

The validity of research concerns the interpretation of observations: whether or not 'the researcher is calling what is measured by the right name' (Kirk and Miller, 1986: 69; cf. Altheide and Johnson, 1994; Silverman, 2001: 232–48).

In the discussions about validity, especially in the context of quantitative research, there is an underlying background assumption about a separation between the 'raw' observations and the issues that these observations stand for or represent. Responses to questionnaires, for example, can be more or less valid representations of underlying social phenomena, such as the respondents' attitudes or values (cf. Alkula et al., 1994). CA is in stark contrast to this kind of approach: the core of its very aim is to investigate talk-in-interaction, not as 'a screen on which are projected other processes', but as a phenomenon in its own right (Schegloff, 1992a: xviii). This commitment to naturalistic description of the interaction order (Goffman, 1983) and the social action taking place within that order (cf. also Sacks, 1984) gives a distinctive shape to the issues of validation in CA. These include the *transparency of analytic claims, validation through 'next turn', deviant case analysis, questions about the institutional character of interaction, the generalizability of conversation analytic findings* and *the use of statistical techniques.*

The transparence of analytic claims

In *Tractatus Logico-Philosophicus*, Wittgenstein pointed out that philosophy, rightly understood, is not a set of propositions but an activity, the clarification of non-philosophical propositions about the world. The method of this activity is complex because the 'knots' in our thinking are complex, but the results of philosophy are simple (see Kenny, 1973: 18, 101–2). A similar kind of paradox between the complexity of method and the simplicity of results is characteristic of CA, too.

The results of (good) conversation analytic research exhibit, in a positive manner, what Kirk and Miller (1986: 22) called *apparent validity*: once you have read them, you are convinced that they are transparently true. A conversational activity called 'fishing' may serve as an example. Anita Pomerantz showed in a paper published in 1980 how participants in a conversation can indirectly 'fish' for information from one another by telling what they themselves know. Descriptions of events displaying their producer's 'limited access' to the relevant facts may work as a device for inviting the other party to disclose his or her authorized version of the same issues (assuming, of course, that the other party is in a position of having privileged access to the relevant facts). Such dynamics are at work in cases like the following:

```
(1)        1 B:  Hello::.
           2 A:  HI:::.
           3 B:  Oh:hi:: 'ow are you Agne::s,
       →   4 A:  Fi:ne. Yer line's been busy.
           5 B:  Yeuh my fu (hh)- .hh my father's wife called me
           6     ..hh So when she calls me::, .hh I can always talk
           7     fer a long time. Cuz she c'n afford it'n I can't.
           8     hhhh heh .ehhhhhh
                                              (Pomerantz, 1980: 195)
```

In Extract 1 above, the description based on limited access to relevant facts given by A (marked with an arrow) works as what Pomerantz called 'a fishing device', successfully eliciting B's insider's report in the next turn. By telling her observations about the line having been busy, A makes it relevant for B to disclose to whom she was talking.

The description of an activity like 'fishing' tends to 'ring a bell' as soon as anyone stops to think about it. 'Fishing' is something in which everybody has participated in different roles. But until Pomerantz's article, this activity had not been described formally. The results of Pomerantz's analysis are very simple. Her argument is transparently true, or, in Kirk and Miller's (1986) terms, it has a genuine 'apparent validity'.

But just as in Wittgenstein's philosophy, 'although the *result* . . . is simple, its method cannot be if it is to arrive at that result' (Wittgenstein, 1975: 52). In CA, the complexities of the method involve other kinds of issues of validation.

Validation through 'next turn'

As Sacks et al. pointed out, research on talk-in-interaction has an inherent methodological resource that research on written texts lacks: 'Regularly . . . a turn's talk will display its speaker's understanding of a prior turn's talk, and whatever other talk it marks itself as directed to' (1974: 728). In other words, in the unfolding of the interaction, the interactants display to one another their interpretations of what is going on, especially of what was going on in the immediately preceding turn of talk (Heritage and Atkinson, 1984). From this fact arises a fundamental validation procedure that is used in all conversation analytic research:

> But while understandings of other turn's talk are displayed to co-participants, they are available as well to professional analysts, who are thereby afforded a proof criterion . . . for the analysis of what a turn's talk is occupied with. (Sacks et al., 1974: 729)

At the beginning of this chapter, it was pointed out that CA differs from those forms of discourse analysis and social constructionism which emphasize the open-endedness of the meaning of all linguistic expressions. Now we can see the reason for this: even though the meaning of any expression, if considered in isolation, is extremely open-ended, any utterance that is produced in talk-in-interaction will be locally interpreted by the participants of that interaction. In the first place, their interpretation is displayed in the next actions after the utterance. Hence, any interpretations that conversation analysts may suggest can be subjected to the 'proof procedure' outlined by Sacks et al.: the next turn will show whether the interactants themselves treat the utterance in ways that are in accordance with the analyst's interpretation.

Therefore in Extract 1 shown above, the utterance produced by B in lines 5–8 provides a proof procedure for the interpretation suggested by Pomerantz concerning A's turn in line 4. (What Pomerantz suggested was that 'telling my side' (what A did in line 4) can operate as a 'fishing device', which indirectly elicits an authoritative version of the events from the interlocutor.) And as we see, Pomerantz's interpretation passes the test: in lines 5–8, B gives her first-hand account of what had happened.

In much everyday conversation analytic work, things are not as nice and simple as in Extract 1: the next turns may be ambiguous in relation to the action performed in the preceding turn. However, the 'proof procedure' provided by the next turn remains the primordial criterion of validity that must be used as much as possible in all conversation analytic work.

Deviant case analysis

By examining the relations between successive turns of talk, conversation analysts aim at establishing *regular patterns* of interaction (Heritage, 1995). The patterns concern relations between actions (such as the relations between 'telling my side' and 'giving an authoritative report' in the case of 'fishing' described above). After having established a pattern, the analyst's next task is to search for and examine *deviant cases*: cases where 'things go differently' – most typically, cases where an element of the suggested pattern is not associated with the other expected elements.

The deviant case analysis in CA closely resembles the technique of 'analytic induction' often used in ethnographic studies (see Hammersley and Atkinson, 1983: 201–4; Silverman, 1985: 111–15; 2001: 237–8). For the analyst, those cases that do not fit the inductively constructed pattern are deviant. Rather than putting aside these discrepant cases, the analyst is encouraged to focus particular attention on them.

In her well-known paper on 'fishing', Pomerantz (1980: 186–7) presents a deviant case in which a description of events displaying its producer's 'limited access' does *not* lead the other party to disclose her authorized version of the event:

```
(2)        1 A:  . . . dju j'see me pull us?=
    1→     2 B:  =.hhh No:. I wz trying you all day. en the line
           3     wz busy fer like hours
    2→     4 A:  ohh:::::, oh:::::, .hhhhhh We::ll, hh I'm g'nna
           5     c'm over in a little while help yer brother ou:t
           6 B:  Goo :d
           7 A:  Goo .hhh Cuz I know he needs some he::lp,
           8     ((mournfully))
           9 B:  .hh Ye:ah. Yeh he'd mention' that tihday.=
          10A:  =M-hm,=
    3→    11B:  .hhh Uh:m, .tlk .hhh Who wih yih ta:lking to.
                                        (Pomerantz, 1980: 186–7)
```

In Extract 2 above, B reports her experience about A's line having been busy (arrow 1). In terms of the interactional pattern identified by Pomerantz, this kind of telling should make relevant a subsequent disclosure of the details of the event by the other, more knowledgeable party. In the extract above, however, this does not happen. Instead, A shifts the topic in her subsequent turn (arrow 2). Therefore, within the framework of the analysis of 'fishing', we can consider Extract 2 as a deviant case. In a more recent paper, Clayman and Maynard (1994) have outlined three different ways that deviant cases can be dealt with:

(1) Sometimes deviant cases can be shown to exhibit the interactants' orientation to the *same* considerations and normative orientations that produce the 'regular' cases. In those cases, something in the conduct of

the participants discloses that they, too, treat the case as one involving a departure from the expected course of events. If the deviant cases show this kind of property, they provide *additional support* for the analyst's initial claim that the regularities found in the first phase of the data analysis 'are methodically produced and oriented to by the participants as normative organizations of action' (Heritage, 1988: 131).

Extract 2 above is an example of this type of deviant case. After A has failed to respond to B's initial 'fishing' turn by an authorized report of the events, B asks directly to whom A had been talking (arrow 3). Through her question, she openly requests the information which the fishing device (arrow 1), according to Pomerantz's analysis, solicited indirectly. This shift to open information seeking after an unsuccessful 'fishing' attempt indirectly confirms B's initial orientation to the 'fishing' as a device which can be used in indirect solicitation of information.

(2) Clayman and Maynard (1994) point out, however, that there are also deviant cases that cannot be integrated within the analysts' construction of the participants' orientations that normally produce the regular cases. In dealing with these cases, the analyst may need to change his or her construction of the participants' orientations. A classical example is Schegloff's (1968) analysis of a single deviant case in his corpus of 500 telephone call openings. In this single case, unlike the other 499, the caller spoke first. The analysis of that single case led Schegloff to abandon his initial hypothesis (according to which there is a norm obligating the answerer to speak first) and to reconceptualize the very first moves of telephone calls in terms of the adjacency pair 'summons (telephone ringing)–answer'. In the deviant case, the answerer did not produce the relevant second pair part, and, accordingly, the caller reissued the summons by speaking first.

(3) There are also, however, deviant cases which cannot be integrated either into the existing or into a reconceptualized hypothesis concerning the participants' orientations (Clayman and Maynard, 1994). In these cases, an explanation can be sought from the individual contingencies of the single case. Normative orientations or strategic considerations other than those that usually inform the production of the pattern may be invoked by the participants in single cases, and these other orientations or considerations may explain the deviance.

In sum, deviant case analysis constitutes a central resource for testing hypotheses in conversation analytic work. Therefore, the researcher should consider the deviant cases not a nuisance, but a treasure. The meticulous analysis of those cases gives impetus, strength and rigour to the development of the analytic arguments.

Validity of claims concerning the institutional character of interaction

In both qualitative and quantitative research, a central dimension of validity involves the correspondence between a theoretical paradigm and the observations made by the researcher. 'Construct validity' is a term that is often used in this context (Carmines and Zeller, 1979: 22–6; Kirk and Miller, 1986: 22). It involves the relations between theoretical concepts and the observations that are supposed to represent those concepts. As was pointed out above, the primary emphasis that CA places on naturalistic description de-intensifies the relevance of many ordinary concerns of construct validity. However, the expansion of conversation analytic research on institutional interaction (see Heritage, this volume; Drew and Heritage, 1992) has reinvoked the need to consider the relation between observations and concepts also in conversation analytic studies.

In conversation analytic research on institutional interaction, a central question of validity is this: what grounds does the researcher have for claiming that the talk he or she is focusing on is in any way 'connected to' some institutional framework? The fact that a piece of interaction takes place in a hospital or in an office, for example, does not per se determine the institutional character of that particular interaction (Drew and Heritage, 1992: 18–21). Institutional roles, tasks and arrangements may or may not be present in any particular interactions; they may or may not be present at particular *moments* in particular interactions. If they are, the conversation analytic programme presupposes their presence is observable to the participants and the analyst alike.

Two basic criteria for the validity of claims concerning the institutional character of talk have been outlined by Schegloff (1987, 1991, 1992b). The first criterion concerns the *relevancy of categorization*. There are indefinitely many aspects of context potentially available for any interaction: we may categorize one another on the basis of gender, age, social class, education, occupation, income, race, and so on, and we may understand the setting of our interaction accordingly. In the momentary unfolding of interaction, Schegloff argues, 'the parties, singly and together, select and display in their conduct which of the indefinitely many aspects of context they are making relevant, or are invoking, for the immediate moment' (1987: 219).

Awareness of this 'problem of relevance' requires the professional analyst to proceed with caution. There is a danger of 'importing' institutional context to data. The professional analyst may be tempted to assume, without going into the details of data, that this or that feature of talk is an indication of a particular context (such as 'medical authority' or 'professional dominance') having affected the interaction. Such stipulation for context may, Schegloff (1991: 24–5) argues, result in the analysis being terminated prematurely, so that the inherent organization within the talk is not thoroughly understood. Phenomena which in the beginning may appear as indications of the workings of an 'institutional context' may in a more thorough examination turn out to be primarily connected to the organization and dynamics of talk which can be even better understood without reference to the 'institutional context'.

Another key issue addressed by Schegloff (1991, 1992b) involves what he calls *procedural consequentiality of context*. He argues that it is not sufficient to say that a particular context is oriented to 'in general' by the participants in interaction, but, instead, it has to be shown how specifiable aspects of the context are consequential for specifiable aspects of the interaction. The goal is to make 'a direct "procedural" connection between the context . . . and what actually happens in the talk' (Schegloff, 1991: 17). What is said, when it is said, and how, and by whom, and to whom, may invoke the context; the goal of the conversation analytic research is to explicate exactly how the things said brought forward the context.

Schegloff's emphasis on the procedural consequentiality of the context has an important corollary. If a piece of research can pin down specific procedural links between a context and talk-in-interaction, it is likely that these observations not only are relevant in terms of analysis of detailed organization of interaction but also contribute to the understanding of the context per se. Standard social scientific understandings of professional and other contexts are often based on rough generalizations concerning the professionals' tasks, clients' roles and the relations between the two (cf. Hak, 1994: 472). Conversation analytic research goes far beyond such generalizations. Thus, for example, the studies of Heath (1992), Maynard (1991a, 1991b, 1992) and myself (Peräkylä, 1998, 2002) on the delivery of diagnostic news have involved not only a detailed description of the specific practices found in medical consultations, but also a specification of a central aspect of that context, namely the dimensions and character of medical authority.

These two fundamental concerns of conversation analytic research on institutional interaction constitute a validity test for the claims concerning the institutional character of interaction. 'Relevancy of categorization' and 'procedural consequentiality of context' are something to be demonstrated by the researcher. In demonstrating them, the researcher will focus on particular phenomena in interaction, such as lexical choice, turn design, sequence organization and overall structural organization (Drew and Heritage, 1992: 29–45; Heritage, this volume). Where the workings of context will be found in a single piece of research cannot be predicted in advance. This unpredictability arises from the inductive character of the conversation analytic enterprise; it causes both the fundamental difficulty and the exceptional fascination of conversation analytic research.

Generalizability of conversation analytic findings

A crucial dimension of validity of conversation analytic (and any other) research concerns the generalizability of the research findings (Pomerantz, 1990; cf. Alasuutari, 1995: 143–57). Owing to their work-intensive character, many conversation analytic studies are based on relatively small databases. How widely can the results, derived from relatively small samples, be generalized?

This character of the problem is closely dependent on the type of conversation analytic research. In studies of ordinary conversation, the baseline assumption is that the results are or should be generalizable to the whole domain of ordinary conversations, and to a certain extent even across linguistic and cultural boundaries. Even though it may be that the most primordial conversational practices and structures – such as turn-taking or adjacency pairs – are almost universal, there are others, such as openings of telephone calls (see Houtkoop-Steenstra, 1991; Lindström, 1994; Schegloff, 1986), which show considerable variation in different cultures. This variation can only be tackled through gradual accumulation of studies on ordinary conversation in different cultures and social milieux. But let us focus now on the study of institutional interaction, where the problem is posed in different terms.

In some (advanced) studies of institutional interaction, explicit comparisons between different settings are made. Miller and Silverman (1995), for example, applied the comparative approach in describing talk about troubles in two counselling settings: a British haemophilia centre counselling patients who are HIV-positive and a family therapy centre in the United States. In particular, they focused on similarities in three types of discursive practices in these settings: those concerned with trouble definitions, trouble remedies and the social contexts of the clients' troubles. In a recent paper, Drew (2003) has gone even further in comparisons of institutional practices. He focuses on *formulations*, i.e. utterances that propose a gist or upshot of the preceding talk (cf. Heritage and Watson, 1979). Drew compares the uses of formulations in four settings – news interviews, workplace negotiations, radio call-in programmes and psychotherapy – and shows how this practice is shaped differently in each setting, so as to serve in its specific contingencies.

It is likely that as the databases and analyses of institutional interaction gradually accumulate, studies like Drew's and Miller and Silverman's will become more common. The comparative approach directly tackles the question of generalizability by demonstrating the similarities and differences across a number of settings. For the time being, however, most of the studies on institutional interaction are more like case studies.

Case studies on institutional interaction are based on data collected from one or a few sites only. The number of subjects involved in such studies usually is relatively small. The problem may be particularly acute if the professional practice that is studied is informed by specific professional theory: for example, psychotherapists working in the framework of 'solution-oriented therapy' (see e.g. Gale, 1991) interact with their clients in ways that are distinctively different from those of psychoanalysts (Vehviläinen, 2003; Peräkylä, *forthcoming*) or therapists with yet different theoretical inclinations (see e.g. Buttny, 1993).[3] For these reasons, it is important to ask whether the results presented in such studies are in any way generalizable. Does everything that is said in case studies on institutional interaction apply exclusively to the particular site that was observed, or do the results have some wider relevance?

In terms of the traditional 'distributional' understanding of generalizability, case studies on institutional interaction cannot offer much. Studying one or a few sites only does not warrant conclusions concerning similarities in the professionals' and their clients' conduct in different settings. In that sense, case studies on institutional interaction have a very restricted generalizability.

However, the question of generalizability can also be approached from a different direction. The concept of *possibility* is a key to this. *Social practices that are possible*, i.e. *possibilities of language use*, are the central objects of all conversation analytic case studies on interaction in particular institutional settings. The possibility of various practices can be considered generalizable even if the practices are not actualized in similar ways across different settings. For example, in my study on AIDS counselling in a London teaching hospital (Peräkylä, 1995), the research objects were specific questioning practices used by the counsellors and their clients. These practices, arising from the Milan School Family Systems Theory, include 'circular questioning' (eliciting one party's description of his or her mind by first asking another party to give his or her account of it), 'live open supervision' (asking questions in such a manner that the delivery of the question is done in two stages, via an intermediary) and 'hypothetical future-oriented questioning' (questions about the patient's life in a hypothetical future situation). These very practices were to a large extent developed in the particular hospital that my data were from, and it is possible that they are not used anywhere else exactly in those specific ways that were analysed in my study (see Peräkylä and Silverman (1991) and Silverman (1997) for some observations on the wide variety of approaches in AIDS counselling in Britain). Hence my results cannot be directly generalizable to any other site where AIDS counselling is done.

However, the results of my study can be considered descriptions of questioning techniques that are possible across a wide variety of settings. More specifically, the study involves an effort to describe in detail how these questioning techniques were made possible: what kind of management of turn-taking, participation frameworks, turn design, sequence organiza- tion, and so on, was needed in order for the participants to set up scenes where 'circular questioning', 'live open supervision' and 'hypothetical future- oriented questioning' were done? The study showed how these practices are made possible through the very details of the participants' action.

As possibilities, the practices that I analysed are very likely to be general- izable. There is no reason to think that they could not be made possible by any competent member of (at least any Western) society. In this sense, this study produced generalizable results. The results were not generalizable as descriptions of what other counsellors or other professionals do with their clients; but they were generalizable as descriptions of what any counsellor or other professional, with his or her clients, *can* do, given that he or she has the same array of interactional competencies as the participants of the AIDS counselling sessions have.

Quantification

Use of large databases and quantification involves another kind of strategy for ensuring the generalizability (and also other aspects of the validity) of the conversation analytical research findings (ten Have, 1999: 144–8). As Heritage shows in his contribution to this book, some of the practices studied by conversation analysts lend themselves to 'coding and counting'. For example, in Clayman and Heritage's (2002) recent study on question design in presidential press conferences in the United States, the journalists' questions were coded regarding the degree of 'adversarialness' that they exhibited. Calculations were made to show how the relative proportions of questions, showing different degrees of adversarialness, changed over time. It was shown that the journalists have become much less deferential and more aggressive in their treatment of the president. Another example of successful quantification is offered in Boyd's (1998; see also Heritage et al., 2001) study on medical peer review. She studied telephone consultations between physicians and the medical representatives of an insurance company. Each consultation yielded a decision concerning the financial coverage of a proposed surgical operation. Using quantitative techniques along with qualitative ones, Boyd showed that the interactional format of the *initiation* of the first topic of the call was a strong predictor of the outcome (the decision concerning the surgery). In other words, the opening of the call set the trajectory for the ensuing review: as a result of the initiation, the participants were either 'collegially' or 'bureaucratically' aligned, and these alignments led to different decisions.

At least two issues are critical regarding the applicability of quantitative techniques in CA. First, straightforward coding of interactional practices is not always possible. Many practices involve such complexity that large numbers of cases cannot be subsumed under simple (and mutually exclusive) categories. If complex cases are forced under simple categories, something that is analytically important may be lost from sight. This kind of consideration has led Schegloff (1993: 117) to propose the possibility that interaction might be orderly 'at the level of the singular occurrence only' and not orderly, in any relevant way, at the aggregate level. The other problem concerns sampling (Silverman, 2001: 249). In order for the quantitative analysis to provide a basis for generalization, the selection of cases to be studied should follow adequate statistical procedures so as to ensure their representativeness. In studies of CA, anything like random sampling is rarely possible. The data collection is too laborious and institutional conditions too strict. In researching medical consultations or psychotherapy, for example, the researcher may have to work with the kind of data that he or she will get access to. If the relation between the sample and the population remains unclear, statistical tests, if they are used, may yield results that should be understood heuristically only (as in Peräkylä, 1998, 2002). This does not need to be a reason not to use quantitative techniques at all, but it is a consideration that restricts their import in terms of generalizability of findings.

Bearing these restrictions in mind, statistical analysis may be useful in particular conversation analytical research designs. These include research designs that concern relations between distinct interactional variables in standardized forms of encounters (like the medical peer review studies by Boyd, 1998), or historical change in such encounters (like the changes of presidential press conferences studied by Clayman and Heritage, 2002), or relations between social categories and interactional practices (like the relations between gender and interruptions studied by West and Zimmerman, 1985). (For a more thorough account on this, see Heritage, 1995). In any case, however, the backbone of conversation analytical work, also regarding generalization of research findings, involves qualitative case-by-case analysis.

CONCLUSION

At the beginning of this chapter, I pointed out that the specific techniques of securing reliability and validity in different types of qualitative research are not the same. The aim of this chapter has been to give an overview of the imperatives faced and solutions found in conversation analytic research, especially when such research focuses on institutional interaction. At a more general level, however, the considerations of validity and reliability in CA are similar to those in any other kind of qualitative research: ˙all serious qualitative research involves assuring the accuracy of recordings and testing the truthfulness of analytic claims˙ In terms of the division of qualitative methods into three main 'branches' suggested by Silverman (2001), it seems that the specific constraints facing CA are closer to those of observational research than those of text analysis. The questions about the quality and inclusiveness of recordings, for example, arise in both, and deviant case analysis is also used in both.

Kirk and Miller (1986: 21, 42) point out that in conducting and assessing qualitative research (particularly ethnography), the primary emphasis has usually been laid on validity rather than on reliability, whereas in quantitative research the emphasis has been on the opposite. Put in simple terms, this may imply that qualitative research is well developed in terms of validity and underdeveloped in terms of reliability. I hope to have shown in this chapter that this is not the case with CA: CA can be considered a serious attempt to develop a method for the analysis of social action that is able to combine concerns of validity with those of reliability.

A serious concern about the reliability of observations was at the very core of the initial motivation of Harvey Sacks in beginning the line of research that we now call conversation analysis. The reliability of recordings remains an inherent strength of CA – but as I pointed out earlier in this chapter, audio or video recording per se does not suffice as a guarantee of the reliability of the observations. The researcher needs to pay attention both to the technical quality and inclusiveness of recordings and to the interplay of spoken language with other modalities of communication and social action.

The main procedures of validation of the researcher's analytic claims in all conversation analytic research include the analysis of the next speaker's interpretation of the preceding action, and deviant case analysis. In conversation analytic studies which focus on institutional interaction, new dimensions of validation have also arisen. These include the validation of the claims concerning the relevance of an institutional context of interaction, and the issue of generalizability of the results of case studies.

NOTES

*   I wish to thank David Silverman, John Heritage and Johanna Ruusuvuori for their comments on the earlier versions of this chapter.

1. For general discussions on the method of conversation analysis, see ten Have (1999), Heritage (1988, 1995), Hutchby and Wooffitt (1998), Pomerantz and Fehr (1997), Silverman (1998) and Wootton (1989).
2. For temporality in organizations, see also Boden (1994).
3. For a general discussion on the study of interactions that are informed by professional theories, see Peräkylä and Vehviläinen (2003).

Recommended reading

Silverman (2001: Chapter 8) offers a compact discussion on reliability, validity and generalizability in qualitative research. A more extensive treatment can be found in Seale (1999). The specific strategies of data analysis in CA are discussed in Chapters 6 and 7 of ten Have (1999).

REFERENCES

Alasuutari, P. (1995) *Researching Culture: Qualitative Method and Cultural Studies.* London: Sage.

Alkula, T., Pöntinen, S. and Ylöstalo, P. (1994) *Sosiaalitutkimuksen Kvantitatiiviset Mentelmät.* Porvoo: WSOY.

Altheide, D.L. and Johnson, J.M. (1994) 'Criteria for assessing interpretive validity in qualitative research', in N.K. Denzin and Y.S. Lincoln (eds), *Handbook of Qualitative Research.* Thousand Oaks, CA: Sage. pp. 485–99.

Atkinson, J.M. and Heritage, J. (eds) (1984) *Structures of Social Action: Studies in Conversation Analysis.* Cambridge: Cambridge University Press.

Boden, D. (1994) *The Business of Talk: Organizations in Action.* Cambridge: Polity.

Boyd, E. (1998) 'Bureaucratic authority in the "company of equals": initiating discussion during medical peer review'. *American Sociological Review*, 63: 200–24.

Buttny, R. (1993) *Social Accountability in Communication.* Newbury Park, CA: Sage.

Carmines, E.G. and Zeller, R.A. (1979) *Reliability and Validity Assessment*. Beverly Hills, CA: Sage.

Clayman, S.E. and Heritage, J. (2002) 'Questioning presidents: Journalistic deference and adversarialness in the press conferences of Eisenhower and Reagan', *Journal of Communication*, 52 (4): 749–75.

Clayman, S.E. and Maynard, D.W. (1994) 'Ethnomethodology and conversation analysis', in P. ten Have and G. Psathas (eds), *Situated Order: Studies in the Social Organization of Talk and Embodied Activities*. Washington, DC: University Press of America. pp. 1–30.

Dingwall, R., Eekelaar, J. and Murray, T. (1983) *The Protection of Children*. Oxford: Basil Blackwell.

Drew, P. (2003) 'Comparative analysis of talk-in-interaction in different institutional settings: A sketch', in P.J. Glenn, C.D. LeBaron and J. Mandelbaum (eds), *Studies in Language and Social Interaction: In honor of Robert Hopper*. Mahwah, NJ: Erlbaum.

Drew, P. and Heritage, J. (1992) 'Introduction: Analyzing talk at work', in P. Drew and J. Heritage (eds), *Talk at Work: Interaction in Institutional Settings*. Cambridge: Cambridge University Press. pp. 3–65.

Drew, P. and Sorjonen, M.-L. (1997) 'Institutional dialogue', in T.A. van Dijk (ed.), *Discourse: A Multidisciplinary Introduction*. London: Sage. pp. 92–118.

Fairclough, N. (1999) *Critical Discourse Analysis*. London: Longman.

Firth, A. (1995) '"Accounts" in negotiation discourse: A single case analysis', *Journal of Pragmatics*, 23: 199–226.

Gale, J.E. (1991) *Conversation Analysis of Therapeutic Discourse: The Pursuit of a Therapeutic Agenda* (Vol. XLI in the series 'Advances in Discourse Processes'). Norwood, NJ: Ablex.

Gergen, G. (1994) *Realities and Relationships: Soundings in Social Construction*. Cambridge, MA: Harvard University Press.

Glaser, B.G. and Strauss, A.L. (1968) *Time for Dying*. Chicago: Aldine.

Goffman, E. (1983) 'The interaction order', *American Sociological Review*, 48 (1): 1–17.

Goodwin, C. (1992) 'Recording human interaction in natural settings', *Pragmatics*, 2: 181–209.

Goodwin, C. (1994) 'Professional vision', *American Anthropologist*, 96 (3): 606–33.

Goodwin, C. (1995) 'Seeing in depth', *Social Studies of Science*, 25: 237–74.

Goodwin, C. and Goodwin, M.H. (1997) 'Formulating planes: Seeing as a situated activity', in D. Middleton and Y. Engeström (eds), *Cognition and Communication at Work: Distributed Cognition in the Workplace*. Cambridge: Cambridge University Press.

Hak, T. (1994) 'The interactional form of professional dominance', *Sociology of Health and Illness*, 16 (4): 469–88.

Hammersley, M. (1992) *What's Wrong with Ethnography: Methodological Explorations*. London: Routledge.

Hammersley, M. and Atkinson, P. (1983) *Ethnography: Principles in Practice*. London: Tavistock.

ten Have, P. (1999) *Doing Conversation Analysis: A Practical Guide*. London: Sage.

Heath, C. (1992) 'The delivery and reception of diagnosis in the general practice consultation', in P. Drew and J. Heritage (eds), *Talk at Work: Interaction in Institutional Settings*. Cambridge: Cambridge University Press. pp. 235–67.

Heath, C. and Luff, P. (2000) *Technology in action*. Cambridge: Cambridge University Press.

Heritage, J. (1988) 'Explanations as accounts: A conversation analytic perspective', in

C. Antaki (ed.), *Analysing Everyday Explanation: A Case Book of Methods*. London: Sage. pp. 127–44.

Heritage, J. (1995) 'Conversation analysis: Methodological aspects', in U.M. Quatshoff (ed.), *Aspects of Oral Communication*. Berlin: Walter de Gruyter. pp. 391–418.

Heritage, J. and Atkinson, J.M. (1984) 'Introduction', in J.M. Atkinson and J. Heritage (eds), *Structures of Social Action: Studies in Conversation Analysis*. Cambridge: Cambridge University Press. pp. 1–13.

Heritage, J. and Lindström, A. (1998) 'Motherhood, medicine and morality: Scenes from a series of medical encounters'. *Research on Language and Social Interaction*, 31: 295–310.

Heritage, J. and Watson, R. (1979) 'Formulations as conversational objects', in G. Psathas (ed.), *Everyday Language. Studies in Ethnomethodology*. New York: Irvington. pp. 123–62.

Heritage, J., Boyd, E. and Kleinman, L. (2001) 'Subverting criteria: The role of precedent in decisions to finance surgery', *Sociology of Health and Illness*, 23 (5): 701–28.

Houtkoop-Steenstra, H. (1991) 'Opening sequences in Dutch telephone conversations', in D. Boden and D.H. Zimmerman (eds), *Talk and Social Structure: Studies in Ethnomethodology and Conversation Analysis*. Cambridge: Polity. pp. 232–50.

Hutchby, I. and Wooffitt, R. (1998) *Conversation Analysis: Principles, Practices and Applications*. Cambridge: Polity.

Kenny, A. (1973) *Wittgenstein*. London: Allen Lane.

Kirk, J. and Miller, M.L. (1986) *Reliability and Validity in Qualitative Research*. London: Sage.

Lindström, A. (1994) 'Identification and recognition in Swedish telephone conversation openings', *Language in Society*, 23 (2): 231–52.

Luff, P. and Heath, C. (2002). Broadcast talk: Initiating calls through a computer-mediated technology. *Research on Language and Social Interaction*, 35 (3): 337–66.

Maynard, D.W. (1991a) 'Interaction and asymmetry in clinical discourse', *American Journal of Sociology*, 97 (2): 448–95.

Maynard, D.W. (1991b) 'The perspective-display series and the delivery and receipt of diagnostic news', in D. Boden and D.H. Zimmerman (eds), *Talk and Social Structure: Studies in Ethnomethodology and Conversation Analysis*. Cambridge: Polity. pp. 164–92.

Maynard, D.W. (1992) 'On clinicians co-implicating recipients' perspective in the delivery of diagnostic news', in P. Drew and J. Heritage (eds), *Talk at Work: Interaction in Institutional Settings*. Cambridge: Cambridge University Press. pp. 331–58.

Maynard, D. (1996) 'From paradigm to prototype and back again: Interactive aspects of "cognitive processing" in standardized survey interviews', in N. Schwarz and S. Sudman (eds), *Answering Questions: Methodology for Determining Cognitive and Communicating Processes in Survey Research*. San Francisco: Jossey Bass.

Miller, G. and Silverman, D. (1995) 'Troubles talk and counselling discourse: A comparative study', *Sociological Quarterly*, 36 (4): 725–47.

Parker, I. (1992) *Discourse Dynamics: Critical Analysis for Social and Individual Psychology*. London: Routledge.

Peräkylä, A. (1995) *AIDS Counselling: Institutional Interaction and Clinical Practice*. Cambridge: Cambridge University Press.

Peräkylä, A. (1998) 'Authority and accountability: The delivery of diagnosis in primary health care', *Social Psychology Quarterly*, 61 (4): 301–20.

Peräkylä, A. (2002) 'Agency and authority: Extended responses to diagnostic statements in primary care encounters', *Research on Language and Social Interaction*, 35 (2): 219–47.

Peräkylä, A. (*forthcoming*) 'Making links in psychoanalytic interpretations: A Conversation Analytical view', *Psychotherapy Research*.

Peräkylä, A. and Silverman, D. (1991) 'Rethinking speech-exchange systems: Communication formats in AIDS counselling', *Sociology*, 25 (4): 627–51.

Peräkylä, A. and Vehviläinen, S. (2003) 'Conversation analysis and the professional stocks of interactional knowledge', *Discourse and Society*, 14 (6): 727–50.

Pomerantz, A. (1980) 'Telling my side: "Limited access" as a "fishing device"', *Sociological Inquiry*, 50: 186–98.

Pomerantz, A. (1990) 'On the validity and generalizability of conversation analytic methods: Conversation analytic claims', *Communication Monographs*, 57 (3): 231–5.

Pomerantz, A. and Fehr, B.J. (1997) 'Conversation analysis: An approach to the study of social action as sense making practices', in T.A. van Dijk (ed.), *Discourse as Social Interaction*. London: Sage. pp. 64–91.

Sacks, H. (1984) 'Notes on methodology', in J.M. Atkinson and J. Heritage (eds), *Structures of Social Action: Studies in Conversation Analysis*. Cambridge: Cambridge University Press. pp. 21–7.

Sacks, H., Schegloff, E.A. and Jefferson, G. (1974) 'A simplest systematics for the organization of turn-taking for conversation', *Language*, 50: 696–735.

Schegloff, E.A. (1968) 'Sequencing in conversational openings', *American Anthropologist*, 70: 1075–95.

Schegloff, E.A. (1986) 'The routine as achievement', *Human Studies*, 9: 111–51.

Schegloff, E.A. (1987) 'Between macro and micro: Contexts and other connections', in J. Alexander, B. Giesen, R. Munch and N. Smelser (eds), *The Micro–Macro Link*. Berkeley and Los Angeles: University of California Press. pp. 207–34.

Schegloff, E.A. (1991) 'Reflections on talk and social structure', in D. Boden and D.H. Zimmerman (eds), *Talk and Social Structure: Studies in Ethnomethodology and Conversation Analysis*. Cambridge: Polity. pp. 44–70.

Schegloff, E.A. (1992a) 'Introduction', in H. Sacks, *Lectures on Conversation*, Vol. 1, ed. G. Jefferson. Oxford: Blackwell. pp. ix–lxii.

Schegloff, E.A. (1992b) 'On talk and its institutional occasion', in P. Drew and J. Heritage (eds), *Talk at Work: Interaction in Institutional Settings*. Cambridge: Cambridge University Press. pp. 101–34.

Schegloff, E.A. (1993) 'Reflections on quantification in the study of conversation', *Research on Language and Social Interaction*, 26: 99–128.

Seale, C. (1999) *The quality of qualitative research*. London: Sage.

Silverman, D. (1985) *Qualitative Methodology and Sociology*. Aldershot: Gower.

Silverman, D. (1997) *Discourses of Counselling*. London: Sage.

Silverman, D. (1998) *Harvey Sacks and Conversation Analysis*. Cambridge: Polity.

Silverman, D. (2001) *Interpreting Qualitative Data: Methods for Analysing Talk, Text and Interaction*, Second Edition. London: Sage.

Smith, D.E. (1974) 'The social construction of documentary reality', *Sociological Inquiry*, 44 (4): 257–68.

Smith, D.E. (1990) *The Conceptual Practices of Power*. Toronto: University of Toronto Press.

Strauss, A.L., Fagerhaugh, S., Suczeck, B. and Wiener, C. (1985) *The Social Organization of Medical Work*. Chicago: University of Chicago Press.

Sudnow, D. (1967) *Passing On: The Social Organization of Dying*. Englewood Cliffs, NJ: Prentice Hall.

Vehviläinen, S. (2003) 'Preparing and delivering interpretations in psychoanalytic interaction', *Text*, 23 (4): 573–606.

West, C. and Zimmerman, D.H. (1985) 'Gender, language and discourse', in T.A. van Dijk (ed.), *Handbook of Discourse Analysis*, Vol. IV. London: Academic Press. pp. 103–24.

Whalen, J. (1995) 'A technology of order production: Computer–aided dispatch in public safety communications', in P. ten Have and G. Psathas (eds), *Situated Order: Studies in the Social Organization of Talk and Embodied Activities*. Washington, DC: University Press of America. pp. 187–230.

Wittgenstein, L. (1975) *Philosophical Remarks*. Edited from his posthumous writings by R. Rhees and translated by R. Hargreaves and R. White. Oxford: Blackwell.

Wootton, A.J. (1989) 'Remarks on the methodology of conversation analysis', in D. Roger and P. Bull (eds), *Conversation: An Interdisciplinary Perspective*. Clevedon: Multilingual Matters. pp. 238–58.

16 Addressing social problems through qualitative research

Michael Bloor

This chapter explores two case studies which provide illustrative details of two different but related approaches for researchers who wish to address social problems and who are also sceptical of the possibilities of extensive influence among the policy-making community. Both of the approaches aim to influence practitioners rather than policy-makers and both link particularly well with qualitative research methods. In the first case study, an ethnographic research project is viewed as an analogue or partial paradigm of successful practitioner work, in this case outreach work among male prostitutes: in effect, the ethnography may be viewed as a demonstration or pilot outreach project. In the second case study, ethnographic work provides the material and the stimulation for practitioners to evaluate and revise particular facets of their own service provision.

SOCIAL RESEARCHERS AS SOCIAL ENGINEERS?

It was rather a shock for me to read in Carey's (1975) social history of the 'Chicago School' of sociology that in the 1920s the foremost practitioners of the foremost school of sociology were divided about how sociological knowledge should be applied. Should it be used to influence policy-makers? Or (and here lay the surprise) should sociologists intervene in social problems directly as consulting professionals, like clinicians or architects? I was vaguely aware that some hundred years earlier Auguste Comte had proposed a similar priestly cadre of sociologists to direct society along enlightened (and Enlightenment) paths. But the realization was somehow monstrous that, as late as the 1920s and contemporaneously with, say, Eliot's 'The Waste Land' and a hundred dystopian diatribes, my intellectual forebears could hanker after the power to re-engineer social life and institutions to their nostrums. It was the absence of that power, rather than humility, which thwarted them: in Carey's analysis (1975: 71–94), it was the lack of the kind of institutionalized authority which medicine exercises over a lay clientele, rather than any acknowledged deficiency in knowledge or in technical competence, which determined the path along which sociology would develop. Sociologists and other social researchers eventually opted to set out their stalls as scientists rather than professionals, and the West was largely spared the directive intervention of social experts (the peoples of the Soviet Union were less fortunate).

SOCIAL RESEARCHERS AS 'ENLIGHTENERS' OF POLICY-MAKERS?

Since the 1960s, the more limited aspiration of sociologists to influence policy-makers has also been under attack. It was pointed out by various critics that the policy community rarely sought *policies* from researchers: instead, research would be commissioned to confirm a preferred policy option, or perhaps to delay a necessary but inconvenient intervention. Bulmer (1982), in *The Uses of Social Research*, was one of those who sought to redefine an influential role for social science in the face of these criticisms. Taking up Janowitz's (1972) distinction between the 'engineering' and 'enlightenment' models of policy research, Bulmer argued that research cannot engineer changes of policy, but it can have an important indirect impact on the policy climate through processes of intellectual association and influence, providing descriptive accounts and theoretical interpretations. Silverman (2001) has termed this the 'state counsellor' role and has gently ridiculed how Bulmer's book on 'the uses of social research' turns out to be solely about the uses of social research for policy-makers.

Both the 'enlightenment' and 'engineering' models have long been under attack from advocates of the 'critical social research' model. Becker (1967), for example, posed the rhetorical question 'whose side are we on?' and argued the case for action-oriented research rather than policy-oriented research, for progressive social change achieved through emancipation rather than policy initiatives. He called for a partisan sociology that spoke up for the underdogs against the elites, elites which would include policy-makers in their number. Today Becker's question is widely believed to defy a simple answer, with researchers experiencing cross-cutting responsibilities to their research subjects, to funding agencies, to gate-keepers and to their colleagues in the scientific community. And Becker's rhetoric of sides is thought to be intellectually disabling, embracing what Silverman (2001: 260) has called 'its prior commitment to a revealed truth' (the plight of the underdog, and so on).

Hammersley (1995) has characterized all three models (engineering, enlightenment and critical) as different varieties of Enlightenment models with a capital E, since they all endorse certain Enlightenment ideas originating with the French 'Encyclopaedists' of the eighteenth century, namely that social life can be improved by planned intervention derived from accumulated scientific knowledge, itself the product of social research. In late modern society all three tenets of the Enlightenment paradigm have come under 'postmodernist' criticism: it is no longer universally accepted that planned intervention is capable of bringing about desirable social change, or that scientific knowledge can facilitate this, or that social research can produce such knowledge. Hammersley's review of these postmodernist criticisms leads him to the assessment that they serve to qualify severely, rather than demolish, the possibility of a social impact for social research: the scope for and feasibility of successful policy intervention has been overestimated in The Enlightenment Project and the role of research in bringing change about has been exaggerated and misunderstood, but this does not mean that social improvement is impossible or that knowledge lacks all authority.

A PRACTITIONER AUDIENCE FOR SOCIAL RESEARCH?

The policy community is not the sole audience for qualitative social research. On the lay audience for qualitative social research, see Silverman (2000: 275–6). Sociologists who have conducted research on sociological aspects of health and medicine have long been aware that there is a role for sociologists as participants in debates on public policy, but that there are also audiences of practitioners (clinicians, nurses and other health professionals) for social research. Practitioner-oriented social research has also been the subject of revisionist criticism. One strand of such criticism is that the researcher becomes the ally of the practitioner in exploitative relationships with patients or clients, servicing the practitioner in practitioner–client relationships which reinforce patriarchy, say, or white supremacy. The other strand of criticism of practitioner-oriented social research is that articulated by commentators such as Schon (1983), who have followed Schutz (1962) in arguing that professional work does not entail the deployment of scientific knowledge, but rather involves the deployment of a different kind of knowledge altogether, knowledge-in-action, which is rigorous but not comprehensive, task-oriented but not systematic, and experiential rather than research-based. In this reading, social research has little of value to contribute to practitioners' work. However, such criticisms hardly apply to that social research which takes practitioners' everyday work as its topical focus: social research which seeks to describe and compare practitioners' everyday work practices self-evidently invites practitioners to juxtapose and weigh their own practices with those reported by the researcher. Qualitative research techniques, with their capacity for rich description, are favoured techniques for research focused on everyday work practices.

The first case study reported in this chapter is a street ethnography of HIV-related risk behaviour among Glasgow male prostitutes. Safer and unsafe commercial sexual encounters were compared: unsafe encounters were found to be associated with control of the sexual encounter by the clients of prostitutes; safer sex was associated with particular techniques of power exercised by prostitutes. These findings indicate possible lines of successful intervention for those engaged in sexual health promotion, while the fieldwork methods and experience offered lessons for the design of successful outreach work in this area. The second case study is a comparative ethnography of variations in therapeutic community practice. The comparative design highlighted a number of features of good therapeutic practice found in particular communities that could profitably be adopted elsewhere, while the researcher's close fieldwork relationships with local therapeutic community practitioners encouraged the practitioners to experiment with particular new methods of working.

CASE A: MALE PROSTITUTES' HIV-RELATED RISK BEHAVIOUR

The need for services

Prior to the HIV epidemic, targeted services for male prostitutes hardly existed in the UK. There were a few notable exceptions: in particular one should note the London-based charity 'Streetwise' and its pioneering drop-in centre for male prostitutes. But certainly there were no targeted services in Glasgow. Indeed, when I and colleagues first began to enquire about male prostitution in Glasgow, we encountered scepticism in some quarters about whether male prostitution actually existed on any scale in Glasgow (it was thought to be much more the sort of thing that might be found in effete, middle-class Edinburgh). Male prostitution, in fact, is a highly diversified activity: the 'call man' in his own tastefully decorated flat, packing for a trip to Brazil with a businessman client, is far removed from the group of swearing, cat-calling, jostling teenagers warming themselves with their bottles of 'Buckie' wine outside the late-night urinal. Not all male prostitutes have much need of services, but others have multiple and complex problems (legal problems, health problems, housing problems, financial problems) which are sometimes unpresented to, or inadequately addressed by, service providers. The illegality of male prostitution has made specialist service development difficult: most Glasgow male prostitutes contacted in our study were below the then age of consent for homosexual acts and many of these acts did not occur in private; although the police adopted a stance of qualified toleration to female street prostitution, whereby female street prostitution was 'policed' rather than suppressed, that toleration was never extended to male street prostitution. And male service providers with an interest in providing services for male prostitutes were vulnerable to misconstructions of their motives.

The harm reduction approach

The HIV epidemic, along with its toll on lives and health, represented an opportunity to change the policy climate in respect of male prostitution. The situation was analogous to that in the drugs services, where a range of services (most notably syringe exchanges) was put in place for existing drug injectors who were not motivated to abstain from drugs or to change their route of administration from injection to smoking or ingestion. This new drugs policy, which became known as that of 'harm reduction' or 'harm minimization', argued that 'the spread of HIV is a greater danger to individual and public health than drug misuse . . . [and that] services that aim to minimize HIV risk behaviour by all available means, should take precedence in development plans' (Advisory Council on the Misuse of Drugs, 1988). In similar fashion, it became possible to argue the case for services targeted at male prostitutes which had as their priority not the elimination of prostitution, but the minimization of individual and public health risks.

Study methods and service provision

These changes in the policy climate are clearer in retrospect than they were in the late 1980s when the fieldwork on male prostitutes' HIV-related risk behaviour was begun. The study was part of a wider programme of research on social aspects of HIV/AIDS supported by the Medical Research Council. The findings and the methodology of the study have been fully described elsewhere (Bloor et al., 1991, 1992, 1993). After pilot work, six different sites – two parks, two pubs and two public lavatories – were selected for time-sampling; non-streetworking prostitutes (escorts, masseurs and call men) were contacted through their advertisements and the study's own advertisement in the gay press. The ethnographic fieldwork was conducted in pairs for security purposes. Prostitutes were contacted by a combination of cold-contacting and snowballing: some of those contacted had never previously spoken to anyone about their prostitution activities. Both gay and self-identified 'straight' prostitutes were contacted, as were both drug injectors and non-injectors, and both novices and experienced prostitutes.

While the fieldworkers' primary objective was research, it was recognized from the outset that the fieldwork also offered opportunities for health promotion: relations between fieldworkers and research subjects can never be scientifically neutral (Hammersley and Atkinson, 1995) and an attempt to preserve a fictional neutrality should never be used as an excuse for failing to attempt to save lives. The Greater Glasgow Health Board provided condoms suitable for oral and for anal sex for the researchers to distribute (when the fieldwork started, condoms suitable for anal sex were not freely commercially available); an advice leaflet was also handed out which gave advice on HIV prevention and also gave contact numbers for HIV/AIDS counselling and for other relevant services such as welfare rights and homelessness.

Study findings

If the handing out of condoms and advice leaflets could be thought to generate a 'reporting bias', discouraging the reporting of unsafe commercial sex, then such discouragement can only have been marginal because at least a third of those prostitutes contacted reported unsafe sex with at least some of their current commercial partners (unsafe sex was defined, following the Terrence Higgins Trust, as anal sex with or without a condom, because of the greater risk of condom failure in anal sex). Unsafe commercial sex was associated with client control. In contrast to female street prostitution, where safer commercial sex is almost always practised and the women assume directive control of the encounter (McKeganey and Barnard, 1992), in many male prostitute–client encounters it is the client who assumes control and decides on matters such as the type of sex and its location. Safer commercial sex among male prostitutes was associated with particular strategies of power to wrest the initiative away from clients. Seeking payment up front (universally practised by female prostitutes) was one such successful strategy. Getting payment up front was not popular with the clients, who feared (with some justification) that the prostitute might 'do a runner', but that the minority of male prostitutes in the sample who *did* insist on prior payment were all currently practising safer commercial sex.

However, getting the money up front was not the only successful counter-vailing strategy of power used by male prostitutes to insist on safer sex. Male prostitution is often a highly covert and ambiguous activity, few words are exchanged and it is not even always clear to both parties that the encounter is a commercial one. Safer sex is likely to be associated with any techniques that serve to dispel the ambiguity that surrounds the encounter and make type of sex (and prices) a matter for overt discussion, as in the following field note:

> His procedure was to stand at the urinal. The client would come and stand beside him. When the coast was clear, the client would put out a hand and he would immediately say 'I'm sorry but I charge.' Some would leave at that point. With the remainder he'd negotiate a rate. He would accept 10 pounds but sometimes got 20 pounds. . . . He always did hand jobs or oral sex. . . . If clients asked him for anal sex he told them to eff off.

Encouragement of overt negotiations between prostitute and client is only one strategy (albeit possibly the most effective strategy) for the promotion of safer commercial sex. Another strategy practised by some respondents was to attempt to screen out those clients looking for anal sex by building up a 'book' of regular clients (with whom safer sex was practised) and refusing all casual commercial contacts. But it is difficult for streetworking prostitutes to confine themselves exclusively to 'regulars' (only one streetworking respondent had succeeded in working thus, although another two respondents had some 'regulars' and supplemented their income with additional casual contacts) and one UK study found that anal penetration was actually more common in encounters with regular clients than with casual clients (Davies and Feldman, 1991), possibly because sexual encounters with streetworkers' regular clients are more likely to take place at the clients' houses with more attendant privacy than semi-public locations such as car parks and back lanes, where disrobing may be difficult, uncomfortable and dangerous.

The substitution of overt negotiations between prostitutes and clients for the furtive and largely non-verbal exchanges characteristic of many encounters would have advantages beyond the prevention of HIV infection and of other sexually transmitted diseases. One considerable advantage might lie in an attendant reduction in the levels of violence surrounding male prostitution. Rapes, muggings and assaults (of clients by prostitutes, of prostitutes by clients and of both prostitutes and clients by 'queer bashing' third parties) are commonplace; during the sixteen-month fieldwork period three of our thirty-two research subjects were charged with assault and a fourth was imprisoned. Many (but not all) of these violent altercations are disputes about money. There were no 'going rates' for the various sexual services on offer: prostitutes took what money they could and, without prior agreement on charges (sometimes without even prior agreement that a charge was to be levied), the scope for violent disputes was considerable, as is illustrated in the following field note:

> ['Sammy' said he'd] never been cheated out of his money: he'd make sure he always got his money (this was said with a sudden hard emphasis . . .). He and 'Kenny' laughingly recalled an altercation with one of 'Colin's' punters [i.e. clients]. Colin was demanding twenty-five pounds and the punter swore he was only due fifteen pounds, refusing to hand over the extra ten pounds. Kenny, in his cynical way, was disinclined to believe Colin, but Sammy said he'd rather believe a mate than some dirty old punter. Sammy had intervened, whipped a knife out and held it in front of his face (this was mimed out for our benefit). The punter instantly pulled out the extra cash, shot off and had never been seen at the toilets since.

Implications for service provision

This research project had two possible policy pay-offs. First, it indicated how both unsafe commercial sex and violence could be reduced, namely through encouraging male prostitutes to engage in overt negotiations with clients. And, secondly, it indicated a possible medium for that encouragement, namely outreach work associated with condom distribution at regular prostitution sites.

Outreach work, taking services to clients rather than waiting for clients to attend at agencies, has a long history but has been little evaluated (Rhodes et al., 1991). It is clear that outreach work is the only means of delivering services to clients who are unable or unwilling to attend agencies and the HIV/AIDS epidemic has greatly stimulated the development of outreach services to stigmatized and victimized populations (drug injectors, gay men, female and male prostitutes) who are judged to be at possible risk of HIV infection and transmission. At the time this study was conducted, Glasgow had no outreach project targeted at male prostitutes: there was a drop-in centre for female prostitutes, but no outreach workers were attached to it and no men were admitted to the drop-in premises. Ethnographic fieldwork, in its protracted and regular contacts with research subjects, has much in common with services outreach work and it was therefore possible for the ethnographic study to take on the character of a local feasibility study for a male prostitute outreach service, demonstrating to the sceptical that appreciable numbers of male prostitutes were working in Glasgow, that levels of HIV-related risk behaviour were high and that outreach contact could be established. Moreover, the nature of the fieldwork contact that was established augured well for a future outreach service: large quantities of condoms were distributed (to clients as well as prostitutes); even highly socially isolated individuals with no contact with other prostitutes proved contactable; working relationships were established with important local individuals such as bar-owners and managers, toilet attendants and (at an appropriate distance) the police, and the project proceeded with no threat to the safety of the ethnographers.

Throughout the fieldwork period I had briefed public health personnel, social work staff and AIDS charity workers about project developments and provisional findings. At the conclusion of the fieldwork period, I had arranged (with the permission of my research subjects) to introduce them to a local social worker who was to be employed as an outreach worker, covering the same prostitution sites that I had covered during ethnographic fieldwork. The introductions were accomplished but the planned outreach post was 'frozen' (along with other local authority posts) owing to a local authority budgetary crisis associated with non-payment of the poll tax. Nevertheless, the commitment to a male prostitution outreach service had been made and the establishment of such a service was merely postponed, taking place at a later date.

No claim is being made here that this ethnographic research made a contribution of any importance to national policy debates about HIV/AIDS services. I did participate in a national colloquium organized to discuss outreach services for men who have sex with men, but by this time a number of outreach services for men who have sex with men were already underway in England, funded under the Health Education Authority's MESMAC initiative (evaluated by Prout and Deverell, 1994). The research project did not fulfil a 'state counsellor' role but, thanks to the sustained contact with research subjects afforded by qualitative methods, the project was able to fulfil a dual research and health promotion function and to act as a demonstration project for the feasibility and content of a local outreach service.

CASE B: PRINCIPLES OF GOOD THERAPEUTIC COMMUNITY PRACTICE

Study methods

Therapeutic communities are found in a variety of shapes and sizes (residential and non-residential, long-term and short-term), catering for a range of client groups (psychiatric patients, ex-psychiatric patients, children with learning difficulties, adults with learning difficulties, drug users and alcoholics, prisoners, and so on), with a range of different staffing arrangements, but having in common an approach to therapeutic work as an essentially cognitive activity which can transform any mundane event in the community (be it lavatory cleaning, or complaining about the noise) by redefining that event in the light of some therapeutic paradigm (Bloor et al., 1988). The nature of the paradigm may vary from community to community, but the redefinition of the event (as showing responsibility, say, or seeking out a new and less pathogenic way of relating to others) as an occasion or a topic for therapy sets it apart and transforms it, much as the profane is transformed into the sacred by religious belief and ceremony.

I and two colleagues (Neil McKeganey and Dick Fonkert) conducted a comparative ethnography of eight different therapeutic communities studied by one or another of us over a period of some ten years. Because all the individual studies involved the collection of similar (participant observation) data on the same general topic (the treatment process), it was possible to reuse those data for a single comparative study which avoided the usual constraint of qualitative methods, namely that breadth of coverage must be sacrificed for depth. As a result, we were able to compare practice across a wide range of contrasting therapeutic community settings – two contrasting residential psychiatric units (studied by McKeganey), a Camphill Rudolf Steiner school for children with learning difficulties (McKeganey), a 'concept house' for drug users (Fonkert), a 'foster family' care facility (Bloor), two contrasting halfway houses for disturbed adolescents (Bloor), and a psychiatric day hospital (Bloor). Accounts of the research methods have been supplied elsewhere (Bloor et al., 1988).

Comparison as a stimulus to practice change

Any ethnography is essentially comparative in approach. When the ethnographer is taking field notes, then he or she is selecting from a cornucopia of continuing sense data those moments that seem to him or her to be of special significance. When analysing the field notes, the ethnographer is juxtaposing and comparing numerous similar and contrasting field note accounts. And when writing the ethnography the writer is weighing various different accounts in order to illustrate and develop the argument in the text. Of course, these comparative judgements are not confined to ethnography: similar evaluative judgements are made on a continuing and routine basis by all

313

research subjects. It therefore follows that one possible *use* of ethnography is to assist in these everyday comparative judgements: a rich description of particular kinds of therapeutic practice, for example, can assist practitioners in making evaluative judgements about their own practices, preserving what seems to them good practice and experimenting with the adoption of new practices where this seems appropriate. In effect, reading an ethnography of therapeutic communities can be like visiting other communities and being drawn to reconsider one's everyday routines in the light of contrasted experience: McKeganey has described how a group visit to a second community led staff and residents at the 'Faswells' psychiatric unit to try to make mealtimes much more of a community and therapeutic occasion, such as they had observed to be the case at the visited community (Bloor et al., 1988: 180).

Provided that the practitioner audience retains some autonomy of function and judgement in its everyday work (arguably a minimum definition of professional practice (Freidson, 1970)), then any ethnography can thus serve as a stimulus to practice change and a number of sociological ethnographies have found their way onto professional training courses for this reason (indeed our comparative ethnography is used on at least one therapeutic community training course). However, my fellow researchers and I wished to go beyond merely passively providing opportunities for such comparative practitioner judgements; we wished actively to draw the attention of readers to particular features of practice in one or two communities which, it seemed to us, might be adopted with profit by other communities. The utility of ethnographic texts for practitioner audiences can be enhanced by making explicit for readers those silent and implicit researcher judgements that have led to particular practices being recorded and analysed in the first place. No authoritative scientific judgement is intended here; I simply list below some practices that seemed to my colleagues and myself to be worthy of wider dissemination. The final test of their utility would lie in whether practitioners themselves shared our judgement and found themselves able to adopt them successfully; successful adoption in the unique circumstances of individual communities may not always be possible, perhaps because of a clash with other valued practices, or inadequate resources, or timetabling problems. The practices we commended were as follows (in no particular order of importance):

1 making fellow-residents responsible for keeping residents in treatment;
2 ways of increasing residents' awareness of the changeability of the community structure;
3 the 'after-group' as a way of promoting resident reflectivity;
4 the attendance of residents at staff change-over meetings;
5 the 'tight house' as a way of countering institutionalism;
6 resident selection of participating staff;
7 the offering of alternative sources of satisfaction to junior staff.

There is no space here to enlarge on all these possible means of improving therapeutic community practice (see Bloor et al., 1988: 172–85, for a fuller account); instead I shall simply expand upon the first listed practice, that of making residents responsible for keeping residents in treatment.

Keeping residents in treatment

All non-custodial treatment institutions face problems associated with the premature departure or self-discharge of residents. It is a commonplace that persons who discharge themselves prior to the completion of their treatment may derive less benefit from that treatment than those who stay to complete the course; indeed self-discharge may be part of a process of relapse to those pathogenic patterns of behaviour that led to the resident's referral to the therapeutic community in the first place. In studies of 'concept houses' for the treatment of drug users, for example, high reported success rates in remaining drug-free among those ex-residents who *complete* their courses have to be set against the fact that up to three-quarters of enrollees may discharge themselves prematurely, against staff advice (see e.g. Volkman and Cressey's (1963) evaluation of the first concept house, Synanon).

No therapeutic community is more vulnerable to premature self-discharge than a psychiatric day hospital, like Aberdeen's Ross Clinic day hospital,[1] where patients who wish to drop out have the simple expedient of failing to turn up for treatment on the following day. Treatment at the day hospital was conducted on a group basis and followed the principle of 'reality confrontation' (Morrice, 1979), the reflection back to patients, informally and in formal group therapy sessions, that their conduct is unacceptable and the depiction of the therapeutic community as a locale where new and less pathogenic social behaviours can be experimented with and adopted. Although confrontation could be manifest in many forms other than angry denunciation, including gentle irony and hesitant concern, staff were aware that the treatment method put pressures on patients which could lead to self-discharge or even to suicidal impulses. To avoid premature discharge and self-harm, there was a convention in the day hospital (understood by staff and all but novice patients alike) that fellow-patients should provide the necessary comfort and support for patients to remain in treatment. In the first field note extract below, 'Lenny' fled after his first ever public disclosure of his sexual orientation; in the second 'Dawn' fled, threatening suicide:

[H]e'd remarked that he couldn't face telling his mother he'd had a sexual relationship with another man . . . he'd walked out on Friday lunchtime and a group of patients had run after him and brought him back and got him talking a bit.

This afternoon considerable pressure was put on 'Dawn': she had spoken of her feelings of hopelessness and depression, her failure to 'work' in the group, and her feeling that she ought to leave the day hospital. Several staff members had already left for prior appointments. 'Edith' (staff) said she had seen Dawn glance at the clock several times: now was her chance to end it (the group). Her voice breaking, Dawn picked up her bag, said she'd end it all right, and rushed out of the room. Edith did nothing to stop her. At 'Harry's' (patient) bidding, 'Olive' (patient) went after her, caught her up in the toilets and made her promise to come again tomorrow. Once before she'd dashed off and her fellow-patients set off after her. Indeed, this dashing after bolting patients is a fairly common occurrence – Edith could predict that Dawn would be looked after.

Moreover, patients who did silently discharge themselves by failing to return to the day hospital could expect a delegation of fellow-patients visiting them at their homes, urging them to return. Determined would-be defaulters had either to announce and defend their decisions in the formal groups or resort to subterfuge – failing to answer the door and even, in one case, leaving the country.

This practice of making patients responsible for keeping their fellow-patients in treatment, albeit effective in the day hospital, is not without potential drawbacks. For example, many patients who stayed away from the hospital were aware that they would be visited and solicited to return: thus, the provision of comfort and support to distressed and defaulting patients could be seen as encouraging attention-seeking behaviour. However, such drawbacks are not overwhelming, since staff who are aware of them can raise them in the formal therapeutic groups.

The patient or resident culture plays an important, even crucial, part in the treatment process in all therapeutic communities: the work of 'reality confrontation', for example, is often seen by practitioners as being more effective when conducted by fellow-patients than by staff, and fellow-residents/patients play an important part in inculcating in new arrivals an understanding of organizational structures and practices. Thus, requiring that patients/residents undertake the responsibility for keeping their fellows in treatment would be simply an extension of the active patient/resident therapeutic role already found in therapeutic communities. Nevertheless, such an extension of patients/residents' responsibilities, if successful, could have an appreciable influence on patterns of self-discharge in many communities. At 'Ashley' for example, one of the two halfway houses for disturbed adolescents in the study, although the residents were prepared to welcome and support new arrivals, established residents who chose to discharge themselves (a procedure sometimes indistinguishable from absconding) were never confronted or persuaded otherwise by their fellows. In one celebrated instance during my fieldwork at the house, almost the entire resident group knew beforehand of one resident's planned 'escape', which involved hanging around on the street outside to intercept the postman and appropriate his 'giro' (welfare benefits cheque) before catching an inter-city bus. No one chose to dissuade him and one fellow-resident even helped him carry his possessions to the bus station.

Feeding back findings

The above list of therapeutic community practices which might be profitably adopted elsewhere (including making residents responsible for keeping each other in treatment) was reported by myself and my research collaborators in the usual way in the academic and practitioner press and in a paper to an international conference of practitioners. But we also fed back findings to individual communities involved in the research. The feedback took various forms: in one community, Neil McKeganey and I used our knowledge of therapeutic community practice at the house to produce a video of everyday practice in the community, which was subsequently used by the house for PR purposes; in the day hospital, I circulated to staff and to some ex-patients (with whom I was still in contact) a research report on the relationship of the patient culture to the formal treatment programme, and that report became the basis for two 'focus group' discussions (Bloor et al., 2001) with staff and ex-patients; in the two halfway houses ('Ashley' and 'Beeches'), I circulated a comparative report to staff of both houses which was used as the basis for a focus group discussion with Ashley staff and for individual staff interviews with Beeches staff (who had largely dispersed to other posts in the meantime), but also at the conclusion of the fieldwork I had previously given staff some impressionistic feedback. At Ashley, this impressionistic feedback focused on how one might combat premature self-discharge:

> I had previously said that I would give the staff some feedback on my thoughts about the house before I left – not a 'scientific' statement, but simply an informed observer's reflections. I'd given some thought to this in advance and had decided to concentrate on one problem I thought was perhaps inadequately attended to – premature departure by residents 'frightened' of the changes expected of them – and a possible solution – a stronger resident culture. I spent an evening talking about this with the warden last night . . . and she brought it up in the staff group this afternoon.
> It led to a lot of discussion: general agreement that the problem was there.
> At the end of the [weekly] community meeting [the warden] said that she'd like (after her return from holiday) a special meeting of the community to discuss the problem of people leaving.

Ashley was not the only study community where the comparative analysis acted as a spur to modifications in practice. Sociological description of everyday therapeutic work can act as a stimulus to practitioners to re-examine their practice and perhaps modify it in response to comparative data. This stimulus to change can be increased by choosing certain forms of dissemination in preference to others, for example by explicit highlighting of examples of good practice, and by personal briefings as well as written reports. It is also possible that the close personal ties that are built up with research subjects over the course of ethnographic fieldwork serve to command an interested and committed audience for the fieldworker's findings. Of course, modes of research dissemination that command an audience among therapeutic community practitioners might not be similarly influential with other practitioner audiences: this should be a matter for empirical experimentation.

CONCLUSION

Policy influence for social researchers is quite possibly a chimera, 'a unicorn among the cedars' which is glimpsed tantalizingly from time to time but always eludes us. Some might say that policy-makers themselves are a chimera: a distinguished epidemiologist of my acquaintance claims never to have met one. In his younger years he would frequently meet senior functionaries in the health service, but they would always claim to be merely implementing policies passed down from above. As he himself grew in seniority, he came to meet the yet more senior functionaries from above, but they, too, claimed merely to be implementing policies passed down from above. Still his seniority grew, but still he encountered only policy implementers. He searched in vain for the fountainheads of health service policy until in old age the truth struck him that no one knowingly makes policy; for reasons perhaps of protective coloration everyone is convinced that they are mere policy-implementers, simply interpreting and elaborating edicts passed down from some more august authority. Analogous, if less colourful, arguments have been constructed by some empirical researchers of policy processes (Manning, 1989; Rock, 1987), namely that policy is a situated discourse, a set of tacit assumptions and implicit meanings found within particular offices and occupational groupings.

It is this policy discourse, this amalgam of committee asides, gossip and unspoken assumptions, that Bulmer would seek to influence through the gentle diffusion of ideas and research findings. But social researchers are rare visitors to these corridors and committee rooms: their capacity for cultural diffusion is minimal. The argument in this chapter has been that the real opportunities for social research influence lie closer to the coalface than they do to head office, that the real opportunities for influence lie in relations with practitioners, not with the managers of practice.

This role for qualitative researchers as practitioner helpmeets will not be found by some to be wholly satisfactory. All practitioner–client relationships (be they outreach worker–prostitute relationships, or therapeutic community staff–resident/patient relationships) are power relationships. In a Foucauldian analysis (see e.g. Foucault, 1980), power cannot be wished or legislated away, it is inherent in all relationships. Therapeutic advance has as its corollary the extension of the controlling therapeutic gaze: the growth of public health medicine since the nineteenth century, for example, has brought great health benefits, but it has also subjected populations to increasing surveillance and regulation (Armstrong, 1983). Surveillance as a technique of power ('the eye that knows and decides, the eye that governs' – Foucault, 1973: 89) is increasingly complemented in the late twentieth century by other techniques, most notably that of 'pastoral care' (Foucault, 1981), whereby clients of agencies find themselves 'shepherded' in disciplinary relationships with practitioners whose avowed goals are merely those of care and advice. Assisting in the extension of outreach work to new populations, or suggesting ways to increase the effectiveness of therapeutic community practice, are each alike analysable as endeavours which tighten the disciplinary grip of experts on citizens. In a new twist on Becker's old 'whose side are we on?' question, it may be argued that researchers should be assisting not in the extension of power, but in the extension of resistance – resistance to meddlesome interference in prostitutes' street dealings, and resistance to expert orchestration of patients' private lives. The opposite of power is not its absence, but the resistance it provokes; researchers, so the argument goes, should be laying the groundwork for citizen resistance rather than fostering the extension and effectiveness of expert power.

However, this critical view of sociological influence on practitioners is a new version of an old song, the song of the Leninist vanguard party which always knows best, having learned the Lessons of History. It matters not, in this critical view, that male prostitutes may welcome the provision of a service where there was none before, or that patients/residents in therapeutic communities may welcome the chance to play a fuller part in the treatment process by providing comfort and support to their fellows. What matters is resistance to experts' disciplinary power. Paradoxically, the critical analyst has become the all-seeing expert: the analyst claims to know better than the practitioners (the outreach workers and the therapeutic community staff), but the analyst also claims to know better than those whose resistance should be stiffened (the prostitutes and the patients/residents). Yet if the critical analysts are themselves experts, what kind of disciplinary relationship do they have with their audience? Should not they too be resisted? It follows that we can skirt these sophistries: where citizens themselves commend the work of practitioners, then it is not the place of researchers to murmur of false consciousness and demand resistance to pastoral care. (See the summary table below)

Unsustainable suggested roles for researchers	Problems
Researchers as 'social engineers'	• Low technical competence • Lack of institutional authority
Researchers as policy formulators/evaluators	• Policy-makers rarely seek policies from researchers • Policy-makers may commission research on policies in order to delay evaluation
Researchers as 'enlighteners' of policy-makers	Researchers have few opportunities to mingle with policy-makers, as opposed to practitioners
Researchers as emanicipators	Involves a prior commitment to an objective reality revealed to the researcher, but not to policy-makers, practitioners or laity

This issue (of whether or not social research should seek to assist the resistance of clients and patients) is part of a broader debate about the epistemological status of social research, about whether value neutrality can and should remain a constitutive principle of social research. The claim that social research can and should be value neutral is under attack from two sides. On one side, battle has been joined by those who argue that research should be explicitly politically participatory, embracing particular political aims, such as combating racism or patriarchy. On the other side, battle has been joined by those who argue that *no* practice or policy prescriptions can be offered by researchers under any circumstances, since all knowledge is socially constructed and there are no grounds for the researcher to claim superior knowledge.

The argument about participatory research is perhaps seen most clearly in the responses which greeted the publication of Foster's (1990) findings on the lack of evidence for racist practices in British schools. Foster found little evidence that black pupils were treated unfairly in lessons or that they were misallocated to ability groups; moreover, he re-examined the evidence of racism found in earlier studies and found it methodologically flawed. The study generated a considerable critical response from those committed to some version of anti-racism. Hammersley's (1995) review of the controversy firmly supports Foster's position against various implicit and explicit charges, notably that as a middle-class white male he was experientially disabled from collecting and understanding evidence of institutional racism, and that the primary objective of research is not the production of knowledge but the changing of society.

The argument of the 'strict constructivists' (the term is Best's, 1989) that researchers should be silent on social problems (having no basis for claiming superior knowledge) was stated succinctly by Woolgar and Pawluch (1985). Best's edited volume (and especially his own concluding chapter) relates some of the responses to Woolgar and Pawluch's paper. He argues the case for a 'contextual constructivist' position in distinction to the 'strict constructivist' position. Best is unclear whether it is practically possible to achieve the strict constructivists' goal of analyses wholly free of assumptions about objective reality; he cites various examples of how such assumptions may creep in at the backdoor of such analyses. Contextual constructivists, in contrast, may collaborate with collectivity members in examining and debating competing policy claims.

It seems, therefore, that qualitative researchers *may* address social problems and that they can address them most effectively by influencing practitioner practice. Qualitative research has a two-fold advantage in these processes of influence: one advantage relates to influencing practitioners who are the researcher's research subjects, and the second advantage relates to influencing practitioners who are the wider audience for the research findings. In respect of practitioners who are research subjects, qualitative researchers can call upon their pre-existing research relationships with their research subjects as a resource for ensuring an attentive and even sympathetic response to their research findings. A close personal and working relationship, based on lengthy social contact and built up over weeks and months, is likely to ensure that not only will practitioner research subjects have a particular interest in the findings (because of the identity of the researcher as much as a particular interest in the research topic), but also they may be willing to devote an unusual amount of time and effort to discussions of the findings. At the day hospital and Ashley halfway house, staff (and a group of ex-day hospital patients) were willing to read a quite lengthy research report and then make their reactions to the report the basis for a special focus group discussion. Where the researcher has become, for research subjects, a person for whom they have a special regard as a result of long familiarity, then it should come as no surprise that those research subjects will have interest in implementing the researcher's suggestions on changes in practice. In effect, the qualitative researcher may become a part of his or her local practitioner collectivity and trades on that position as a collectivity member to disseminate research findings.

In respect of other practitioners (who are not research subjects), the qualitative researcher has the advantage that the research methods allow rich descriptions of everyday practice which enable practitioner audiences imaginatively to juxtapose their own everyday practices with the research description. There is therefore an opportunity for practitioners to make evaluative judgements about their own practices and experiment with the adoption of new approaches described in the research findings. Qualitative studies of everyday practice offer sufficiently detailed descriptions of practice to act as a spur to judgement and experimentation. If Schon (1983) is correct in his argument that professional work involves the deployment of knowledge-in-action rather than scientific knowledge, then qualitative research allows professional practitioners to reflect upon that, previously taken-for-granted, knowledge-in-action. Relatedly, where specialist services (such as male prostitute outreach services) do not currently exist, qualitative research can provide detailed descriptions of the circumstances and behaviour of potential service-users such that material assistance is given with the design of targeted services. In the special case of outreach services, ethnographic fieldwork shares so many similarities with outreach work that a successful ethnographic project can act as a feasibility study or demonstration project for an outreach service. Shaw (1996) has recently developed at length the argument that qualitative methods can provide a paradigm or examplar for practitioners seeking to reflect upon and modify their work practices.

Practitioner autonomy is variable in its extensiveness but universal. Practitioners may not always have the local autonomy to develop new services to new target populations of clients, but all practitioners have the autonomy to modify their everyday work practices. In seeking the chimera of policy influence, sociologists rather neglected how research findings can address social problems through the encouragement of modifications and developments in practitioners' everyday practices. The effectiveness of research in addressing social problems has been increasingly questioned and even the legitimacy of social research in addressing those problems has been queried.

Of course, these questions and queries have been raised most loudly *outside* the research community, by pundits and politicians. However, this chapter is concerned not with punditry or politics, but rather with those questions and queries raised *within* the social research community. It is suggested that the addressing of social problems is indeed a legitimate objective of social research and that, although the effectiveness of social research as an agency of social change may be somewhat limited, it is certainly not wholly ineffective. Moreover, if the impact of social research on service providers' practices is considered alongside the impact on formal policy, then social research clearly has the potential to be more effective yet as an agency of change. (See the summary table below)

Qualitative researchers addressing social problems through influence on practitioners' practices

Advantages	Alleged disadvantages
• Qualitative researchers can capitalize on fieldwork relationships with practitioners to stimulate interest in their findings	• Assisting practitioners in improving service delivery may be viewed as conspiring with experts against the laity
• The rich descriptions of everyday practice found in qualitative research allow practitioners to compare their own practices with those reported in the research	• Researchers should be silent on social problems having no basis for superior knowledge
• New practices can be adopted from research descriptions	• The scope for successful changes in practice is frequently overestimated
• Ethnographies may even provide a partial model for new outreach services	• Practitioner autonomy is limited, especially in the creation of new services

ACKNOWLEDGEMENTS

I wish to thank Ian Shaw, Anssi Peräkylä and David Silverman for their helpful comments on an earlier draft of this chapter. All the research reported on here was supported by the Medical Research Council. I wish to thank Marina Barnard, Andrew Finlay and Neil McKeganey for their help as my co-fieldworkers in the male prostitution study and I wish to thank Dick Fonkert and Neil McKeganey for their help in the comparative analysis of the therapeutic communities data.

NOTES

1. This therapeutic community has since been relocated from the Ross Clinic to Kingseat Hospital, near Aberdeen.

Recommended reading

The section on 'generalizability' in Anssi Peräkylä's chapter elsewhere in this volume addresses cognate issues.

M. Hammersley (1995) *The Politics of Social Research*. London: Sage.
A comprehensive guide to the inevitable limitations researchers face in influencing policy.

C. Heath and P. Luff (1992) 'Collaboration and control: crisis management and multimedia technology in London Underground line control rooms', *Journal of Computer Supported Cooperative Work*, 1: 69–94.
A good early example of 'workplace studies', analysing workplace interaction and claimed by conversation analysts and video analysts to have high practical utility for practitioners and managers.

I. Shaw (1996) *Evaluating in practice*. Aldershot: Ashgate.
Offers suggestions on a closer relationship between research and practice.

D. Silverman (Second Edition, 2004) *Doing Qualitative Research: a practical handbook*. London: Sage.
Chapter 26 considers the different audiences for social research.

REFERENCES

Advisory Council on the Misuse of Drugs (1988) *AIDS and Drug Misuse: Part One*. London: Department of Health and Social Security.
Armstrong, D. (1983) *Political Anatomy of the Body: Medical Knowledge in Britain in the Twentieth Century*. Cambridge: Cambridge University Press.
Becker, H. (1967) 'Whose side are we on?', *Social Problems*, 14: 239–48.
Best, J. (ed.) (1989) *Images of Issues: Typifying Contemporary Social Problems*. Hawthorne, NY: Aldine de Gruyter.
Bloor, M., McKeganey, N. and Fonkert, D. (1988) *One Foot in Eden: A Sociological Study of a Range of Therapeutic Community Practice*. London: Routledge.
Bloor, M., Finlay, A., Barnard, M. and McKeganey, N. (1991) 'Male prostitution and risks of HIV infection in Glasgow: Final report', *ANSWER*, A.212: 1–3.
Bloor, M., McKeganey, N., Finlay, A. and Barnard, M. (1992) 'The inappropriateness of psycho-social models of risk behaviour to understanding HIV-related risk behaviour among Glasgow male prostitutes', *AIDS Care*, 4: 131–7.
Bloor, M., Barnard, M., Finlay, A. and McKeganey, N. (1993) 'HIV-related risk practices among Glasgow male prostitutes: Reframing concepts of risk behaviour', *Medical Anthropology Quarterly*, 7: 1–19.
Bloor, M., Frankland, J., Thomas, M. and Robson, K. (2001) *Focus Groups in Social Research*. London: Sage.
Bulmer, M. (1982) *The Uses of Social Research*. London: Allen and Unwin.

Carey, J. (1975) *Sociology and Public Affairs: the Chicago School*. London: Sage.

Davies, P. and Feldman, R. (1991) 'Male sex workers in South Wales', *Project Sigma Working Paper No. 35*. Colchester: University of Essex.

Foster, P. (1990) *Policy and Practice in Multicultural and Antiracist Education*. London: Routledge.

Foucault, M. (1973) *The Birth of the Clinic*, trans. A. Sheridan. London: Tavistock.

Foucault, M. (1980) 'The eye of power', in *Power/Knowledge: Selected Interviews and Other Writings 1972–1977*, ed. C. Gordon. Brighton: Harvester.

Foucault, M. (1981) '*Omnes et singulatim*: Towards a criticism of political reason', in S. McMurrin (ed.), *The Tanner Lectures on Human Values II*. Salt Lake City: University of Utah Press.

Freidson, E. (1970) *Profession of Medicine*. New York: Dodds Mead.

Hammersley, M. (1995) *The Politics of Social Research*. London: Sage.

Hammersley, M. and Atkinson, P. (1995) *Ethnography: Principles in Practice*, 2nd edition. London: Routledge.

Janowitz, M. (1972) *Sociological Models and Social Policy*. Morristown, NJ: General Earning Systems.

McKeganey, N. and Barnard, M. (1992) *AIDS, Drugs and Sexual Risk: Lives in the Balance*. Milton Keynes: Open University Press.

Manning, P. (1989) 'Studying policies in the field', in J. Gubrium and D. Silverman (eds), *The Politics of Field Research: Sociology Beyond Enlightenment*. London: Sage. pp. 213–35.

Morrice, J.K. (1979) 'Basic concepts, a critical review', in R. Hinshelwood and N. Manning (eds), *Therapeutic Communities: Reflections and Progress*. London: Routledge & Kegan Paul. pp. 94–111.

Prout, A. and Deverell, K. (1994) 'MESMAC: Working with diversity – building communities: An evaluation of a community development approach to HIV prevention for men who have sex with men'. London: Health Education Authority.

Rhodes, T., Hartnoll, R., Johnson, A., Holland, J. and Jones, S. (1991) 'Out of the agency and on to the streets: A review of HIV outreach health education in Europe and the United States', *ISDD Research Monograph No. 2*. London: Institute for the Study of Drug Dependence.

Rock, P. (1987) *A View From the Shadows: Policy Making in the Solicitor General's Office*. Oxford: Oxford University Press.

Schon, D. (1983) *The Reflective Practitioner*. London: Temple Smith.

Schutz, A. (1962) 'Commonsense and scientific interpretation of human action', in *Collected Papers*, Vol. 1, ed. M. Natansson. The Hague: Martinus Nijhoff. pp. 17–38.

Shaw, I. (1996) *Evaluating in Practice*. Aldershot: Ashgate.

Silverman, D. (2000) *Doing Qualitative Research, a practical handbook*. London: Sage.

Silverman, D. (2001) *Interpreting Qualitative Data: Methods of Analysing Talk, Text and Interaction*, 2nd edition. London: Sage.

Volkman, R. and Cressey, D. (1963) 'Differential association and the rehabilitation of drug addicts', *American Journal of Sociology*, 64: 129–42.

Woolgar, S. and Pawluch, D. (1985) 'Ontological gerrymandering: The anatomy of social problems explanations', *Social Problems*, 32: 214–27.

17 Using qualitative data and analysis

Reflections on organizational research

Gale Miller, Robert Dingwall and Elizabeth Murphy

There are growing demands in contemporary societies for transparent organizational governance and quality assurance based on evidence of efficiency, effectiveness, equity and civility. These demands are related to a number of practical and ideological changes affecting the structures and operations of such public and private organizations as corporations, schools, hospitals, factories, criminal justice agencies and social service agencies. The changes include the reorganization of organizational work around new technologies (particularly information technologies), implementation of re-engineering programmes in business and non-business organizations (Hammer and Champy, 1993), concern for better managing of knowledge creation and learning within organizations (Chawla and Renesch, 1995; Wenger et al., 2002), and the emergence of new management theories emphasizing the complex, paradoxical, interactive and self-organizing features of organizational processes (Stacey et al., 2000; Streatfield, 2001).

In this environment, organizational stakeholders – policy makers, planners, managers, professional staff and clients – cannot afford to ignore valid sources of information about outcomes and processes. Qualitative social scientific research is a useful – but underutilized – tool for addressing many of the problems and dilemmas facing contemporary organizational stakeholders. Perhaps the best-known contemporary example of how qualitative social scientific research may have practical organizational applications is Lave and Wenger's (1991) analysis of situated learning and communities of practice. Lave and Wenger (1991: 65) based their analysis on five qualitative studies of apprenticeships

> among Yucatec Mayan midwives in Mexico ..., among Vai and Gola tailors in Liberia ..., in the working-learning settings of U.S. navy quartermasters ..., among butchers in U.S. supermarkets ..., and among "nondrinking alcoholics" in Alcoholics Anonymous.

Wenger (1998) has extended this perspective in his study of the social organization of medical claims processing. More recently, Wenger et al. (2002) have developed the practical implications by showing how organizations (especially business organizations) might better achieve their goals by *Cultivating Communities of Practice*.

These studies build on an abundant history of theoretically informed and practically applicable qualitative organizational research in the social sciences. Classic examples include Roy's (1959) research on industrial machine operators and Dalton's (1959) work on business and industrial managers. More recent studies include Kanter's (1977) qualitative research in a multinational corporation, Lipsky's (1980) study of street-level bureaucrats, Dingwall et al.'s (1983) analysis of public agency responses to child abuse and neglect cases, Vaughan's (1983) study of corporate fraud by Revco Drug Stores, Inc. and her later (1996) examination of the organizational failures implicated in the loss of the Space Shuttle, *Challenger*.

This chapter draws general lessons from the applied contributions made by these, and other, qualitative researchers in the social sciences. It is also informed by the social scientific literature on qualitative evaluation research (for example, Patton, 2002; Shaw, 1999; Shaw and Lishman, 1999). We emphasize four related and overlapping applied contributions of qualitative research:

- Qualitative researchers' standpoints for observing and analysing organizational processes.
- The flexibility of design and focus on discovery in qualitative research.
- Qualitative social scientists' orientations to organizational complexity and holism.
- How qualitative research is used to reframe organizational problems and paradoxes.

We shall discuss each of these contributions in turn. The discussion will also identify how qualitative organizational research differs from quantitative – outcomes-oriented – research, as well as to note how they can be usefully combined. We conclude by considering how social scientifically informed qualitative research differs from other qualitative approaches to organizations, particularly in its ethic of 'fair dealing' (Dingwall, 1992).

INSIDE ORGANIZATIONAL PROCESSES

Quantitative research designs are particularly useful for examining relationships between inputs and outputs in organizational work. They can provide detailed and reliable outcome data, which, in principle at least, allow administrators, policy makers and other stakeholders to decide whether a particular action was worthwhile. However, while these studies can report the probability that action A will lead to outcome B, they are rarely able to tell us much about *how* A was transformed into B or *why* an action that proved effective in one work site was ineffective in another. Quantitative researchers are not, however, alone in these difficulties. High-level organizational officers are also frequently at a loss to answer how and why questions about organizational outcomes.

According to Brown and Duguid (2000), these problems are easily explained. Outcomes researchers and high-level officers look at organizational work processes from the outside. The outside perspective often blinds observers from seeing the importance of worker improvisations and 'local' knowledge in shaping outcomes. Brown and Duguid suggest that this is why high-level officers (and perhaps outcomes researchers) are prone to place too much faith in formal responses (such as work 're-engineering') to organizational problems.

Brown and Duguid contrast the outside perspective with the inside perspective, which focuses on the details of workers' shared organizational knowledge and their everyday actions and interactions. This is the domain of qualitative organizational research. Social scientific qualitative researchers describe and explain the social conditions under which organizational work is, and is not, done effectively. Both the descriptions and explanations answer questions about the how and why of organizational outcomes. They also often make fundamental components of organizational processes visible to outside stakeholders like regulators or other public policy agents.

A classic example is Orr's (1996) study of the practical knowledge and activities of technicians who service and repair Xerox copy machines. From the outside, the technicians' work was straightforward, if not predetermined by technological and organizational factors. The technicians were supposed to travel to the customer's office, collect information about the problem at hand (the machines were programmed to provide some of this data) and fix the machine by following instructions found in documents produced by Xerox. For Orr, however, 'how is the work supposed to be done?' proved a less interesting question than 'how do the technicians actually get the job done?' The latter question asks what goes on inside this work process.

Based on his observations of, and conversations with, the technicians, Orr discovered that copy machine service and repair is a complex, contingent and improvisational process. While their training emphasizes technical competence, effective copy machine technicians are also managers of knowledge and relationships. The technicians must build and manage effective working relationships with the machines (many of which are distinguished by their idiosyncrasies and seeming unpredictability), the customers who operate and often misuse the machines, and the larger technician community. The technician community is an important source of practical knowledge about how to respond to troublesome copy machines.

The community's knowledge is 'local' and unofficial. It is often conveyed as stories and certainly cannot be found in Xerox's technical manuals. This shared knowledge addresses the distinctive problems posed by the idiosyncrasies of individual copy machines. 'There is an assumption on the part of all participants in the service world that technicians can solve any machine problem' (Orr, 1996: 71). Thus, the problems posed by a seemingly un-repairable copy machine are treated as challenges to the collective wisdom and competence of the entire technician community.

Orr's study is ironic and perhaps debunking. It shows how the actual work of servicing and repairing copy machines requires that technicians sometimes ignore official (and authoritative) organizational instructions and procedures. Some readers might conclude that the study teaches us that the 'real' authorities on how organizational work is done are the people who do the work. We do not necessarily disagree. But, for us, the more important lesson taught by Orr's study involves the way in which the technicians' improvisations and apparent rule violations advanced the company's most important interest, effective customer service. Orr's research is a study of the social organization of *best practices* in copy machine service and repair.

This study documents how and why Xerox's copy machine service and repair programme is effective. Such information is vital to stakeholders who might contemplate changing work processes. No one can know for sure what all the consequences of a change in a work process will be: however, the chances of unintended consequences emerging increase when managers, policy makers and planners cannot see the existing process from the inside. Changes that seem small and limited when proposed and discussed may have far-reaching and unexpected consequences when implemented.

Thus, another practical use of qualitative organizational research is that it provides an inside standpoint for anticipating possible unintended con-sequences of new policies and procedures. Consider, for example, Wiener's (2000) work on quality assessment in US hospitals. One part of this reports an attempt to apply the concepts and practices of 're-engineering' and 'work redesign'. The plan promised to reduce the hospital's costs while increasing customer satisfaction, quality of care and market share. It redistributed hospital staff members' work assignments in order to reduce labour costs (by eliminating unnecessary specialist positions, such as phlebotomists), increase the efficiency of hospital staff in serving patients, and reduce unnecessary idle time for staff members.

A major unanticipated problem involved taking blood samples from patients, a job that was previously done by the phlebotomists but was now assigned to other staff. Problems with the new arrangement soon became a recurrent theme at meetings of the troubleshooting committee. The laboratory representative reported that staff were having difficulty in drawing blood. Since she no longer had a team of phlebotomists available, she was unable to offer assistance and could only advise callers to approach a doctor. 'Flexible working' had actually led to the reallocation of tasks previously carried out by relatively cheap specialized staff (phlebotomists) to more expensive doctors. Moreover, lack of skill in drawing blood led staff to use more expen-sive equipment that could more easily be operated by relatively untrained and inexperienced people. Similar problems arose in relation to cuts in respiratory-therapy staff and the reallocation of their work. Almost two years after implementation, the hospital concluded that the plan had failed to deliver on its promises.

Wiener's prolonged immersion in the setting and careful documentation of the processes involved in the emergence, design, implementation, and eventual breakdown of the redesign initiative allowed her to identify some of the factors that turned a seemingly rational and efficient organizational change into a costly, protracted and disruptive failure. She classified these factors into two major types: deficiencies in the execution of the work redesign plan and hospital managers' unrealistic assessments of the medical staff's knowledge, analytical skills and potential for administrative leadership. The latter assessments were the basis for management decisions to assign new and expanded responsibilities to nurses and other staff members. A close qualitative analysis of the medical staff's work should have flagged up the risks of disruption accompanying the proposed changes and challenged the costs of properly retraining the medical staff to meet their new responsibilities.

Qualitative research is not a panacea for administrative planning and decision making. As Brown and Duguid (2000) observe, though, organizational managers and other stakeholders need to balance the information available to them as outside observers of work processes with information obtained from inside.

DISCOVERY

Wiener's study illustrates another feature of qualitative research: its ability to deal with unanticipated factors or issues and to provide organizational stakeholders with information that they do not expect to be relevant. Qualitative study design is a flexible, iterative process, allowing qualitative researchers to respond to unanticipated opportunities that arise in the course of the research. Wiener (2000: 10) describes how a valuable source of data arose from a 'combination of the accident and sagacity that marks unstructured research'. Early in her research, while attending a conference sponsored by the Patient Care Assessment Council, an organization of quality assessment/improvement professionals, she was invited to observe future meetings of the council. These meetings proved to be a key source of data. Similarly, towards the end of her research, she discovered an online network where quality assessment/improvement professionals discussed common problems and sought or offered advice and assistance to one another. She subscribed to the network and obtained important data that allowed her to assess the generalizability of her findings to other hospital settings where similar policies were being implemented.

The evolution of Wiener's study reflects the general emphasis placed on discovery in qualitative research. Qualitative researchers approach settings or phenomena of interest without assuming that they know in advance what will turn out to be important. Qualitative research in the social sciences is an empirical orientation focused on discovering how organizational worlds are socially organized and operate. Wiener's study shows how this orientation includes a readiness to take advantage of fortuitous circumstances by developing new and unexpected sources of data. In referring to 'fortuitous circumstances', however, we do not mean to endorse the unfortunate, but common, impression that the discoveries of qualitative research are isolated and unverifiable cases. While the expectation of discovery underlies many of the methodological and analytic practices of qualitative research, these strategies also include procedures for double-checking and verifying discoveries.

Researchers use checkpoints in their designs to assess what they have discovered and to adjust their data collection and analysis in response. For example, data coding and analysis are carried out alongside data collection in qualitative research. Preliminary analysis of data guides ongoing decisions about strategies for future data collection. The design may be adjusted, for example, to test out the scope of a generalization derived from one part of the research setting by considering whether it holds under different circumstances (Dingwall et al., 1998). This approach to qualitative data collection and analysis echoes Glaser and Strauss's (1967) proposals for building grounded theory. It is often forgotten, indeed, that Glaser and Strauss included a chapter about the use of qualitative data to develop grounded applications of qualitative knowledge (see also Patton, 2002).

Qualitative researchers also use multiple research methods (including quantitative methods) and informants in collecting, double-checking and verifying their discoveries. An example is Kanter's (1977) study of Indsco, a multinational corporation. From the outset, her research goals were to produce an ethnography that would both advance the development of structural understandings of organizational behaviour and produce practical recommendations for change that would be useful to high-level corporate managers and improve the career opportunities for lower-level corporate workers and managers. Kanter reports that her findings and recommendations are based on survey data from 205 sales workers and sales managers, interviews with a variety of Indsco employees and managers, examination of corporate documents (including performance evaluations of Indsco personnel), group discussions, and participant observation of corporate meetings and training sessions. Finally, Kanter (1977: 296) notes that she double-checked her findings with

> A small group of people with whom I built close working relationships over the years. These people were largely in functions where they were well placed to see a large number of people in a large number of levels at Indsco. They could tell me as well as provide information about the issues in their own careers. I could also use them to check out stories I gathered elsewhere.

Kanter's study of Indsco shows how researchers sometimes incorporate quantitative research within qualitative studies. There are also practical benefits to including discovery-oriented qualitative components in quantitative studies of organizations. As Shaw (1999) notes, applied qualitative research is one way to balance quantitative researchers' traditional concern for rigour with a concern to do research that is relevant. But qualitative research can also enhance the rigour and credibility of quantitative research. An example is Kaplan and her colleagues' study of the impact of computerization on clinical laboratory services in a large teaching hospital (Kaplan, 1986, 1987; Kaplan and Duchon, 1988, 1989). The researchers studied the introduction of a computer system, which replaced manual systems for managing testing, and the reporting of results to clinicians, in nine laboratories.

The researchers used a combination of qualitative and quantitative methods. The quantitative measures were designed to test pre-existing theory about job characteristics and satisfaction and their relationship to reactions to the new computer system. Qualitative data were gathered from a combination of interviews, observation and open-ended questionnaire responses, carried out before, during and after the installation. The researchers compared and contrasted laboratory staff members' responses to the new computer systems in each of the nine laboratories. If the quantitative study had been carried out in isolation, the researchers would have concluded that differences in evaluation of the new system were unrelated to job characteristics. However, the qualitative study both raised doubts about the validity of these findings and suggested a means of resolution.

Revisiting the qualitative data, Kaplan was able to identify variation among the laboratory technicians, which was not reflected in the quantitative measures of job characteristics and job satisfaction. The variation did not relate to the objective nature of the work but to the ways in which the technicians understood their jobs. Kaplan and Duchon (1988: 49) described these differences:

> One group saw their jobs in terms of producing results reports, the other in terms of the laboratory bench work necessary to produce those results reports. The group who saw its job in terms of bench work was oriented towards the work of producing lab results, whereas the group who viewed its work in terms of reporting results was oriented towards the outcomes of the lab work: the members of this group saw themselves as providing a service.

This distinction became central to the subsequent analysis of both qualitative and quantitative data. The difference in work orientation was associated with different evaluations of the impact of the computer system. Those who saw their work primarily in terms of producing results tended to view the new system as having a negative impact by increasing workload and interfering with established ways of working. The others, who defined their task in terms of reporting results, were more likely to offer favourable assessments. They saw the new system as a means of improving the service they offered.

The qualitative work's flexibility allowed the researchers to discover local differences in job orientation that had more explanatory power than the quantitative indicators derived in advance from general theories. The existence of these orientations suggests different strategies for managers dealing with the consequences of the change, particularly a need to focus on the technicians' understandings of their work rather than on attitudinal measures at the point of recruitment.

HOLISM AND COMPLEXITY

The complex and contextual nature of all human activity is a central issue for organizational research. In much quantitative work, contextual factors are considered to be potentially threatening contaminants to a research design's integrity. The aim is to establish valid and reliable relationships, which by definition hold irrespective of context. Such researchers are sensitive to the difficulties posed by the complexity of the social world and the ever-present risk of spurious correlations. Their aim is, however, to nullify the context and to try to eliminate the merely situational (Stake, 1995). Mishler (1979) describes this practice as *context-stripping*.

By contrast, complexity and context are placed at the centre of qualitative social scientific research on organizations (Miller and Dingwall, 1997). Context is stressed, not stripped. Consider, for example, Bosk's (1979) study of how surgeons detect, categorize and sanction medical error by junior house staff in training. Bosk identifies several shortcomings in the way that junior staff were evaluated and held accountable, particularly the way in which medical institutions are overly reliant on surgeons' individual judgements and consciences. The credibility of his recommendations for change (and those made by other policy-oriented researchers), however, rests on his detailed ethnographic knowledge of the complex organizational settings and practices.

> Any programmatic change which intends to make professionals more accountable to clients must of necessity start with a complex phenomenological understanding of what currently passes for accountability and how it is achieved. Field research such as this informs policy by grounding it in a firm understanding of how participants construct their social worlds. It is only from this concrete understanding of the present, practical order that any changes in the existing interactional politics of social control can be negotiated. (Bosk, 1979: 6)

Bosk's emphasis on basing organizational policy on 'concrete understanding of the present, practical order' echoes our earlier discussion of inside perspectives. However, his study shows how this can also sometimes be the best place from which to see the 'big picture', in this instance possible solutions to the problem of professional governance and accountability.

Qualitative research can clarify the social, cultural and structural contexts associated with organizational problems and dilemmas. As Lipsky (1980: 193) states, 'There is a necessary and inevitable tension between the desire to have an impact in the short run, and the recognition that problems are not reducible to short-term incremental manipulations.' While the contextual clarifications provided by qualitative researchers do not always lead to easy solutions to organizational problems, the findings can stimulate stakeholder discussions about the better management of ongoing problems and dilemmas. Lipsky's (1980) study of street-level bureaucrats exemplifies such a contribution.

Another example is Vaughan's (1983) study of corporate misconduct by Revco Drug Stores, Inc. The company was found to have falsely billed the state of Ohio for prescriptions that were neither ordered by physicians nor delivered to patients. Part of Vaughan's study examined the organizational context that made it possible to commit the fraudulent acts. She showed how this related to Revco's growth and development, and the consequent leakage of authority within the company. *Authority leakage* occurs when members of upper-level management no longer know or control what is happening in organizational subunits. Vaughan explains that leakage is not in and of itself a sign of organizational problems: it is a rational response to the changing circumstances faced by successful organizations.

Vaughan's advice for stakeholders wishing to minimize the negative potential of authority leakage focuses on two general issues. First, she identifies four aspects of interorganizational transactions that create opportunities for corporate misconduct. Second, she distinguishes between widespread authority leakage in large, complex organizations and the more narrowly dispersed opportunities for illegal activity by their members. Only some organization members (two in the case of Revco) both have the necessary skills and occupy organizational positions that provide them with opportunities to engage in undetected illegalities. While Vaughan does not offer remedies to the problem of organizational misconduct, her holistic approach helps her to identify factors relevant to organizational stakeholders attempting to anticipate and respond to potential unintended consequences of organizational growth.

Marlaire's (1990) conversation analytic study of bias in educational testing is also instructive. Although controversial, the testing of children's intellectual abilities and achievement is widely practised in US schools. These tests have practical importance for teachers, school administrators and counsellors who use the scores to assign children to classes and programmes that are judged to suit their abilities. Educators rely on the findings despite substantial public debate about the tests' potential cultural biases.

Marlaire analysed video tapes and transcripts of ten educational assessments conducted by special education clinicians. Interaction between the clinicians and the children was central to the testing process: the clinicians asked questions and made statements to which the children responded. The clinicians then evaluated the children's responses as appropriate or inappropriate. Marlaire's data show that the issue of bias in testing is more complex than public debates suggest. Indeed, she concludes that bias is unavoidable in such interactions. This arises from an invisible collaboration between children and clinicians, a collaboration that is essential if they are to interact effectively.

This study illustrates how conversation analytic research investigates the present, practical order stressed by Bosk. More precisely, Marlaire shows how educational testing is complex, collaborative and contingent (Rawls, 1987). Context-stripping by both educators and their critics oversimplifies the interpretive skills displayed by both children and clinicians in testing situations. She notes, for example, that the clinicians' questions were often phrased to give the children minimal information about what might count as correct answers. 'Thus, deciphering the formula for a correct answer is no simple matter and the child must often "second guess" clinicians' intentions' (Marlaire, 1990: 254).

Although Marlaire (1990: 257) might have concluded that all testing of children's intellectual abilities should be eliminated, she acknowledges its organizational context and importance: 'Even if we were to cease using particular assessment tools . . . , we would still have the problem of how to sort and select children for appropriate program slots.' Based on this practical reality, Marlaire makes several recommendations for reorganizing educational testing interactions to assess more comprehensively the abilities displayed by children and to take better account of interactional factors affecting the children's scores.

REFRAMING

One way in which stakeholders experience organizational complexity is as practical paradoxes, which sometimes seem to be irresolvable. This is the central theme of Streatfield's (2001) book about *The Paradox of Control in Organizations*. Streatfield, a long-term corporate manager, states that his experiences have taught him that

> managers find that they have to live with the paradox of being "in control" and "not in control" simultaneously. It is this capacity to live with paradox, the courage to continue to participate creatively in spite of "not being in control" that constitutes effective management. (Streatfield 2001: 140)

The paradox of control is an example of what Ker Muir (1977) calls mutually contradictory truths. The assertions that managers are in control and not in control are contradictory, yet 'each is a premise for many decisions' (Ker Muir 1977: 283). He explains that the study of true but mutually contradictory truths is both a curse and a blessing for social scientists. It is a curse when others interpret social scientific findings and analyses as common sense and belabour the obvious. This is a frequent response when researchers assume that they must privilege one mutually contradictory truth over another. The study of mutually contradictory truths becomes a blessing, however, when social scientists focus on the social conditions under which each of the assertions is true. For example, when are managers in control and when are they not in control? This is an empirical question that can be addressed through qualitative research.

The formulation of the paradox of control as a question about differing social conditions is similar to the reframing techniques used by family therapists (Fisch et al., 1982). Family therapists base their work on the belief that family members continue to act in ways that sustain their problems because they lack alternative languages for formulating what is possible in their lives. Reframing introduces new languages for describing and orienting to problematic conditions. The problem-sustaining patterns noted by family therapists resemble the persistent public debates about bias in educational testing. As Marlaire (1990) notes, these rest on the assumption, shared by professional educators and their critics, that it is possible to have unbiased tests. She reframes the debate, and points to new options, by calling attention to the collaborative organization of testing situations.

Ker Muir's (1977) study of how twenty-eight randomly selected police officers responded to volatile police–citizen encounters is a further example of how qualitative researchers reframe organizational problems and para-doxes. He draws upon both political theory and his qualitative data in reframing police–citizen encounters as legal extortionate transactions. He explains that both legal and illegal extortionate transactions involve antag-onistic relationships in which one party (in this case, the police) explicitly or implicitly threatens to take a hostage (the citizen's liberty) if the requested ransom (citizen acquiescence with the police officer's requests or demands) is not paid.

Effective extortionate transactions (that is, the effective exercise of police authority) rest on two related conditions. The first is that citizens value the hostage sufficiently to be willing to bargain with the police to keep it. The second is that citizens are able to pay the requested ransom. 'In the absence of either hostage or ransom, the extortionate relationship will break down' (Ker Muir, 1977: 38). When the extortionate transaction breaks down, police officers and citizens are faced with a paradox having profound practical implications, not the least of which is that officers sometimes then assert control by illegal and brutal means.

Breakdown can occur in four circumstances: police encounters with very poor citizens who have few resources with which to bargain; highly emotional family disputes; crowds intent on protecting their honour and achieving their goals; and juvenile activities oriented towards proving one's manhood and/or gaining prestige within a group. Police threats of physical force and arrest take on a different significance in these situations compared with encounters that satisfy all the conditions necessary for the extortionate transaction. In volatile situations threatening behaviour increases the potential for violence and may advance the agendas of provocateurs.

Ker Muir uses his interviews with, and observations of, police officers to assess the practical effectiveness of their responses to situations where the extortionate transaction breaks down. He notes that ten of the twenty-eight officers, who he classifies as 'professional', were most effective in dealing with these situations. Although these professional officers accepted their responsibility to arrest citizens sometimes, they initially searched for other, often highly creative, solutions. One of Ker Muir's (1977: 82) interviewees describes another officer:

he'd come into a family beef with a husband and wife throwing and yelling at each other. Then he'd set down on the couch and take his hat off, and he didn't say a word. Sooner or later the couple felt kind of silly. He'd take 45 minutes in each of these situations, but he never had to come back.

Even where they believed arrest was necessary, professional officers still attempted to defuse volatile situations.

Professional officers were distinguished by their enjoyment of conversation. They liked to talk with people, both other officers and citizens. In the process, they learned about others' concerns and needs. Professional officers also recognized the importance of language in police–citizen encounters. Ker Muir describes these officers as eloquent, not because they possessed particularly extensive vocabularies or were adept at figurative language but because they were effective in using language to inform, instruct and sometimes manipulate others. Ironically, Ker Muir's observations were supported by data already collected by the police department. The department's application form included the question: 'If you had the opportunity, and if nothing of the kind existed in the community where you live, would you prefer to found (*a*) a debating society or forum; (*b*) a classical orchestra?' (Ker Muir, 1977: 231). Professional officers were overwhelmingly more likely than the other officers in his study to choose 'founding a debating society'.

Ker Muir also considered the larger organizational context of police–citizen encounters by asking, 'How did the police chief's management of the organization foster or inhibit the professional orientation to policing?' He concluded that the chief's most important contribution would be by paying greater attention to the role of sergeants. Most day-to-day work by patrol officers is invisible to high-ranking police department officials. Sergeants, on the other hand, are uniquely positioned to identify effective and ineffective patrol officers, as well as to teach the conversational techniques used by professional officers. Ker Muir makes several suggestions about how the police department might increase the professionalism of sergeants and, by extension, the professionalism of patrol officers.

This study shows how social scientific perspectives and questions offer alternative languages for describing problematic situations and for seeing new responses. The focus on language is more than a theoretical exercise. Ker Muir begins from systematic and credible qualitative data that he uses to identify officers who are effective in managing difficult encounters with citizens. His skill lies in specifying just what it is that makes these officers different from their peers and in reformulating this in ways that make their skills portable, generalizable and teachable. Police sergeants can be offered these general descriptions and then encouraged to develop them through practical instruction, translating them back into the here and now of everyday work.

However, these generalized accounts also make the lessons of policing available to others who have to negotiate with difficult citizens – other emergency workers, for example. The same skills may be of value to fire crews attempting to extinguish fires that citizens are happy to see burn or to paramedics trying to evacuate injured people from tense crowds or riots. They may also be useful to people like reception desk clerks who have to control queues in stressful environments such as airline check-ins. Finally, Ker Muir's data and analysis should be of interest to the corporate managers to whom Streatfield's (2001) book is directed. The professional officers in Ker Muir's study illustrate one way that managers might guide and shape situations in which they see themselves as not in control.

CONCLUSION

This chapter has examined the contributions that qualitative research based in the social sciences can make to informing debates among organizational stakeholders about the most efficient, effective, equitable and humane means of achieving their various goals. Whether in private or public sector organizations, the prevailing expectation in contemporary societies is that these debates will take place in a rational and transparent fashion meeting legally imposed standards of corporate governance. Qualitative research has a particular part to play in exploring issues of process, in explaining how outcomes are achieved – or not, as the case may be. Although stakeholders retain responsibility for the outcomes that reflect the balance of their interests and bargaining strengths, qualitative evidence may help them to see new strategies and possibilities for conciliation that advance their goals.

Many different people do qualitative research in organizations for many different reasons. Kunda (1992) discusses the relationship between Lyndsville (a high-tech corporation that he studied) and 'tech watchers'. The latter include various academic researchers, consultants, journalists and other organizational outsiders who regularly observe and comment on aspects of Lyndsville. Kunda (1992: 254) explains that it is not possible clearly to differentiate between different kinds of tech watchers.

> Published scholarly work of the "applied" sort resembles the popular genre, and journalists often cite the popular literature in lieu of their own brand of research and theory. Consequently, these forms of observation, analysis and reporting do not always fall into distinct categories, but belong on a continuum.

In a conversation with GM, a management consultant remarked that she found it useful to spend a few days observing in the organizations that hired her. At the very least, these observations usually revealed occasions when organization members, at all levels, routinely used their time in inefficient ways.

There is, then, a sense in which the applied skills and services of the consultant and of the social scientific qualitative researcher are similar. But they are not identical. Clearly, most social scientific qualitative research in organizations involves more than spending a few days talking with organization members and observing their actions and interactions. Social scientists are more likely than other qualitative researchers to immerse themselves in the organizations that they study by doing in-depth interviews with members, carefully examining relevant records, and making extensive observations of members' activities and/or audio or video recordings of meetings, events or routine practice. They also bring distinctive background knowledge from their reading of previous research reports or of theoretical literature that seeks to generalize from an array of particular findings.

Roy's (1959) analysis of the social organization of time in a machine shop points to a related difference between social scientific and other qualitative approaches to organizations. The primary purpose of social scientific qualitative research is to understand how organizations work rather than to expose malpractice or to advise some stakeholders on how to achieve their preferred goals at the expense of others. In the process of understanding, of course, important information may be uncovered relevant to either of these objectives. Social scientists also tend to be more concerned with the general than with the specific: even where the research only involves a single organization, this is typically seen as a case study that stands for a class of organizations, whether already documented in the literature or to be documented by future studies.

However, the biggest difference lies in social scientists' governing ethic. Dingwall (1992) proposed that this could be described as 'fair dealing', the notion that the researcher's role is not to sit in judgement but to represent as dispassionately as possible the contribution of each participant to the production of the setting that is being studied. The resulting analysis may be a source for moral outrage but it should not be a vehicle for this: effective reform demands an understanding of how morally outrageous things come to happen, which is rarely the result of deliberate wickedness at all levels. We see a concern for this aspect of fair dealing in virtually all of the qualitative studies discussed in this chapter.

This chapter has added another dimension to Dingwall's (1992) initial conceptualization of qualitative research as fair dealing. We have called the additional dimension 'best practices' to highlight qualitative researchers' distinctive vantage point for observing how solutions to organizational problems are often already evident in the everyday practices of organization members. Ker Muir's (1977) discussion of the distinctive orientations and practices of professional police officers is an example of how qualitative researchers can identify best practices hidden by dominant problematic patterns, effective work within a troubled environment. Orr's (1996) study of copy machine technicians, on the other hand, shows how qualitative research can reveal widespread (but officially unrecognized and discouraged) best practices developed by organization members in order to achieve organizational goals.

Fair dealing in qualitative organizational research involves dispassionately analysing how organization members contribute to the production of efficient, effective, equitable and humane work processes and relationships as well as how they contribute to undesired organizational outcomes. It is important that organizational stakeholders receive both messages from qualitative researchers.

Recommended reading

Renée R. Anspach (1993) *Deciding Who Lives: Fateful Choices in the Intensive-Care Nursery*. Berkeley, CA: University of California Press.
Anspach uses observational data to analyse how life and death decisions are made in intensive-care units for newborn infants. She emphasizes the social organization of decision making in the units (including the structural obstacles that parents faced in participating in the decision making) and how decision makers' decisions are shaped by their location within the structure of the intensive-care unit. Anspach's analysis raises a number of practical ethical questions about how life and death decisions are made and identifies several paradoxes in public policies relating to such decision making.

Diane Vaughan (1996) *The Challenger Launch Decision: Risky Technology, Culture, and Deviance at NASA*. Chicago: University of Chicago Press.
This is an historical ethnography of the Space Shuttle *Challenger* disaster of 28 January 1986. The practical circumstances of the research dictated that Vaughan begin with detailed analyses of documents about the disaster; later she augmented the documentary data with interviews. Vaughan describes her study as a contribution to the sociology of mistakes because it focuses on how this and other organizational mistakes are socially organized and produced through organizational structures.

Deirdre Boden (1994) *The Business of Talk: Organizations in Action*. Cambridge: Polity Press.
While Boden's study is primarily intended as a contribution to organizational theory, she does discuss some of the practical implications of the study at the end of the book. Most importantly she shows how ethnomethodological and conversation analysis of organizational interactions (in this case meetings) can be useful in identifying the interactional and managerial skills that are needed in flexible, changing and 'information-rich' organizational environments.

Ian Shaw (1999) *Qualitative Evaluation*. London: Sage.
This is a very useful overview of many of the most important issues surrounding qualitative evaluation research today. Shaw gives serious attention to theoretical and philosophical issues associated with qualitative evaluation as well as to the concrete methods used by qualitative evaluation researchers.

REFERENCES

Bosk, Charles L. (1979) *Forgive and Remember: Managing Medical Failure*. Chicago: University of Chicago Press.

Brown, John Seely and Paul Duguid (2000) *The Social Life of Information*. Boston: Harvard Business School Press.

Chawla, Sarita and John Renesch (1995) *Learning Organizations: Developing Cultures for Tomorrow's Workplace*. Portland, OR: Productivity Press.

Dalton, Melville (1959) *Men Who Manage: Fusions of Feeling and Theory in Administration*. New York: John Wiley & Sons.

Dingwall, Robert (1992) 'Don't mind him – he's from Barcelona: qualitative methods in health studies', pp. 161–75 in Jeanne Daly, Ian McDonald and Evan Willis (eds), *Researching Health Care*. London: Routledge.

Dingwall, Robert, John Eekelaar and Topsy Murray (1983) *The Protection of Children: State Intervention and Family Life*. Oxford: Basil Blackwell.

Dingwall, Robert, Elizabeth Murphy, Pamela Watson, David Greatbatch and Susan Parker (1998) 'Catching Goldfish: Quality in Qualitative Research', *Journal of Health Services Research and Policy*, 3: 167–72.

Fisch, Richard, John H. Weakland and Lynn Segal (1982) *The Tactics of Change: Doing Therapy Briefly*. San Francisco: Jossey-Bass.

Glaser, Barney G. and Anselm L. Strauss (1967) *The Discovery of Grounded Theory: Strategies for Qualitative Research*. Chicago: Aldine.

Hammer, Michael and James Champy (1993) *Reengineering the Corporation: A Manifesto for Business Revolution*. New York: HarperBusiness.

Kanter, Rosabeth Moss (1977) *Men and Women of the Corporation*. New York: Basic Books.

Kaplan, Bonnie (1986) 'Impact of a Clinical Laboratory Computer System: Users' Perceptions', pp. 1057–61 in B. Blum and M. Jorgensen (eds), *Medinfo 86: Fifth World Congress on Medical Informatics*. Amsterdam: North-Holland.

—— (1987) 'Initial Impact of a Clinical Laboratory Computer System: Themes Common to Expectations and Actualities', *Journal of Medical Systems*, 11: 37–47.

Kaplan, Bonnie and Dennis Duchon (1988) 'Combining Qualitative and Quantitative Methods in Information Systems Research: A Case Study', *MIS Quarterly*, 12: 571–86.

—— (1989) 'A Job Orientation Model of Impact on Work Seven Months Post Implementation', pp. 1051–5 in B. Barber, D. Cao, D. Quin and G. Wagner (eds), *Medinfo 89: Sixth World Congress on Medical Informatics*. Amsterdam: North-Holland.

Ker Muir, Jr, William (1977) *Police: Streetcorner Politicians*. Chicago: University of Chicago Press.

Kunda, Gideon (1992) *Engineering Culture: Control and Commitment in a High-Tech Corporation*. Philadelphia: Temple University Press.

Lave, Jean and Etienne Wenger (1991) *Situated Learning: Legitimate Peripheral Participation*. Cambridge: Cambridge University Press.

Lipsky, Michael (1980) *Street-Level Bureaucracy: Dilemmas of the Individual in Public Services*. New York: Russell Sage Foundation.

Marlaire, Courtney L. (1990) 'On Questions, Communication, and Bias: Educational Testing as "Invisible" Collaboration', pp. 233–60 in Gale Miller and James A. Holstein (eds), *Perspectives on Social Problems: A Research Annual*, Vol. 2. Greenwich, CT: JAI Press.

Miller, Gale and Robert Dingwall (eds) (1997) *Context and Method in Qualitative Research*. London: Sage.

Mishler, Elliot G. (1979) 'Meaning in context: Is there any other kind?', *Harvard Educational Review*, 49: 1–19.

Orr, Julian E. (1996) *Talking About Machines: An Ethnography of a Modern Job*. Ithaca, NY: Cornell University Press.

Patton, Michael Quinn (2002) *Qualitative Research & Evaluation Methods*. Beverly Hills, CA: Sage.

Rawls, Ann (1987) 'The Interaction Order Sui Generis: Goffman's Contribution to Social Theory', *Sociological Theory* 5: 136–49.

Roy, Donald F. (1959) '"Banana Time": Job Satisfaction and Informal Interaction', *Human Organization*, 18: 158–68.

Shaw, Ian (1999) *Qualitative Evaluation*. London: Sage.

Shaw, Ian and Joyce Lishman (eds) (1999) *Evaluation and Social Work Practice*. London: Sage.

Stacey, Ralph D., Douglas Griffin and Patricia Shaw (2000) *Complexity and Management: Fad or Radical Challenge to Systems Thinking?*. London: Routledge.

Stake, Robert E. (1995) *The Art of Case Study Research*. Thousand Oaks, CA: Sage.

Streatfield, Philip J. (2001) *The Paradox of Control in Organizations*. London: Routledge.

Vaughan, Diane (1983) *Controlling Unlawful Behavior: Social Structure and Corporate Misconduct*. Chicago: University of Chicago Press.

—— (1996) *The Challenger Launch Decisions: Risky Technology, Culture, and Deviance at NASA*. Chicago: University of Chicago Press.

Wenger, Etienne (1998) *Communities of Practice: Learning, Meaning, and Identity*. Cambridge: Cambridge University Press.

Wenger, Etienne, Richard McDermott and William M. Snyder (2002) *Cultivating Communities of Practice: A Guide to Managing Knowledge*. Boston: Harvard Business School Press.

Wiener, Carolyn (2000) *The Elusive Quest: Accountability in Hospitals*. Hawthorne, NY: Aldine de Gruyter.

Part IX Postscript

18 Who cares about 'experience'?
Missing issues in qualitative research*

David Silverman

We know too much about people in these days; we hear too much. Our ears, our minds, our mouths are stuffed with personalities. (Henry James, *The Portrait of a Lady*, 218)

Isabel found it difficult to think of Madame Merle as an isolated figure; she existed only in her relations with her fellow-mortals. . . . Madame Merle was not superficial – not she. She was deep; and her nature spoke none the less in her behaviour because it spoke a conventional language. 'What is language at all but a convention?' said Isabel. 'She has the good taste not to pretend, like some people I have met to express herself by original signs. (ibid.: 167)

What is qualitative research? Given the disparate nature of the topic, how are we to answer such a question? Rather than add to the unending textbook debates, this chapter will focus on one feature where there appears to be a consensus. Using examples drawn from ethnographic work on organizations, I will then show why I disagree with this consensus and offer a reasoned alternative drawing upon the neglected work of Harvey Sacks (Sacks, 1992; Silverman, 1998; Baker, this volume).

The consensual position is well set out in a recent authoritative work. The Editorial Introduction to the Second Edition of *The Handbook of Qualitative Research* puts it this way:

Both qualitative and quantitative researchers are concerned with the individual's point of view. However, qualitative investigators think they can get closer to the actor's perspective through detailed interviewing and observation. They argue that quantitative researchers are seldom able to capture their subjects' perspectives because they have to rely on more remote, inferential empirical methods and materials. (Denzin and Lincoln, 2000: 10)

Denzin and Lincoln's portrayal of what qualitative researchers 'think they can [do]' (above quotation) is a deadly accurate characterization of much contemporary qualitative research. It appears to differentiate us beautifully from those benighted number-crunchers whose concern for mere 'facts' precludes a proper understanding of what Denzin and Lincoln call 'the actor's perspective'. By contrast, our research concerns itself with '[the] perspectives of the participants and their diversity' (Flick, 1998: 27) and attempts 'to document the world from the point of view of the people studied' (Hammersley, 1989: 165). When we study entities like organizations, then, the key question is: 'How to get at and document the lived experience of organizational members?' (Eberle and Maeder, 2002).

This attention to the 'perspective', 'point of view' and 'lived experience' of the people we study reveals a rarely challenged consensus about the nature of our enterprise and its analytical targets. Although, as Flick points out (1998: 17), it is often associated with the symbolic interactionist tradition, it extends itself much more generally throughout qualitative research.

For instance, within most organizational ethnography, 'experience' is the prized object. As Aldrich suggests:

the various interpretive views have in common their focus on an actor's perspective on life in organizations. (Aldrich, 1992: 23)

Yet what Aldrich calls 'the actor's perspective' is a very slippery notion as his intellectual ancestor, Max Weber (1949), was well aware. For instance, it is by no means clear how such 'perspectives' relate to our actions. Indeed, is there a 'point of view' or 'perspective' lying behind every act?

Most qualitative researchers who champion the subject's point of view or privilege experience simply do not question where the subject's 'viewpoint' comes from or how 'experience' gets defined the way it does by those very individuals whose experience we seek to document. Do these not emerge, in some way or other, from the varied contexts out of which we 'draw from experience' to convey accounts of who and what we are?

A telling example is provided in an anecdote about one of Jay Gubrium's doctoral students (Gubrium and Holstein, 2002: 21–2). The student interviewed pharmacists who had engaged in substance abuse. His aim was to understand how those who 'should know better' accounted for what had happened to them. As it turned out, what these pharmacists said closely fitted the familiar recovery rubric of self-help groups. Indeed, many had attended groups like Alcoholics Anonymous (AA) and Narcotics Anonymous (NA). So in what sense were these accounts the pharmacists' 'own' stories? As Gubrium pointed out, do these stories not 'belong' less to individuals than to particular organizational discourses which are merely 'voiced' here?

By contrast, a concentration on 'lived experience' (rather than 'voices') can lead to an essentialist, 'romantic' conception of inner meaning (Silverman, 1989). We can see this romanticism at work in Aldrich's references to:

> the *expressive* side of participation (which) is as important as the task-related side, as organizations do not operate solely on the basis of a rational economic model. (Aldrich, 1992: 25, my emphasis)

We might ask Aldrich: why are 'task-related' activities necessarily moulded according to an economic model; why do we have to assume that activities are guided either by a 'rational' logic or a logic of sentiment? Does this not return us to the 1930s and the Hawthorne studies?[1]

Two examples of organizational ethnographies will serve to illustrate my point.[2] Hassard (1993) calls his study of a fire station an 'interpretive ethnography'. His data 'involved accompanying firefighters during the working day and asking them to explain their activities before, during and after each event' (1993: 99). Hassard claims that this represents an 'ethnomethodological' stance (98) which:

> portrays the everyday work of a fire station in terms of how firefighters make sense of and enact the task system. (101)

Yet his use of interviews, analysed in terms of 'recurrent theme(s)' (100), hardly challenges the consensus I have outlined since it fully concurs with the latter's focus on how people 'view' or 'experience' the social world.

Linstead and Thomas's (2002) use of a 'poststructuralist feminist reading' to define their research on middle managers might seem to threaten the consensus more effectively. Yet, as it turns out, like Hassard, in this study interviews are used and analysed in terms of themes.

In both my examples, apparently non-orthodox positions happily fall within the consensus. Although ethnomethodology, poststructuralism and feminism would appear to have little in common with qualitative research's symbolic interactionist roots, here they do, sanctified by the siren call of 'lived experience'.[3] The roots of such a stubborn consensus surely extend beyond social science theories and say something about the world around us. One inescapable fact about the cultural milieu of the Western world is that 'lived experience' must be pursued and interrogated. One aspect of this is seen in the work of the 'psy' professions, notably in the methods of the skilled counsellor (see Peräkylä, 1995).

Of course, not everybody visits a counsellor or psychiatrist. But many of us avidly watch 'reality' television shows, soaps and chat shows in which people's 'experience' is very much the target (see Atkinson and Silverman, 1997). TV news programmes also increasingly cater to our demand to get inside people's heads. Take the example below, garnered more or less at random:

> Mother 'relieved' at son's release from Camp X-Ray. (BBC TV teletext headline)

You might say: how on earth can a mother be anything other than relieved by her son's release from internment? Surely, it would only be newsworthy if such a mother wanted her son to stay in Camp X-Ray and was upset by his release?

Yet our media (and, to be fair, most of us) demand such snippets of apparently 'lived experience'. The fact that they turn out to be entirely predictable seems to be of no account. Indeed, it is demanded of us all that we should have the appropriate response. Think, for instance, how successful athletes so often tell interviewers that 'it has not sunk in yet'. After all, they need to be seen like we perceive ourselves, as decent people, surprised by good fortune.

Rarely does the absurdity of these kind of responses sink in. For instance, after the rescue of some men from a recent mine disaster in the USA, a TV interviewer asked a mine official:

> Int: How did people feel after the men were released?
> Official: Actually I was too busy talking to people like you.
>
> (US TV report)

This is a rare example of an interviewee refusing to play the Experience Game. The mine official shows us that this kind of feelings discourse is a product of media demands.

Occasions like mine accidents and murders (particularly of children) are marvellous grist to the media mill. Referring to the reporting of the immediate aftermath to the murder in Soham, England, of two young girls, a critic wrote:

> How do you feel about the abduction and murder of those two ten-year-old girls? Come on, how do you really feel? Yes, you're right, it's a crassly stupid, pointless and insensitive question. So why have much of the media spent the past fortnight demanding answers to that and similar questions from everybody in Soham and beyond? (Hume, 2002)

Mick Hume's questions should equally be posed to researchers who are tempted by the lure of 'experience'. Perhaps, as Henry James suggested more than a century ago, in the words of his character Ralph Touchett, 'we know too much about people in these days'? (The full quotation is given at the start of this chapter.) Put at its starkest, must qualitative research privilege 'experience' and 'feelings' when, in so doing, it is responding to the same imperatives as a soap opera or a therapy session?

There is, of course, an obvious response to my rhetorical question: not necessarily. Let us take one example of an organizational ethnography which dispenses with interviews and makes no Aldrich-like distinction between task and expressive organization.

Zimmerman (1992) was concerned with the interactional organization of the talk occurring in calls to US 911 emergency telephone numbers operated by the emergency services. His research was based on data from three centres (one in the Mid-West, two on the West Coast). His study focused on calls to two of the centres which have a computer-assisted dispatch system (CAD).

At all times, call-takers (CTs) have to attend to callers' (Cs) talk in terms of what is reportable via the CAD codes. This means that response tokens from the CT are often replaced by the sound of the computer keyboard. CTs must also orient both to what Cs are saying and to what they are *about* to say. Hence they may defer initiating enquiries if their monitoring of the C's talk suggests the upcoming delivery of a piece of pertinent information. Some of these kinds of organizational 'solutions' are oriented to by Cs.

So, here, unlike other telephone calls, the opening sequence does not routinely contain a greeting or a 'how are you?' sequence. Both parties typically seek to reach the 'reason for the call' sequence as soon as possible.

We see these features in Extract 1 below, where a caller is reporting an incident:

```
1   ([kb=sound of keyboard being used)
C:  hhh Uh there's uh (0.2) oh I think it's uh (.) white jeep
    (.) hh jeepster tha[t pulled up here uh in front.
                       [kb - - - - - - - - - - - - - - - -
C:  =An there's about (0.1)] five Nihgro guys tha' got out, I
    - - - - - - - - - - - - - ]
    heard=um tal[kin about (0.1) hh going (.) to thee] next
               [- - - - - - - - - - - - - - - - - - - - -]
    apartment building uh fur uh fight (0.2) [hh a]n I jus'
                                             [- - -]
    am going down tuh check it out
```
                                                (Zimmerman, 1992: 4)

Zimmerman notes about this extract:

> At the possible conclusion of C's account of the trouble . . . (on line 8) CT [the call-taker] says nothing while she continues her keyboard activity. After a pause of 0.2 second, C initiates (an) elaboration . . . which, in the absence of a receipt of acknowledgment from CT, may be oriented to the possibility of some problem with his narrative. (1992: 427)

This absence of response tokens, one expected feature of hearers' activities when not taking a turn at any given possible turn-transition point in ordinary conversation, has observable consequences in these calls. As Zimmerman suggests, the absence of such a response token may be heard by C as indicating a trouble in the report. Thus it can lead to hedges and downgrades. These are seen less than ten lines later (data not shown), when C hedges, stating that 'it might not be anything'.

Zimmerman's approach to the use of a computer-assisted technology reveals how a particular task-structure is enacted. Without using interviews, he is able to show us in real time how people communicate and make decisions (see the chapters by Heritage and Potter in this volume). Put another way, unlike Aldrich (and the Hawthorne researchers) who place human beings and machines in two different boxes, Zimmerman shows us how machines come to have a presence in human interaction (see also Heath's chapter in this volume and Heath and Luff, 2000).

Of course, Zimmerman's study did not emerge out of a clear blue sky. Several decades ago, the pioneering work of Harvey Sacks set out the template for a new model of qualitative research. I will now, therefore, provide a taste of what Sacks has to offer (for a book-length introduction, see Silverman, 1998). Throughout, I will attempt to show you that Sacks is more than the founder of what you may take to be a sect ('just one of those ethnos') but has much to teach researchers who will never want to do conversation analysis or ethnomethodology. In this spirit, let us look at Sacks's insistence that 'activities are observable' and contrast it with ethnographers who privilege 'experience'.

ACTIVITIES ARE OBSERVABLE

As I have already noted, a popular activity in everyday life is to wonder about people's motives. Indeed, in the case of talk shows, the motives of the rich, famous or just plain unlucky or deviant become a central topic. Yet, in many respects, social science has picked up this habit, taking as its task the revelation of other people's 'motives' and 'experiences'.

Even in the 1960s, Sacks seemed fully aware of these issues. His kind of social science always turned away from the insides of people's heads and towards their observable activities. Like Madame Merle, as viewed by Henry James's Isobel Archer (see quotation at the start of this chapter), Sacks saw that we exist in our relations with others and express ourselves through a conventional language. In this sense, Sacks was a self-proclaimed behaviourist who announced that his task was to elucidate how people did whatever they did. As he put it:

> For Members, activities are observables. They see activities. They see persons doing intimacy, they see persons lying, etc. . . . And that poses for us the task of being *behaviourists* in this sense: finding how it is that people can produce sets of actions that provide that others can see such things. (Sacks, 1992, Vol. 1: 119)

As examples of such 'sets of actions', Sacks offers 'describing' and 'questioning'. These are interesting activities because each may be seen as a *resource* for social scientists, e.g. ethnographers 'describe' cultures and 'question' informants. However, Sacks wants to make both activities a *topic* by examining them as forms of behaviour which, through some methods awaiting inspection, are produced and recognized.

It follows that how societal members (including social researchers) 'see' particular activities is, for Sacks, the central research question. In this respect, together with Garfinkel (1967), he offers a unique perspective in social science which 'seeks to describe methods persons use in doing social life' (Sacks, 1984: 21).

When researchers 'describe' and 'question', very often they are tacitly using members' methods. If we are to study such methods, it is, therefore, crucial that we do not take for granted what it is we appear to be 'seeing'. As Sacks says:

> In setting up what it is that seems to have happened, preparatory to solving the [research] problem, do not let your notion of what could conceivably happen decide for you what must have happened. (115)

Here Sacks is telling us that our 'notion of what could conceivably happen' is likely to be drawn from our unexamined members' knowledge. Instead, we need to proceed more cautiously by examining the methods members use to produce activities as observable and reportable. Let us see what Sacks meant by looking at his study of an organization.

In his very first transcribed lecture, given in Fall 1964, Sacks begins with data from his PhD dissertation on telephone conversations collected at an emergency psychiatric hospital. In the following two extracts, A is a member of staff at the hospital and B can be somebody either calling about themselves or calling about somebody else.

```
1
A:  Hello
B:  Hello
```
                                                          (Sacks, 1: 3)

```
2
A:  This is Mr Smith may I help you
B:  Yes, this is Mr Brown
```
                                                          (Sacks, 1: 3)

Sacks makes two initial observations about these extracts. First, B seems to tailor his utterance to the format provided by A's first turn. So, in Extract 1, we get an exchange of 'hellos' and, in Extract 2, an exchange of names. Or, as Sacks puts it, we might say that there is a 'procedural rule' where

> a person who speaks first in a telephone conversation can choose their form of address, and . . . thereby choose the form of address the other uses. (1: 4)

Sacks's second observation is that each part or turn of the exchange occurs as part of a pair (e.g. Hello–Hello). Each pair of turns may be called a 'unit' in which the first turn constitutes a 'slot' for the second and sets up an expectation about what this slot may properly contain. Given this expectation, A is usually able to extract B's name (as in Extract 2) without ever having to ask for it directly. The beauty of this, as Sacks points out, is that it avoids a problem that a direct question might create. For instance, if you ask someone their name, they may properly ask 'Why?' and, in this way, require that you offer a proper warrant for asking (1: 4–5). By contrast, providing a slot for a name cannot be made accountable. So to answer a phone with your name has a function in institutions where obtaining callers' names is important (1: 5–6).

Of course, the fact that something may properly happen once a slot has been created does not mean that it *will* happen. Take this further example cited by Sacks:

3
A: This is Mr Smith may I help you
B: I can't hear you
A: This is Mr <u>Smith</u>
B: Smith.

(1: 3)

Sacks's two procedural rules do not mean that speakers are automatons. What seems to happen in Extract 3 is that B's reply 'I can't hear you' means that the slot for the other party to give their name is missed. This does not mean that their name is 'absent' but rather that the place where it might go is closed. As Sacks puts it:

> It is not simply that the caller ignores what they properly ought to do, but something rather more exquisite. That is, they have ways of providing that the place where the return name fits is never opened. (1: 7)

Put at its simplest, researchers must be very careful how they use categories. For instance, Sacks quotes from two linguists who appear to have no problem in characterizing particular (invented) utterances as 'simple', 'complex', 'casual' or 'ceremonial'. For Sacks, such rapid characterizations of data assume

> that we can know that without an analysis of what it is (they) are doing. (1: 429)

Such an analysis needs to locate particular utterances in sequences of talk (1: 430 and 622). So an ethnographer who reports that (s)he heard someone tell a 'story' only raises a further question: how the ethnographer (and presumably the members of the group studied) heard an activity as a 'story'.

THE COMMENTATOR MACHINE

Through Sacks, let us now look more closely at how ethnographers use informants to support their findings, for instance in interview studies or by means of 'respondent validation'. By doing so, Sacks suggests that they treat people's ability to give and receive 'sensible' descriptions in different contexts as entirely non-remarkable. As he puts it:

> The essential 'message' of this paper is: even if it can be said that persons produce descriptions of the social world, the task of sociology is not to clarify these, or to 'get them on the record' or to criticize them, but to describe them. (Sacks, 1963: 7)

Sacks's (1963) paper is rightly famous for the example of a machine with its own built-in commentator. He tells us that this hypothetical machine might be described by the layman in the following terms:

> It has two parts; one part is engaged in doing some job, and the other part synchronically narrates what the first part does. . . . For the commonsense perspective the machine might be called a 'commentator machine', its parts 'the doing' and 'the saying' parts. (5)

For a native-speaking ethnographer, the 'saying' part of the machine is to be analysed as a good, poor or ironical description of the actual working of the machine (5–6). However, Sacks points out this sociological explanation trades off two kinds of unexplicated knowledge:

(a)   knowing in common with the machine the language it emits
      and
(b)   knowing in some language what the machine is doing. (6)

But to know 'what the machine is doing' ultimately depends upon a set of pre-scientific, commonsense assumptions based on everyday language and employed to sort 'facts' from 'fancy'. It follows that our ability to 'describe social life', whether as lay people or sociologists, 'is a happening' which should properly be the 'job of sociology' (7) to describe rather than tacitly to use.

Sacks's insistence on the priority of describing the everyday 'procedure employed for assembling cases of the class' radically separates his position both from Durkheim *and* from romantic ethnographers.

Despite their apparent differences, both Durkheim and Goffman take for granted some social 'reality' to which people respond (e.g. 'suicide') or describe a process (e.g. 'labelling') identified on the basis of tacit commonsense reasoning. Their common failing is, as Sacks puts it, that they work with 'undescribed categories':

> To employ an undescribed category is to write descriptions such as appear in children's books. Interspersed with series of words there are pictures of objects.

For Sacks, most sociologists get by through simply 'pointing' at familiar objects (what philosophers call 'ostensive' definition). So they are able to give an account of what Sacks's 'commentator machine' is 'doing' by invoking 'what everybody knows' about how things are in society – using what Garfinkel (1967) refers to as the 'etcetera principle'. They thus pretend to offer a 'literal' description of phenomena which conceals their 'neglect [of] some undetermined set of their features' (13).

Moreover, such neglect cannot be remedied, as some researchers claim, by assembling panels of judges to see if they see the same thing (e.g. inter-coder agreement as a basis for claiming that one's descriptions of data are reliable). Such agreement offers no solution because it simply raises further questions about the *ability* of members of society to see things in common – presumably by using the 'etcetera' principle as a tacit resource (see Clavarino et al., 1995).

Sacks's problem is how we can build a social science that does better than this. In some way, we must free ourselves from the 'common-sense perspective' (10–11) employed in our use of 'undescribed categories'. For Sacks, the solution is to view such categories 'as features of social life which sociology must treat as subject matter' rather than 'as sociological resources' (16).

What looks like a complicated theoretical solution turns out, however, to involve a quite straightforward direction for research. We must give up defining social phenomena at the outset (like Durkheim) or through the accounts that subjects give of their behaviour (Sacks's 'commentator machine'). Instead, we must simply focus on what people *do*. As Sacks puts it:

> whatever humans do can be examined to discover some way they do it, and that way would be describable. (1992, 1: 484)

We now see why Sacks should have referred to sociology's 'peculiar stance'. Quite properly, he suggests, sociology seeks to be a science. In doing so, it needs to seek a 'literal' description of its subject matter. However, this search is undercut, in Sacks's view, by sociology's use of concepts ('a descriptive apparatus') based on unexplicated assumptions (1963: 2).

By contrast, Sacks asks us to make this descriptive apparatus our topic. For:

> whatever humans do can be examined to discover some way they do it, and that way would be describable. (1992, 1: 484)

Sacks concedes that this kind of research can seem to be 'enormously laborious' (1: 65). However, he denies critics' claims that it is trivial. You only need to look at the ability of both lay persons and conventional researchers consistently to find recognizable meaning in situations to realize that social order is to be found in even the tiniest activity. The accomplishment of this 'order at all points' (1: 484) thus constitutes the exciting new topic for social research.

Beginning with the observability of 'order at all points', our first task should be to inspect the

> collections of social objects – like 'How are you feeling?' – which persons assemble to do their activities. And how they assemble those activities is describable with respect to any one of them they happen to do. (1: 27)

This version of our research task clearly sets Sacks apart from most qualitative researchers. However, despite his radical perspective, Sacks was too sophisticated a thinker to believe that any approach, including his own, could learn nothing from its predecessors. Let us now consider what Sacks believed we can still learn from more conventional forms of ethnography.

THE VALUE (AND LIMITS) OF ETHNOGRAPHY

Sacks's lectures make many favourable references to the tradition of ethnographic work that originated in the 1930s in the Sociology Department of the University of Chicago. This work represented the first flowering of an empirical school of sociology concerned with observing what it termed the 'subcultures' to be found in the buildings and the streets of the modern city (see Hammersley, 1989).

Despite taking a different theoretical tack, Sacks found much to admire in the Chicago School's attention to detail. As he comments:

> Instead of pushing aside the older ethnographic work in sociology, I would treat it as the only work worth criticizing in sociology; where criticizing is giving some dignity to something. So, for example, the relevance of the works of the Chicago sociologists is that they do contain a lot of information about this and that. And this-and-that is what the world is made up of. (1992, 1: 27)

Like the older ethnographers, Sacks rejected the crass empiricism of certain kinds of quantitative sociology. In particular, as we have seen, its assumptions that research is based on finding some indices and explaining why they rise and fall by *ex post facto* interpretations of significant correlations.

Sacks had taken courses with Erving Goffman at Berkeley in the early 1960s and found much to admire in his work. Unlike Bales, who mainly used laboratory data, Goffman was interested in the complexities of naturally occurring behaviour. Unlike Homans, he did not want to 'correct' everyday understandings but to show the complex way in which they functioned. In fact, Goffman cites as his intellectual ancestor the German sociologist Georg Simmel, commending his penetrating analyses of the 'forms' of social interaction.

So Goffman's work was important to Sacks. Like Goffman, Sacks took Simmel's work very seriously, referring to him as 'one of the greatest of all sociologists' (Sacks, 1992, Vol. 2: 132). Like Goffman, Sacks had no interest in building data-free grand theories or in research methods, like laboratory studies or even interviews, which abstracted people from everyday contexts. Above all, both men marvelled at the everyday skills through which particular appearances are maintained.

We can catch sight of Sacks's use of Goffman's ideas in his paper 'Notes on Police Assessment of Moral Character' (Sacks, 1972) which was originally written as a course paper for Goffman's course at Berkeley in the early 1960s (Sacks, 1972: 280n.). For Sacks, police officers face the same kind of problem as Goffman's Shetland Islanders (see Goffman, 1959): how are they to infer moral character from potentially misleading appearances?

To solve this problem, police 'learn to treat their beat as a territory of normal appearances' (Sacks, 1972: 284). Now they can treat slight variations in normal appearances as 'incongruities' worthy of investigation, working with the assumption of the appearances of 'normal' crimes (cf. Sudnow, 1965).

Sacks's point of departure from Goffman can be seen if we compare their work on ceremonial orders. Although parts of Sacks's early lectures draw directly from Goffman, it soon becomes clear that Sacks wants to understand 'ceremony' not by reference to concepts like 'impression management' or 'frames' but to the sequential analysis of conversations (see Heritage, this volume).

For instance, we know that the proper return to 'how are you feeling?' is 'fine'. This means that if you want to treat it as a question about your feelings you have to request permission (e.g. by saying 'it's a long story' where the next party may say 'that's alright, I have time'). This means that 'everyone has to lie' because people attend to 'the procedural location of their answers' and, in part, produce answers by reference to 'the various uses that the answer may have for next actions that may be done' (Sacks, 1992, Vol. 1: 565).

This focus on 'procedural organization' means that Goffman's (1981) attempt to separate the 'ritual' and 'system' requirements of interaction would have been a non-starter for Sacks. Contrary to Goffman's (1981) suggestion that Sacks has the focus of a 'systems engineer', Sacks shows that behaviour is *not* rule-governed but rule-guided. In this sense, you can do what you like but you will be held accountable for the implications of your actions. Moreover, unlike an engineering model, social order is merely a *by-product* of social interaction, an 'offshoot of a machine designed to do something else or nothing in particular' (Sacks, 1992, Vol. 2: 240).

Unlike Goffman, Sacks's stock in trade was not anecdotes or invented examples but detailed transcriptions of tape-recorded conversations. By using this kind of data, Sacks claimed that he was able to look at interaction in a much more detailed way.

A good example of this is when a student at one of Sacks's lectures suggests that Sacks's example of a visitor interpreting appearances in a household is fully explained by Goffman's concept of the incongruous impressions that people 'give off'. Sacks replies that, in fact, he has a basic difference from Goffman's approach. As he puts it:

> Goffman talks about responses to incongruity but he does not tell us what incongruity is. That's what I think I'm beginning to see here in this stuff [data]. *How* it is that one sees it. He has not analyzed how it is that you do 'an incongruity', what makes it an incongruity. (Sacks, 1992, Vol. 1: 92)

Another way of putting this is that Sacks wanted to study the local production of social order in far greater detail than Goffman. Sacks was convinced that serious work paid attention to detail and that, if something mattered, it should be observable.

For instance, in a fascinating passage, Sacks noted the baleful influence on sociology of G.H. Mead's proposal that we need to study things which are not available to observation, e.g. 'society', 'attitudes' (see Mead, 1934). As Sacks comments:

> But social activities are observable, you can see them all around you, and you can write them down. The tape recorder is important, but a lot of this can be done without a tape recorder. If you think you can see it, that means we can build an observational study. (1992, 1: 28)

Despite ethnographers' attention to the logic of writing their field notes (see Emerson et al., 1995), most do not confront fully the problematic character of how we describe our observations. Put at its simplest, this relates to what categories we use. As Sacks says:

> Suppose you're an anthropologist or sociologist standing somewhere. You see somebody do some action, and you see it to be some activity. How can you go about formulating who is it that did it, for the purposes of your report? Can you use at least what you might take to be the most conservative formulation – his name? (1: 467)

As Sacks suggests, this apparently trivial problem is actually not resoluble by better technique, like detailed note taking. Rather it raises basic analytic issues:

> The problem of strategy . . . may not be readily handleable by taking the best notes possible at the time and making your decisions afterwards. For one, there is an issue of when it is for the Members that it turns out who did the thing. (1: 468)

In fact, many contemporary ethnographers, now aided by advanced software packages, ignore this problem. In the way Sacks suggests, they simply put in some set of categories derived from lay usage (1: 629). By doing so, of course, we are no wiser of how, *in situ*, categories are actually deployed and enforced, nor how violations in category-use are actually recognized (1: 635–6).

TAPING INTERACTION

As we have seen, both Goffman and the early Chicago School ethnographers had generally relied on recording their observations through field notes. Why did Sacks prefer to use an audio recorder?

Sacks's answer is that we cannot rely on our recollections of conversations. Certainly, depending on our memories, we can usually summarize what different people said. But it is simply impossible to remember (or even to note at the time) such matters as pauses, overlaps, inbreaths and the like. Think back to Extracts 1–3 above for a good example of this.

Now whether you think these kinds of things are important will depend upon what you can show with or without them. Indeed, you may not even be convinced that conversation itself is a particularly interesting topic. But, at least by studying tapes of conversations, you are able to focus on the 'actual details' of one aspect of social life. As Sacks put it:

> My research is about conversation only in this incidental way, that we can get the actual happenings of on tape and transcribe them more or less, and therefore have something to begin with. If you can't deal with the actual detail of actual events then you can't have a science of social life. (Sacks, 1992, Vol. 2: 26)

Tapes and transcripts also offer more than just 'something to begin with'. In the first place, they are a public record, available to the scientific community, in a way that field notes are not. Second, they can be replayed and trans-criptions can be improved and analyses take off on a different tack unlimited by the original transcript. As Sacks told his students:

> I started to play around with tape recorded conversations, for the single virtue that I could replay them; that I could type them out somewhat, and study them extendedly, who knew how long it might take. . . . It wasn't from any large interest in language, or from some theoretical formulation of what should be studied, but simply by virtue of that; I could get my hands on it, and I could study it again and again. And also, consequentially, others could look at what I had studied, and make of it what they could, if they wanted to disagree with me. (Sacks, 1992, Vol. 1: 622)

A third advantage of detailed transcripts is that, if you want to, you can inspect sequences of utterances without being limited to the extracts chosen by the first researcher. For it is within these sequences, rather than in single turns of talk, that we make sense of conversation. As Sacks points out:

> having available for any given utterance other utterances around it, is extremely important for determining what was said. If you have available only the snatch of talk that you're now transcribing, you're in tough shape for determining what it is. (1: 729)

This is why Sacks worked with long sequences of tape-recorded interaction. As he put it:

> the kind of phenomena I deal with are always transcriptions of actual occurrences in their actual sequence. (Sacks, 1984: 25)

Sacks liked to work with such material because he could use it to try to access the machinery through which people put their interactions together as they try to make sense of each other's actions. Even the activity of 'coding' is not the preserve of research scientists. All of us 'code' what we hear and see in the world around us. This is what Garfinkel (1967) and Sacks (1992) mean when they say that societal members, like social scientists, make the world observable and reportable.

Put at its simplest, this means that researchers must be very careful how they use categories. For instance, Sacks quotes from two linguists who appear to have no problem in characterizing particular (invented) utterances as 'simple', 'complex', 'casual' or 'ceremonial'. For Sacks, such rapid character-izations of data assume that we can know that [such categories are accurate] without an analysis of what it is [members] are doing. (Sacks, 1992, Vol. 1: 429)

At this point, the experienced researcher might respond that Sacks has characterized conventional research as over-naive. In particular, most researchers are aware of the danger of assuming any one-to-one correspondence between their categories and the aspects of 'reality' which they purport to describe. Instead, following Weber (1949), many researchers claim that they are simply using hypothetical constructs (or 'ideal types') which are only to be judged in relation to whether they are *useful*, not whether they are '*accurate*' or '*true*'.

However, Sacks was aware of this argument. As he notes:

> It is a very conventional way to proceed in the social sciences to propose that the machinery you use to analyze some data you have is acceptable if it is not intendedly the analysis of real phenomena. That is, you can have machinery which is a 'valid hypothetical construct', and it can analyze something for you. (1: 315)

By contrast, the 'machinery' in which Sacks is interested is not a set of 'hypothetical constructs'. Instead, his ambitious claim is throughout 'to be dealing with the real world' (1: 316). The 'machinery' he sets out, then, is not to be seen as a set of more or less useful categories but the *actual* categories and mechanisms that members use.[4]

A TEXTUAL EXAMPLE

We saw earlier an example of the kind of work on conversation that Sacks inspired in Don Zimmerman's study of emergency telephone calls. However, it would be misleading to assume that Sacks's work is only of interest to researchers who want to study talk.

Sacks was interested in naturally occurring data of all kinds.

Whether we are looking at audio or video tape or textual material, according to Sacks, we can still do good analyses providing we study how participants (members) 'put some category in' (in different ways, this is the concern shared by all the authors whose chapters appear in this book). In this respect, for Sacks, the discipline of sociology has failed to grasp the analytic nettle. As he puts it:

> All the sociology we read is unanalytic, in the sense that they simply put some category in. They may make sense to us in doing that, but they're doing it simply as *another Member*. (Sacks, 1992, Vol. 1: 41–2, my emphasis)

The availability of alternative category collections (e.g. first names, surnames, occupational or family titles) means that any sociology that aspires to do more than reiterate commonsense understandings must specify how members categorize (1: 803). Only in this way can sociology be 'a natural observational science' (1: 802).

Let us take a concrete example. In two of Sacks's lectures, he refers to a *New York Times* story about an interview with a navy pilot about his missions in the Vietnam War (1: 205–22, 306–11). Sacks is specially interested in the story's report of the navy pilot's reported answer to a question in the extract below:

THE NAVY PILOT STORY

How did he feel about knowing that even with all the care he took in aiming only at military targets someone was probably being killed by his bombs?

'I certainly don't like the idea that I might be killing anybody,' he replied. 'But I don't lose any sleep over it. You have to be impersonal in this business. Over North Vietnam I condition myself to think that I'm a military man being shot at by another military man like myself.'

Source: Sacks, 1992, Vol. 1: 205

Sacks invites us to see how the pilot's immediate reply ('I certainly don't like the idea . . . ') shows his commitment to the evaluational scheme offered by the journalist's question. For instance, if the pilot had instead said 'Why do you ask?', he would have shown that he did not necessarily subscribe to the same moral universe as the reporter (and, by implication, the readers of the article) (1: 211).

Having accepted this moral schema, Sacks shows how the pilot now builds an answer which helps us to see him in a favourable light. The category 'military man' works to defend his bombing as a category-bound activity which reminds us that this is, after all, what military pilots do. The effect of this is magnified by the pilot's identification of his co-participant as 'another military man like myself'. In this way, the pilot creates a pair (military man/ military man) with recognizable mutual obligations (bombing/shooting at the other). In terms of this pair, the other party cannot properly complain or, as Sacks puts it:

there are no complaints to be offered on their part about the error of his ways, except if he happens to violate the norms that, given the device used, are operative. (1: 206)

Notice also that the pilot suggests 'you have to be impersonal in this business'. Note how the category 'this business' sets up the terrain on which the specific pair of military men will shortly be used. So this account could be offered by either pair-part.

However, as Sacks argues, the implication is that 'this business' is one of many where impersonality is required. For if it were the case that, that you had to be impersonal in this business held only for this business, then it might be that doing this business would be wrong in the first instance. (1: 206)

Moreover, the impersonality involved is of a special sort. Sacks points out that we hear the pilot as saying not that it is unfortunate that he cannot kill 'personally', but rather that being involved in this 'business' means that one must not consider that one is killing persons (1: 209).

However, the pilot is only *proposing* a pair of military man/military man. In that sense, he is inviting the North Vietnamese to 'play the game' in the same way as a child might say to another 'I'll be third base'. However, as Sacks notes, in children's baseball, such proposals can be rejected:

if you say 'I'll be third base', unless someone else says 'and I'll be . . . ' another position, and the others say they'll be the other positions, then you're not that thing. You can't play. (1: 307)

Of course, the North Vietnamese indeed did reject the pilot's proposal. Instead, they proposed the identification of the pilot as a 'criminal' and defined themselves as 'doing police action'.

As Sacks notes, these competing definitions had implications which went beyond mere propaganda. For instance, if the navy pilot were shot down then the Geneva Conventions about his subsequent treatment would only properly be applied if he indeed were a 'military man' rather than a 'criminal' (1: 307).

Unlike more formalistic accounts of action (Parsons, 1937; Mead, 1934), Sacks's analysis shows us the nitty-gritty mechanisms through which we construct moral universes 'involving appropriate kinds of action and particular actors with motives, desires, feelings, aspirations and sense of justice' (J. Gubrium, personal communication). Like Garfinkel (1967), Sacks wanted to avoid treating people as 'cultural dopes', representing the world in ways that some culture demanded. Instead, Sacks approached 'culture' as an 'inference-making machine': a descriptive apparatus, administered and used in specific contexts. Although their language is different, the chapters by Atkinson and Coffey and by Prior in this volume imply much the same approach to description.

Sacks's take on 'culture' underlines a radical position that may be unsettling to some readers. After all, many of us are wedded to particular methods and approaches and are unlikely to be prepared to abandon them overnight. So why take account of what Sacks had to say?

I will try to answer such an understandable response in two ways. Shortly, I will summarize what I take to be Sacks's contribution to 'mainstream' qualitative research. First, however, I will address the repeated criticism that Sacks's position (and, more generally, ethnomethodology) leads to an arid, purely theoretical take on institutions which glories in its lack of substantive input into social problems. I will call this the 'so what?' line of criticism.

SO WHAT?

On the face of it, teachers of social problems and, even more so, caring professionals would seem to be a very unlikely audience to appreciate Sacks's work. Indeed, Sacks refused to respond to suggestions that social science must justify itself by its contribution to 'society', as this question and answer session with a student shows:

> Q: Will it ever have any possible relevance to the people who were involved in producing it?
> A: It needn't have any relevance . . . I take it that there's an enormous amount of studies that are not intended to be relevant. For example, studies of how cancer does cancer is not intended to build better cancer.
>
> (Sacks, 1992, Vol. 1: 470)

In this answer, Sacks closely follows what Garfinkel terms 'ethnomethodological indifference' to questions of how things (whether cancer, social problems or, indeed, social science itself) *should be*. As I have already noted, his answer depends on a degree of sophistry – presumably the student did not intend that research should help cancer!

However, we do not have to judge Sacks's potential contribution to social problems by this answer. In particular, recent applied work using methods that ultimately derive from Sacks, has, in my view, undoubtedly contributed to the solution of several practical issues, most notably in the field of institutional interaction (see Heritage, this volume; Drew and Heritage, 1992b; Peräkylä, 1995; Silverman, 1997; Heath and Luff, 2000).

The practical relevance of such 'applied' conversation analysis (CA) shows 'why language and interaction matter to the sociology of social problems' (Maynard, 1988: 312). As Maynard points out, CA (and Sacks) can be useful precisely because it avoids any 'abstract formulation' of interaction (e.g. in terms of social science concepts like 'role', 'label', 'deviance'). So, if 'labelling' and 'societal reactions' set careers of deviance in motion, such motion depends upon 'the ordered activities of telling troubles and proposing problems' (325).

Such ordered activities can be made visible because, as Maynard puts it, CA demands

> [the] observation and scrutiny of the details of actual talk and interaction. (320)

Maynard concludes that CA is able to make a basic contribution to the study of fundamental social processes and problems. As he argues:

> To the extent that we have learned about such interactional phenomena as diversity, conflict, domination, troubles and problems, the institutional processing of deviance, and mediated versions of social problems, it is because we have propositions about systems of vernacular talk, turn-taking, troubles-telling, commonsense knowledge, conversational sequencing, rhetoric and so on. (326)

Moreover, it is not just what Sacks said about turn-taking that is relevant to contemporary studies of social problems. Sacks's work on 'description' has inspired a generation of ethnographers who have studied topics as diverse as mental illness hearings (Holstein, 1988), schemes to get the unemployed into work (Miller, 1993), family therapy (Miller, 1987; Gubrium, 1992), the care of the elderly (Gubrium, 1980) and business meetings (Boden, 1994).

At this point, the reader may still ask: where does this get me? Although there is a lively tradition of ethnographic work that follows Sacks, I am aware that many readers are unlikely to want to abandon more mainstream ethnographic work in order to learn CA or membership categorization analysis.

Let me conclude, therefore, by underlining the implications that Sacks's work contains for 'mainstream' qualitative research.

IMPLICATIONS FOR METHODOLOGY

Qualitative researchers are becoming increasingly sensitive to assessing the quality of their work. Even if arguably sloppy work is still accepted in some journals (Silverman, 2000: 283–96), 'quality' issues are central to many qualitative methodology textbooks (see Peräkylä, this volume; Miles and Huberman, 1984; Seale, 1999; Seale et al., 2004).

Sacks's (posthumous) contribution to this debate can be summarized in terms of three issues: the quality of our methods, the quality of our data and the quality of our data analysis. I will briefly deal with each area below.

Quality of methods

I have shown elsewhere the extent to which interviews are by far the most common method used in qualitative research (Silverman, 2000: 290–2). Although I certainly would not wish to argue that interviews are never appropriate, the romantic auspices of some interview studies should give us pause for thought.

In interviews, as Heritage puts it, the mistake is to treat the verbal formulations of subjects

> as an appropriate substitute for the observation of actual behaviour. (Heritage, 1984: 236)

Drew and Heritage (1992a) show how this has a direct impact on the kind of data we think are relevant. Most qualitative researchers use such data as interviews, focus groups and diaries. They thus attempt 'to get inside the "black box" of social institutions to gain access to their interior processes and practices' (5). However, such studies may suffer from two problems:

- the assumption of a stable reality or context (e.g. the 'organization') to which people respond;

- the gap between beliefs and action and between what people say and what they do (Webb and Stimson, 1976; Gilbert and Mulkay, 1984).

Qualitative researchers' preference for interview studies ironically respects a division of labour preferred by quantitative researchers. According to this division, while quantitative research focuses on objective structures, it falls to qualitative researchers to give 'insight' into people's subjective states.

The unfortunate consequence of this division of labour is that *both* approaches neglect a great deal about how people interact. Put more strongly, both kinds of research are fundamentally concerned with the environment around the phenomenon rather than the phenomenon itself.

Moreover, we need to question the argument that observational or other naturally occurring data are 'unavailable' in the supposedly 'private' sphere of human interaction (e.g. in domestic life). As Gubrium and Holstein have noted:

> The formulations of domestic order that we hear outside households are treated as authentic as are those heard within them. . . . As a practical matter, this means that the analyst would treat *private* and *public* as experiential categories – constructed and oriented to by interacting persons – not actual geographic or social locations. . . . [This implies that] methodologically, we should not take for granted that privacy implies privileged access – that those occupying the private sphere are taken to be experts on its description, the final arbiters of its meaning. (1995: 205)

Such a situation suggests that we need to look twice at the unthinking identification of the open-ended interview as the 'gold standard' of qualitative research. Note that this is not to reject each and every interview study. I merely suggest that the choice of any research instrument needs to be defended and that the pursuit of people's 'experience' by no means constitutes an adequate defence for the use of the open-ended interview.

Quality of data

Whatever material Sacks analysed, he was scrupulous about working with long sequences of text or transcript and providing those sequences intact to the reader. By this means, he provided a public forum in which to assess the reliability of his data.

Of course, data quality is also something that concerns 'mainstream' qualitative researchers. Yet how often are textbook discussions translated into practice? How often are we given details about the auspices of field note extracts? How frequently do interview studies provide sequences of talk (including that of the interviewer)?[5]

Of course, some of this negligence can be ascribed to the ever-increasing demands of journal editors for shorter research articles. How can we satisfy these pragmatic constraints and yet provide credible data extracts? Using Sacks's work as our example, we might use fewer but more detailed extracts.

As I tell my research students, saying 'a lot about a little' is not a bad maxim for qualitative research.

Quality of data analysis

Analysing long, well-transcribed data extracts, as Sacks did, helps both the reliability and likely validity of our data analysis. Sacks was no revolutionary in this respect. He merely followed the path prescribed since the 1950s at least through the method of analytic induction (AI) (see Denzin, 1989: ch. 7).

AI involves the use of the constant comparative method allied to deviant case analysis. Yet, only rarely is it explicitly applied in mainstream ethnography (see Bloor (1978) for a rare example). More commonly, there is an anecdotal quality to many published qualitative research studies, first noted by Mehan (1979: 15). This problem is succinctly expressed by Bryman:

> There is a tendency towards an anecdotal approach to the use of data in relation to conclusions or explanations in qualitative research. Brief conversations, snippets from unstructured interviews . . . are used to provide evidence of a particular contention. There are grounds for disquiet in that the representativeness or generality of these fragments is rarely addressed. (1988: 77)

Bryman's complaint is mirrored ten years later by Paul ten Have. The latter notes the complaint that in CA, like other kinds of qualitative research:

> findings . . . are based on a subjectively selected, and probably biased, 'sample' of cases that happen to fit the analytic argument. (ten Have, 1998: ch. 7, p. 8)

This complaint, which amounts to a charge of anecdotalism, can be addressed by what ten Have, following Mehan (1979), calls 'comprehensive data treatment'. This comprehensiveness arises because, in qualitative research, 'all cases of data . . . [are] incorporated in the analysis' (Mehan, 1979: 21).

Such comprehensiveness goes beyond what is normally demanded in many quantitative methods. For instance, in survey research one is usually satisfied by achieving significant, non-spurious, correlations. So, if nearly all your data support your hypothesis, your job is largely done.

By contrast, in qualitative research, working with smaller data-sets open to repeated inspection, you should not be satisfied until your generalization is able to apply to every single gobbet of relevant data you have collected.

The outcome is a generalization which can be every bit as valid as a statistical correlation. As Mehan puts it:

> The result is an integrated, precise model that comprehensively describes a specific phenomena [*sic*], instead of a simple correlational statement about antecedent and consequent conditions. (1979: 21)

To anyone who cares to read them, Sacks's own data analyses (Sacks, 1992) are a model of comprehensive data treatment. His work serves to underline an aspiration of quite conventional 'mainstream' qualitative research and to provide a shining example.

CONCLUDING REMARKS

Sacks's endeavour ultimately resists any formulation which I might offer. As he himself put it:

> I can tell you something, but you have to be careful what you make of it. . . . The upshot of what I've said is this: I make no commitment to what kind of placing anyone makes of what it is that I do, nor to whatever recommendations anyone might provide me, which turn on such a treatment. (1992, 1: 621)

Like the work of Wittgenstein and Saussure before him, Sacks's work is largely available to us in notebooks and lectures published posthumously. Like these other two great thinkers, Sacks will continue to exert an influence on many subsequent generations.

However, although Sacks can inspire, he cannot tell us all that we have to do. Following Wittgenstein's (1971) analogy of the 'ladder', we can use Sacks's work to climb up higher, but we have to proceed carefully and thoughtfully. To repeat his words:

> I can tell you something, but you have to be careful what you make of it.

NOTES

* I am most grateful for the comments of Judith Green, Jay Gubrium and Geraldine Leydon on an earlier draft.

1. Aldrich also makes the common assumption that open-ended interviews are central to all paradigms which reject functionalism: 'to study organizations an analyst must . . . understand its organizations as members do. In practice, this means conducting unstructured interviews, doing fieldwork (and) participant observation' (1992: 25).

   Gergen reveals very clearly the romanticist auspices of Aldrich's language of 'sides': 'the chief contribution of the romanticists to the prevailing concept of the person was their rhetorical creation of *the deep interior* . . . the existence of a repository of capacities or characteristics lying deeply within human consciousness' (1992: 208–9).

   Romantic accounts can be seen, as Gergen suggests, as 'forms of language, not in themselves derived from what is the case (and) achieving their impact through rhetorical artifice' (1992: 210). Although Gergen takes this argument in a post-modernist direction, we could use it to support ethnomethodology's focus on the properties of actual language use (e.g. in members' descriptions). Indeed, this is implied in Gergen's discussion of 'representation as a communal artifact' (214).

2. Since the authors of both these studies refer favourably to my own work, I may seem to be very ungracious in using their work as examples of a consensus which I reject.

Let me emphasize that I believe that their work is good of its kind, unlike some easier targets.

3. A hidden aspect of this consensus is that data gathered are under-analysed. A focus on 'themes' can conceal researchers' preference for 'telling' examples, i.e. examples that support their case (see Silverman, 2000: especially 283–96). Moreover, very little attention is usually paid in interview studies to how interviewer and interviewee co-construct agreed meanings (see Rapley, 2004).

4. Goodwin and Heritage (1990: 301) refer to 'the great debate between cognitive anthropology and cultural materialists on the status of emic analysis'. The debate turns on the relative reliability of native and analysts' understandings of culture. However, as both Garfinkel and Sacks show, commonsense and analytic understandings are in no way *competitive*. Instead, the point is to see how members produce the sense that they do without confusing commonsense interpretations with social science explanations.

These imperatives have been taken on board in two major ethnographies by anthropologists (Moerman, 1988; Goodwin, 1990). As Goodwin and Heritage argue, these writers do not appeal to natives' accounts, 'but instead rel[y] upon the actions of participants themselves' (1990: 301) as they interactively and sequentially make sense.

In terms of my argument above, we might call such studies examples of non-romantic ethnography.

5. Neither of the organizational ethnographies discussed earlier (Hassard, 1993; Linstead and Thomas, 2002) give us anything more than brief extracts of what interviewees said. We therefore get no information on how these responses are contextualized within an interaction.

Recommended reading

Sacks (1992) presents most of his previously unpublished lectures. 'Doing being ordinary' (1992, 2: 215–21) should be read by every ethnographer. The story of the navy pilot, discussed in this chapter, is analysed in Volume 1: 205–22. Sacks's well-known discussion of a child's story ('The baby cried. The mommy picked it up') appears in Volume I: 223–31 and 236–66. My book (Silverman, 1998) offers an introduction to Sacks's work intended for non-specialists. For a sophisticated defence of the (non-romantic) use of interview data as narratives, see Atkinson and Coffey (2002).

REFERENCES

Aldrich, H.E. (1992) Incommensurable paradigms? Vital signs from three perspectives. In M. Reed and M. Hughes (eds), *Rethinking Organization: New Directions in Organization Theory and Research*. London: Sage, 17–45.

Atkinson, P. and Coffey, A. (2002) Revisiting the Relationship between Participant Observation and Interviewing. In J. Gubrium and J. Holstein (eds), *Handbook of Interview Research*. Thousand Oaks, CA: Sage, 801–14.

Atkinson, P. and Silverman, D. (1997) Kundera's Immortality: The Interview Society and the Invention of Self. *Qualitative Inquiry*, 3 (3): 304–25.

Bloor, M. (1978) On the analysis of observational data: a discussion of the worth and uses of inductive techniques and respondent validation. *Sociology*, 12 (3): 545–57.

Boden, D. (1994) *The Business of Talk: Organizations in Action*. Cambridge: Polity Press.

Bryman, A. (1988) *Quantity and Quality in Social Research*. London: Unwin Hyman.

Clavarino, A., Najman, J. and Silverman, D. (1995) Assessing the quality of qualitative data. *Qualitative Inquiry*, 1 (2): 223–42.

Denzin, N.K. (1989) *The Research Act* (Third Edition). Englewood Cliffs, NJ: Prentice Hall.

Denzin, N.K. and Lincoln, Y. (2000) *Handbook of Qualitative Research* (Second Edition). Thousand Oaks, CA: Sage.

Drew, P. and Heritage, J. (1992a) Analyzing Talk at Work. In Paul Drew and John Heritage (editors), *Talk at Work*. Cambridge: Cambridge University Press, 3–65.

Drew, P. and Heritage, J. (1992b) (eds) *Talk at Work*. Cambridge: Cambridge University Press.

Eberle, T. and Maeder, C. (2002) 'The goals of the conference', Conference Proceedings, Conference on Ethnographic Organization Studies, University of St Gallen, Switzerland.

Emerson, R., Fretz, R. and Shaw, L. (1995) *Writing Ethnographic Fieldwork*. Chicago: Chicago University Press.

Flick, U. (1998) *An Introduction to Qualitative Research*. London: Sage.

Garfinkel, H. (1967) *Studies in Ethnomethodology*. Englewood Cliffs, NJ: Prentice Hall.

Gergen, K. (1992) Organization Theory in the Postmodern Era. In M. Reed and M. Hughes (eds), *Rethinking Organization: Directions in Organization Theory and Analysis*. London: Sage, 207–26.

Gilbert, G.N. and Mulkay, M. (1984) *Opening Pandora's box: A Sociological Analysis of Scientists' Discourse*. Cambridge: Cambridge University Press.

Goffman, E. (1959) *The Presentation of Self in Everyday Life*. New York: Doubleday Anchor.

Goffman, E. (1981) *Forms of Talk*. Oxford: Blackwell.

Goodwin, M.H. (1990) *He-Said-She-Said: Talk as Social Organization among Black Children*. Bloomington: Indiana University Press.

Goodwin, C. and Heritage, J. (1990) Conversation Analysis. *Annual Review of Anthropology*, 19: 283–307.

Gubrium, J. (1980) Patient Exclusion in Geriatric Settings. *The Sociological Quarterly*, 21: 335–48.

Gubrium, J. (1992) *Out of Control*. Newbury Park, CA: Sage.

Gubrium, J. and Holstein, J. (1995) Qualitative Inquiry and the Deprivatization of Experience. *Qualitative Inquiry*, 1 (2): 204–22.

Gubrium, J. and Holstein, J. (2002) *Handbook of Interview Research*. Thousand Oaks, CA: Sage.

Hammersley, M. (1989) *The Dilemma of Qualitative Method: Herbert Blumer and the Chicago Tradition*. London: Routledge.

Hassard, J. (1993) *Sociology and Organization Theory: Positivism, Paradigms and Postmodernity*. Cambridge: Cambridge University Press.

ten Have, P. (1998) *Doing Conversation Analysis: A Practical Guide*. (Introducing Qualitative Methods Series). London: Sage.

Heath, C. and Luff, P. (2000) *Technology and Action*. Cambridge: Cambridge University Press.

Heritage, J. (1984) *Garfinkel and Ethnomethodology*. Cambridge: Polity Press.

Holstein, J. (1988) Court ordered incompetence: conversational organization in involuntary commitment hearings. *Social Problems*, 35 (4): 458–73.

Hume, M. (2002) These mawkish tears are an insult. *The Times*, 19 August.

James, H. (n.d.) *The Portrait of a Lady*. London: Heron Books.

Linstead, A. and Thomas, R. (2002) 'What do you want from me?' A Poststructuralist Feminist Reading of Middle Managers' Identities. *Culture and Organization*, 8 (1): 1–20.

Maynard, D.W. (1988) Language, Interaction and Social Problems. *Social Problems*, 35 (4): 311–34.

Mead, G.H. (1934) *Mind. Self and Society*. Chicago: Chicago University Press.

Mehan, H. (1979) *Learning Lessons: Social Organization in the Classroom*. Cambridge, MA: Harvard University Press.

Miles, M. and Huberman, A. (1984) *Qualitative Data Analysis*. London: Sage.

Miller, G. (1987) Producing Family Problems: Organization and Uses of the Family Perspective and Rhetoric in Family Therapy. *Symbolic Interaction*, 10: 245–65.

Miller, G. (1993) *Enforcing the Work Ethic*. Albany, NY: SUNY Press.

Moerman, M. (1988) *Talking Culture: Ethnography and Conversation Analysis*. Philadelphia: University of Pennsylvania Press.

Parsons, T. (1937) *The Structure of Social Action*. New York: McGraw-Hill.

Peräkylä, A. (1995) *AIDS Counselling*. Cambridge: Cambridge University Press.

Rapley, T. (2004) The Qualitative Interview. In C. Seale, G. Gobo, J. Gubrium and D. Silverman (eds), *Qualitative Research Practice*. London: Sage.

Sacks, H. (1963) Sociological Description. *Berkeley Journal of Sociology*, 8: 1–16.

Sacks, H. (1972) Notes on Police Assessment of Moral Character. In D. Sudnow (ed.), *Studies in Social Interaction*. New York: Free Press, 280–93.

Sacks, H. (1984) Notes on methodology. In J.M. Atkinson and J. Heritage (eds), *Structures of Social Action: Studies in Conversation Analysis*. Cambridge: Cambridge University Press, 21–7.

Sacks, H. (1992) *Lectures on Conversation*, edited by Gail Jefferson with an Introduction by Emmanuel Schegloff. Oxford: Blackwell, 2 vols.

Seale, C. (1999) *The Quality of Qualitative Research* (Introducing Qualitative Methods Series). London: Sage.

Seale, C., Gobo, G., Gubrium, J. and Silverman, D. (eds) (2004) *Qualitative Research Practice*. London: Sage.

Silverman, D. (1989) The Impossible Dreams of Reformism and Romanticism. In J. Gubrium and D. Silverman (eds), *The Politics of Field Research: Sociology Beyond Enlightenment*. London: Sage, 30–48.

Silverman, D. (1997) *Discourses of Counselling: HIV counselling as social interaction*. London: Sage.

Silverman, D. (1998) *Harvey Sacks and Conversation Analysis* (Polity Key Contemporary Thinkers Series). Cambridge: Polity Press; New York: Oxford University Press.

Silverman, D. (2000) *Doing Qualitative Research*. London: Sage.

Sudnow, D. (1965) Normal crimes: sociological features of the penal code in a public defender's office. *Social Problems*, 12: 255–76.

Webb, B. and Stimson, G. (1976) People's Accounts of Medical Encounters. In M. Wadsworth (editor), *Everyday Medical Life*. London: Martin Robertson.

Weber, M. (1949) *Methodology of the Social Sciences*. New York: Free Press.

Wittgenstein, L. (1971) *Tractatus Logico-Philosophicus*. London: Routledge.

Zimmerman, D. (1992) The interactional organization of calls for emergency services. In P. Drew and J. Heritage (eds), *Talk at Work*. Cambridge: Cambridge University Press, 418–69.

Appendix

Transcription conventions

The examples printed embody an effort to have the spelling of the words roughly indicate how the words were produced. Often this involves a departure from standard orthography. Otherwise:

→	Arrows in the margin point to the lines of transcript relevant to the point being made in the text.
( )	Empty parentheses indicate talk too obscure to transcribe. Words or letters inside such parentheses indicate the transcriber's best estimate of what is being said.
hhh	The letter 'h' is used to indicate hearable aspiration, its length roughly proportional to the number of 'h's. If preceded by a dot, the aspiration is an in-breath. Aspiration internal to a word is enclosed in parentheses. Otherwise 'h's may indicate anything from ordinary breathing to sighing to laughing, etc.
[	Left-side brackets indicate where overlapping talk begins.
]	Right-side brackets indicate where overlapping talk ends, or marks alignments within a continuing stream of overlapping talk.
°	Talk appearing within degree signs is lower in volume relative to surrounding talk.
> <	'Greater than' and 'less than' symbols enclose talk that is noticeably faster than the surrounding talk.
((looks))	Words in double parentheses indicate transcriber's comments, not transcriptions.
(0.8)	Numbers in parentheses indicate periods of silence, in tenths of a second – a dot inside parentheses indicates a pause of less than 0.2 seconds.
:::	Colons indicate a lengthening of the sound just preceding them, proportional to the number of colons.
becau-	A hyphen indicates an abrupt cut-off or self-interruption of the sound in progress indicated by the preceding letter(s) (the example here represents a self-interrupted 'because').

___ Underlining indicates stress or emphasis.

dr^ink A 'hat' or circumflex accent symbol indicates a marked pitch rise.

= Equal signs (ordinarily at the end of one line and the start of an ensuing one) indicate a 'latched' relationship – no silence at all between them.

Fuller glossaries may be found in Sacks, H., Schegloff, E.A. and Jefferson, G. (1974) 'A simplest systematics for the organization of turn-taking for conversation', *Language*, 50: 696–735; and Atkinson, J.M. and Heritage, J. (eds) (1984) *Structures of Social Action: Studies in Conversation Analysis*. Cambridge: Cambridge University Press.

Name Index

Subject Index